THE STANDARD BEARERS

AUSTRALIA V INDIA, PAKISTAN AND SRI LANKA 2018-19

GIDEON HAIGH

Published by:
Wilkinson Publishing Pty Ltd
ACN 006 042 173
Level 4, 2 Collins Street
Melbourne, Vic 3000
Ph: 03 9654 5446
www.wilkinsonpublishing.com.au

NATIONAL LIBRARY OF AUSTRALIA

A catalogue record for this book is available from the National Library of Australia

Planned date of publication: 05-2019
Title: The Standard Bearers
ISBN(s): 9781925642933 : Printed - Paperback

Design by Spike Creative Pty Ltd
Ph: (03) 9427 9500
spikecreative.com.au

Printed in Australia by Griffin Press, part of Ovato

CONTENTS

INTRODUCTION

'It's Your Game' promised advertising slogans for the cricket summer of 2018-19 in a slightly plaintive tone – the apostrophe was dropped for the inevitable hashtag. In the campaign devised by Saatchi, Australian cricketers wandered in on and interacted with everyday cricket fans, with lots of wholesome fondling of baggy greens, misty looks and 'aw shucks' moments.

But whose game was it really? Whose team and whose history? What did ownership even mean? And how do you sell things to the public they already own? Such was the mood of introspection in Australian cricket, and at Cricket Australia, as a season commenced certain only in its dimensions: eight Tests, eleven one-day internationals and ten T20 internationals at home and abroad. Otherwise, everything was up for grabs, still, many months after the crisis of Cape Town, and the suspensions imposed on ball tampering conspirators Steve Smith, David Warner and Cameron Bancroft. The game was under growingly new management: by the start of November, the slow-motion tsunami had swept away not just Australia's best batsmen, but coach Darren Lehmann, CEO James Sutherland, senior director Bob Every, chairman David Peever, high-performance boss Pat Howard and commercial chief Ben Amarfio. Left in charge of a depleted XI were skipper Tim Paine and coach Justin Langer. En route to Australia were an Indian team led by a charismatic, omnicompetent captain, Virat Kohli, determined to win a series in this country for the first time.

The Standard Bearers collects some of my writings over the course of 2018-19, mainly for *The Australian*, although also for *The Times, Wisden Cricketers' Almanack and Wisden India*. It's a real time record: you'll see that I narrowly favoured Australia coming into the Border-Gavaskar Trophy, in addition to getting one or two things right. You might get a sense of writing's daily challenges — of finding something fresh to say about, for example, Kohli, of whom so much was being said, and Cheteshwar Pujara, of whom so much was being seen. It's a challenge still satisfying to rise to, which is why the task of writing about cricket has continued engaging me these many years.

At best, 2018-19 was going to be a two steps forward and one back sort of season. The ratio was reversed against India, but a hearty victory over Sri Lanka in the Warne-Muralitharan Trophy engendered feelings of optimism for the beckoning defence of the World Cup and the Ashes. And while the mercurial Justin Langer had his moments, Paine grew in stature, as a captain, keeper, batsman and personality, at an age where, too often in the recent past, Australian cricket has been apt to grow antsy about age and advancement. Assuming Smith and Warner return to the colours this year, Paine will remain – not something one might have tipped in the immediate, febrile aftermath of Cape Town. Did he and his team persuade Australians that they represented more than themselves? They did not, at least, do the opposite, a success of sorts.

On a personal note, this was my eighth season covering cricket alongside my colleagues and friends Peter Lalor and Andrew Faulkner, whose good fellowship has kept me in the role of columnist at *The Australian* longer than I ever expected, for which I thank them sincerely.

CRICKET AUSTRALIA

THE CONTINUING CRISIS

3 September 2018

Six months after Australia's cricketers crossed their 'line', Cricket Australia is headbutting its own.

Since Bob Every left the board of CA in May, the venerable former chairman of Wesfarmers and Boral has kept his own counsel; likewise, the organisation.

Every has declined to discussed why he, CA's most experienced and prestigious director, departed so suddenly; having acknowledged his resignation in belated, grudging and muted fashion, CA has yet to replace him.

But journalistic nature abhors an information vacuum. Yesterday's scoop by my colleague Peter Lalor has cast further unflattering light on the chequered chairmanship of CA's David Peever.

Every's acerbic letter and email of resignation, accusing Peever of 'sub-standard' performance, accord with an impression already open to outsiders: that CA's chairman has unnecessarily and pointlessly complicated work in three vital areas.

By his own admission, Peever spent 'two years' discussing the best time for CEO James Sutherland to conclude his long tenure, only to fail to advance a credible replacement, internal or external, leaving the organisation now in caretaker mode. Glaciers have better succession planning.

Peever's stamp was already all over last year's divisive pay confrontation with the Australian Cricketers' Association. He also blundered into broadcast negotiations earlier this year with an intemperate message to the owners of Channel Ten, then a key media partner.

After this last pratfall, we learn from Every's sign off to fellow directors, Peever offered his resignation — a gesture Every interpreted damningly as 'fake'.

At around the time, of course, Peever's colleagues had other seemingly more urgent concerns to address. When Sandpapergate shielded him from what otherwise might have become Bottomfeedergate, Peever sailed on with a sorry-not-sorry for the ages: 'I made an apology to the executive in question for the tone of the email... and that apology was accepted. But it was in the context of a negotiation.'

Funny thing, context. It was no excuse when Steve Smith, David Warner and Cameron Bancroft transgressed in the context of a high-pressure Test match at the end of an exhausting season. Peever, by contrast, was free to provide the context for the Ethics Centre's review of the 'culture, processes and governance' of CA in the same breath as he pre-empted its findings by announcing that the board had 'asked' him to remain for a second three-year term and that he had 'agreed to do that.' We now know that the most experienced board member had so disapproved of Peever's second term that he chose to step down as a 'matter of principle' — which invites consideration of the contrasting principles of other board members.

To say the least, this does not play well in the Test match of public opinion, where onlookers have also been bemused lately by the unfolding he-said-she-tweeted saga of sacked Cricket Tasmania staffer Angela Williamson.

Nor does it burnish CA's reputation in the corporate suites where it likes to hob nob, but where Bob Every's is a name to reckon with.

Above all, however, it draws attention to a weakness besetting the governance structure at which CA arrived with the advent of an 'independent board' six years ago — that said structure is supremely difficult to change. In theory, CA is owned by the state associations, and answerable to them; in practice, those state associations rely on CA for their funding and strategic direction, at the expense of their local identities and practical autonomy. If change was necessary at the top of Australian cricket, from where would the impetus come? From a seemingly supine board where the chairman sits on the nominations committee? From states neutered by an increasingly centralised system? If neither, who else? Structures unable to reform themselves arouse interest from outside.

Last year it was government and commercial partners who exerted pressure on CA to strike an accord with disaffected players after months of pointless conflict; in March, the prime minister and sponsors swiftly made plain their dismay at events in Cape Town.

A CA board that lost the confidence of stakeholders might find itself in a similar position. It could especially be a focus of the state in the event of a Labor government, to whom a former executive of Rio Tinto like CA's chairman might not appear like such a pillar of rectitude.

Last week, coincidentally, CA expressed hopes of shaking loose taxpayers' money for the sake of investment in community cricket. Nice idea. But if it wants the patronage of democracy, it will want to be looking a mite more democratic itself.

This month, the Ethics Centre is scheduled to complete its soundings among cricket's great and good — the process Peever set in motion in April. The report will be presented to the CA board. What comes out the other side will significantly influence that board's ongoing credibility.

The following month will see CA's annual general meeting, historically a rubber stamp, a mutual back pat and a loyal toast. A 'line' here, though, is ever more observable, and that's the line drawn between the standards of accountability on the pitch and in the boardroom.

CRICKET AUSTRALIA

BOARD GAMES

6 September 2018

An iron law of realpolitik is never to commission a review whose conclusions one does not know already. Cricket Australia is growingly aware of its cynical wisdom.

In mea culpa mode back in April after the crisis of Cape Town, chairman David Peever announced an 'overarching review' of 'culture, processes and governance' of Cricket Australia, albeit that the arch didn't seem to quite cover his own job, which he was keen to extend.

Anyway, Sydney's Ethics Centre, corporate Australia's go-to guys for made-to-measure morality, got to work, carried out fifty or so interviews, surveyed a further 500 persons, and are shortly to present the fruit of their labours to a sub-committee of the CA board, including Mark Taylor, Michael Kasprowicz, Earl Eddings and Jacqui Hey.

So then what? After the year CA has had, one would have thought, the review deserves the widest possible circulation. The involvement of the Ethics Centre and its founder Simon Longstaff was to a significant degree a response to disquiet about a game that CA holds in trust on behalf of the public. The review will hardly serve this purpose if it is kept from that public, sanitised, bowdlerised or suppressed.

Some squeamish souls at Jolimont, however, are now having second and third thoughts about the prudence of releasing the Ethics Centre's work. These include Mark Taylor, who last week on Nine's *Sports Sunday* worried aloud about the review containing 'warts-and-all reporting'. Said Taylor: 'We are going to get stuff that's going to dredge up stuff from the players' pay dispute from last year, TV rights negotiations, we've got a new CEO coming on, it'll be very juicy. But do we want to go back and have a look at all this stuff from the last 18 months, which has, to be honest, been quite tumultuous?'

In other words: no.

But why not? Because it's 'juicy'? What does that even mean? You seek a review, presumably, because you think there are things, complicated and perhaps contentious things, that need further consideration. What did Taylor think the Ethics Centre were going to review? The photocopier?

The pay dispute, the broadcast negotiation and the changes to the executive are not 'stuff' being 'dredged up' — they are core functions of CA. They go, moreover, straight to the effectiveness of the unimpressively accident-prone Peever, who aspires to an eminence not even attained by Sir Donald Bradman in seeking consecutive three-year terms as chairman despite an intimate association with the 'tumult' to which Taylor is referring.

An alternative solution, as Taylor explained it, was the publication of the Ethics Centre's recommendations alone. 'We won't censor it,' he insisted. 'I think we've either got to put it out there or use what is recommended by the Ethics Centre. That's my opinion: we've either got to say, 'it's all out there, warts and all', or put out what he recommended we should do going forward, because to me, that's the key.' Actually, that's not an opinion: it's two mutually exclusive options laid side by side to provide the illusion of balance.

The available inference is that Taylor, having already expressed misgivings about the former, favours the latter, as he implied in his final remark: 'It's about what we can do in the future to make the game better, not necessarily what we've done wrong in the past.'

But is it really about that? Just to remind ourselves: the Ethics Centre is involved in a Re-View, which by definition looks at things again.

It may see what has been done wrong. It may also identify what has been performed adequately or well so it can be continued. But to publish recommendations without facts is tantamount to providing answers without reasoning, and arguably renders them worthless. The approach Taylor seems to favour, furthermore, would subvert the status of the review as 'independent': nothing could be more 'dependent'.

Now, let's be frank here. Chances are that the Ethics Centre will not take full advantage of the wart-rich environment. Longstaff's cultural review of the troubled Australian Olympic Committee a year ago was a squib from its opening sentence: 'The Ethics Centre wishes to acknowledge the assistance of the AOC in the production of this report, not least the courage of the AOC's executive, its President and CEO for their commitment to understanding and improving their organisational culture.'

'Courage'? Never mind Lone Pine and Long Tan, eh? Those diggers never had to suffer the withering firepower of a sub-optimal organisational culture. How will the Ethics Centre begin its reflections on CA? With a tribute to Peever's fearless commitment to healthy ergonomics?

Let's just say that Longstaff did not got where he is by championing radical reform agendas. We know already that the Ethics Centre did not trouble to interview departed director Bob Every, Peever's most astringent critic. We also know that CA and the Ethics Centre cosily share a director, Michelle Tredenick. But what Longstaff is almost bound to recommend to CA — because it is de rigueur on assignments like this, sounds vaguely impressive, and nobody ever argues for less — is 'greater transparency'.

Publication of the entire review, then, will be a good start on measuring up to a new standard. CA could then get to work on its risible annual report, which has shrunk in detail as the organisation has grown in size.

One reason, however, eclipses all others for full and frank disclosure, which is that the review concerns a game, mattering very much and not at all. Can we maybe leave the customs of redaction and expurgation and secrecy to creepy corporations, venal governments and self-protecting bureaucracies? Let cricket live up again to its good name and be an example of honesty and straight dealing. Let those involved be prepared to take responsibility, hear criticism, wish to learn and to improve.

Last week, CA unveiled its new slogan for the summer: *It's Your Game*. You bet it is. Which makes it especially difficult to turn around and say: but it's our review.

CRICKET AUSTRALIA

KILLER APP

9 September 2018

Recently I sat down with an Australian cricketer and caught sight on his phone of the Cricket Australia app – his two-way communication with the organisation's team performance department. I had seen these before, but when I expressed interest he offered, with a tone of good-humoured chagrin, to take me through its various functions.

The app, developed by Microsoft to replace an analog version, serves every player in CA's elite system as a diary – conveying details of games, training, travel et al. In the whirl of the ceaseless Australian cricket season, all but a tiny well-organised minority would be lost without it. Its other purpose is as a real-time monitoring system, collecting data on the players' physical and mental states for synthesising at Brisbane's National Cricket Centre. In the jargon it goes to the cricketer's IPP (Individual Player Profile) of the AMS (Athlete Management System).

The app's dashboard presents eight options accented to playing and training workloads, calibrated to a fine degree. If a player has batted on a certain day, for example, they must account for the elapsed time and balls faced, and whether the activity was 'very easy', 'easy', 'moderate', 'moderately hard', 'very hard', 'very, very hard', 'extremely hard', 'sub maximal' or 'maximal'.

A wellness section solicits information about sleep, soreness, stress and fatigue. 'How do you rate your fatigue?' the app asks with quiet insistence: are you 'always tired', 'more tired than normal', 'normal', 'fresh' or 'very fresh'? Other pages surveyed 'reflections', on training and on games. Did the player have a 'Clear Plan'? Did the player 'Stick to the Plan'? How had they gone 'Creating a Contest'? Did they achieve 'Focus' and 'Execute Skills'? I was struck by one tiny box on this screen: 'Enjoyment'. 'Remember that?' I asked. 'Not really,' he laughed. Underneath was an instruction: 'Submit'. The choice of word could hardly have been more appropriate.

We were talking cricket, so it wasn't quite the moment to chew on French philosophy, but I reckoned Michel Foucault could have mined that app for tens of thousands of words. Foucault's famous study of the prison, *Discipline and Punish*, originated the concepts of surveillance and panopticism by exploring Jeremy Bentham's scheme for a circular penitentiary, designed in such a way that the inmates could never be sure whether they were being observed from a central tower. Foucault saw this as prefiguring modes of surveillance in modern society so internalised that every man became effectively their own overseer, policing themselves for fear of punishment.

The concept is almost a bit hoary now in a world of social media's mass voluntary data collection and personalised content creation. Incessant scrutiny, of course, is what keeps cricket's economy afloat — from the everyday business of putting big cricket to air to the minute interest in every moment of Virat Kohli's day. Cricketers have locked themselves in a gilded jail, consenting to supervision by a staggering profusion of technologies, from pitch microphones to infra-red cameras; CCTV even pursues them into stairwells, as David Warner and Quinton de Kock learned at St George's Oval.

But there is expanding an unseen realm of control that presents itself benignly, in the guise of greater efficiency and improved welfare. It is not yet fearfully efficient; it is data being collected mainly because it can be, and not yet that meaningful because there is so little to compare it to. But it is a phenomenon that in cricket is not to be removed, only expanded and refined, edging cricketers along to road to the status of automata, regulated and perhaps even one day selected by machine-learning algorithms. For a generation of cricketers is emerging whose life has been altogether pervaded by technology, who show off their digital ankle bracelets as jewellery, to whom the word 'submit' has no unsavoury connotations.

The CA app also has two self-reporting features related to psychic wellness: players must regularly update their EPQ (Eysenck Personality Questionnaire), an inventory of character traits, and K10 (Kessler Psychological Distress Scale), an index of depression and anxiety. Interested, I asked around other players to see how they related to this. Shoulders were shrugged: one basically filled in whatever it was felt would keep CA off one's back. To them, the exercise felt tokenistic. I was told the story of a female player who failed to fill in her EPQ and K10 in for a couple of weeks because she was depressed. All she received was a call admonishing her for delinquency. So she resumed, reporting low levels of mental wellness for the next fortnight. Nobody contacted her. What mattered, clearly, was ticking her boxes.

Early days yet too, I dare say. But what does it prelude? Players as individuals confiding in a distant database rather than their peers? Players turning aside from one another on the assumption that the system will palliate all suffering? Resourceful and resilient teams have always picked up and carried along their vulnerable members. But what is a 'team' in this schema? Simply a temporary vehicle for self-expression remotely tended by all-seeing, all-knowing superintendents?

As one bonded with cricket a lifetime, I often feel incomparably blessed, spoiled for choice, stimulated by the game's growth, excited by my watching opportunities. But what

I'm watching also feels less free, less spontaneous, more contrived and constricted.

There are giants who rise above it, and in some ways they are magnified more than ever; the rewards for the mass, too, have happily never been greater. Yet I cannot help a feeling that these developments have come at the cost to the cricketer's dignity, independence and pleasure. They sometimes seem merely to be passing one another by, units of production, never at rest. The cricketer with whom I was chatting was nearer the end of his career than the beginning but did not regret it. 'Cricket's changed so much even in the last five years,' he said. 'I know it's always changed, but there's become something about it that's so…' As he reached for a suitable sentiment, I interpolated: 'Joyless?' He nodded. 'That's the word,' he said, looking down at his phone. 'Joyless.'

MOISES HENRIQUES

CAPTAIN'S KNOCK

11 September 2018

The gas bottle. The barbeque wouldn't light. It must be that the gas bottle was empty. Now he'd have to do something about that. But he couldn't, just couldn't.

It was the afternoon of Christmas Eve last year, and Moises Henriques was in the backyard of his comfortable Clovelly home readying for an evening visit from friends and family. Thirty-year-old Moises — tall, strong, handsome, financially secure, widely respected — had been among Australia's elite cricketers nearly a decade. He had led his country in an under-19 World Cup. He had faced the world's fastest bowlers, dismissed the world's best batsmen, represented his country twenty-six times, appeared before the teeming stands of no fewer than five Indian Premier League franchises. He was captain of New South Wales Blues; he had, just the day before, skippered the Sydney Sixers in a Big Bash League match watched by more than three-quarters of a million people.

Now he was on his knees and had tears pouring down his face at the prospect of refilling a gas bottle. Coming into the backyard, his fiancée Krista rushed to his aid. What was wrong? The service station was close. The bottle was not a problem. And, of course, it wasn't. But Moises could feel his chest constricted, his pulse racing, his thoughts cramming up against each other. He began pleading with Krista to cancel the gathering. The truth was that he'd been feeling this way for weeks, maybe even years. He could not let people see him like this.

Krista calmed him, arguing that he would be better for the company. She'd do everything. He could relax. The cylinder was refilled. The night proceeded. Moises strove to keep it together, but there was no mistaking his subdued mood. As he and his wife left, the former England batsman Michael Lumb paused with Krista by the door. 'Is Moey OK?' he asked quietly. 'He seems… dark.' When Krista repeated the remark afterwards, Moises again felt his chest tighten. 'He knows,' he thought. 'Everyone knows. But if only they knew *how it felt*.'

Nine months after his gilded life as an alpha athlete crumbled last Christmas, Moises faces a new season more hopefully — but 'how it felt', and what lay behind a withdrawal from cricket explained as for 'personal reasons', he feels bound to share. That instant when the tiniest task seemed insuperable came at the end of years of depression suffered silently, and perhaps for decades endured unacknowledged.

In a cricket scene in which they do not abound, Moises Henriques is a leader. He was a precocious junior all-rounder — more advanced in his teens than either his contemporaries and friends Steve Smith and David Warner. If he has not quite fulfilled the buoyant hopes for his talents as a top-order batsman and pace bowler, he has stood out for his pacific temperament and interpersonal skills. He first led NSW aged twenty-two. 'Some people like being captain, but don't like rolling up their sleeves, having tough conversations,' says his teammate Ed Cowan. 'Moey has been doing that since he was a really young man.' Says the state's assistant coach Geoff Lawson: 'He's a good man to the core.'

Like a good man, Moises soldiered on through Christmas, stressfully split into three visits, to Krista's family, and to each of his long-estranged parents. On Boxing Day, he trained with the Sixers at the SCG. When he returned home, he cried for three hours. By now,

Krista was insistent. Moises had to 'see someone'. She messaged the player welfare manager at Cricket NSW, Justine Whipper.

Novacastrian Whipper had been at CNSW for five years and become something of an institution — warm and empathetic, a trusted confidante of male and female players alike. She had worked closely with Moises, notably in the aftermath of the death of Phillip Hughes: 'He was in deep grief, but so rational and so fair with everyone.' At times, Moises had confided worries and sensitivities. But when she asked him to rate his distress on a scale of one to ten, Whipper was shocked by his answer of 'seven' — adjusted for Moises' stoicism, that was near the top of the range. Whipper was already dealing with one horrendous duty: the boyfriend of a member of the NSW Breakers had been killed in a car accident on Christmas Eve. Now she went in search of a diagnostician for her men's captain, but in the holiday season could find no appointment earlier than the morning of 28 December — hours before Moises was due to captain the Sixers in their next game. It would have to suffice.

Psychiatrist Greg de Moore is associate professor of psychiatry at Sydney's Westmead Hospital. He works from a dour facility on the site of the old Parramatta Hospital for the Insane — a museum there contains all the instruments popularly associated with the treatment of the mentally ill, from straitjackets to an electroshock machine. Arriving with Krista, Moises couldn't help thinking of the movie *One Flew Over the Cuckoo's Nest*. But he was determined to do his best: he must keep it together.

De Moore recognised Moises: a cricket lover, he penned a fine life of the troubled colonial sporting prodigy Tom Wills. He also recognised Moises' type — a high-functioning 'coping individual', suddenly overwhelmed. He has seen surgeons operating one day, completely prostrated the next; he has known barristers proceed almost straight from court to collapse. They can be awkward patients. 'In psychiatry, you only ever get a "version" of the person,' he notes. 'And the coping individual can reconstitute quickly: they want the psychiatrist to give them a "good report". But as that interview went on, you saw all the little red flags.' The flat affect, the helpless cognitions, the poor sleep, the lost appetite: they spelt out 'major depression'.

'The people who picked this up had done an excellent job,' de Moore reflects. 'But he was probably in a worse way than they realised.' De Moore was struck by Moises' carriage. He stood straight, tall; his body was athletically sculpted; his bearing was 'almost military'. But he walked as though sore: 'Moises was a man who limped both inside and outside.'

Such limping is ever more public, and no respecter of reputations, here (Ian Thorpe, Greg Inglis, Barry Hall) or abroad (Serena Williams, Michael Phelps, Andrew Flintoff). An episode of *Four Corners* last year, 'After the Game', shone a light on the difficulties experienced by elite athletes in leaving their sporting identities behind, with an accent on the suicide of former Wallaby Dan Vickerman. But the mid-career 'leave of absence' to deal with mental demons is increasingly common in the AFL: last year it was Western Bulldogs star Tom Boyd; this year it has been Brisbane Lions' captain Dayne Beams. For its part, Cricket Australia has been researching the prevalence of mental maladies for about five years. Data collected recently by mental health consultancy Orygen suggests a 'caseness' (a level of symptomatology warranting treatment by a health professional) of about a quarter of the elite playing population — roughly in line with the general population. We may exalt our cricketers, hold them to lofty standards, imagine them to be 'living the dream', but they are as susceptible to malignant sadness as anyone. And given that Moises is the first Australian to talk openly about his troubles, that suggests a good deal of silent suffering.

To young Moises, born on the Portuguese island of Madeira but raised in the Sydney's industrial Peakhurst, sport was the world. His parents separated, acrimoniously, when he was eleven. Moises remained with his father Alvaro while his younger brothers Nicholas and Robert lived with their mother Anabeth. Alvaro worked punishing shifts at a sheet metal factory but was a taciturn parent, never violent but sometimes brooding and withdrawn. Moises would get himself off each morning to Endeavour Sports High School, where cricket reciprocated his love and he flowered into a hard-hitting, fast-bowling prodigy, first representing Australia at under-17 level. Picked for his state at eighteen, he became the youngest Blue to take five wickets in an innings since Doug Walters.

Then Moises was hit by injury. His young hamstrings and calves tore; his shoulder had to be reconstructed; the changed kinaesthetics affected his confidence; cricket did not 'feel' the same. He finally broke into the Australian team in January 2013 and played three Tests in tough conditions in India, making 68 and 81 not out on debut. But he slipped back almost as quickly and on an Australia A tour in his mid-twenties began experiencing almost existential doubts: 'I remember looking around and thinking: "I don't even know why we're here. What are we doing this for? Everyone's playing for themselves." There was nothing on it. There was no trophy. We weren't really a team. We hadn't trained together. I didn't know the person next to me. I started to notice the selfish traits in other people, got a bit obsessed with them. I just wanted to go back and play for NSW, because it was something I felt part of.'

Sometimes, when Moises parsed the comments he heard from coaches, cricket even seemed a bit ridiculous: 'They would say: "You've always got more time than you think." Then they would say: "Take the game on." Well, which was it? Next it would be: "Try to get them doing something they're not comfortable doing." Well, what are these "somethings" exactly? "Have a clear mind." But you're never going to have a clear mind: you'll always be thinking something. "Go to your strengths." What does that even mean? We were just saying words.'

Moises kept a lid on these dissatisfactions. But about his cricket, much of the time he felt frustrated. He would get in a funk about his batting when he fell short of an imagined perfection. He would punish himself by the standards he set his bowling. The strange thing was that these behaviours were effectively endorsed: he was admired by his peers for his dedication and self-sufficiency. 'I trained hard — probably too hard,' Moises recalls. 'I wasn't outwardly emotional. I kept a level head. I made sensible decisions in facets of my life, like buying a house. Then I'd go through stages where I'd think: "I'm struggling here. Can someone just help me?" 'But he felt incapable of asking. In hindsight, Moises grasps that his desire for help and his resistance to seeking it involved more than cricket — they simply localised and concentrated in what was the chief source of his self-definition. At the time, there was a simpler recourse: hating the game.

Cricket did not simply lose its lustre for Moises; it became a torment. Short-form cricket at least was over quickly. Long-form cricket left him sick with sleepless dread: 'I never slept during Sheffield Shield matches. I'd dwell on a day for four hours, then fear the next day for three.' Success alleviated these agonies only temporarily, and only ever provided respite, never satisfaction. He would find himself thinking: 'You used to love this game. You still love training, trying to master your craft. Why are you not enjoying what you used to thrive on?'

Beneath it all lay a sub-stratum of thought he barely understood. Like most cricketers, for example, Moises was devastated by the death of Phillip Hughes. Yet, as Justine Whipper noted, it brought forth his best, turning him outward from his own preoccupations. 'For the first 36 hours I was an absolute mess,' Moises recalls. 'Then I thought: "Maybe I can help other people." I wasn't getting satisfaction from doing what I had to do, but I've always felt valued when my friends have thought they could rely on me.'

Moises handled the incoming calls, took the soundings in the dressing room, deflected the pressure to rush back to competition: 'You had the officials all saying: "You've got to get out there again. It's the best way to deal with things." And I was saying: "Hey, you don't know what the best way to deal with this is. It might be for some people, but it won't be for others. There's no precedent here. Let individuals make their own decisions."'

Personally, Moises did not want to play the Shield round finally scheduled for twelve days after Hughes' death, but as captain felt he owed it to those who did. He remembers vividly dismissing Usman Khawaja caught in the gully, punching the air in delight, then as he was walking back to his mark breaking into tears, so wrong did pleasure feel.

Moises was inclined to such tangled thinking anyway. In a T20 at Arundel in June 2015, he collided with a Surrey teammate going for a catch so violently that three surgeries were needed to reconstruct his broken jaw. His first thought on coming to was of Hughes: 'I'm so lucky that wasn't worse.' His second was relief:

'I'd been anxious before every game over there, and we were just about to play twenty-one days of cricket in the next twenty-four. I had been dreading the weeks to come. At least now, I thought, I didn't have to play.'

By this time, Moises had sought help from various psychologists, who had treated his thoughts mainly as challenges of motivation — not uncommon among mid-career athletes, for whom the end is now distantly looming. Yet the mechanism most helpful to him had always been counterintuitive: he would accept no contract longer than a year. For many athletes, insecurity is a bane. Moises welcomed it, arguing that he 'played better under pressure'. In fact, he now says, he liked the reassuring sense that the exits were not sealed.

It seemed to work. The night before the first Sheffield Shield game of 2016-17, Moises was panic-stricken: 'It was the worst headspace I had ever been in. Not only did I not want to play, I wanted to give the game up completely.' He located a new psychologist, who recommended a number of practical tools, from meditation to a gratitude diary, and including cognitive behaviour therapy to promote more positive thoughts. It correlated with the best season of his career: 775 first-class runs at 64.6, 414 one-day runs at 69, 615 T20 runs at 38.4.

Inside, Moises often still felt terrible, caught up in a cycle of lacerating thoughts. No sooner had he been dismissed in matches that he would start to fret over his bowling; when he finished bowling, he would commence brooding on his batting. 'It was the four-day grind that spun me out,' he says. 'You're just looking for a place to hide, but the game comes back at you again and again.' Yet outwardly, he was at last the dominant player he had always threatened to be. It was an equilibrium he could just about live with. In April 2017, he defied his old custom and signed a four-year contract with the Blues and the Sixers. There was rationale for certainty: Moises and Krista were planning to marry, to buy a matrimonial home and start a family.

Not all at once, but over the course of winter with Sunrisers Hyderabad and Surrey, signer's remorse set in. Caught up in the busyness of the day-to-day, Moises let his therapeutic regime slip, while the psychologist who had helped him went on maternity leave. As the home season began, Moises felt stale, drained; he craved a break, but the solace of possible escape was gone. Just when he needed them, too, the runs and wickets dried up. A couple of good deliveries, a couple of ordinary pitches, and suddenly he was 'out of form', and not just with the bat: 'My head was in such a bad space. I really had no idea. I was second guessing everything… After four matches, I'd scored 100 runs in seven bats. I thought: "I'm nowhere here. Fuck, I hope they drop me. But they won't because I'm captain."'

So Moises had to keep going. One day at training, Lawson caught a sidelong glimpse of him. He had often worried about Moises' masochistic dedication to practice, and sometimes physically pried the ball from his hand. Now, Lawson felt, the cricketer looked exhausted, his eyes dead: 'It was the 1000-yard stare.' When the Blues arrived in Hobart for the year's last Shield match, the cricketer's body rebelled. 'It was freezing cold and pissing down,' Lawson recalls. 'Maybe three players went into the indoor nets. Moises, as Moises does, batted far too long, then he wanted a bowl and third ball he pulls up feeling his groin.' Lawson groaned: 'Oh, for fuck's sake, you shouldn't even be bowling.'

Again, Moises' immediate sensation was relief, but this quickly gave way as the Blues were beaten out of sight. Returning home racked with guilt at letting his teammates down, he shunned company, dedicated himself penitently to physical recovery. It did nothing for his mental state, increasingly clawed by panic. When his groin recovered sufficiently for him to lead the Sixers' in their first two games, he did so in terror of suffering an anxiety attack on the field. The gas cylinder finished the job.

On 28 December, Moises spent two hours with De Moore, the last forty minutes with Krista. De Moore urged him to consider anti-depressant medication and take a break from the game. Prepared to accept the former, Moises was resistant to the latter. 'You don't understand,' he insisted. 'I'm the captain.' Krista drove them home: 'It was lucky she came. I couldn't have done it. I felt ten times worse leaving than arriving.' They sat in a Clovelly café for half an hour in a desperate search for normality before Moises could bear it no longer, and he spoke to team doctor John Orchard, who urged him not to play that evening. Orchard, whose father is a psychiatrist and mother a psychologist, has developed a strong interest in mental health, and the taboos around it. He reassured Moises: 'This won't count as a black mark against you. You'll be supported all the way.'

At last, Moises rang Sixers' coach Greg Shipperd. They agreed to meet early at the SCG. In more than fifty years' cricket, Shipperd had never seen a player so obviously distressed: 'He went into a back story about having had these feelings for a long time, that he was at the point he couldn't deal with them anymore. He'd be lucid for a bit, then he'd be in tears.' The coach took the decision out of Moises' hands. 'I'm shutting you down,' said Shipperd. 'You're in no shape to play. I'm going to walk you to your car and we'll talk tomorrow.' Sixers' physiotherapist Daniel Redrup, who'd witnessed the exchange, hugged Moises and rang Ed Cowan: 'Moises is in trouble and he'll need someone with him.'

The Sixers' support staff now discussed how to handle the

announcement. Orchard thought it might be tactful to report a recurrence of Moises' groin strain; Shipperd disagreed, and so, when consulted, did Moises. Two other players in the Sixers squad, Nic Maddinson and Jordan Silk, had quietly opted out of the game to deal with stress-related conditions during the preceding two seasons. 'They've owned it,' said Moises. 'So should I.' His absence was explained as stemming from 'personal reasons.' Ironically, Silk played in Moises' place that evening, and top-scored. But the Sixers lost heavily. 'I watched it at home,' Moises recalls. 'It was terrible.'

So was the next week. Moises could not sleep, could not eat; he paced the halls at night, elaborately envisioning the worst; no career, for he could not bear it; no fiancée, for he was sure Krista would leave. He stayed in touch with Shipperd; he continued consulting De Moore and Whipper; Orchard and Cowan visited daily. 'He was a walking skeleton,' says the last.

It was worst when the Sixers played without him. Moises feared going out, being seen, being judged. But the harshest judge was himself, for falling short of his own standards. Thinking he needed to intensify and accelerate his recovery, he had De Moore recommend a treatment facility, and checked in to the Northside clinic in St Leonards. He checked straight out, stricken with embarrassment. The people here had real problems: 'I thought about going into a group session and saying: "Hi, my name's Moises. I earn a lot of money, I own a beautiful house in Clovelly, I'm engaged to a beautiful woman who cares about me and yeah… my life's shit."'

Yet this also proved something of a turning point, for Moises chose to consider his condition as a kind of mental 'injury'. Injuries, he reasoned, don't always need a hospital, but they do need 'rehab'. He would dedicate his every waking moment to getting better. He read voraciously on the subject of depression and discussed it with friends and teammates when they called. He interrupted cycles of damaging thought by simple gestures such as swimming at Coogee, putting at Bonny Doon, and walking the dog. He spoke daily to the Australian team's psychologist Michael Lloyd, who encouraged him to think in progress by increments. 'One out of ten to two out of ten is a hundred per cent improvement,' Lloyd would remind him. He even broached the subject with his father, of whose response he had always been slightly fearful. When Moises mentioned he was suffering depression, Alvaro grew upset: it was his fault, all his fault. Moises hastened to assure him otherwise. Indeed, the experience had changed his sense of his upbringing. For the sake of his son, Moises reflected, his father had kept going, kept working, kept struggling, when at times it must have felt impossible. In its way, it was a heroic achievement.

Having ceased to be something Moises had to do, cricket started looking more like something he wanted to do. He rejoined the Sixers' squad on a trip to Hobart without playing, remaining to one side, but to Shipperd clearly calmer. Finally, on 16 January, Moises batted again in Sixers' colours, and scored the winning run against the Stars at the MCG. De Moore, down from Sydney, was in the crowd: 'I felt so proud for him, of him, because people didn't know what he'd been going through. Relieved as well.'

Yet perhaps the key phase of Moises' recovery was the resumption of the Sheffield Shield season, because it did not go to plan. Though he had stood down from the Blues' captaincy, Moises scrounged just 32 runs in four hits, and was now staring at the poorest season of his career. All the same, Moises felt over the worst: 'I thought, "Y'know, this is exactly what we've been working on. The sun's still coming up in the mornings. They might drop me, but I hope they don't, because I actually really want to play".' On the afternoon of 24 February at the SCG, he went to the middle against Tasmania and by the close had zoomed to 116 not out. 'There was no way I would have had the mental skills to do that previously,' he says. In the season's concluding games, he bowled as fast and as well as he had in two years.

Fixed? No, but better — married too. And here, for all the trauma and toll, is a story of mental travail leavened with hope. Moises suffered many gruelling years before he was more or less forced to seek help, but it was there for him, and the game rallied round. 'This could have gone on a lot longer and been a lot worse,' observes De Moore. 'Moises was very open about how he thought which made my task a lot easier.' But the stigma around seeking help remains, partly because of a sense that mental illness, by its seeming invisibility, is uniquely intractable. De Moore is anxious that this should be better understood — that while a strained mind is assuredly harder to treat than a strained hamstring, it can be addressed. 'Major depression is a common condition,' he says. 'None of us are immune. But it is also eminently treatable.'

At the Blues' recent pre-season camp on the Sunshine Coast, their coach Phil Jacques asked each player to bring an object that meant something to them. Many, inevitably, brought junior cricket bats; Moises brought a copy of *The Courage to be Disliked*, a work of popular psychology by Ichiro Kishimi and Fumitake Koga whose words had proved soothing at a low point ('Why is it necessary to be special? Probably because one cannot accept one's normal self'). 'I'm showing you this because I can't show you my brain,' he explained.

Colleagues young and old listened intently as Moises described his self-interrogations, his dread and panic, his final breakdown. Afterwards, he had private messages from four squad members in their twenties — they too were wrestling with loss of focus and lack of enjoyment. Things can change, he told them. One need not suffer alone.

ALASTAIR COOK

FAREWELL TO CRICKET

13 September 2018

My first glimpse of Alastair Cook was at a dinner of England's venerable Cricket Writers Club after the 2005 Ashes. Midst the Flintoff-flavoured euphoria, the twenty-year-old Essex opener diffidently accepted an award for Young Cricketer of the Year. 'Any good?' I asked a local sage. 'Too limited to be a great batsman,' I was told. 'But he'll do a job.'

Now he has retired as Test cricket's fifth highest run scorer, that sounds like the precursor to oh-so-many underestimations. But it might not be far off the unassuming Cook's self-evaluation. Like no other batsman of the modern era, Cook constructed himself as a resistance machine, a sometimes-ungainly contraption of angles and elbows, hard mind and soft hands. Nobody has faced as many as the 26,562 deliveries he received at Test level or survived as many as 26,287.

Cook did not seek runs so much as let them settle on him, although settle they did. Over the last few years, with a modesty rooted in a very English aversion to fuss, he looked uncomfortable with the statistical company he was keeping. 'I feel sorry for him,' Cook said during the Boxing Day Test when told he had passed Brian Lara's run tally during his toiling double-hundred. Of his career, he philosophised: 'The longer it goes, the harder it gets.'

This affords him, I think, a certain uniqueness. Cricket exalts individuals, is strewn with greats, classically dominating and masterful. Cook's cricket was of a different quality, that of the infinitely good, the hugely competent. He was resilient, reliable, equable, exemplary, undemonstratively fit, seldom even hurt. He stabilised every team he was part of not only by his performance, but by giving no trouble, by taking less than his share, from teammates, coaches, selectors, medical staff, leaving more for others.

This Cook did in much the same spirit as he occupied the captaincy, first slip and short leg — not perhaps because he was brilliant, but because there was nobody better, because if there was a brunt around he was prepared to bear it, in the interests of general gain. He thought in collective terms always. When England recaptured the Ashes at Trent Bridge in 2015, I recall, Cook had the presence of mind on the fall of the last Australian wicket to collect two souvenir stumps, for his feisty young charges Ben Stokes and Mark Wood. Afterwards he thanked not only his present coach, Trevor Bayliss, but the previous coach, Peter Moores, who had been unceremoniously sacked.

Cook was appreciated, therefore, most of all by those he played with. Reaction shots from player balconies on the achievement of individual milestones have become one of television's corniest staples, a formulaic as salutes at parades. But the images on Monday were noteworthy, dour, grizzled James Anderson jumping up and down like a child at a fair.

Ornery Jimmy first met placid Cook as a county opponent, and the story is that when they sat down in an airliner to commence their first tour together, Cook introduced himself wryly: 'The last time we met you called me a cunt.' Anderson is usually thought of in terms of his partnership with Stuart Broad, but his light-and-shade combination with Cook in that English dressing room is not be ignored.

Cook last week summed up his 'whole life' as invested in 'trying to play for England'. The remark rather passed listeners by — well, duh. Yet the singularity of the ambition was notable. Cook did not hanker for a title ('I want to win a World Cup'), or competition ('I want to play IPL') or a format ('I want to play Test cricket'): indeed, 'playing for England' also encompasses one-day cricket, where Cook strove manfully to improve, only to have to accept that he could not keep pace with a fast-evolving game. In these cosmopolitan times, of instant teams and of portable allegiances, a profession such as Cook's seems almost antiquely patriotic.

Watching him it was almost possible to forget that the world had changed so much, although not quite. In some ways, his cricket was a casualty of the game's trend towards transnationalism and corporatism, involving a kind of lucrative obscurity — because his arrival coincided with Sky's cricket ascendancy, not a single ball of his career was seen by his countrymen on free-to-air television.

What Cook resisted as well as rivals was the demand that cricket need be swept along by the on-rush of time, that it fall in step with the world's hurry, bustle and instantaneity. To get his measure, he compelled you to stop a while, for his chief gear, low and energy-efficient, was uniquely attuned to the business of cricket stretched over five days.

I once watched Cook drag his bag across Lord's from the Nursery to the Pavilion on a morning he was due to resume batting. He stopped to talk to a former teammate in the media, chatted smilingly until the man hurried on. He paused at the square for another word with ground staff busily involved in tidying the creases, with the air of an ordinary passer-by. Cook continued steadily, neither slowly nor quickly, neither striding nor strolling, as though he did everything in life at the pace of a Test match. He batted skilfully that day in a losing cause, in the same space through which in the morning he had quietly wended his way.

His retirement leaves a disturbingly large vacancy, not just in English cricket but in Test matches more generally. In the top fifty Test run scorers, there remain only two active players: Hashim Amla at fifteen and Chris Gayle at forty-three, currently playing some of the most forgettable cricket of their careers in the Caribbean Premier League. International cricket is a game with a few stars but no giants.

If Cook did not suggest looming greatness thirteen years ago, at least there was a place for him; a coach spying a junior version of Cook today, I suspect, would write him off at once. Cook set forth to do a job and fulfilled it on an epic scale. The succeeding generation will enjoy many opportunities, but not perhaps this one again.

THE JLT CUP

ONE DAY AT A TIME

20 September 2018

Cricket usually rejoices in anniversaries, but one is passing at the moment with muted notice: the JLT One-Day Cup that began last week commenced the fiftieth season of domestic limited-overs cricket in Australia.

You'd be pardoned missing it, this being the sixth consecutive year in which fifty-over cricket between the states has been only a spring bloom briefly glimpsed at outgrounds, leaving summer split between more telegenic Test matches and the Big Bash League.

The 2018-19 schedule, quietly rolled out a year ahead of Australia defending its hard-won World Cup, may also be the strangest yet. To the outcome of the event, the fifteen-match round robin is of zero significance, every state going through to three-stage finals.

That a team could lose every preliminary game and still lift the trophy is a quaint possibility even by Cricket Australia's eccentric fixturing standards — paradoxical even. Executive general manager, team performance Pat Howard often talks of promoting 'high-pressure game time' at domestic level, yet here he is rendering the first fortnight of the JLT One-Day Cup as necessary and consequential as ABC Life.

After the Blues lost their second game on Thursday, captain Kurtis Patterson observed lightly that it didn't really matter providing they finished well — so much for the Aussie anathema of defeat.

For some time, of course, it's not been entirely clear what purpose is served by domestic one-day cricket at all. Squeezed together, it is easy for players to miss in its entirety, as this instalment will be by the likes of the injured James Faulkner and Peter Nevill.

Played essentially in pre-season, coincident with football finals, it is not a lead-in to the summer's one-day internationals. Nor does it seem to have strong bearing on the composition of Australia's fifty-over team. The tournament has been dominated over the last three years, for example, by the likes of Nic Maddinson (1070 runs at 56) and Callum Ferguson (1043 at 52), neither of whom have played ODI cricket in that time — Maddinson, of course, ended last season axed by his state.

D'Arcy Short, by comparison, vaulted into Australia's ODI side as opener despite a record of 109 one-day runs in seven hits for Western Australia interrupted by a single thrash against the Cricket Australia XI — and thereby hangs a tale.

It's partly the CA XI's last-minute axing from the competition that's led to the peculiar futility of this season's round-robin. The CA XI, composed of young elite players not chosen by their states, was introduced to domestic one-day cricket in 2015, with Howard explaining: 'We know we've got the talent and we want to be able to expose these players to more high-pressure game time to help the states and to help the overall national cause.'

In three years, the team lost sixteen of eighteen games. In this there lay no disgrace — on the contrary, it suggested that the states had it pretty right, that the players concerned were not quite up to snuff. The principle of the XI, nonetheless, was a sore point among interstate cricketers, who saw the quality of domestic cricket, and the idea of selection on merit, diluted. They greeted news that the JLT One-Day Cup would revert to six teams with relief as a timely reflation of elite cricket values.

Yet in June, in one of those articles on cricket.com.au barely distinguishable from a press release, Howard's offsider Peter Roach presented the CA XI as having been an unmitigated triumph. Thanks to its influence, Roach claimed, the states had at last got with the programme and started advancing young talent.

In that way CA has developed of presenting everything as one strategic masterstroke after another, Roach chalked up as credits the Test cap for Hilton Cartwright, and the T20 caps for Mitchell Swepson and Jack Wildermuth — although it is hard to believe that these cricketers would not have emerged anyway.

A little more humility might be in order. Correlation may not be causation, but since Howard began dickering with domestic one-day cricket, Australia's ODI ranking has slipped from number one to number six — our lowest ever.

Persons of goodwill may disagree about potential correctives to this decline, but the most obvious would not be redesigning your domestic limited-overs competition so that three-quarters of the fixtures are basically exhibition games. And yet… here we are.

Underlying this is a broader and longer trend: CA's steady effacement of the notion that domestic cricket involves six states in red-blooded competition with a reductive conviction that it is simply a form of glorified match practice and fitness testing for individuals auditioning before national selectors and T20 scouts, a system in which the states no longer exist to develop their own winning cultures so much as to provide 'game time' to pampered favourites. It may well expedite a few careers; it also sounds like a prescription for selfishness, entitlement, frailty.

It is set to continue too. Another brainstorm recently entertained at Jolimont is that all elite coaches should be employed by CA rather than engaged by the state associations themselves — this on the theory that such streamlining would progress cricketers more seamlessly and clarify expectations for those rising to the top.

Because this is so difficult? Because cricketers have not for nearly 150 years been able to work this out for themselves?

What Australian cricket could do with right now is the opposite of this perhaps well-meaning but frankly muddle-headed helicopter parenting: less uniformity among the states, more contention and rivalry, fewer artificialities and contrivances, greater respect for the meaning and integrity of its domestic competitions, and a general roughing of a few of its smooth edges.

One of the appeals of the excellent Alex Carey is that he found his own way rather than having a primrose pathway laid before him — he quit, returned, failed, reskilled and re-emerged. It's a career such as might have been led fifty years ago. He is the better for it, and so would others be.

NEW CEO

WE NEED TO TALK ABOUT KEVIN

3 October 2018

Well, what was all that about? Having paid good money to head hunters at Egon Zehnder, it turns out that Cricket Australia only needed the internal phone directory.

If he just scribbles 'Executive' over the top of 'Operating', Kevin Roberts won't even have to invest in a new business card — and he'll appreciate that saving because it will free up more funds for grass roots cricket.

Fourteen months have now elapsed since the resolution of last year's pay dispute, which was marked by a hurried press conference in the demilitarised zone of the nets at Melbourne Cricket Ground attended by CA's then-CEO James Sutherland and his Australian Cricketers' Association counterpart Alistair Nicholson.

The instigators of that fiasco, Roberts and his chairman David Peever were then nowhere to be seen. Yet there they were yesterday, across the road in the CA boardroom, toasting their joint futures. To the losers the spoils, eh?

Peever read his opening remarks as usual — he's starting to make Sutherland look like Christopher Hitchens.

Roberts responded, more impressively — better than on video, for sure. A claque of staffers then applauded when he had finished. They stopped short of handing out bucket hats at least.

Two questions were obvious: how an organisation looking to 'drive cultural change' could best be led by a representative of the prevailing culture; and why an organisation about to receive an independent assessment of said culture from a highly-paid external consultant, Simon Longstaff of the Ethics Centre, would effectively pre-empt its findings by pushing on regardless with its most significant appointment.

But if you bothered asking, you can't follow CA that closely: this is what they do and how they do it, accountable only in theory, transparent to only a few.

In fact, most people already know. Normally when a job as prestigious as that of CEO of a major sport falls vacant, there is a swirl of ear-catching names. Not in this case.

Peever essentially ruled it out on the day Sutherland foreshadowed standing down: 'It is a Cricket Australia role, so we're probably going to have a little bit of a bias towards an Australian, and it is a role in cricket so we're probably going to have a bias towards someone of cricket. But… I don't want to put constraints around that.'

Chairman, you just did.

Two outsiders mentioned, David Gallop and Todd Greenberg, eliminated themselves early, guessing correctly that Roberts was already choosing furniture for the corner office.

The final short-ish list — Roberts, John Harnden, John Warn and Christina Matthews — were all 'of cricket' and 'of Australia'. Roberts v Harnden was one former director versus one current director. That only doesn't look incestuous if your standard is the Borgias.

Not that Roberts lacks the attributes of a successful executive. He is confident, polished and presentable. He has played good cricket; he clearly has his chairman's full confidence, which is naturally better than the alternative

Anyone in his role deserves a measure of goodwill. A CA that 'won't be perfect but will be genuine', as he put it, is a wholesome aspiration.

Roberts identified as a challenge an improved relationship with players in the periods between collective bargaining. Richly ironic coming from CA who tried to isolate and intimidate the ACA in the lead-up to the last negotiations… but not wrong.

Yet Roberts should also know that he has significant ground to make up. He has hardly made every post a winner on his corporate journey, and his reputation is as a better upward manager than sideways or downwards. Since he took over 'people, culture and strategy' at CA, many people have left, the culture is a source of contention and the strategy has never seemed more accented to commercial outcomes.

Asked a question about the futures of Steve Smith and David Warner yesterday, Roberts offered the dodge that he is 'not a selector'. Well, nor is his chairman, but Peever and fellow director Mark Taylor were part of the ersatz committee that just chose Australia's new twin vice-captains.

For his part, Peever offered a closing benediction about the game's administrative classes: 'I see the role of administrators as being a lowly servant of something much greater than ourselves. We get the privilege of being part of these things for short times and our job is to make sure and do everything we can to make sure that the game is as strong and as sound in 30 years, and stronger in fact, as it is today.'

What to make of this word salad? CA is replacing a CEO who served seventeen years, and on a top whack too; Peever himself has served six years and wants another three as chairman.

'Lowly servants'? Without wishing to be unkind, they are something Peever seems likelier to employ than to be.

In the offing are the interlocking Longstaff and McCosker reviews, which seem to have been complete for weeks yet which

Peever insists 'have not landed'. Frankly, one must now question their point, except to retroactively bless decisions already taken — from which a permissible inference is that they were designed that way all along.

What was all that about? It might be that the question answers itself.

NEIL HARVEY

NINETY NOT OUT

5 October 2018

Governor of New South Wales David Hurley seldom steps out of vice-regal character. But when he invested Neil Harvey as a member of the Order of Australia a month ago, he gave the system a little gratuitous feedback: 'Should have happened years ago.'

Harvey was chuffed. Chuffed by the whole thing actually: 'I've tried to do the right thing right through my whole career, and it's culminated with this Order of Australia, which I treasure, and I was delighted to have the kids at Government House for it.'

There could be no rushing his 90th birthday, of course, which falls on Monday, and finds him the last survivor of the Invincibles, the oldest member of the Australian Cricket Hall of Fame, and a candidate for the best living Australian batsman, though the last of his 79 Tests were played sixty-five years ago.

Harvey's has been an astonishing life, memorably incised by that once-in-a-lifetime experience of touring England under the captaincy of Sir Donald Bradman in 1948, but also spanning generations. As a youth, Harvey was introduced to England's Sir Jack Hobbs, who had debuted against W. G. Grace; as a selector, Harvey picked Allan Border.

It's a life blessed with three children, three grandchildren, five great-children, and the admiration of hundreds of thousands of people unknown to him, including those who witnessed his Test hundreds at sixteen venues in six countries.

Watching him, said his captain and confrere Richie Benaud,

was like being instructed in 'the meaning of the word "batsmanship".' For fifteen years, he was 'the most difficult man in the game to bowl to.'

Harvey's is also a life, as Hurley noted, curiously neglected. There were no plush commentary gigs or fawning biographies for him when he retired. He sold Tupperware — quite successfully thanks.

Harvey did not become one of those biddable and cuddly veterans who endeared themselves to the modern generation with praise and platitudes; he developed none of the polish of Richie Benaud or the avuncularity of Bill Lawry. In an age inclined to the emollient and oblique, he has given straight answers to straight questions.

Were Matthew Hayden or Ricky Ponting playing on too long? Yep. Should Shane Warne make a comeback? Nope. Asked by a journalist to rate a player or critique on-field behaviour, he always would.

For that, Harvey makes no apology: 'I don't like the way some of them behave. And the way they carry on about things on the field, that's what gets me most riled. This garbage that goes on, abusing people, I just can't have that. As for the current guys saying that it's gone on forever, that's a lot of garbage. They say that it's always been part of the game, and it certainly hasn't.'

Some were used to more deference. Mark Taylor, now a Cricket Australia director, once dismissed Harvey as 'the boy who cried wolf.' But since the wolf turned up at Australia's cricket door in Cape Town, Harvey would have been excused a sense of 'I-told-you-so.' Coach Darren Lehmann, who once decried Harvey as 'a joke' and said he 'wouldn't be allowed in' to the Australian dressing room, has himself moved on from it. David Warner, who like Harvey served thirty Tests as Australian vice-captain, languishes under a year's suspension.

When others were nodding at Warner's promotion three years ago, Harvey was a dissenting voice, telling the *Telegraph*: 'I don't like

(Warner's) attitude, I don't like the way he behaves himself and I think he's the wrong man for the job.'

Harvey is still firmer today: 'I hope he's not allowed back in the game, and his penalty wasn't long enough as far as I'm concerned.' Have Cricket Australia been too weak? 'Oh, no doubt…'

All the same, this doesn't keep him up nights. Harvey has simply hewed to a lifelong code of saying what he thinks. 'I've always had strong opinions,' he says. 'If they take no notice it doesn't bother me.'

The same code probably cost him the chance for a long reign as captain of his country. Harvey was working-class — real working class, when the expression actually meant something, one of six sons of a factory caretaker. All of them played first grade for their local club, Fitzroy.

Cricket lifted Harvey from his station. Yet its establishment, as it did with Keith Miller, remained keener on his talent than his character. The same establishment, chary of such a straight shooter, even now remains a little cool towards him.

'No,' he chuckles when asked. 'Nobody's asking me to present baggy greens.'

Sounds like an idea, actually. In fact, as the governor said, it should have happened years ago.

NEIL HARVEY
A LIFE WORTH LIVING

5 October 2018

Today, the world's best batsman is a twenty-nine-year-old multi-millionaire with a sizeable portfolio of premium Sydney real estate — he also, of course, languishes under a year's ban from cricket. Sixty-five years ago, by contrast, the world's best batsman shared a bedroom with his younger brother.

That summer of 1952-53, Neil Harvey had a season even more prolific than Steve Smith's last: 834 runs in five Tests against South Africa and 1659 runs in sixteen first-class matches, a total exceeded only by Bradman.

Between times, Harvey returned to the upstairs bedroom he occupied with Brian, four years his junior. Horace and Elsie Harvey did not even own their cramped terrace with the concrete backyard at 198 Argyle Street, Fitzroy; it was the property of Lifesavers, at whose factory Horace was caretaker.

Neil, who turns ninety on Monday, has in his bones a forgotten Australia. The area that today votes Green and skews hipster was in those days an industrial suburb of factories, railyards, gasholders, slums, and a general poverty so dire that the newly-formed Brotherhood of St Laurence chose to base itself there.

Luckier than many, the Harveys were frugal, unostentatious and, as Methodists, abstemious. Neil inherited their temperance, eschewing alcohol until he was nearly thirty, their thrift, becoming a scrupulous saver, and above all their household's love of sport.

All six Harvey boys played at least first-grade cricket, Neil and brother Merv going on to represent Australia, while their sister Rita was uncomplainingly enlisted as scorer for Horace's local club, Felix Socials, in the North Suburban Cricket Association.

The cobblestone lane in which the boys learned the game with a cut-down bat, a tennis ball and a deal box for stumps was for decades afterwards a local landmark. 'We had a lot of fun,' says Harvey. 'Made our own fun. One of the great things about large families — you make your life together.'

Not that even then Fitzroy was homogenously Anglo, already acknowledging influences from the Mediterranean and Ireland: Neil's brother Clarence was known as Mick for being born on St Patrick's Day. There was an indigenous population as well, and Harvey's boyhood hero was Doug Nicholls, lay preacher, secretary of the Australian Aborigines' League and another abstainer, who played basketball with the local boys in between starring on the wing for Fitzroy Football Club on Saturdays.

'I suppose I was conscious of it [Nicholls' heritage], but it was more that he treated everyone alike,' says Harvey. 'He was a great advocate of getting people together and playing sport. He did a fantastic job at that and I was just so proud to be part of it.'

Harvey emulated Nicholls by joining the Lions, playing in the reserves. Aged fourteen, he also played full-forward in the XVIII of the Collingwood Technical College, kicking 112 goals in ten games; teammates Len Fitzgerald, in the centre, and Harold Shillinglaw, at centre half forward, both went on the VFL. But Harvey was by then more interested in the Lions' co-tenant at Brunswick Street Oval, the Fitzroy Cricket Club, where he and his brothers would pile up more than 25,000 runs in nearly 800 games.

As the only left-hander amongst them, he already stood out; he quickly proved the most precocious. Starting the 1941-42 season in the Fifths, Harvey finished it in the Thirds. Still batting in short pants, he compiled 101 and 141 not out in the competition final.

These formative seasons were the basis of everything that followed. Harvey's coaches, Joe Plant and Arthur Liddicutt, were two old salts who exhorted him to come down the wicket to slow bowling — the same skill for which the English cricket writer Neville Cardus would call him 'the Cavalier on Swift Feet.'

In those days, too, the Australian cricket team hardly felt so far away. On his first night at training, twelve-year-old Harvey was introduced to Morrie Sievers, barely coming up to the Australian pace bowler's waistband. Within three years they were playing together in Fitzroy's Firsts and working together at West Melbourne power station, where Harvey was apprenticed to the Melbourne City Council's electrical supply division as a fitter and turner. Sievers would be there to shake Harvey's hand when the nineteen-year-old was himself chosen for Australia. At the time, Harvey still did not own his own bat, having to borrow one from Fitzroy's club kit.

Donald Bradman's post-war Australian team was heavily weighted towards pre-war players desperate to make up for years forgone. Yet Harvey was so extravagantly gifted that his maiden Test was his twelfth first-class match.

His second Test, against India, was on the Melbourne Cricket Ground, at its uncompromising vastest — no moribund drop-in pitch and no roped off boundaries then. Harvey remembers the cry of his partner Ray Lindwall when, on 95, he drove into untenanted space: 'Run five! Run five!' One for the stattos: has anyone else reached a Test hundred with an all-run five, unassisted by overthrows?

Actually, it's easy to come up with remarkable statistics for Harvey. He averaged a neat 50 in first-class cricket over sixteen years, nearly 60 in the first innings of Test matches, spread his twenty-one Test hundreds across sixteen grounds.

What's harder to convey is the crackling alacrity he lent a sometimes staid era, from the moment he made his Ashes debut in 1948. 'What's going on, Nugget?' Harvey said to his partner Keith Miller when they met in the middle at Headingley, with Australia three for 68 chasing England's 496. 'Let's get into 'em.' Which he did, orchestrating Australia's fightback with 112 in 183 balls.

Standing only 171cm in size 6 boots, Harvey batted dashingly, fielded nimbly, exuded competitive spirit, good humour, good health. 'His cricket,' said Bradman, 'used to flow.'

Above all, Harvey was a true cricketer's cricketer. 'You have to get close to the pulse of Australian cricket to appreciate its debt to Harvey,' noted the gnomic cricket writer Ray Robinson late in the player's career. 'Everyone has been inspired by this trim, alert, candid, battle-wise man of action, whose sportsmanlike outlook, from his first brisk step into the field to his last stride out of the gate, makes cricket a game worth playing… and watching.'

There is a memorable photograph of Sir Robert Menzies in an Australian dressing room in December 1954, come to congratulate Harvey on a scintillating unbeaten 92 to bring Australia within an ace of victory in a Sydney Test that had long looked lost.

Menzies is all double-breasted bulk, cigar and homburg in his left hand; Harvey, lean and sun-bronzed, has a towel round him. Their right hands clasp meatily; about both men there is a breezy unselfconsciousness and intergenerational affinity.

It is not, of course, an entirely faithful reading of the era or its social mobility, even in cricket. Harvey saved carefully for his first car, a four-door wire metal MG, and his first home, which he built on a block of land in Heidelberg after marrying in January 1954.

But three years later, at the age where Steve Smith is today a property magnate, Harvey was struggling. He was captain of Victoria and in line for the top job, but his former skipper Lindsay Hassett was winding up the sports store where Harvey worked, and opportunities allowing him time off for cricket were suddenly scarce.

Job offers came from Sydney, as once they had for his mate Miller, and he decided quickly: 'Got a couple of kids, gotta feed them, better up sticks.' Harvey joining a firm, John Dynon & Co, who sold crockery and cutlery to hotels, and employed several sportsmen, including the boxer Fred Hannebury and North Sydney wing Kenny Irvine. In starting to play for NSW, however, Harvey let his preferment for the Australian captaincy slip, behind first the youthful Ian Craig, then the suave Richie Benaud. Nor did he receive support from the Victorian Cricket Association: 'I don't really know why. I think they took a dim view of the fact that I moved.' Harvey settled for being the staunchest deputy he could be.

Once in a while you hear it said that either Miller or Shane Warne were the best captain Australia never had. The title may more properly belong to Harvey, notwithstanding that he did serve in the role for a single Test, leading Australia to a stirring victory at Lord's in 1961 when Benaud was injured. 'Hundred per cent record,' Harvey notes.

Perhaps the Australian Board of Control was worried about his lack of polish. Hassett (Geelong College), Ian Johnson (Wesley College) and Craig (North Sydney High and Sydney University) had the graces; Harvey (Falconer Street Central School) had no airs. Perhaps they were concerned by Harvey's trenchancy. When they applied to the Australian Board of Control for permission to write about the 1962-3 Ashes series, interestingly, Benaud was approved and Harvey refused.

Harvey had a last word of sorts when he marked his retirement with some newspaper articles scathing of the negativity of England's captain Ted Dexter. Those who associate Harvey with astringent criticism of modern players might be reassured to know that he was just as caustic about his contemporaries.

Retirement? To Harvey it was no big deal. Where players today agonise privately and sometimes publicly about the right and proper circumstances of farewell, Harvey's decision followed a brief interior monologue. A unique fifth tour of England beckoned, and Harvey made 154 in his penultimate Test, and 231 not out in his last Sheffield Shield innings. 'I felt as though I could make the effort, and I obviously had something left,' he says. 'But I thought: "Oh, I've had a go."'

Quite coincidentally, Harvey's great teammate and close friend Alan Davidson had independently reached the same conclusion, and they bowed out in the same Sydney Test. Not for more than twenty years, when Greg Chappell, Dennis Lillee and Rod Marsh also chose Sydney as a chose the same Test to retire did Australian cricket sustain such a loss at a single stroke.

Today, Harvey wishes others were similarly decisive. As an Australian selector from 1967 to 1979, he set many careers in motion, including those of Chappell, Lillee, and Marsh, not to mention Jeff Thomson, Kim Hughes and Allan Border. But he also felt the need to curtail a few, including Bill Lawry's as captain in January 1971.

'Old Phantom, he didn't like it,' recalls Harvey. 'And I've criticised people since for playing too long. I used to have a go at Allan Border about it, for instance. Some blokes they don't want advice like that. They don't want to be told their time's up.'

Time might not be felt on the side of a ninety-year-old either, but who knows what the fates have in store? Harvey has been a widow four years, the last surviving Invincible for three, and knows longevity owes as much to luck as genes. In June 1969, Harvey's boyhood roommate Brian fell from a ladder at work for the State Electricity Commission and was electrocuted as he grabbed hold of a live wire. He was 37.

Sport, however, offers continuity, even a semblance of immortality. Harvey's grandson David represented the Western Force in Super Rugby, played Sevens for Australia and four Tests for Brazil; his grand-nephews Robert and Anthony were star Australian rules footballers for St Kilda and Norwood respectively; his grand-niece Kirby Short maintains the blood tie with cricket as captain of the Queensland Fire and Brisbane Heat.

Short's first sport was softball, at which her mother Pauline represented Australia: Harvey, joining her grandfather Mick, did not watch her play cricket until November 2009 at North Sydney Oval. Since then, he's pleased to see, she has gravitated towards the top of the order. 'Mick would be proud of her continuing the family tradition,' he says.

At the oval on Brunswick Street that Harveys first trod in the mid-1920s, meanwhile, current tenants Edinburgh CC, recently named Victoria's best community club, will this weekend field twenty-eight junior sides from under-10s to under-18s. That takes Harvey back. 'It was one of the great cricket grounds in Melbourne,' he remembers. 'They had a beautiful wicket.' For all that's changed, some things are being held onto and others recreated; I report that the club has raised the money to replace the turf pitches dug up when Fitzroy moved to Doncaster in 1986.

'Oh,' says Harvey, 'that's fantastic news.' And he beams.

CROSSING THE LINE

CULTURE CLASH

5 October 2018

Tim Paine's Australians return to a Test match field tomorrow for the first time since slinking out of Johannesburg having had their baggy green arses handed to them by nearly 500 runs. Three players are set to debut in Dubai; so will Justin Langer as a Test coach.

Some are predicting a pantsing. Despite forebodings justified by Australia's record in Asia, it may not be so bad. They find Pakistan, post-Misbah and Younis, in a familiar state of flux, under a new administration sunk in a worsening feud with India, into a tenth year without international cricket at home. Australia's challenges are deluxe by comparison.

Hereabouts, in fact, exist signs of renewal. Steve Smith and David Warner have resumed grade cricket; Cameron Bancroft is working his passage back by good deeds; a commentary mic has been thrust into Darren Lehmann's hand. As of Wednesday, there is a new CEO at Cricket Australia, Kevin Roberts, elected unanimously by a board restored to strength by the recent addition of Dr Lachlan Henderson.

Still coming down the pike are the 'cultural reviews' of organisation and team, led by Simon Longstaff and Rick McCosker respectively, by now in need of a portmanteau word to summarise them. Yet it is hard now to see the point of Longcosker, except to sprinkle holy water on changes already made, whether or not this was intended. That's because we're all 'moving forward', as CA's chairman David Peever declared last week, perhaps inspired by Julia Gillard's success with that construction.

With the past's rapid recession in mind, I last week tendered my own shoestring cultural review of Australian cricket, *Crossing the Line*, produced on scant budget and in a haste hopefully not too obvious. An extract, involving a contemplation of the lived experience of the elite cricketer, runs in these pages. Despite the (Bunnings) sandpaper on the cover, it's not intended to anatomise events in Cape Town in detail; in time, these will be the protagonists' to narrate.

Rather is it a study of the forces at work in Australian cricket, sometimes dimly understood even by those under their influence. The focus falls on the three anathematised players only insofar as they are fruit of a system geared to success, in market share and financial surpluses as well as the cricket field.

'*Smash the boundaries... be relentless... play to win.*' That's not from a Nike ad, but from CA's Australian Cricket Strategy 2017-2022, drafted by none other than the new CEO.

Not that this was a mandate to cheat. But when cricketers and coaches are constantly enjoined to muscle up to a 'line' of conduct, and indeed to bash at it, then maybe we shouldn't be so primly shockable when it ends in televised tears. On Wednesday, interestingly, Roberts' 'vision' was all about 'creating good people' as well as good cricketers. He'll be invoking the 'spirit of cricket' before he knows it...

The views in *Crossing the Line* aren't mine alone. They reflect gleanings from background conversations with fifty respected individuals in and of cricket, none of whom I quote directly, all of whom contributed something candid and constructive. A joy of this game is that it contains so many excellent people — players, coaches, officials, observers — so passionate about its welfare.

I'll not summarise my findings here. But one concluding reflection I had was the growing difficulty of obtaining a total view of cricket in Australia.

Everyone I encountered understood their own segment of the scene well; many grasped the playing of the game in ways more subtle and acute than I ever will. Yet there was also a feeling of being dwarfed by the whole, and of direction from the top that was autocratic where it was not bureaucratic, transfixed by corporate visions, mired in arbitrary metrics.

Perhaps that is the inevitable trajectory of professional sport, towards requiring ever greater degrees of specialisation and ever narrower niches, like Adam Smith's pin factory. But with its multiple outposts, purposes, functions and formats, overlain with centralised decision making occurring ever further from actual outcomes, Cricket Australia can feel like a house divided against itself. Coupled with this is CA's curious sovereignty, where the ostensible owners, the state associations, are strategically and financially beholden to it, and the board more or less appoints itself.

In relative turnover terms, Cricket Australia and its satellites actually do not constitute a massive entity. But the organisation is a good deal larger, much wealthier and far less personal than it was even five years ago, and rushing so headlong into an imagined future that the past and even the present trade at something of a discount. Old-style custodianship seems less a priority than new-fashioned entrepreneurship.

Blame, meanwhile, is an orphan. There was undoubtedly deep regret at CA about events in Cape Town, but scant evidence of genuine contrition from anyone except the players, while introspection was essentially outsourced to Longcosker. And… oh look, there's a cricket game…

Well, yes. But one of cricket's tendencies in Australia — it is abiding rather than new — is to equate its health with the fortunes of the national team. It's understandable and rooted in history. But the relationship is perhaps more like that between the stock market and the real economy, with leads and lags, the temporary distortions of accident, individual genius, human frailty.

So the forthcoming Tests in the UAE loom as both very important and kind of trivial. There should be neither too much glee at success or horror at setbacks. At least as important this summer will be experiences like the live and television audience for last Saturday's women's international at North Sydney Oval — those moments that spread joy, restore connection, aren't merely to be marketed and monetised. Meanwhile, cricket can take a good hard look at itself, and 'the line' can be consigned to cliché oblivion.

AUSTRALIA IN THE UAE

DRAWN OUT DRAMA

12 October 2018

Welcome to Australian cricket's age of diminished expectation.

Back in the day, it was England who used to specialise in Dunkirk-inspired draw fantasies, Barmy Army whistling the theme from *The Great Escape*.

Australia has historically scorned the draw. We discountenanced them in our first-class cricket until after World War II; Mackay and Kline at Adelaide in 1961 and Border and Alderman at Port-of-Spain in 1984 remain two of our few such stories. Now we have another, and know how they feel, those moments where anything other than abject defeat is experienced like deliverance.

For Nathan Lyon, batting at the end with captain Tim Paine, this was just a fifth draw in his last forty test matches, one of which was a washout, another last Boxing Day's crime against cricket.

Lyon is the man charged with leading Australia's victory song. For this team in transition, moving beyond its former crash-through-or-crash ways, he might want to work up a stalemate shanty.

There was cause for Australian optimism coming into the Dubai Test. This is not the Pakistan of Imran and Zaheer, or Wasim and Waqar, or even Younis and Misbah. This is a country that hardly plays Test cricket — eight matches since Sydney at New Years' 2017 — and has not hosted an international this decade. Its most experienced batsman is out of form; its most experienced pace bowler is out of time; its star spinner is, just returned from injury, underdone; its captain is, frankly, flaky. In the field it can look lackadaisical, and sometimes haphazard.

To lose all ten wickets for 60 to such a combination, as Australia did on the third day, largely to an off spinner on debut, actually took some doing.

Between times, however, Australia exhibited a lot of spirit, especially after losing the toss — something that must have caused Paine's heart to sink. While the last day will live in memory, the first two days should not slip from it.

The main bowlers were disciplined, the change bowlers serviceable, Marnus Labushagne a handy resource, a Swiss Army pocket knife of a cricketer. The catching was satisfactory, the outcricket excellent, and the keeping from Paine probably his best in the year since being recalled to the colours.

Keeper/captains are rare; head to head, they are rarer still. Sarfraz Ahmed reminds you why, making the twin tasks look like a physical and mental ordeal, alternately irritable and lugubrious, bungling bowling changes and referrals. On Paine in this Test match, the burden sat lightly.

Above all was Australia's physical conditioning impressive, and perhaps an early dividend of the regime of Justin Langer, who regards it as non-negotiable. Lyon and Peter Siddle are already made to order for him: stoic, uncomplaining, reliable. Usman Khawaja looks to be reconstructing himself along similar lines.

Khawaja has hardly been the acme of fitness at any stage of his eight years as an international, not helped by a knee reconstruction following an anterior cruciate ligament tear in December 2014. At times in the last little while, in fact, he has looked rather on the outer, not naturally flinty or abrasive in the endorsed Australian modes of the moment. Accordingly, he has seemed to mark time, especially while being dragged through Asia as a supernumerary.

In Dubai, Khawaja batted nearly thirteen hours, and fielded sixteen more, in temperatures nudging 40 degrees and humidity around 60 per cent. Above all, he looked unflustered, unhurried, as secure and soft-handed in defence as peak Alastair Cook, but also deploying his repertoire of sweeps as disruptively as Andy Flower at his best.

With the unavailability of Steve Smith and David Warner, Khawaja is the best batsman in Australia, arguably by some distance. At thirty-one, with the experience now of no fewer than five national coaches, the mantle suits him.

The message about the coach's expectations does not, meanwhile, seem to have reached Matthew Renshaw, languishing now a little conspicuously and perhaps confusedly, given a system that has previously lavished him with 'opportunities'.

Nor is Langer without his own challenges. His seeming motto of In Marshes We Trust, for example, may begin to cloy if they do not click in Abu Dhabi. Though they brought runs from the tour match, the brothers also trailed longer-term records: twenty-three of Shaun's fifty-seven completed Test innings and nineteen of Mitchell's forty-four have ended in single figures.

Coupling them at three and four in the Australian order in Dubai, then, looked more like a gamble than an investment, especially as it left Labuschagne and Travis Head to take their new caps to the crease consecutively. And for all the pluck on show, let us remember, five of top six produced two half-centuries between them, on a pitch that scuffed but did not crumble, as perhaps it should.

Australia will take a good deal from this match, nonetheless.

What is done once can be again. For all the exciting, virile cricket that Australia has played in recent years, it was also prone to overconfidence and brittleness in ways that foreshadowed the moral reckoning of Newlands.

Under Darren Lehmann's charge, batting a hundred overs in the third innings at Ranchi last year was as close as Australia came to a genuine concerted staving off of defeat. Otherwise the talk was always 'moving the game on', 'taking the aggressive option', 'entertaining the crowd' etc, with official corporate imprimatur. Quoth the Cricket *Australia Australian Cricket Strategy 2017-2022:* 'Smash the boundaries… Be Relentless… Play to Win'.

While Australia adjusts to new realities, of our best two batsmen suspended for six further months, and two of our most skilled pacemen feeling their way back into competition, we'll need more living to fight another day. This at any rate has been an encouraging start.

SHANE WARNE

SPIN CYCLE

15 October 2018

Last Thursday, Shane Warne told an interviewer that the current Australian batting line-up was 'the worst' he had seen, and that Steve Smith and David Warner would 'walk back in'. He followed this up on Friday with a tweet of lavish praise for their 'guts and spirit', their 'outstanding performance'.

On social media, this reverse ferret was thought a bit rich. Yet there was also something inimitable about it. Even in his fiftieth year, nearly twelve years on from his retirement from international cricket, he is prepared to throw it up, tempt fate, risk embarrassment, but take events insouciantly in his stride.

In a branded, guarded, circumspect world, Warne remains a giver, nearing 18,000 tweets at a rate of 2000 a year, with as many followers as Warner and Smith put together. As he used to say of bowling: 'No matter how far they hit it, it always comes back.'

Warne knows this. And his new book *No Spin* suggests that inhabiting his public persona is ever more of a challenge for him. 'Believe it or not, I'd take the quiet life over the red carpet any day,' he insists as early as the third paragraph.

Just as quickly, however, he also consents: 'Lying low hasn't been my thing. I have lived in the moment and ignored the consequences.'

Later Warne pauses for reflection: 'A lot of people spend their life trying to be in the newspaper or magazines. I've spent most of my life trying not to be in them.'

Moving on he relates a story of suing the *Herald Sun* for

defamation and as part of the settlement agreeing to write a column for them. Huh? 'People close to me... wonder why I open myself in such a public way,' he concludes. 'So I'm going to keep things to myself a lot more and live less of my life on the edge.'

Only Warne could make the act of publishing a tell-all autobiography into an act of reclaiming his privacy: what do they say about genius being the capacity to continue functioning while holding two contradictory ideas in one's head?

Little purpose is served reviewing *No Spin*. It is not a reflective book; his has not been an examined life. He narrates a tale of John Buchanan's 2006 pre-Ashes boot camp, where Australian team members fell to discussing one another's foibles. 'The verdict on me was that I'd never give up on the cricket field,' Warne recalls, 'but that I was too quick to be judgemental about others and never prepared to change my mind once I'd formed an opinion.' It is the essence of *No Spin* that the judgements seem to have been formed long ago and progressively rationalised rather than arrived at after mature deliberation.

That also means that the values are constant. Warne is to the suburbs as Bradman to the bush, and has a sentimental attachment to the suburban virtues, of courtesy ('Manners are free'), punctuality ('I can't stand anyone who is late for anything'), plainness ('If there's an opposite to a foodie, I'm it'), and filial piety. His mother is 'tough as they come' and 'the most honest person I know'; his father, with his 'soft heart', is 'my other hero'. In most autobiographies, parents recede after the first few chapters. Brigitte and Keith Warne are there at every step.

Even in some of *No Spin*'s most outrageous tales, there is a hint of a code, even if discerning it might require a second look. For example, in a widely reported excerpt, Warne recounts a 2006 tabloid sting in which he was filmed wearing Playboy undies cavorting with two models whose SMS siren song lured him to a London address in the middle of a county match for Hampshire. The story is silly if not tawdry, but the signature detail is that rather than return to his hotel and risk sleeping through the alarm, Warne drove straight back to the county ground and grabbed a few zzzzs in his car before being woken by the physio. He then went out and took seven for 99.

Where Warne seems most determined is to retell the story of Australia's long global supremacy as other than that of a baggy green band of brothers. His disparagement of Steve Waugh, the animosity deriving from Waugh leaving Warne out of the 1999 Antigua Test, has become something of a shtick.

No Spin offers a few additional details: Warne says he was promised the Australian captaincy during the subsequent World Cup by chairman of selectors Trevor Hohns in the event Waugh did not 'get a score' or the team did not progress to 'the next stage of the tournament'; Warne reports that a few months later he voted against Waugh playing the Galle Test while his skipper was still suffering the after effects of an on-field collision with Jason Gillespie.

Clinging to ancient grievances? Or testifying honestly to the 'element of bitterness' he harboured, and went on harbouring? One might wish Warne had paused introspectively at this point. Why did Waugh's making this selection call cause him so much hurt, and so poison the relations between them that he continues carping almost two decades later? With what insecurities and vulnerabilities did it resonate? But that may be to miss something imperishable about Warne: that he did not play the game so much as live it.

The best chapter in *No Spin* is the one that belies the title, being all about spin. It is fun, and fresh, alternately practical and venturesome, shrewd and flamboyant, and written entirely in the present tense, as though Warne still pulls on his bowling boots every morning and takes the field of play. And although the chief outlets for that urgency and vitality are now soundbites and tweets, that may be the way he still sees it.

AUSTRALIA IN THE UAE

TRAVEL SICKNESS

19 October 2018

Australians enjoy an excellent reputation as travellers: hearty, energetic, adventurous, resourceful. Our batsmen not so much.

Which is counterintuitive. Unlike all those plucky backpackers inured to hardship and happy to make do, Australian batsmen are cocooned in comfort, amply resourced, extensively trained. Yet each passing year brings another misadventure abroad, the cricket equivalent of an outbreak of amoebic dysentery in a blazing youth hostel about to be crushed by an avalanche.

For all the semblances of encouragement, UAE 2018 has gradually joined the annals of India 2013, UAE 2014, England 2015, Sri Lanka 2016, India and Bangladesh 2017 and South Africa six months ago: series throughout which Australia failed to exceed 350 in consecutive first innings.

There have been better moments between times: after victories in South Africa in 2014 and New Zealand in 2016, Australia briefly regained its ICC Test match blue riband. Success, though, has depended largely on the bowlers, who on many occasions have done double duty at the crease: for example, it was the lower order runs of Peter Nevill and Peter Siddle that enabled Adam Voges to render Australia unassailable at Wellington in February 2016.

When it goes wrong, too, it goes badly. We all remember the postlude of Cameron Bancroft's spontaneous sandpaper storage — the overhasty press conference, the drawn-out agonies of the punishments, and now the interminable suspensions. But the prelude was just as significant, Australia making a bright start to chasing South Africa's 311, then losing eight wickets for 132, with Bancroft actually the solitary resister until Nathan Lyon flung the bat about at number ten.

Before it was a moral failure, then, Newlands was a batting failure, with the pressure to make the difference up passed on to the bowlers and fielders. Steve Smith called the Australians 'desperate' to coax a response from the ball; would the same desperation have existed had the team not so often found themselves in a similar corner?

Many problems faced by cricket teams are variations on abiding themes. This is too, but only sort of.

Over time, most accomplished batsmen have averaged slightly less away than at home. Greg Chappell's greatness is evinced by minimal discrepancy between his home and away averages (55 versus 53); somewhat greater differences can be found in the records of, say, Ponting (57 versus 46), Hayden (58 versus 43) and Langer (49 versus 41).

The exceptions are noteworthy, and probably merit greater regard: Allan Border averaged 45 at home, 55 away; Steve Waugh 48 at home, 56 away.

In other words, seen in the terms of their time, they produced runs when most needed and least noticed, in Test matches tucked away in football seasons, often untelevised and usually underreported. An outlier of the recent past was Marcus North, who averaged 43.5 abroad with hundreds in four countries, but one fifty in eight Tests at home.

Australia, however, now has precisely nobody in really either category. Michael Clarke might be thought a harbinger of the trend, dominant at home (62), far less a force away (39). Coincidentally or not, Clarke was the first Australian batsman of substance in many years to shy from county cricket, with its great range of conditions, need for professionalism and leadership, demands of travel and of tiredness — he played a dozen nondescript games in 2004.

An attitude set in at this zenith in Australian performance, in fact, that English cricket was a little beneath our best players. It would take John Inverarity to notice the runs that Chris Rogers had spent the better part of a decade stockpiling, and to give him his due.

In the last five years, the gaps between the records of Australian batsmen at home and away have yawned. David Warner's figures are a match for Clarke (64 versus 39). Usman Khawaja's (67 versus 30) and Shaun Marsh's are worse (59 versus 25). Minus two hundreds, that average slips to less than 17.

Throughout these troubled tours, Steve Smith set his own standards, ever more extraordinary. Between 2013 and 2018, he averaged 53 away, in addition to a staggering 84 at home. But there perhaps your problem lies. A batsman has no business averaging 84 in their own driveway let alone in Test cricket. It's arguable that a kind of inverse correlation is at work: that as batting has grown progressively easier in Australia, we have tended to find it ever harder away, and after a while have expected to.

Our increasingly stereotyped flat wicket cricket — lots of boundaries, lots of airspeed — simply does not transfer readily elsewhere. Truncated series with a bare minimum of preparation, such as this rubber with Pakistan, militate against learning. Batsmen straddling three formats, in the shorter two of which almost everything is geared in their favour, might struggle to do so anyway.

For also going steadily by the board in Australia is domestic competition of variety and consequence, on pitches with local characteristics, in circumstances where winning really matters. Instead, to carve out more of the calendar for T20, states play fifty—over cricket which counts for ever less, and four-day matches bunched up against one another shaped by the latest points vogue, with an elite few offered sterilised auditions in the controlled environments of Australia A tours.

We 'get cricket into' cricketers as though they are vessels to be filled up, rather than organisms to be stressed, seasoned and matured, thereby broadening the jump to Test match cricket, with its duration, demands, and public and media attention. Nowadays, too, thanks to pay television, our foreign failures are more visible and therefore culpable.

It took long decades to nurture institutional structures and career paths that built batsmen steadily to excellence and equipped to play in all conditions; we have dismantled them blithely, thinking all the while that we could fix it with an extra warm-up match here or net session there. Justin Langer has a lot going for him. But the travel experience is only partly enriched by a better tour guide.

ROD MARSH

IN SAFE KEEPING

24 October 2018

Only forty-six men have captained Australia in a hundred and forty-two years of Test match cricket, leaving a big field from which to choose the best candidate not to have done so.

Keith Miller has his backers; likewise, Shane Warne. An independent observer in Mike Brearley, quite possibly England's best captain, ventures another name: Rod Marsh.

The judgement appears in a handsome new illustrated book by and about Australia's indestructible wicketkeeper of the 1970s and 1980s celebrating his half a century in first-class cricket, where one might be expected to read nice things, but Brearley says them abnormally well. 'If you were to summon up a picture of the essence of belligerence, of pugnacity, on a cricket field, Marsh would be a prime candidate,' Brearley notes.

Yet there was also, says Brearley, a Marsh who was not only 'thoughtful, empathic and dynamic' but 'genial, modest, respectful of the skills of others'. Australia is captained by its wicketkeeper today; why not then?

Marsh does not know, nor is he much fussed. 'No, I have no regrets about that,' he says lightly. 'All good.' Turning seventy-one a week from tomorrow and residing in Adelaide, he is these days as much engaged by being a grandfather of six: thus the book, in fact, in case they eventually 'wonder what I did with my life'.

The moustache is gone; likewise, a knee. But the hands are good. In all his years, Marsh never reported a broken finger — albeit by the simple expedient of never submitting to an X-ray.

Today he's on the board of the South Australian Cricket Association, which is fitting. In March 1982, the SACA voted in favour of Marsh's appointment as Australian skipper, only to be thwarted.

The story is this. On a tour of New Zealand, Marsh was advised by team manager Alan Crompton that he would inherit the job for the subsequent trip to Pakistan, Greg Chappell having decided to stay at home. But when hands were raised, the Australian Cricket Board chose Kim Hughes by the odd vote.

Something clearly went awry. Was he regarded as a bit too much his own man? 'Probably.' Was his standing as one of the sans-culottes of World Series Cricket held against him? 'WSC wouldn't have helped,' he agrees. 'They were nice and dark about that in Perth.'

Then again, Marsh reasons, perhaps it was a lucky escape: in Pakistan, the Australians were whitewashed. 'If I'd been given the job, I'd have ended up with the worst record of any Australian captain,' he jokes. 'I enjoyed captaincy. But knowing what it does to a man I was better off not having the job.'

What does it do to a man? In the year of the fall of Steve Smith and David Warner, it seems a timely question to ask, and the right person to ask it of. Few rival Marsh in their breadth and depth of cricket service, as player of ninety-six Tests, and administrator of cricket academies in Australia, England, India in Dubai. Justin Langer was a protégé; so, too, every current state coach bar one, and Australia's women's coach to boot. Captains? He played international cricket under four, was a mentor to three (Ricky Ponting, Adam Gilchrist and England's Andrew Strauss), and a chairman of selectors to two (Michael Clarke and Steven Smith).

Marsh had, he observes, an instant initiation in the stakes: 'I realised pretty quickly how tough it was. My first captain Bill Lawry got sacked and heard about it on the radio; my next one, Ian

Chappell, was pretty cranky about that. So it was a helluva job and anything you could do to help you should. I guess the way I wanted to contribute was making sure everyone was happy, pulling in the same direction as best I could.'

Talking to Marsh, you wonder whether we fetishise captaincy a little much, at the expense of seniority and collegiality — notions that, with our multiple vice-captains and 'leadership groups', we're groping to recapture.

Marsh might not have been a captain, but he was indisputably a leader, a buffer for an Australian team of sizeable egos. Behind the stumps, he would listen to Ian and Greg Chappell bicker as only brothers can, and keep things jovial; between overs, he was regularly required to soothe the fevered brow of his great mate Dennis Lillee.

The book contains a priceless photograph of Lillee sidling truculently towards fine leg after finishing an over in a Test at the MCG. Marsh is solicitously at his elbow. The great bowler was apparently complaining about the fields Greg Chappell had set for him. Was Marsh agreeing? 'I disagreed with Dennis on a few things, but I never let him know,' he chuckles. 'And I could get him to change his mind without him being aware of it.' (Pause) 'The best I could.' (Laughs) 'He could have been double bluffing me.'

The other relationship Marsh effectively managed was with other teams. This could, of course, be complicated. The Australians in his playing career were a tough bunch; but they were not, he insists, a mean bunch. 'We were very competitive,' Marsh says. 'We were called 'the ugly Australians'. But that was more because we were winning and we were arrogant and we had fast bowlers who could intimidate and did. If it ever got nasty on the cricket field, it was quickly worked out.'

Marsh remains a strong proponent of socialising at the end of the day's play with opposition. Why, I wonder, have we convinced ourselves that this is impossible without somehow dulling our competitive edge? 'I'm a bad person to ask,' says Marsh. 'Because I cannot imagine playing cricket without interacting with the opposition after the day's play.

'It's just common sense that's what you should do. They'll say that they can't do it because of the ice baths, but you can get that over with in ten minutes. And then you sit down and have a drink. Doesn't have to have a beer; can be a soft drink. You just have to look each other in the eye and if there has been a problem out there fix it up.'

Marsh's observation of the strain on captains leads him in his book to an interesting conclusion, that 'there is a long history of captains totally losing the plot after about thirty Tests'. The most pronounced case in his experience was Michael Clarke.

'I always thought Michael was a terrific bloke,' says Marsh. 'Western suburbs. Simple soul. Good young man. I'd known him at the academy, taken him on tour to England, got on really well with his dad. He was a loveable brat really. Always called me "Uncle Rodney". Still does. But over the course of the captaincy, his personality changed completely. I just think he became bitter with things if they weren't going his way, angry at the press, angry at people.'

Steve Smith? The strains on him were quickly palpable, during Australia's calamitous tour Sri Lanka in 2016, where he was controversially rested. 'Steve didn't want to go home but he was shot,' says Marsh. 'He needed to go home for a rest mentally. With Steve it would have been good had he had another year as player. But then, of course, he just raised his batting to another level.' To argue on the basis of Newlands that Smith should not have been promoted to the captaincy is to Marsh simply wisdom after the event.

If some things abide, what has changed? Marsh has spent a lifetime among young men. How would he compare a twenty-five-year-old of his playing days to one of his selecting days? 'At twenty-five, most of the guys in my era were married, had children, had jobs,' Marsh notes. 'We'd learned from being mentored by older people. We'd played first grade alongside thirty-five-year-olds. We'd played Sheffield Shield cricket among lots of older players and, frankly, you're taught the game much better by peers than by coaches.'

With that opinion, how did Marsh approach coaching? With an unconscious proviso: it was not an end in itself. There were cricketers, he felt, who were great trainers, who actually did their best work in the controlled and sterilised environment of the nets, the gym, the practice match. 'When I was playing, we used to say that about Kerry O'Keeffe,' Marsh recalls. 'Greg [Chappell] reckoned what he should have done was put some netting on either side of his cap, and then he would have been a champion. When I was a coach, there was Dominic Thornley [of New South Wales]. I could never understand why he didn't play a lot of cricket for Australia. As an under-17 he was an absolute champion, the next best thing to Ricky [Ponting].'

The enigma was deepened by the players who didn't look so great, but somehow were. England's Strauss, whom Marsh groomed during his years at the England Cricket Board's academy in Loughborough, was one.

'I didn't think Andrew Strauss was going to be a Test match player,' admits Marsh. 'I told him that and he didn't like it. In fact, I think it became a motivation of his to prove me wrong, which I was very happy about. Helluva good cricketer and a very good captain.'

Testing his intuition has to Marsh always been part of the allure. 'It's the eyes,' he insists. 'The eyes give it away, how interested a guy is in what you're saying. Doesn't matter whether he agrees with you — in fact, I was always happy when players thought for themselves. But you see something about a guy's demeanour that says he wants to become a player.'

What worries Marsh about coaching now is its ceasing to see players as people. In hindsight, he regards 2011's high-profile Argus Review as a low point. As chairman of selectors, Marsh reported to the review's foremost evangelist, CA's high-performance technocrat Pat Howard — not always with utmost faith.

Last week, Marsh raised hackles at Jolimont with lines from his book blaming CA for nurturing a culture in which 'nothing counted except results' which 'all came to a head that fateful day in March 2018.' He sees no reason to resile from them: 'Every meeting, every phone hook-up, it was continually drummed in that we had to be number one in each format, because that's what it said in the Argus Review.'

While Marsh liked his boss personally, appreciating his energy and commitment, he was never convinced of the former Wallaby's affinity for cricket. 'He's a decent bloke,' says Marsh. 'I'll always have a conversation with him. But, Christ, he knows nothing about the game. Poor old Pat, he struggles to understand it. He just goes around repeating what other people say.'

Not that Howard would perhaps be alone in this. To Marsh, much about the game now seems mechanical: the gradgrindian obsession with work ethic; the intricate mesh of metrics; the robotic routines of throwdowns; the resource-rich National Cricket Centre in Brisbane. 'There are very few outcomes as far as I can see [at the NCC],' says Marsh. 'They're shovelling a lot of people through there but to me it almost hasn't got its own identity...'

The part that sticks with me is that they moved from here [Adelaide] to Brisbane allegedly because of better weather. So what do they do? Build a $28 million indoor centre.'

On the fashionable obsessive-compulsive practice methods of Steve Smith, meanwhile, Marsh detects the watermark of Ricky Ponting — one of his own great favourites, but with whom on batting he somewhat differs. 'Ricky always used to say that pro golfers just hit hundreds of thousands of balls,' explains Marsh. 'That was why they were so good, so why didn't the same thing apply to cricket? But a golf swing is a golf swing. In a round it hardly varies. With cricket there's a whole range of swings. You're not actually grooving them in the same way. You're trying to adapt to different conditions, and hitting a moving rather than a stationary ball.'

Is this why Australian teams disintegrate when the ball does deviate? Because we do. 'You've got to keep the good ball out,' Marsh sighs. 'And that's one thing we continue struggling with. If it's moving or spinning we haven't learned anything.' One thing's sure at any rate: Marsh could never have practised the Steve Smith way. 'I would've been bored shitless.'

Marsh is such a dedicated sceptic, that it's hard to resist asking him about another fashion, to do with the role he so adorned. The Test match after Marsh stood down from the national selection panel in November 2016, Australia dumped its unobtrusively effective keeper Peter Nevill in favour of the less reliable but more aggressive Matthew Wade. Would it have happened had Marsh still been in the chair?

Marsh laughs. 'Put it this way,' he says. 'I don't ever think that the wicketkeeper's job is to talk incessantly on the field. The wicketkeeper sets the example for the fielding team. To me the way you do that is: you are the man that wants to get up to the stumps and take the returns; you encourage them when they field well; you raise your eyebrows when they don't; you just continually work on raising the standard of the fielding group, which goes a long way to the bowlers bowling better. But you don't have to talk incessantly, saying stupid things, like 'well bowled' when someone's sent one four-foot-wide of off stump.' Marsh laughs. 'The nonsense they come up with now…'

Nonsense — there is a lot of it about. On Monday, some of the game's latter-day nonsense will come up for external scrutiny, with post-Cape Town independent 'cultural reviews' of CA and the Australian team to be released after almost seven months. What did Marsh tell them? 'Actually, nobody contacted me,' he reports.

Really? 'Really.'

Reminiscent of Marsh's brush with the Australian captaincy: sometimes what doesn't happen in cricket is as telling as what does.

* *Rod Marsh: The Complete Illustrated Autobiography is published by Affirm Press ($45, 304pp).*

CRICKET AUSTRALIA

ANNUAL GENERAL RUBBER STAMP

25 October 2018

It took, by my watch, 75 seconds to re-elect the board of Cricket Australia at the MCG this week, a third the time needed to read the audit and risk report aloud.

Three hands were perfunctorily raised at the mention of each name. Not so much democracy in action as democracy inaction.

To open his second three-year term, chairman David Peever then thanked his fellow directors, including departing Tony Harrison, although not departed Bob Every, who slated Peever's performance as 'sub-standard' on resigning six months ago.

The chairman moved on to express satisfaction with the new broadcast deal with Seven/Fox (whose negotiation he disastrously intervened in), the new memorandum of understanding with the Australian Cricketers' Association (whose negotiation he needlessly prolonged) and the winning of male and female 'Ashes titles'.

Amid the pastries and pleasantries in the Harrison Room, one's mind drifted back to the tenth-rate Moomba float on which a mortified Steve Smith and his colleagues had to pose after their Ashes… err… title… at Sydney in January.

Ah, innocent days of *schadenfreude*. Since then, Australia has won a single Test in six and a single one-day international in nine, slipping to fifth and sixth in those formats' rankings respectively. Asked later about the team's recent record, Peever limply offered that one was only as good as one's last performance — hardly the best-chosen cliché, as Australia had hours earlier been dismissed for 89 in a T20 international by Pakistan. Hell, the last time Australia's rankings sank so low, CA called it a crisis and commissioned a review. Oh yes, that reminds us…

For there was an elephant in the room with a sandpiper hide: the parallel external reviews of CA, led by Simon Longstaff, and of the Australian cricket team, led by Rick McCosker, occasioned by what Peever glancingly referred to as the 'incident in Cape Town'.

By all accounts these reviews have been substantially complete for many weeks, yet somehow *not quite done*, with the result that they could not be consulted by the state associations who own CA until *after* the annual meeting finished.

Of course, this could happen so easily. Perhaps the photocopier was out of toner. Perhaps Every sealed Peever's stapler in jelly as a prank. But, well, a little odd, wouldn't you say? After all, shareholders seeking to exercise their prerogative as owners of an organisation in an informed fashion might have found an independent assessment of said organisation's governance useful *before* voting.

CA is a sporting body, not an intelligence directorate, not a top-secret defence contractor. Its latest slogan is: 'It's Your Game.' Peever himself has told us that he is merely cricket's 'humble servant'. The public is positively gagging on unction.

But no, Peever insists that the reviews be released 'properly'. And so, on Monday at 10am, your correspondent will be joining colleagues in a lock-up at CA where we will peruse the reviews and be privately briefed — although not, puzzlingly, by either Messrs Longstaff or McCosker. Lloyd Pope could hardly impart more spin to his wrong 'un.

Just what can these reviews say, furthermore, that is remotely significant? They land, at last, with all the doings done. The critical positions of CEO, coach, captain and vice-captain(s) have all been refilled; the directors have all been reappointed; Peever at the annual meeting foreshadowed 'no change in the high-performance structure.'

Team performance boss Pat Howard last week foreshadowed his leaving… in basically another year when his contract expires. That's a longer farewell tour than Steve Waugh. What with CEO James Sutherland's one-year notice period, CA has become only slightly easier to leave than Hotel California.

Speaking of Sutherland, the annual meeting was his last day after twenty years of dark suits and uncomfortable doorstops. He is a good man, a tactful negotiator and skilled incrementalist: I realised that T20 was a revolutionary force when I saw him watching a game at the MCG without a tie.

Cricket owes him a good deal, although let's not forget he has also done exceedingly well out of it. In his valedictory address, Sutherland asked pardon for making some 'personal' remarks, which in the next breath he rendered impersonal by referring not to cricket's meaning for him but 'how much it means to so many Australians.' Hard to break the habits of a lifetime, eh James?

Sutherland then offered a curious comment about the 'romantics and nostalgics who would like it [cricket] not to change.' Hmm. This from the guy with the Lord Harris quote — 'You do well to love cricket, for it is more free from anything sordid, anything dishonourable, than any game in the world' etc — on his office wall…

Anyway, I would like to meet these people, these 'romantics and nostalgics'. I dare say they are out there somewhere. But they have bugger-all influence on the running of the game. There may once have been some rheumy-eyed retrospectors in the media, but they're long gone. After all, nothing must stand in the way of the sale.

This is one of cricket's zombie myths: that only the forces of reaction prevent its confident surge into the streamlined, rational and beckoningly lucrative corporatist future. It is belied by the fact that no game in the world could have changed so much in the last decade, in some ways for the better, although also in ways that have smacked of change for change's sake.

In any case, what is a game without romance or nostalgia? Actually, I'll tell you. It is Cape Town, where all that mattered was the desperate search for the next minuscule advantage… and not getting caught.

We must await Monday to learn what the Longstaff and McCosker reviews contain. But it's a fair guess that they will not be fingering romance and nostalgia as two of Australian cricket's biggest problems.

So farewell James Sutherland, with gratitude, and welcome successor Kevin Roberts, with goodwill, for all cricket has a stake in his success. But all cricket will not be convinced by a game where underinformed shareholders re-elect directors in less time than it takes to boil an egg.

CRICKET AUSTRALIA

CULTURE WARS

29 October 2018

As the clock ticked towards the Cricket Australia press conference at the MCG yesterday, a group of journalists who had been in the lock-up reading the independent review fell in behind the entourage of chairman David Peever en route to the designated venue, the Yarra Park Room.

The two loosely connected parties began walking… and walking. After passing through several doors and some minutes threading darkening corridors, realisation dawned: we had gone too far; we had taken a wrong turn somewhere; we were lost. A simple soul, I found it impossible to pass this gift metaphor up: the chairman has no idea where he's going.

Nor did it get much better from there. Perhaps not since Cape Town has there been a more hopeless press conference, and at least Steve Smith and Cameron Bancroft had weariness, confusion and youth as excuses; Peever found it completely impossible to explain how CA could now commit to a mission of cultural change without a solitary personnel change.

Peever described the review by Simon Longstaff of the Ethics Centre as motivated by the organisation's desire to 'look in the mirror'. But what to do when the mirror, as mirrors are wont to do, fails to flatter? He gave one convincing answer at least: that he's looking forward to this weekend's one-day international. I'll bet he is.

A 147-page report on culture and governance would not normally be considered a must read: Tim Paine, a little disappointingly, admitted to not having done so. But it repays study. Don't worry about the recommendations: they're ineffectual. Flick over the diagrams: they're superfluous. Try, if you can, to ignore the redactions: they are ridiculously extensive. CA is blaming the lawyers. Because that's what lawyers are for.

Instead, turn your eye to passages that I dare say we will be quoting from for the next decade, or the next review, whichever comes first. Longstaff finds that the ball-tampering incident at Newlands was not an aberration but 'an extreme example of a latent tendency growing out of the prevailing culture of men's cricket in Australia', players having 'internalised the belief that winning is the only thing that matters', and 'led to believe that their worth resides entirely in their capacity to meet CA's strategic and commercial goals'.

CA blithely 'assumed that the core values and principles of cricket would generate the ethical restraint needed to offset the focus on competition' within the Australian team. They were wrong. As an unidentified state administrator quoted by Longstaff puts it: '[Bancroft] should have said no, but he had no foundation on which to say no whatsoever.'

Yet this makes complete sense in organisational terms, says Longstaff, for CA is externally perceived as 'controlling and arrogant', and internally as 'an environment where people struggle to say "no" to people in positions of power and influence, which further enables leadership and power to be centralised'. And while players cop bans for their transgressions, 'the same standards do not apply to those who administer and govern the game.'

Longstaff hardly draws a more effective illustration than this: that CA's code of conduct for players extends to seventy 'legalistic' pages, that its code of conduct for staff runs to four including a dress code, and that it is not even clear the latter applies to the board.

'The bubble' is a widely-used metaphor for those wishing to describe the circumscribed world of the players, and elite athletes generally. But the bubble, Longstaff observes, is a phenomenon of administration too, and one passage could really have been written only with CA's team performance boss Pat Howard in mind: 'That is the tragic circumstance of those who live in the bubble. They are blinded by their noble intentions. They are desensitised by the logic of their arguments and the science that informs their principles. They believe that they are the clear-eyed realists and that others are deluded. They just cannot see the unintended effects of what they do — yet for which they are ultimately responsible.'

Howard, of course, merely implemented 2011's Argus Review; he had no say in its creation, or that of the Crawford-Carter review of CA's governance, conducted simultaneously, ushering in the independent board of which Peever was an original member and now chairs.

These reviews do not come off well. 'CA is a not-for-profit organisation,' Longstaff observes. 'However, the effect of both reports served to graft on a corporate model designed exclusively to generate a profit for the sport's 'shareholders' (the States) that was positioned as critical for the very survival of the sport in Australia.'

Here, arguably, Longstaff falls short, although the evidence is in his hands. He fails to make the obvious point that a system in which the shareholders are the strategic and financial vassals of the organisation they ostensibly own is almost impossible to reform.

Yesterday's press conference was all the proof you needed. While Peever deflected questions and repeated rote-learned responses, state chairmen who last week voted him another three-year term without the benefit of reading Longstaff's report sat there like waxworks dummies.

That's not a 'corporate model'. In a corporate model, there are external agents, such as regulators, such as institutions, such as government. Chairs resign; boards reconstitute; executives get fired, and even have bonuses clawed back. At Jolimont, somehow, a small elite award themselves promotions, new terms, fat benefits, cheery farewells. Let's not forget that the only reason we have been afforded this glimpse of the degree of cricket's organisational dysfunction is because a vigilant cameraman spied a cricketer scratching a cricket ball; otherwise CA would still be stumbling along counting its millions, oblivious to the players' discomfiture and the public's discontent.

Sometimes it is tempting to read between the lines of Longstaff's review — the sections that haven't been redacted anyway. One obiter dictum deserves a wider audience: 'One of the hard truths of leadership is that a person may need to accept responsibility for matters over which they do not exercise direct control — both for acts and omissions in the conduct of one's leadership.'

And if that truth is not understood? Then it needs to be reinforced until it is. You didn't need to be in that corridor yesterday to know it. David Peever is lost. Cricket needs to find another guide.

CRICKET AUSTRALIA

PEEVER AGONISTES

30 October 2018

The venerable mining chief John Ralph used to tell this story to prospective company chairmen.

One day, a chairman was handing over to his successor. 'If you get in trouble, go to the safe,' he said. 'In it, you'll find two numbered envelopes. They'll help you.'

So the new chairman took office, duly faced his first crisis, went to the safe and opened the first envelope. Inside was a piece of paper that read: 'Blame me.' So the chairman heaped blame at his predecessor's door, and crisis duly abated.

It worked so well that when in time a second crisis broke out, the new chairman could hardly wait to return to the safe. What pithy wisdom would the second envelope impart? Inside was a piece of paper that read: 'Prepare two envelopes.'

Which brings us to another mining man, coincidentally from the same group where Ralph was a tribal elder. David Peever spent twenty-seven years at Rio Tinto before becoming a member of the inaugural 'independent' board of Cricket Australia in 2012, succeeding to the chairmanship in 2015. Ralph's observation that chairs will generally be indulged one crisis but seldom more is presently being put to the test.

Last year, Peever was the key string-puller in CA's breathtakingly maladroit campaign to end the revenue share agreement with the Australian Cricketers' Association that had underpinned twenty years of sporting industrial peace.

Now he finds himself embroiled in another fiasco largely

of his own making. It was not Peever who applied sandpaper to a cricket ball at Newlands — he was, in a rare moment of good timing, flying in the opposite direction, away from South Africa. Peever did, however, put faith in an independent review of the 'culture and governance' of CA by Sydney's Ethics Centre — and independently does it read.

Dr Simon Longstaff's 147-page report is detailed, blunt and often scaldingly critical. In the case of Newlands, Longstaff concluded, CA were culpable for their failure to 'create and support a culture in which the will-to-win was balanced by an equal commitment to moral courage and ethical restraint.'

More generally, CA were widely regarded as 'arrogant and controlling', perceived to 'say one thing and do another', understood to be a place 'where people struggle to say "no" to people in positions of power and influence'.

The organisation would need 'to address the perception that it is (or believes itself to be) the sole or principal custodian of Australian cricket.' Like the Australian team in March, then, CA has been jolted to a realisation of their pent-up unpopularity.

In mitigation, one might observe that there but for the grace of God would go many a large Australian sporting organisation. How would the cultures and governance of various football codes emerge from similar scrutiny?

The difference was, however, that CA gave the Ethics Centre the keys to the shop, perhaps in expectation of a relatively gentle ride, as one of Longstaff's key findings is that really only the board and the senior executive of CA think they are going well — nobody else.

When CA did not get what they bargained for, the report appears to have stalled for some weeks. One reason for this, it is now apparent, was legal. As published, the review features no fewer than thirty-eight redactions to save the blushes of individuals named, causing it to resemble a copy of *Ulysses* as expurgated by the Kansas Board of Education.

Were there other reasons? Suffice to say that the delay was long enough for CA to appoint as its new CEO Kevin Roberts, Peever's preferred candidate, and to hold its annual meeting last Thursday, at which CA's state associations owners re-elected Peever for a second three-year term.

Then, and only then, were those associations permitted to partake of Longstaff's unsparing judgements — to which some of them, as respondents to his interviews and questionnaires, had contributed. As the state chairman sat there watching Peever hem and haw at Monday's review press conference, how many of them experienced buyers' remorse? Because it was, frankly, mortifying.

Peever's corporate career was mainly a corridor affair — he was instrumental in the lobbying against Labor's 2010 mining tax. To a public facing position, he has never looked particularly suited; to the role of cultural commissar he now appeared not only acutely out of his depth, but to incarnate the attitudes Longstaff described. He spoke of 'respecting' the findings, while evidently some distance short of accepting them. He claimed not to be 'embarrassed at all', in the next breath quibbling about 'reality' and 'perception'. In one rhetorical flight, Peever invoked 'the light on the hill', which he defined 'for all of us…that we want cricket to be the best that it can be.' He stopped short of asking cricket fans to maintain their rage and enthusiasm. Australian Associated Press reported him afterwards as 'adamant that he is going nowhere.' Quite.

Nothing being quite official until it happens on television, Peever concluded his day with a final *mea minima culpa* on the

ABC's 7.30 in which Leigh Sales made him resemble one of those inflatable clowns weighted in the bottom with sand who bounce upright when punched in the face.

'The work was never about, umm, ahh, dwelling on negatives,' Peever volunteered, *a propos* of nothing. 'This is a very important day for cricket and we are moving forward from here.'

'If you don't want to address the negative, how do you move forward from here?' Sales asked.

'Indeed, we're not dwelling on the negatives,' Peever continued in his impervious monotone. 'But we're, umm, ah, taking very seriously what has been written in the review and indeed, forty-two recommendations from the review, and already many of those are being actioned.'

Sales continued with the simplest question of all: 'How can the very same people who presided over this toxic culture now be the ones to change it, particularly when as the report explains you're the only people who couldn't identify the problems?'

Peever's was not an answer: 'Yeah cultural change comes about by understanding where some of the gaps are. This report identifies those gaps. And we will certainly, as I said, be using it to improve the game.'

The clincher, however, was Peever's contention that cricket was strong despite having experienced a 'hiccough in South Africa'. If it was merely a hiccough, what was this exhaustive review process about? If it was merely a hiccough, why have Australia's best two cricketers been sidelined for a year? Train wreck? This was the *Southern Aurora* colliding head on with the *Spirit of Progress.*

Peever's name, incidentally, does not appears in the review, leaving readers to wonder which redactions it may lurk beneath, because his influence certainly registers. Longstaff specifically addresses the contribution to the souring culture of last year's collective bargaining negotiations between CA and the ACA, which involved 'negotiation tactics described as arrogant' and which were 'cited as having contributed to dysfunction in relationships between CA and the players.' This pointless and destructive campaign was to a significant degree Peever's handiwork — it also acted as an opportunity for his protégé Roberts to audition to succeed James Sutherland.

Longstaff elsewhere makes mention of a bullying culture at CA 'said to be evident in other stakeholder relationships' and in 'the tactics employed when negotiating commercial outcomes', to which 'a blind eye' was turned. No more spectacular example of this exists than Peever's March intervention in the course of television rights negotiation, when he lambasted CA's broadcast partner the Ten Network as 'not prepared to challenge their operating model to be anything other than bottom feeders.'

Peever's scolding message to Armando Nunez, president of Ten's owner, CBS Studios, subsequently became public: 'Unfortunately your team has completely messed this up. I expected much more given our discussions and the unique position we were affording 10. Franky [sic], the tactics are appalling on a number of levels.'

Privately, according to fellow director Bob Every, who subsequently quit the board protesting his chairman's 'sub-standard' leadership, Peever offered to resign at the time, but in such a way as to cast doubt on his sincerity.

Publicly, Peever expressed regret, with the qualification that the message had been sent 'in the context of a negotiation' — the commercial counterpart to the time-honoured sledging cliché of 'what-happens-on-the-field-stays-on-the-field'.

Although only time will tell what the Longstaff review means in the longer-term, some are already exploring its potential — including the cricketers' trade union. Longstaff wants CA to 'establish a constructive working relationship involving a mediator' with the ACA, and to commence 'confidence building measures' — summoning up the image of Peever falling backwards into association president Greg Dyer's arms.

For the time being, rapport remains elusive. Dyer was yesterday arguing that the review's 'new evidence' justified a relaxation of the penalties imposed on Smith, Warner and Bancroft, which are, as has been widely observed, significantly out of proportion with those clapped on previous ball manhandlers.

Prima facie the case is good; second impressions are less flattering. Australia's ball tampering at Newlands was uniquely flagrant and egregious. There is some ambiguity about the use of a fingernail or the application of mint-flavoured saliva; Bancroft, with the connivance of Warner and acquiescence of Smith, premeditatedly undertook a clearly illegal practice, causing teammates, as well as the game, needless distress and financial loss.

The suspensions, furthermore, were not imposed for ball tampering alone — the trio were also sanctioned for evasions after the fact, at the press conference and with the investigator. They had the opportunity to appeal and did not take it.

Longstaff's review is helpful context rather than 'new evidence', and context is of necessarily limited value. We now understand, thanks to the Hayne Royal Commission, that ripping people off, dead and alive, was a cultural norm at banks and insurers. But this makes no difference to our distaste for individual depredations. The public seemed satisfied with the sentences on the three cricketers six months ago, and if fury has abated it still lurks beneath the surface.

That said, it would be a good deal easier for CA to reinforce the players' accountability were their board and officers held to some material form of account as well. That they have not merely reinforces Longstaff's view that 'the same standards [as apply to players] do not apply to those who administer and govern the game'. Indeed, they're hardly donning hair shirts at Jolimont. Sutherland concluded his seventeen-year tenure as CEO last week, leaving the cricket system financially richer yet in other respects spiritually weaker, while the ranks of well-paid executive general managers remain unchanged.

A new deputy chairman and heir apparent has been appointed, Earl Eddings from Victoria, which, looking forward, implies that CA's board will be chaired by a wealthy, conservative, middle-aged, suit-wearing white man out to 2024. The advent of the independent board six years ago was meant to expose CA to the winds of change and the rigours of the marketplace. Yet there is a case it has simply installed a new elite, less accessible and accountable than before, allowed for the unthinking assimilation of corporate values, for steady deterioration in the working environment, for flimsier relations with stakeholders, and, most publicly, cricket's public denigration.

'I serve as chairman at the pleasure of the board and I serve as a director at the pleasure of our owners, the states,' Peever reminded all present on Monday. A group of people, in other words, much like him. The game? The public? The nation? The spirit of cricket? Not so much. Yet on what we have seen this week, it's hard to avoid the conclusion that David Peever should set about preparing two envelopes.

CRICKET AUSTRALIA

DROPPING THE PILOT

1 November 2018

A school of thought is that Australian cricket teams need to reacquaint themselves with the crafts of batting long and batting ugly. They could look for an example to Cricket Australia's chairman David Peever.

For days he has provided a masterclass in chairing ugly, dimly inept in public, deaf to calls for his resignation from some of Australian cricket's most distinguished names and calls for his remaining from absolutely nobody.

But after the administrative equivalent of three from 167 balls, Peever has realised he is out, hit-wicket, having dropped a copy of the cultural review he commissioned in April on his stumps.

The irony is that the review, which this week caused such angst with its unsparing portrait of an 'arrogant and controlling' Jolimont junta, may be the one thing Peever got right — as potentially salutary and constructive for the organisation as Cape Town was for our cricketers.

The problem was that while the cricketers accepted their humbling public verdict, Peever's pettish response to the review on Monday became an exhibit of the self-same culture, unaccountable and high-handed, that the Centre's Dr Simon Longstaff described.

Peever's innings should never have been prolonged. The rigmarole around delaying distribution of the review to the state associations until *after* his re-election at last week's annual meeting brought discredit on everyone involved, including the associations themselves.

When Peever in June foreshadowed his seeking of a second three-year term, he did so in terms of 'continuity', at the outset of the executive search for a new CEO. To paraphrase *Lucky Jim*, this was a pseudo-solution to a non-problem. When a CEO departs like James Sutherland after seventeen years, the challenge is not stability but regeneration — even more so when that CEO is eventually succeeded by his chief operating officer.

Peever also spoke of having been 'asked by my colleagues' to extend his tenure to six years. We now know that one colleague was dead set against, Bob Every preferring to resign from the board than continue to serve on a board with a 'sub-standard' chairman.

But that left seven other directors, happy to leave it to Peever. And let's remember that he did not arrogate this role to himself; it took a whole board to acquiesce in the farcical annual meeting. Peever was elected unopposed except by common sense.

Now the first CA chairman to serve the entirety of his term as an independent becomes the first CA chairman to get the boot. This is not what the ace consultants David Crawford and Colin Carter had in mind when their January 2012 report ushered in the 'skills-based' nine-member board, to replace the old fourteen-member federal argy-bargy.

Peever Agonistes has now highlighted some potential weaknesses in the system. In theory the arrangement was meant to promote a cleaner division of responsibilities between board and executive; in practice it may have encouraged a division all too clean. Questions were raised last year about how well-informed directors were of the rancorous pay negotiations; one might equally ask whether directors troubled themselves sufficiently to get informed. The review implies a board that took residence in its own version of Longstaff's 'gilded bubble', oblivious to CA's deteriorating profile among stakeholders and the Australian team's declining stature.

Here is a further irony: that an organisation which preened itself on its customer focus — 'fans first' — saw them increasingly through a consumerist fuzz of its own making. When Cape Town happened, there remained no reserve of goodwill to draw on.

The chief problem, however, is that the board, having ceased to be directly representative of the states, became representative largely of itself. One of Longstaff's most reverberating conclusions reads: 'While those who lead "on the field" are held personally accountable for their performance — liable to be "dropped" for poor results or dismissed for bad conduct. The same standards do not apply to those who administer and govern the game. The issue here is one of consistency in relation to the obligations of leadership. One of the "hard truths" of leadership is that a person may need to accept responsibility for matters over which they do not exercise direct control — both for acts and omissions in the conduct of one's leadership.'

This has been an inglorious week in Australian cricket. An obdurate CA and supine state associations have shared the limelight with an opportunistic Australian Cricketers' Association, overeager to argue for lenience in the cases of Steve Smith, David Warner and Cameron Bancroft.

Again, this was the picking out of a non-problem. Were their bans too long? How about the length of this piece of string? People of goodwill can differ. The Longstaff review furnished valuable context but no 'new evidence' per se, no sandpaper being discerned on the Grassy Knoll.

It's arguable that it was precisely the trio's preparedness to accept their bans that exerted regime change pressure on Jolimont. By their compliance and contrition, Smith, Warner and Bancroft may have done the game a good governance turn.

It is customary in the event of a departure to utter a few words of commendation. In Peever's favour, it should be conceded that he genuinely loves the game and his job — perhaps a little too much, inasmuch as he was noted for tendencies to micromanagement. About his commitment to grass roots cricket, there was no reason to doubt his sincerity.

His misfortune, perhaps, is that the CA chairmanship, especially after Cape Town, required someone different, capable of building confidence and embracing change. In the end, the simplest way for him to do that was to leave.

CRICKET AUSTRALIA

WHO'S NEXT?

2 November 2018

In one of my favourite episodes of *The Thick of It*, the apoplectic Malcolm Tucker reassures a recently appointed minister that the prime minister won't sack her for a colossal media gaffe. 'Sacked after twelve months, looks like you've fucked up,' he explains. 'Sacked after a week, looks like he's fucked up.'

So before too many high-fives are exchanged about the de-election of Cricket Australia's ex-chairman David Peever a week after his re-election, let's call recent events by their proper name: a right royal fuck up, by a board who should know better, and involving a system that remains intact.

To reinforce the Ethics Centre's conclusion of a cultural malaise in the Australian game, CA went ahead and role played it before the eyes of a disbelieving public, buying into Peever's vision of change with continuity — after all, it had worked so well for Malcolm Turnbull. Then… well, you don't need me to tell you. But one take away seems pretty clear; whoever should succeed Peever in the long-term must come from outside.

CA musters some experienced directors. Jacqui Hey and John Harnden come well credentialled. But their main qualification for the chairmanship is that they are already on the CA board and, frankly, that's not a great one, especially when a 'core complaint' identified by Ethics Centre is 'that the organisation does not respect anyone other than its own.'

CA recently spent a reputed half a million dollars on a search for a new CEO that ended next to where it started. Something akin will invite ridicule which the game, after this week, can ill afford. So far, unfortunately, the push seems to be for circling the wagons. Former CA grandees threw their weight behind Mark Taylor, a distinguished former captain and board member since 2004. And, despite his visible reluctance to fill the role, it's true that he has more credibility than the rest of board's faceless men and women put together. Nineteen Test centuries will do that for you.

Everyone likes good old Tubby: when he lost his board seat in the spill of positions with the creation of the independent board in 2012, he was quickly found another. His dual role as CA powerbroker and Nine pundit — his contract was extended in June — has tended to occasion only low-level grumbling.

After all, we're all pretty relaxed here, eh? This is a country where national selectors act as commentators and talent managers and the national cricket body is a media outlet. What was it Taylor's old boss used to say? Oh yes: 'If you don't have a conflict, you don't have an interest' But maybe that hasn't been entirely to the good; maybe he is in a bit of a 'gilded bubble.'

Amid the present discontents, Taylor sat on the board sub-committee which liaised with the Ethics Centre. When asked about the review on Nine two months ago, he talked about its 'juicy' content and 'warts-and-all-reporting', then confusingly insisted it might be sealed.

Which hat was Taylor wearing here? Presumably his boardroom baggy green, for it is the business of the media to be on the side of maximum disclosure. It should be non-negotiable. Then, last Sunday, ahead of the review's release, Taylor offered: 'I'm sure that those in the media, people like ourselves, will enjoy the stuff in those reviews. That will come out.'

'People like ourselves.' Taylor now had on his porkpie hat with a ticket reading 'Press'.

Lastly, just days ago, as reactions roiled to Peever's pratfalls, Taylor was busily opining on Nine that it was 'far too early to be making any rash decisions', insisting that everyone was 'jumping the gun in terms of wanting to make widespread changes' and should 'wait for things to settle down in the coming weeks.'

It wasn't a hat he was wearing this time but a helmet — and, as Thursday's events proved, he was certainly not reading cricket's room. Taylor is a likeable man whose contribution to Australian cricket commands respect. But the rush to endorse him suggests that we're still blinkered by what might be called the 'good bloke' factor.

So who might take the chair? It is easier to come up with a range of useful attributes than someone who fits them all. Some favour a distinguished ex-player, although such an individual might be short of organisational experience; some incline to a public figure, a former politician or mandarin, although this might alienate as many supporters as it engages.

A key responsibility of whomever is tapped will be to restore relations between CA and the state associations, which have in recent years been aggravated by Jolimont's tendencies to centralisation and unilateralism. The deterioration was dramatised last week by the (belated) push back of the board of Cricket NSW in response to the content of the Ethics Centre review.

In that sense, recent administrative events can be read in terms similar to those of the public response to Cape Town, which for many fans was a last straw, a final insult — out of proportion to the specific offence, the reaction representing the achievement of a critical mass of dismay. The review was not be ridden out by a few monotone 'moving forwards' and 'very importants'.

What's also necessary, because it has been conspicuously lacking at Jolimont just lately, is a sense of urgency. At stages this year, CA has seemed to want to slow down time. Time has stubbornly declined to wait. Long notice periods. Drawn out contract completions. Grinding bureaucratic processes. And they have been set at nought by what Harold Macmillan warned politicians of: 'Events, dear boy, events.'

So let's have a chairman sooner rather than later — in fact, as Malcolm Tucker was known to put in text form, 'ASAFP'. The F standing, of course, as a character remarked, for 'feasibly'.

CRICKET AUSTRALIA

HOWARD'S END

3 November 2018

In his cool appraisal of the culture and governance of Cricket Australia released last week, the Ethics Centre's Simon Longstaff includes a piquant paragraph about the 'tragic circumstance' of sporting officials caught up in their corporate mission.

'They are blinded by their noble intentions,' observes Longstaff. 'They are desensitised by the logic of their arguments and the science that informs their principles. They believe that they are the clear-eyed realists and that others are deluded. They just cannot see the unintended effects of what they do — yet for which they are ultimately responsible.'

Who Longstaff had in mind specifically might have been clear but for the review's 38 lengthy redactions, but it was hard to avoid the thought that he was describing Pat Howard, CA's guru of high performance through seven years of frequently mediocre performance that has left the men's team ranked more or less where it started.

Howard, with whom CA yesterday parted company as part of an executive reshuffle that looked more like a game of 52 Pick Up, was recruited from rugby to a role created by 2011's Argus Review to be the cricket's 'single point of accountability'.

Twice Howard managed to push this accountability down, consecutively moving on Mickey Arthur and Darren Lehmann. Yet, energetic and driven, he kept the confidence of his board and CEO James Sutherland, and never looked other than completely convinced of his rightness — reminiscent in his way of *The Quiet American*'s

Alden Pyle, in being 'impregnably armoured by his good intentions and his ignorance'.

Howard asked many useful questions of the way cricket has historically developed young talent. Unfortunately, he could never sit still long enough to listen to the answers. He preferred systems to sentiments, algorithms to intuition. His infatuation with youth and obeisance to data were well-intentioned notions carried to excess.

Yet in some ways, Howard was as much a captive of the system as anyone. As Longstaff noted, Howard's unit was 'given virtual carte blanche in its quest to produce a winning national team'. Everything and everyone had to bow down before it, leaving first-class and first-grade cricket simultaneously overmanaged and under-resourced.

Instead, fortunes have been lavished on pathways cricket with precious little to show for it, in the men's game at least. Anecdotally, too, not even those on the right side of the velvet rope enjoy it all that much. There is talk of teens struggling with overpraise, unable to process criticism, disenchanted by favouritism, burned out by the busy work of 2km time trials and skinfolds, yanked from their local support networks by the need to push numbers through the National Cricket Centre.

Frankly, however, this is precisely what CA wished Howard to do, and in which it urged him on at every step, even as bureaucracy, as bureaucracy is wont to do, developed a stake in its own survival, and as the old organic processes, subverted or suspended, slipped into neglect.

There were economic imperatives too. Cricket must now churn out lots more cricketers than of yore — sufficient for three international formats, and a domestic season radically expanded by the Big Bash League. Howard's confidence in Australia's ability to be number one in Test, one-day and T20 cricket never faltered, but even he must have felt the pressures of mission creep.

So, we must ask again, where were directors? As Ian Chappell pointed out last week, CA's board has never been long on cricket experience. But with the game in a phase of accelerated change, this has become a conspicuous lack. Whatever one may think of the changes wrought to talent management in Australian cricket, they have lacked genuine contestation. It's all very well to criticise Howard's ideas. But who, except behind their hands, was prepared to challenge them?

The management changes announced yesterday bear the imprint of new CEO Kevin Roberts, whom the Ethics Centre in its unsparing critique has effectively handed a mandate for change. It now requires little imagination to conclude which persons featured in most of the report's redacted matter — Howard and Ben Amarfio, CA's executive general manager commercial, also ushered out the door yesterday after developing a problematic reputation among commercial partners and in the columns of the *Financial Review's* Joe Aston.

The issue for Roberts now is to separate himself from the 'culture and governance' that has brought CA into disrepute. After all, he served on the board from 2012 to 2015, and has been a senior executive since. Can one offer solutions if one has been part of the problem? The jury is out. And suffice it to say that some of that jury's members are still thinking.

An executive purge is one way of appeasing a clamour for change. But as they say in business, it isn't who you fire but who you hire. Restoring faith in CA's bona fides will require a high-performance chief of high calibre, one capable of listening as well as talking.

It's also possible that, especially with the growth of women's cricket, the role has grown too large for a single person and could do with a serious cricket thinker reinforced by a skilled administrator. Alternatively, it could be scaled down to a role on par with that of the national coach. Above all, however, what CA could do with in this role is someone who sees cricket for what it is rather than what they want it to be, with a feeling for outcomes as well as intentions.

CRICKET AUSTRALIA

THE MESS WE'RE IN

8 November 2018

How broken is Australian cricket? That depends on how you evaluate its health. It has $1.2 billion of television money to look forward to. Pity about the fragile Australian men's team and an administration turning cannibal.

Far harder to obtain a measure of is the club system on which the game has immemorially been built. Anecdotally, it is far from well. In Brisbane last week, in fact, it came to a point that may well be a test case of Cricket Australia's stewardship of the game.

Brisbane has a dozen first-grade clubs, and they are fed up. Dictated to by a bureaucracy that claims always to know best, they are mounting a resistance.

It is no small thing to bring together clubs that are fierce on-field rivals, but presidents met on Wednesday night to form a committee to directly lobby the board of Queensland Cricket over the heads of a management that insists its hands and purse strings are tied from Jolimont.

Their message: in the worship at the high-performance altar, the integrity of local competition has been sacrificed. It is nearly beyond repair.

First-grade clubs play almost a third more days of cricket than they did twenty years ago, fixtures bloated by T20. Yet, paradoxically, results are chronically distorted by workload restrictions on individuals, in a Goldilocks-like search for quantities of cricket that are 'just right'.

These restrictions are partly to allow for elite pathways cricket, from Futures League to junior carnivals, where it is not uncommon to see twenty paid support staff, on grounds that the first-grade clubs are compelled to provide for next to nix.

At the same time as distributions to volunteer-run clubs are declining in real terms, so is the busywork increasing, with first-grade essentially operating seven days of the week for eight months of the year, much of the time filling out forms.

Five years ago, QC required clubs to sign off on a governance, management and administration checklist with sixty sub-headings; now there are twice as many, including such requirements as 'align strategic plan to National Performance', which presumably doesn't meant to go seventeen weeks without winning a game.

Despite this, first-grade performances seem to have negligible significance in state selection, and if you are over twenty-five and haven't broken through then you might as well give up: the system has a vampiric preference for young blood.

As John Buchanan asked recently on his return to coaching Wests and finding one player over thirty-five in his top four grades: where are the older players? 'That used to be where you got your best coaching — playing with and against the older guys,' he noted. 'All the talk about ethics in Australian cricket traces back to this because the older guys may have played it tough but they pretty well played within the rules and they would sit down and have a beer at the end and talk through the day.'

The other obsession is with junior participation — the deployment of game development officers to plump numbers and hit head office KPIs, so as better to tickle the fancy of sponsors. As part of their obligations, QC now requires first-grade clubs to go 'into schools' to widen the CA catchment. Cricket has always been a numbers game, but it's at the point where it seems that the attached bodies and souls matter far less.

What antagonises the clubs mainly, however, is the attitude — the establishment's arrogance and condescension, which Simon Longstaff of the Ethics Centre nailed as the core complaint of CA's stakeholders.

Let's remind ourselves that CA last year presented itself as on the side of the battlers, going to war with its elite players over the parlous state of 'grass roots cricket'. Yet in Queensland, home state of cricket's $200,000-a-year 'humble servant' David Peever, it's been happy to mow grade cricket to ground level.

Those who run grade cricket are the not just the salt of the game; they are often smart, practical, well-informed, highly-motivated and, because they have lives and knowledge bases outside the game, worldly wise. The system, however, treats them as peasants. And as governance gurus have lauded 'independence' as a panacea for a forward-looking game, so clubs have found themselves disenfranchised in every state, maligned as parochial and conservative in the headlong pursuit of 'new markets' and aspirations to out-AFL the AFL.

One of the initiatives discussed at Wednesday night's meeting was especially interesting: a national club representative body to lobby CA, and maybe provide a bit of that new-fangled elite honesty. Brisbane has it worse than most cities, with minimal local government support. But premier competitions all over Australia have variations on similar complaints.

In the medium-term, the real challenge is to CA's barely-concealed desire to control everything in cricket not nailed down plus quite a lot that is. The abrupt exit of team performance boss Pat Howard last week hinted at a change of tack, although he leaves behind a talent management diagram resembling that of a UN agency.

This will be interesting task for new CEO Kevin Roberts, whose chief role at CA, apart from kicking sand in the Australian Cricketers' Association's face, has been knitting the state associations ever more tightly into a centralised model, in which all wisdom flows from postcode 3002.

Now CA wants us to know, via its marketing mouthpieces, that 'It's Your Game'. It's hardly a persuasive message if the high-performance boffins are preventing your club using first-choice quicks for more than a few overs because they have an imminent state second XI commitment, thereby effectively penalising you for having a strong attack and souring the match for their teammates.

As with everything, as with life, as with the title of Longstaff's report, these things are 'a matter of balance'. But there's good evidence that CA has had this out of whack too long and grown indifferent to the practical consequences of its actions. Wealth is not health, and never was.

CRICKET AUSTRALIA

CLUBBED TO DEATH

15 November 2018

Last Saturday, in a top of the table clash in Perth first-grade cricket, Claremont-Nedlands took the field to defend 283 against University of Western Australia at picturesque University Oval.

Claremont-Nedlands, the Tigers, formed in a merger thirty years ago but with roots preceding Federation, are the competition's reigning two- and one-day premiers, with serious sponsors, a strong culture and a well-organised junior programme. Their first-choice attack features state opening bowlers Matt Kelly and Joel Paris, and Futures League all-rounders Tim David and Brad Hope.

Except it didn't work out that way. As occurs late every week in the premier competition in each capital city, the local association advised clubs of those bowlers whose workloads were to be 'managed' — and it happened that this covered the entire Tigers' attack.

David was allowed to bowl ten overs, and 'accidentally' snuck in an extra couple, dismissing University's Warriors opener Will Bosisto. But Kelly was forbidden from playing after bowling thirty-odd overs each in two Sheffield Shield games, while Paris and Hope were allowed to play only as batsmen.

Paris has been minutely managed since injuries after a brief international exposure almost three years ago; Hope had reported soreness after a gym session. They looked on as their youthful stand-ins were put to the sword, University piling up six for 446 including a double hundred by Surrey import Will Jacks. So pointless did the contest grow that the last dozen overs were bowled by part-timers. The game was attended by West Australia's talent development manager David Fitzgerald. One wonders what on earth he could have learned from such a catchweight contest.

I relate this story not because it is unusual but because it isn't. As observed, such strength and conditioning restrictions on players in Cricket Australia's high-performance stream are imposed every week and passed on by the likes of Fitzgerald with a 'sorry-mate-them's-the-rules' shoulder shrug.

The system has operated for most of Pat Howard's recently-concluded reign as executive general manager, team performance — and let us say with pure intentions. Yet whatever injuries it may have prevented, it has taken toll in other ways, less measurable but more meaningful.

'Workload management': the very expression is dismal, a beautiful game described in terms better suited to treadwheeling or hod carrying. Worse actually: 'workload management' reduces the cricketer to a kind of externally-controlled mechanism, without a will of his own, and alienated from his body, which is essentially leased back to him on certain prescribed terms.

Workload management is meant, of course, to be in bowlers' interests, to protect them from the suasion of peer pressure and excesses of zeal and adventure, including the desire to explore their limits. The troubles with the regime are various while also obvious. Games are debased. Competitions cease to be decided by merit. Cricketers' dignity is infringed. Who is a bowler who cannot bowl? Who is a batsman who makes hay against second-liners? They are participants in a cricket charade.

The restrictions impinge further, impacting the quality of practice, even the point of it. The bowler who arrives at a net session with a quota of thirty permissible deliveries is in no position to experimentally vary intensities or to hone skills. The exercise becomes one of quantity, as though the cricketer is merely a vessel to be filled with cricket up to a sharply drawn line.

Some strength and conditioning gurus are reputedly so anxious to sterilise interaction of bat and ball at the moment that they are encouraging bowlers to commence bowling in empty nets, lest they enter too willingly into a contest before being adequately warmed up.

Yet reduce the quality of practice bowling, and you also reduce the quality of practice batting, setting the scene for a skills race to the bottom. Some modern batsmen are fine with this: they look to nets only for 'confidence'. But it's a fragile confidence, with nothing much learned and still less improved.

Coincidentally, there exists a school of thought in Australian cricket about the baleful influence on our batting stocks of throwdowns, delivered manually and by sidearm — such methods, it is claimed, have deskilled our batsmen, whose grooved swings cannot cope with a ball deviating untowardly.

It echoes a line of argument of the 1980s — the last time Australian batting was in so parlous a state, although a veritable golden era compared to today — about the impact of bowling machines, which it was feared would beget robotic batsmanship.

I'll present no finding here. But both reasonings overlook why we turn to mechanical aids in the first place. It's because batting and bowling impose such unequal physical burdens — it being far easier to face 10,000 balls than bowl them, we will always be shorter of bowling than batting. There are no batting machines or side bats.

The throwdown, I suspect, established itself as means of making up for that difference; since artificial limitations on bowling loads began to be imposed, it has spread like lantana.

In addition, there now exists a form of the game, T20, in which the contest between bat against ball is arguably less meaningful than that between bat against bat.

When batting is about hitting, when the supply of quality bowling is limited anyway, and when any game failure will be excused as arising from the stress and chaos of the format, what incentive exists to do more than gorge on the sidearm anyway?

Last week in Australian cricket were reported two seemingly separate concerns: a limited-overs batting line-up which its captain Aaron Finch deemed 'one-dimensional', and pace bowling reserves regarded as so valuable to as to necessitate their deafening to the siren song of Indian Premier League.

Or were these flip sides of the same problem, that cricket is being compromised by its steady industrialisation and bureaucratisation, that artificial expedients have supplanted natural balances and that quantity is thinning quality, but that too many jobs depend on the continuity of current practices for this to be seriously questioned? What transpired last week at University Oval, then, was a bad game, may have been a useful case study.

GEORGE BAILEY

ALL IN THE FAMILY

20 November 2018

What goes in to making an Australian cricketer?

The question could be answered any number of ways, and the formula is one the boffins would dearly love to work out — imagine a eugenics department at the National Cricket Centre, cloning its own baggy green master race.

Until then, it's worth consulting an intriguing new case study of a family tree with green and gold sprigs thirteen decades apart.

Aged thirty-six, Tasmania's captain George John Bailey looks to be on a last playing lap after an honourable career including only five Tests but 120 other international caps; his great-great grandfather George Herbert Bailey also led Tasmania, and represented Australia on their non-Test tour of England in 1878.

This much I knew, but an utterly unique book by Tasmanian journalist Martin Rogers reveals so very much more. It is called *Cricket in the Genes*, updating for the genome generation such tales of consanguinity as Dudley Nourse's *Cricket in the Blood* and John Edrich's *Runs in the Family.*

At 263 copiously illustrated pages, it's the most comprehensive Bailey genealogy one could imagine, tree boughs almost breaking with detail, with cricket such a recurrent theme that had the current George done anything else with his life there would almost have been reason to doubt his patrimony.

Of course, as in every family chronicle, there is much more besides, including the obligatory convict quotient: George's great-great-great-great-great-grandmother was the First Fleet's youngest female prisoner; his great-great-great-great grandfather was twice sentenced to death, for theft in England commuted to transportation, and for piracy in the colonies, having stolen a boat during one of his three escapes from jail.

But cricket quickly pervades the picture. George Gibson, whose father David it was who twice dodged the noose before becoming a successful pastoralist, represented Tasmania in the very first game of first-class cricket in the colonies, when the colony hosted a Victorian XI at Launceston Racecourse in February 1851. He later became a member of parliament, and father-in-law to George Herbert Bailey.

George Herbert's clergyman father was also a votary of cricket. Before his recruitment by Tasmania's Anglican Church, Rev Brooke Bailey had fostered the game as headmaster of Ceylon's prestigious Royal College and insisted on an English boarding school education for his son heavy on the sport.

Born in Colombo, George Herbert grew into a polished specimen of Anglo-Australian manhood: a fine cricketer, footballer, diocesan lay reader and senior bank employee. These were excellent credentials when the original colonial team to tour England was chosen, and it was arguably Bailey's inclusion which entitled the combination to that proto-national descriptor 'Australia', he being the only player not from Victoria or New South Wales.

There might have been a second Tasmanian, thirty-year-old opening batsman John Lake Allen Arthur, but two days after receiving an invitation to join the party he dropped dead of 'brain fever'.

As it was, George Herbert Bailey alone carried the hopes of Tasmania, and discharged them honourably, finishing third in the batting averages, and might have played Test cricket but for the prior calls of the Union Bank. His gifted sporting sons with Isobel nee Gibson then ran into the generational calamity of the Great War.

Keith, lucky in that a cleft palate prevented his enlistment, played first-class cricket and senior football. But Guy, who appeared in first-grade cricket for Melbourne University while studying medicine, was blown to atoms by an artillery shell; Roy, captain of Tasmania's football team, never recovered from two exposures to poison gas; Alan, in the first XI at Hutchins, was invalided home from the Dardanelles with typhoid.

Pardon here a personal digression, substantiating the cliché about every Tasmanian being somehow related: turns out that Alan, George John's great-great grandfather, married Marjorie Elvie Walch, whose great uncle was my great-great-grandfather Charles Edward Walch. So next time I see George I'll be addressing him as 'cuz'.

But what's chiefly striking about the unfolding tale is the many different ways that the house of Bailey has shaped and been shaped by cricket. This is not a saga in the vein of the Mohammeds, the Chappells or the Waughs. The Bailey family's relationship with cricket is not built around success alone but on a deep and abiding love.

George's mother Carmen had a great-great grandfather, Joseph, among the founders of Melbourne's Brighton CC. Joseph's four sons then played staggering volumes of school, club and social cricket, travelled miles to watch big games, collected cricketana, served as club officials. One son accomplished the notable double of playing club matches against W. G. Grace and during the Battle of Britain.

George Bailey's father John, proud owner of a complete set of *Wisden*, has given a lifetime to cricket. A player and captain at Launceston Grammar, he returned as coach for fifteen years, where his son led a first XI team that included James Faulkner and Tom Triffitt; today, he leads Tasmania's over-60s team.

At the end of *Cricket in the Genes*, George reflects that he has enjoyed the game so much he is unsure what will 'replace cricket' in his life. The lesson of his heredity is that there is no need. Cricket is a lifetime's companion. There are numberless ways to savour and serve it, and they do not end with the hanging up of a cap or the passing on of a captaincy. A concluding thought bubble: the background that made George Bailey an exemplary Australian cricketer equips him perfectly to succeed Mark Taylor on the Cricket Australia board.

AUSTRALIA A

TRASHING THE BRAND

22 November 2018

From Jolimont last week were handed down two nationally representative cricket teams. Attention fell on one; the other told a tale too.

Australia picked a fourteen-member squad for the First Test in Adelaide. Such is local pessimism that some would favour us being allowed to play all of them at once.

The combination is not so much weak as clearly uncertain, with so many moveable parts and inherent variables. None of the batsmen are genuinely grooved in their slots — it's almost a team of natural number fives. Shaun Marsh should bat there, perhaps designated 5a, having finally achieved consistency in that role last season. But, seven years into his Test career, Australia is also entitled to expect more of him.

The pace bowling is set for such a punishing schedule that, dare one say it, rotation must be an option. Twenty days' Test cricket in thirty-three? Only a sadist, or a batsman, could come up with such a regime. This renders likelier the inclusion of Mitchell Marsh, to provide auxiliary overs as well as to bolster the team's quotas of Marshes and of vice-captains. After that, who knows? We are searching for omens, trusting in providence.

One figure who should have been walking a little taller on Thursday, and deservedly, was Victoria's coach Andrew McDonald, whose state seems at last to have been acknowledged as Australia's domestic bellwether.

Having won three of the last four Sheffield Shields, and again streeting the competition this season, Victoria rightly provides more than a third of the Test squad.

Confusingly, however, this same notion, that domestic performance counts, did not filter down into the second team the selectors picked — the Cricket Australia XI, led by Sam Whiteman, who'll take the Indians on at the Sydney Cricket Ground from next Wednesday.

Passing little remarked on Thursday, it is a genuine oddity, the names reading like the answers to a list of very difficult cricket trivia questions.

Three years ago, Whiteman appeared to have good prospects of succeeding Brad Haddin as Australia's gloveman. Injury and form have confined him to two T20 and one List A match since January 2017. Only he and fringe New South Wales pace bowler Harry Conway in the CA XI have played more than ten first-class matches.

Non-Test matches on tours, it should be said, are a vexed area. Our visitors do a good deal of the vexing. In England this year, the Board of Control for Cricket in India demanded that their tour match against Essex be called off after three days rather than four, thinking it too hot; on this trip, they have demanded the opposite, that this match against the CA XI be extended from three to four days.

They are, meanwhile, poor hosts, recently denying the visiting West Indies any more than a single two-day warm-up match in out-of-the-way Vadodara, and forcing the West Indies Cricket Board to pay for their own preparatory camp in the UAE.

Mind you, India are hardly on their own in such stunts. A recent communiqué from the ICC cricket committee concerned 'clear expectations for the treatment of visiting teams particularly around practice facilities, warm-up matches and logistical arrangements.' It evidently did not reach the Pakistan Cricket Board, who in the UAE offered a warm-up game against a Pakistan A team without a single specialist spinner. The Marshes put on 207, which looked like a classic rope-a-dope when they then eked out 44 runs in eight Test innings between them.

Anyway, in that slightly preachy way it has of telling the world its business, Jolimont announced in June that it intended doing better. Head of operations Peter Roach said that CA would 'set an example for everyone else to follow' by committing to 'good warm-up games, suitable conditions and standard of opposition' and 'play a real part in helping international teams prepare as best they can.'

So how does a CA XI of pet projects and foragings from down the back of the couch square with that?

It's pleasing to see Whiteman back; the team contains some handy young cricketers, and good luck to them. But have they really earned the privilege of mixing it with international opposition? For it is a privilege, or at least should be.

Time was when there existed a sense of occasion around the touring team readying for Tests forthcoming. Tour matches were chances for the next rung of players to stake claims, for keen followers to see the visitors in more intimate surrounds.

Until quite recently, the visitors versus Australia A, composed of the next best outside the Test team, was a showpiece event, almost an additional Test, broadcast on free-to-air television. But we last did that in 2013-14; since then we've offered flecks from our gilded pathways, like the unlamented CA XI that for three seasons debased the domestic fifty-over competition.

How much more worthwhile would India's SCG fixture have been had it involved an Australia A of those nearer the head of queue for international selection, such as Marcus Stoinis, Jake Weatherald, Jhye Richardson and Jackson Bird, or rewarding those in good domestic form, like Alex Doolan and Joe Mennie; Marcus Harris or Peter Handscomb might even have been chosen, for a taste of their looming challenge.

Rather than the zombie version of a bad idea in prospect, such a match would have offered an opportunity to gauge such players against quality opposition, maybe to set the Indians back on their heels a little.

As it is, we will roll into Adelaide in a cloud of hopeful vagueness. Perhaps that is the underlying sentiment — our need to clutch this as long as possible. It's a strategy, but not a terribly robust one.

TEST MATCH CRICKET

OUR GAME

30 November 2018

'It's Your Game' runs the condescending folksy advertising campaign for the summer's cricket, at odds with the pretensions of elite honesty and processes of stealth privatisation. But next week, it will make a last make a little sense, with the coming of a Test match, which you will be able to watch, the old-fashioned way, for free.

Here's a paradox at cricket's heart: that the formats most allegedly demotic are those it's been deemed most economically expedient to cordon off, and that the format often maligned as exclusive and esoteric remains most democratic.

Unlike India with its inconvenient grounds and weird ticket rackets, and England with its astronomical admission prices and chronic scarcities, Test cricket in Australia remains of the people, by the people, for the people.

Even better, Adelaide offers a Test in sunlight again — thanks to the obduracy of the Board of Control for Cricket in India, but bully for them.

Whatever its merits as a television product, pink ball cricket has so far been a squib for live spectators: muted days and half-deserted nights to follow the wasted mornings.

The games' most constructive outcomes have been indirectly sought — the extra grass thatches to make up for the ball's deficiencies, sharpening the contest between batsman and bowler. But to have evenings back in Adelaide, however temporarily, will be a blessed relief, not least to the local economy, in the pubs, restaurants, functions and events where the play of days has historically been savoured and debated — again, all part of the Test match's democratic, communitarian character.

Let's extend this further. The First Test looms large in what's widely regarded as a summer in which cricket will fight to restore credibility forfeited in a game-threatening controversy.

Controversy is an outcome of untoward events in contexts of significance. It serves to reveal what we value, what we wish to defend.

The underarm ball is recalled today as a conspicuous sporting scandal. But it was also, in its way, the moment one-day cricket in this country came of age, demonstrating that it too was capable of generating passions, splitting opinion.

You can argue that T20 cricket, for all its thrills and spills, has yet to engage imaginations the same way. With the possible exception of the spot-fixing murk that marred the Indian Premier League five years ago, its scandals have been temporary, local, jejune.

One-day cricket, meanwhile, has turned into too much of a commodity product to matter overly anymore. Where it has seemed to involve bigger stakes — the 1996 Eden Gardens riot, the 2003 armbands of Andy Flower and Henry Olonga, the 2007 death of Bob Woolmer — it has needed the contextual enrichment of a World Cup.

So let's say this for Sandpapergate — it testified to the abiding resonance of Test cricket. The live events, broadcast on pay television in the early hours of the morning, were actually seen by relatively few, and are recalled now in somewhat of a jumble. Yet what a moment. Would it have mattered quite so much had Cameron Bancroft dropped sandpaper down a pair of canary yellow strides while wearing a shirt whose replica you could purchase at the merchandising kiosk? No, the offence drew its shock value from the transgressors being so representative — in pristine white, beneath their revered caps, and thereby performing in the nation's name.

Nor, thanks to the Test match's duration, was there any escaping to seclusion. Steve Smith and David Warner began their penance in full public gaze the following morning, when they returned to the field stripped of their hard-won titles. In no other format of any sport, I think, was such a scenario possible, and, if it may seem scant consolation, it had the quality of momentousness that brings sport to life.

That being so, redemption can only begin in similar circumstances, on a Test match field. Even had they not been behind a pay television rampart, would any of the summer's internationals have mattered all that much? We turn to such stuff for excitement, for distraction, for fun — not that there's anything wrong with that. But still it is the Test match that slows us down, makes us dwell, forces us to think, causes us to remember — and just occasionally stirs us to fury. Which, incidentally, is why the future of Test cricket really does matter, rather than simply being something it would be kind of nice to have around the place, like an attractive lamp or fresh flowers.

The exquisite burden of Test cricket, it should be added, does not fall on us alone. It imposes on our visitors too. Steve Waugh used to speak of India as Australia's 'final frontier'; with our manifold and appreciable home advantages, we are theirs. Across more than seven decades, India have won five Tests in Australia out of 44, two of them against Bob Simpson's 1977-78 cadet corps; they have not won a Test here in more than a decade.

So if Australia is at less than full strength, history also bears down on Virat Kohli, for stronger Indian teams than his have failed in these parts. If India retain the Border-Gavaskar Trophy, they will have earned it.

That's another strengthening facet of Test cricket — that its continuity imbues it with the quality of the quest, with further quests within. Nothing in the northern summer was quite so compelling, for example, that Kohli's recurrent duel with James Anderson, who had the better of him four years ago but this year had to bend the knee.

So let's go to Adelaide contemplating something greater than Australia's prospects, which will at all events wax and wane, with some feeling for the rich, layered drama that only five-day cricket provides, for it will only be our game if we make it so.

FIRST TEST PREVIEW

TWO UNDERDOGS?

5 December 2018

This summer's Border-Gavaskar Trophy starts with a novel feel as a contest that seems to involve two underdogs.

Each team, one suspects, would like the other to be regarded as favourite, easing the burden of expectation, affording them slightly greater licence. Each team has a disconcertingly good case.

India sits atop the International Cricket's Test ladder, but in an era where quality is being stretched thin by the game's various mutations, and this year have lost six of eight Tests on the road.

Australia, depleted, ranks fifth, but in this decade has lost only five and won 27 Tests on home soil.

Both combinations are bowling bulls, batting bears.

Australia's top order, with Smith and Warner out of calculations for obvious reasons, and Renshaw and Maxwell out of favour for less obvious reasons, looks as temporary as a shantytown awaiting a bulldozer.

With the Sheffield Shield on hiatus until 23 February, moreover, there will be no up-to-date red ball batting data for selectors to work off. Look forward to more hunches, favourites being petted and kites being flown. There will, of course, be bucket hats, so that's all fine…

India, meanwhile, have problems very nearly as pressing. This week's scads of armchair Kohliology — and seriously, can we generate any more? — is as much about the limitations of the rest of his order, now deprived of the precocious Prithvi Shaw, nor balanced by Hardik Pandya.

Kohli is clearly the most coveted wicket on either side — the one likeliest to touch off a mardi gras of celebration. Daylight separates his away average (47.4) from those of Chetheshwar Pujara (36), KL Rahul (33) and the enigmatic Rohit Sharma (25). Superior Indian line-ups than this have come to grief here.

The figure whose influence may be almost as great as Kohli's is his vice-captain Ajinkya Rahane. Four years ago in these climes, admittedly in a flat pitch series bossed by batsmen, Rahane looked like the next big thing — cool, compact, disarmingly powerful. Yet he had an indifferent time at last start against Australia and has not scored a Test century since August last year. A return to form would be timely; it could even be decisive.

If nobody aspires to the mantle of front runner in this series, who deserves it? On balance, and it is a very fine one, Australia. In this country, fast bowling affords a team a keen edge.

Don't underestimate India's bowling unit. It has strength in depth. But coming off a home series against West Indies faces an acclimatisation challenge. Tim Paine has the right toolkit in the most suitable workshop.

Mitchell Starc, Josh Hazelwood and Pat Cummins are only a year older than when they hoovered up 66 English wickets in last summer's Ashes, and they have been vacuum-sealed since in anticipation of a demanding home summer.

Coach Justin Langer clearly esteems Peter Siddle and has been prepared to overlook prior reservations about Chris Tremain.

On the sidelines loiter sprightly Jhye Richardson and sharpish Brendan Doggett, not to mention the dependable Scott Boland and Joe Mennie, neither of them thirty, both at peak proficiency. Nathan Lyon, meanwhile, has quietly helped himself to 20 Shield wickets at 21.5 so far this season,

So as raggle taggle as Australia's batting is, the team's bowling should be capable of keeping targets within bounds. And sublime as he is, Kohli also made only 46 runs in five hits against Australia last year, cutting a distracted and skittish figure before he was overtaken by injury — just saying.

Yet this does, quite legitimately, add to the pressure on the home team, and on Langer, under whom the Australians have so far played twenty-four international matches, winning only six, and half of these T20 international victories over Zimbabwe and the UAE.

Like his predecessor Darren Lehmann, Langer had the paradoxically good fortune to inherit a shambles, with proportionately diminished expectations. Unlike Lehmann, he has no Mitchell Johnson lurking just out of view to bend the world to Australia's will.

Cricket Australia took a sizeable bet on Langer — a four-year contract to coach in all three formats including selectorial responsibilities and splendiferous resources. He embarked on his task with ample goodwill and evangelical zeal.

So far, apart from the enjoyably whacky 'elite honesty' meme, the pay-off has been disappointing. Judgement, rightly, will be suspended until evidence is in from a home series. But don't be surprised if, in the event of setbacks, it is unsparing. Players can redeem themselves by individual attainments; the coach, implicated in every collective failure, has an unavoidably harder lot.

On his appointment in May, Langer embraced the idea of odds stacked against him. 'We [Australians] love to win, but we don't like to win by too much because we like to be the underdogs,' he said. Winning by too much has not been a challenge for him since. And the status of underdog, for all its romance, is not one you can build a career on.

FIRST TEST, DAY 1

INDIA TRIPS UP

6 December 2018

When you're number one, at anything, there will exist a temptation to behave accordingly. After all, leaders proverbially have a presence, project an aura.

Plus, let's be frank, it's fun. In Australia's long cricket primacy, they exuded a mentally disintegrating air, a self-reinforcing expectation of success.

India have enjoyed cricket's yellow jersey for four of the fifteen years in which rankings have been officially calculated — a good run, all things considered. But they have not toured here with that status before, and yesterday, as their top four sacrificed themselves in 20 overs with swishing, open, diagonal blades, they looked like a team expecting the world to bow down before them. Never mind going hard at the ball. These were hands of stone to rival Roberto Duran's.

Virat Kohli, his arrival at the crease preluded by a week-long media drum roll, was as culpable as anyone. Answering questions after winning the toss, he slouched behind his shades, hands in pockets, endangering an interlocutor with his charisma. An hour later, he drove avidly, greedily, was expertly pouched in the gully by a cartwheeling Usman Khawaja and could hardly compute it. He stood surveying his dismissal with a mix of dismay and disapproval, as though entitled to a multimillionaire's mulligan.

As 'good, hard cricket' has been an Australian trope these last few years, with opinion differing about the proportions of goodness and hardness, so 'fearless cricket' has been a leitmotiv for Kohli. 'Virat Kohli fearless cricket' returns 226,000 Google hits. But just as there has proven a fine line between hardness and abrasiveness, so can the fearless turn reckless. Chesteshwar Pujara alone displayed the requisite reck, guarding off stump against pace like a sentry, deploying his front pad against Nathan Lyon like a sandbag. Thirty balls did he need to get going after lunch — more deliveries than his opening pair survived between them.

A wallflower at the Indian Premier League since 2014, Pujara has been scolded in India these last few years for slow scoring — a bit like expressing disappointment in a watch for not ticking faster. What he has is the courage to be his own man, which is the very definition of fearlessness.

Did Kohli and his men underestimate the Australians? They certainly underestimated Australia — the early seam movement offered to the pace bowlers, the baked-in bounce available to Lyon, the need to be secure as batting conditions reach their best. Many a fielding team has been broken by a long, hot, fruitless afternoon at Adelaide Oval. The Indians hardly gave themselves a chance of lasting so long. Instead they scattered five sixes in the first 100 runs. Having just cleared the boundary with the fourth six from Lyon, Rohit Sharma miscued an attempted fifth from the next ball. Having achieved the fifth with a ragged leading edge, Risabh Pant went down on his haunches to heave Mitchell Starc in the direction of the Victor Richardson Gates. Youth is his pardon, but it is not an indefinite one.

Only Ravi Ashwin seemed capable of embedding alongside Pujara, although the comfort with which he defended for nearly two hours underlined how his colleagues, repenting at leisure, had squandered the advantage of first innings. With number ten for company, Pujara provided two further sixes, cleaving 30 runs from his last 18 deliveries.

Australia? The Australians hung in, their rope-a-dope bowling in the morning, hitting full lengths with upright seams against batsmen determined to assert themselves, good enough for the scenario. They maintained their heart and hydration through an enervating afternoon, whites clinging to sweat-soaked sides — Peter Handscomb, wearing his protective gear at slip, and Marcus Harris, donning a helmet at leg gully, even looked a tad overdressed.

The collective effort actually bore strong resemblance to that elusive 'good, hard cricket' that Australian players have been on about these last few months — disciplined bowling, alert catching, phlegmatic captaincy and sure-handed keeping, with no need for snarling and scarely a 'line' in sight.

A uniformly excellent day's outcricket concluded with a quicksilver run out, Pat Cummins finding Pujara short of his ground from side-on despite the strain of nineteen overs. It is early days for their comeback campaign, but they could scarcely have done more.

They have now seen an Indian armour with a good deal of chink. And for all the talk of the visitors 'never having a better opportunity' in Australia, they are flattered by their ranking, derived as it is from a phase of home success since eaten away by comprehensive series defeats in South Africa and England.

Most of Test cricket's number ones this decade have been much the same, falling upwards into the slot because someone must fill it — Australia's last spell there was ended by seventh-ranked Sri Lanka. Nobody really has built to last. It seems an idea from a bygone era.

At tea, the big screen showed highlights of the Adelaide Test here fifteen years ago, when rankings were a new thing, and there was seldom a reason to refer to them anyway, daylight occupying second place behind Australia.

In that match, Rahul Dravid batted fourteen hours, with a yogi's serenity. The footage was like something from recovered from a time capsule along with a copy of the day's paper, a collected Shakespeare and a New Testament.

India were then building, patiently and resourcefully, towards an all-weather, all-terrain cricket that would win a World T20, then a World Cup, and lead to two spells atop the world Test rankings. But if they tackle this tour as they tackled yesterday morning, they will not hold onto that ranking long.

FIRST TEST, DAY TWO

MARSH MELLOW

7 December 2018

Some teams do 'ave 'em. This Australian team's is Shaun Marsh.

What is he? The country's oldest promising batsman or its youngest veteran? The selectors' pet science experiment? Cricket's version of the proverbial broken watch retained on grounds it is right twice a day?

Some imaginative suggestions were made on social media as he emerged to bat yesterday, even unintendedly. When Marsh was one off 18 balls at lunch, Bet365 tweeted inviting odds for a score over 40, with the postscript: 'Bet responsibly'. Good advice. Wonder if it reached Trevor Hohns?

It was something of a surprise to see Marsh at number four, another left-hander for the delectation of Ravi Ashwin. He prospered last summer at numbers five and six; at numbers three and four, his average dwindles into the twenties.

This should not matter, but for some batsmen somehow does — thus, for example, Michael Clarke's discrepant records at numbers four (average 30) and five (average 60). But Australian cricket's circumstances no longer conduce to acting as Marsh's community support group.

That is a heavy burden for any cricketer to bear, and one sensed it bore on Marsh, as Ashwin commenced the afternoon session, eventually floating the last ball of the first over invitingly wide. Marsh's drive was a last-minute snatch, like the lunge Mr Bean might make at a tray of hors d'oeuvres just as it slipped out of reach, leading to a spilt drink, a groped waitress and a cringe-inducing pause.

The inside edge, to be fair, might have gone anywhere — into a pad, into the ground, between keeper and slip. But the stumps seemed to beckon, the bails fell, and social media seethed and roiled — a gift wicket for all save Marsh's circle of boosters, momentarily subdued. Statistics tightened round the batsman's throat. In his last half-dozen Tests, Marsh has now averaged 8; his overall Test average, which in January exceeded 40, has dwindled to less than 35.

Averages, of course, can obscure as much as they reveal, and in Shaun Marsh's case they are a veritable masking agent. His career has been composed of soaring peaks and longer, gloomier foothills, two in his every five innings ending in single figures.

Few batsmen have made batting appear both so simple then so complicated, sometimes in consecutive weeks. Because of the former, he has gone on being selected for what he is known to be capable of rather than what he has achieved.

Marsh is the kind of cricketer who excites coaches and selectors: imagine resolving the enigma! Enigmas, however, drive fans to distraction. Periodically, they charm. Otherwise they smack of unearned opportunity; of a lack of seriousness, of durability, of heart.

Harsh verdicts were rendered on Shane Watson; they continue to reverberate around Rohit Sharma. Marsh's current batting coach Graeme Hick never achieved what he seemed capable of; might the same prove true of Marsh's brother Mitchell?

Yet nor are fans consistent. Consider Shaun's father Geoff. He played fifty Tests, averaged 33, made four hundreds. His failures excited no howls of execration. On the contrary, he was thought a doughty fighter, a solid citizen, a suitable vice-captain. When Australia's selectors finally left him out after a barren series against India, his skipper Allan Border stormed and sulked.

This signifies something about at least the perception of his son. Geoff was felt to add something beyond runs to the Australian teams in which he played — a steadiness, an honesty, a work ethic. Shaun? He bats. He is an average fielder. He has an indifferent fitness record. He has never looked like captaincy material. He is not regarded as a character or a joker or a foil. It is only his cricket that leaves an impression; otherwise he feels more absence than presence.

Of course, it is not Shaun Marsh's fault he has gone on being chosen. In some respects, his career testifies to the dearth of alternatives. He has not kept out of the side a Brad Hodge, Jamie Siddons or Stuart Law; perversely he might be regarded as a better player had he not so often been picked.

What to make of him now? It is a shock to realise that Marsh turned thirty-five in July — otherwise almost pensionable age in Australian cricket.

Usually deathwatches over senior players start earlier. Age gives failures a context — they are seen as evincing fading powers, slowing reflexes, dimming eyes. The difference is, perhaps, that Marsh is not descending from a discernible standard of excellence — he is pretty much doing what he has always done, eliciting the same complaints, inducing the same chagrin.

For what it's worth, I suspect Marsh has been the Australian player most unsettled by the absences of this year of Steve Smith and David Warner: he is a Fortinbras unsuited by nature for promotion to Hamlet. Australia lost more than the talents of its captain and vice-captain in South Africa; it was forced to redistribute responsibilities, in a hurry, in a vacuum. Others did rise to their various challenge yesterday afternoon. Travis

Head survived a testing initiation by Ashwin, settled in against some waspish seam bowling from Ishant Sharma, and pushed on past tea to a crisp and well-organised half-century.

Heaven knows, Marsh may yet rise to an occasion to come. Three weeks ago he made an exquisite unbeaten 163 in a fourth-innings here to guide Western Australia to victory over South Australia. The attack was neither so formidable nor the circumstances so fraught, but Marsh remains in touching distance of rare heights — a source of further exasperation, to champions and detractors alike. The fact is that he owes them both.

FIRST TEST, DAY 3

KOHLI COMES TO STAY

8 December 2018

The day before this First Test, a one-minute video of Virat Kohli preparing in the nets went aggressively, almost flesh-eatingly, viral. A little Diwali of devastating strokes, it rapidly accumulated a million views, and perhaps as many gasps of awe and rapture.

There was actually the odd stray boo from the Adelaide Oval crowd yesterday as India's captain came to wicket just before tea with his team two for 76, although perhaps more for local morale than out of active hostility. The match was at a hinge point. His appearances will in any case be the main event throughout this Border — Gavaskar Trophy — the big production number, the show stopper.

And so he did — stop the show that is. In deference to the narrowness of India's fifteen-run first innings lead, this was Virat rather than Viral Kohli. Cummins and Hazlewood tested him on a full length looking to have him play across the line, but he took his stance a step forward and sternly defended the stumps; Starc ostentatiously posted two men out and bounced him, but he swayed out of trouble.

Nathan Lyon offered an inviting gap at cover and the occasional ball thrown wide, but Kohli stayed coy after an early waft, either deep in the crease or stretching elastically forward, and Lyon tightened his line; when the Australian spinner dropped short, Kohli pulled prudently, at zero feet, for a single. Not until Travis Head offered him a half-tracker did Kohli attempt a stroke of real violence, although again he kept the ball to ground.

With Cheteshwar Pujara, Kohli progressed at a sober run-for-run. Between overs they enjoyed quiet communion; between deliveries, Kohli mimed defensive shots. Mileposts were lightly brushed: Kohli became the fifth Indian to pass 1000 Test runs against Australia. More importantly, more than a decade has passed since India's last Test victory in Australia, and that was the stake here — quite enough to stimulate Kohli's competitive juices.

Third innings of Test matches take more forms than any other. It can turn a match, set a scene; it can be a long haul to erase a deficit or a helter-skelter jaunt to build a lead; since the decline of the follow-on, it has sometimes served strategic purpose, as it did a year ago in Adelaide, as essentially a rest period for bowlers ahead of their fourth innings missions.

Yesterday, with the respective first innings having virtually cancelled out, it almost began the match anew, play slowing to something like a saunter after twenty wickets in fewer than 200 overs.

Having sacrificed themselves impulsively on the first morning, KL Rahul and Murali Vijay commenced like repentant sinners, abjuring strokes wherever possible — and Starc, arguably, made this more possible than he should have, continuing a curious lull in his penetration if not in his pace.

There were three scoring strokes in the innings' first fifty deliveries, but no false ones. With Vijay and Rahul not making runs, Starc not taking wickets and spectators not taking notice, there was time to appreciate a few incidental phenomena, such as the burning lights, as if in defiance of the Board of Control for Cricket in India, and the extraordinary growth in batsmen's peripheral vision in the last twenty years, the demand for white background at the Cathedral End and the encroachment of seats having reduced the oval's once welcoming hill to two perfunctory hillocks.

At least the old scoreboard remains, the numbers rolling forward and backward to update the scores, the helpful 'C' after each captain's name, the Anglo politeness of acknowledging the umpires, the defiantly Australian 'Sundries' above the total.

As the opening bowlers gave way, it registered more activity. The Ritalin of restraint wearing off, Rahul tried to carve Cummins over cover, slashed over slip, drove high and wide over point for six, swayed back from a rapid rejoinder. The pair seemed through the worst when Vijay stretched for something too distant, and Rahul flailed at something too close, adding to the Test's lengthening catalogue of batting misjudgements. The next would be a long time coming.

As the day entered extra time, Kohli drove Starc on the up — the same shot Kohli had looked to play after fifteen deliveries in the first innings, bringing about his own destruction. Now he had soaked up eighty-five, and the ball zoomed soundlessly through covers. Then, four overs from time, Kohli slightly misjudged Lyon's length, and perished to a catch at short leg, leaving Pujara to prolong the match's third innings into the fourth day.

An innings of 34 from 104 deliveries will not stand out in a storied career; still less will it stimulate a viral video. But had the Australians dismissed Kohli early again, their hopes would have soared; as it is, with India now 165 runs ahead, the innings may prove a contribution out of all proportion to its size.

FIRST TEST, DAY FOUR

LYON HEARTED

9 December 2018

You can no longer see the Cathedral from Adelaide Oval, but you can still watch Nathan Lyon.

In his eighty-first Test, he is perhaps the nearest thing Australian cricket has to an institution — recognisable, durable, reliable. As the First Test threatened to slip away from his team altogether yesterday, he kept them in touch; they were still, just, holding on at the close.

Notably, Lyon is the only Australian player remaining from the corresponding Border-Gavaskar Trophy Test four years ago, when he took twelve wickets, seven of them after tea on the final day to secure a memorable victory.

Here the task was different, the need for patience greater. It had taken Lyon twenty overs to make his first breakthrough the day before; he did not strike again yesterday until his thirty-third over; he had a stumping missed, an lbw and a short leg catch granted then rescinded; he'd have been running his hands through his hair had he any left.

The lot of the slow bowler in such circumstances is thankless. He must lead and support, penetrate and contain. Lyon had no Marnus Labuschagne to complement him, as in the UAE, and was pitted against batsmen who learn to play finger spin with their rusks.

But having at length dismissed the world's best batsman on Saturday, Lyon became the first bowler in the match to get Cheteshwar Pujara's better, after 450 balls. From his day's work he extracted five for 74, 18 of these slogged in an over by Rishabh Pant whom he dismissed soon after.

He did not make this look easy. Lyon makes nothing look easy, with his pipe cleaner man physique, the little towel in his permanently scuffed pants worn like a tradie's toolkit. Instead he creeps up on statistics and taps them politely on the shoulder, yesterday passing Bob Willis's 325 Test wickets, taken in nine more games.

Of indeterminate age to look at, Lyon has just turned thirty-one. His *Cricinfo* profile image is old enough that it shows him with tangled mop and a slightly startled expression, as though surprised by the necessity to be photographed, and the company in whom he has been gathered.

Among Australian cricketers over the last seven years he has been the most mis-underestimated, not least by himself — unassuming, unostentatious, takeable for granted in the best way possible, by his sheer consistency.

Not unappreciated mind you. Lyon's useful undefeated 24 on the second day was cheered to the echo. Through the filter of the stumps mics as he bowled yesterday could be heard a ceaseless chorus of encouragement; as he grazed at fine leg between overs, he met a non-stop demand from young fans with paraphernalia to autograph and phones to pose for. With a wave of his hand, he acknowledged his retinue's grateful applause as he concluded his spell.

Only half a dozen slow bowlers have now taken more Test wickets than Lyon. As it happens the spinner who ranks ahead of him is in this match his head-to-head rival.

Behind his shades, as if attempting to go incognito, Ravi Ashwin wheeled away until forty-two of the day's ninety overs were of spin.

What Ashwin did was underline Lyon's excellence, extracting

comparatively slow turn from the same pitch and less bounce. He obtained two wickets and might have had a third had a difficult short leg catch offered by Handscomb stuck. But the drop-in pitch is playing no real tricks. The deviation is consistent, the footmarks are shallow, and nothing is keeping low.

So there remain glimmers for Australia. As often when his place is threatened, Shaun Marsh played with some little skill after tea. He might have dragged Mohammad Shami onto his stumps toward the end, but the cricket gods winked and he survived.

Elsewhere, the recently muted form of Mitchell Starc continued. His knots were down. He looked a little ginger. There were sets of byes down the leg side, which Tim Paine might as well have tried shooting out of the sky like clay pigeons for all the hope he had of stopping them.

At one point in the morning, a drive from Lyon bisected the bowler and Starc at mid-off. Starc took some jogging steps towards it but slowed as Hazlewood took up the chase from wide-on most of the way to the boundary. Paine then shuffled Starc to coverpoint, where he caught Ajinkya Rahane's reverse sweep off… Nathan Lyon.

On the day, that was to whom and to where it all went back. And for all the abiding anxiety around wear and tear on Australia's gilt-edged pace attack, it is Lyon whom his team would most struggle to replace at present.

The only other spinner in Australia with more than ten first-class wickets this season, Queensland's Mitchell Swepson, is paying nearly 50 runs for each of them, while the enigma of Ashton Agar continues.

So on Lyon's narrow shoulders much weight bears. The selectors might be well advised to drop in at St Peters' and offer a prayer nothing untoward happens to him.

FIRST TEST, DAY FIVE

INDIA OUTPACES AUSTRALIA

10 December 2018

Under the entry 'snakes', the fabled Irish encyclopedia was said to read: 'There are no snakes in Ireland.' Time was when the encyclopedia of Indian cricket contained a similar entry for 'fast bowling.' The climate was too hot, the pitches too dry, even the national diet too deficient in protein.

That time, to be fair, was long ago — India has brought fine pace bowlers to Australia, such as Kapil Dev, Javagal Srinath and Zaheer Khan. But it has never verifiably outpaced Australia in its own conditions, until this first victory here in almost eleven years.

Ishant Sharma survives from that victory; Mohammed Shami was here four years ago; Jasprit Bumrah is new, fresh, and will take some getting used to, with his rasping pace, oblique angles and low but strong front arm, his saunter and surge style like a meandering sentence concluding in an exclamation mark.

It was not merely the wickets the trio divided here that so impressed, but their consistent hostility and hostile consistency, challenging the stumps and the Australian defensive techniques, but also clanging headgear, banging gloves, menacing splices and clavicles.

India have, moreover, something in reserve. Umesh Yadav, probably the quickest among them, and Bhuvenshwar Kumar, perhaps the swingingest, have been drinks wallahs here, but will almost certainly get their turn this summer. Virat Kohli is still feeling his way in managing such equipment, but he is learning.

This was the tenth Test match out of a dozen this year in which India have taken twenty wickets. They have not won as many as they should have with such a record, but if they prolong it will finish more often first than second.

With as many as 98 overs possible yesterday, the gold dollars dropped into their donation buckets in the morning like coins into a wishing well. Each run, however sketchy, drew a ripple of applause; each passed edge and half shout drew a little intake of collective breath. An enclave of flag-waving Indians swooned every time Kohli handled the ball.

When India's captain won the toss and batted on Thursday, he'd probably have envisioned a rather different-looking fifth day pitch — darker, dustier, more deeply eroded. But the mission of pressing for victory in a fourth innings, always akin to drawing teeth from an unwilling mouth, was on this drop-in surface even harder yakka than usual, especially for a four-man attack with overs on the clock already, who eventually enjoyed but one break during the day.

Kohli clapped till his hands must been sore; Rishabh Pant bore three helmets back and forth like an overburdened waiter; Ravi Ashwin wasted a review, as if in a hurry for a kettle to boil. It was not Ashwin who particularly harried the Australians, though he kept it tight and taut, bustling through his overs. Rather did Ishant set India on its road with a bouncer that, from round the wicket, would have done more than muss Travis Head's hair had his gloves not got in the way; he later hit Mitchell Starc's helmet for good measure.

Shaun Marsh looked the part as always, in the leanness of his physique, the geometry of his stance, the daintiness of his defence. He turned the strike over effectively, middled a pull, played the shot of the day off his pads.

A corollary of Marsh's being a poor starter is that he has been an effective goer on — he is some duck and some dinner. Before this game, one in six of his Test innings had ended at 0, one in ten with a hundred; between 70 and a century, he had fallen only thrice. If he could just get there… but at 60 he was nicked off by Bumrah, who also bounced out Tim Paine.

Shami had by then nearly had the greatest impact of all, with a seething lifter jamming Paine's finger against his bat handle — with his awful surgical misfortunes, Australia's captain must feel queasy every time he hears a door slam. In the event, blessedly, he was cleared of injury.

If Australia's pacemen were outbowled, they arguably held their own with the bat. Starc showcased his 360-degree swing; Pat Cummins displayed a scholar's diligence in defence; Josh Hazlewood applied himself bravely.

Above all was there Nathan Lyon, who met some scepticism on Sunday night when he stated that 'the wicket's good enough for us to really knuckle down tomorrow and have the belief we can score these runs' but looked intent on doing the job himself. He had a superb match.

For all their pluck, however, Australia have lost five of their last six Tests, and will not change that trend if they can scratch together only two half-centuries and a best partnership of 50 across two innings. Man of the match Cheteshwar Pujara provided an object lesson in batting discipline, so abstemious against Starc, Hazlewood and Cummins, so nimble against Lyon, so trusting in his defence that his could afford to hasten slowly.

Individuals have problems to solve, but there is a confidence lacking that can only be stimulated by achievement and example. Aaron Finch's porous defence is one thing; his strange reticence about reviewing his second innings decision offers a suitable case for treatment. Had Australia gone into tea on Sunday without losing a wicket, there's no telling how yesterday's chase would have turned out. An imaginary encyclopedia of Australia would confirm that there are still batsmen. But they need to believe it themselves.

TEST BATTING

SLIM PICKINGS

13 December 2018

Words such as 'even', 'tense' and 'competitive' have been applied to describing the First Test in Adelaide. But perhaps the most literally accurate description is: 'average'.

In four innings, Australia and India accumulated 1083 runs, or 27.1 runs per wicket — a near-perfect match for the 27.3 runs per wicket in the calendar year's other 42 Tests.

Not since 1959 has this per capita rate been so poor, which seems remarkable in view of the many advantages modern batsmen enjoy, from the quality of their equipment, including more powerful bats and lighter protective gear, to their rich financial rewards and ample preparatory resources.

Nor does it seem so long since we were pronouncing the general hegemony of the bat. With the turn of the century, batting seemed to achieve a new stability of productivity, with a floor in the mid-30s, and peaks over 50.

Some of us wondered, in fact, whether the bloated scores were all to the good. Ten years ago, when averages were twice as great as they are now, more than a third of all Tests were drawn. This year only four Tests in 43 have ended in stalemate.

This proceeds in parallel with a contrasting observable reality, that, with the spread of T20, batting today is more dynamic, the players stronger, more versatile, more innovative. Mike Atherton, who has observed many of the greatest and at close quarters, thinks Virat Kohli the best batsman he has seen.

So what underlies this seeming overthrow of the batriarchy, at least in general and quantitative terms?

Could it be the bowling? Probably not — after all, the personnel has hardly changed year-on-year.

Could it be the pitches? Maybe — the tendency of countries to roll out surfaces tailored to their own bowling advantage is widely remarked on.

Could it be practice methods? Some complain of the substitution of the empty calories of throwdowns for nutritious net practice, partly because of the workload restrictions on bowlers, although also because of the growing preference for preparation being about feeling 'confident' rather than actively challenged or problem solving.

Perhaps the simplest explanation — it's so simple as to sound axiomatic, but bear with me — is that there aren't as many top-class Test batsmen around.

In the period 2012-2015, there was a quite extraordinary twilight of the idols, perhaps unprecedented: Sachin Tendulkar, Rahul Dravid, VVS Laxman, Virender Sehwag, Kumar Sangakkara, Mahela Jayawardene, Tillekeratne Dilshan, Shivnarine Chanderpaul, Jacques Kallis, Graeme Smith, Kevin Pietersen, Ricky Ponting, Michael Clarke and Mike Hussey all bid farewell to Test cricket, the majority in favour of a few extra years of T20.

To this list has since been added the likes of AB de Villiers, Alastair Cook and Younis Khan, reinforced by the involuntary ineligibility of Steve Smith and David Warner. Among Test cricket's top 30 run scorers, only one current player remains: Hashim Amla.

Even if seldom in such profusion, of course, players are always retiring. But what's happened, one suspects, is that a fresh generation of Test talent has failed to emerge. In Adelaide, Cheteshwar Pujara became the 96th player to make 5000 Test runs, but he is one of only seven with that many who are currently active and available.

Why have successors to that gilded generation not emerged? It seems obvious to observe, again, that the game has changed, but that makes it no less true, and also belies the strain of nostalgia for the good old days when men were men, a ramp was something you drove up, it was only newspapers who had scoops, and everyone averaged 50 in the Sheffield Shield.

First-class cricket, performances in which have always been the most reliably predictive measure of top-level success, is in eclipse, here and everywhere, played in fits and starts, weakened by international calls, debased by high-performance jiggery-pokery.

When Rohit Sharma stepped out at Adelaide, he had not played a first-class match since being dropped from the Indian Test team in February, and frankly it showed — a batsman caught in the deep at 86 in the first innings and caught at silly point at four for 248 in the second is falling between two tall and shaky barstools.

T20, which has supplanted four-day cricket as the game's most profuse variant, is no training for anything other than itself, technically or temperamentally. The biomechanics of Aaron Finch driving over cover in a T20 and bending his front leg to hit along the ground through cover in a Test match are radically different — as we learned in Adelaide.

Equally suspect is the mentality that sees moving the game on as an end rather than a means. Four years ago, KL Rahul made a painstaking debut Test century in Sydney over six hours. In Adelaide, like Finch, he presented an intriguing study, flailing away from his body at the top of the first innings, getting away from himself in the second: while KL Jeckyll defended dourly, KL Hyde periodically rose to full height and carved impossible arcs in the air with which he luckily failed to connect.

We should not look too censoriously on this secular shift. After all, the fallibility of the batting in Adelaide made for compulsive viewing. Does anybody seriously regard Matthew Hayden's 380 against Zimbabwe as batsmanship's fullest flowering?

Perhaps what we grew used to watching in the noughties was the anomaly — the culmination of a long phase of relative stability, an equipoise between five- and one-day cricket, leading to a bubble economy that fetishized big scores.

This, by contrast, is the first generation that has had to stretch its techniques over three quite distinct games. There is already an underestimated gap between T20 and one-day cricket, which is challenging the likes of Chris Lynn to bridge; Test cricket is exponentially more complicated.

Administrators mandating constant format changing then wondering why batsmen aren't 'grinding out big hundreds' is cricket's version of cakeism — the expectation fuelled by populist politics that we should not only have cake and eat it too but lose weight at the same time.

This carries entailments, though. Test cricket is a big game. It requires big feats, which build big names, and these have most commonly been accomplished with the bat. Next year's Ashes commences the first cycle of the new World Test Championship. A championship in which everyone prepares decks to give their own bowlers a chance of taking twenty wickets will soon pall. And an average game will not generate those extraordinary accomplishments that, even if it is only every now and again, Test cricket needs to verify its uniqueness.

SECOND TEST, DAY 1

THE WILD WEST

14 December 2018

During his 1960s apprenticeship as the nation's favourite con man, Alan Bond notoriously bought several miles of sand dunes at Yanchep, applied bitumen and green paint, and sold the lots as grassy coastal frontages. Perth Stadium followed yesterday in the same West Australian real estate traditions.

Since the retirement of the WACA Ground was foreshadowed five years ago, there has been much concern about the preservation of its vital spark at cricket's new premises. The project manager insisted that the new drop-in pitch would provide 'speed and bounce' because 'that's what cricket in Western Australia is famous for', the curator this week described his mandate from Cricket Australia as being 'to get that fear in the eyes of the opposition turning up and seeing it fly'.

As Virat Kohli and Tim Paine walked out yesterday morning, the pitch was discernible on the square mainly thanks to the presence of stumps, and the talk was of green mambas, shifting plates of turf, and three-day Tests.

When Kohli handed over his team sheet, it offered little change out of 140kmh. When Paine won the toss, he took first innings with just a tremor of insecurity. It turned out that India had bought a sandhill.

Not that Marcus Harris and Aaron Finch were to know that as they set out to sink foundations for Australia's innings. They'd first have noticed the radical change in cricket's neighbourhood, from the WACA, with its feel of an old suburb before the processes of gentrification, to the Stadium, more like a gated community built for a multinational.

No doubt it will serve Australian rules well. But compared to the WACA it has all the atmosphere of an aircraft hangar, all the history of a 7/11, and its largely deserted terraces yesterday featured more shades of grey than a novel by Graham Greene.

As far as the pitch was concerned, it took only a few overs to discount the presence of too many demons; by the time the pair had raised none for 100 in the 34th over, doubling Australia's best partnership in Adelaide, the surface appeared positively benign.

Finch battled away with his technique, rising above it by dint of his temperament. Harris enhanced the favourable impression he made in Adelaide with decisive footwork and versatile strokes, punching down the ground and square of the wicket with equal facility.

One end at Perth Stadium is named for Justin Langer. Harris perpetuates his coach more actively. The compact left-handedness; the wafture of the bat as he abjures a stroke; the turn of the head that brings the left eye into play: with a Matthew Hayden at the other end, he would be almost a dead ringer.

'Mediocre with flashes of brilliance', Langer once called him; the coach's judgement yesterday could have been revised to 'composed and competent with flashes of me'.

In the end, more sere and yellow by the hour, the pitch played well — interestingly, at least.

Much attention focused on a full ball from Mohammed Shami that rose no higher than Harris's ankle and a bouncer from Umesh Yadav that cleared the keeper's outstretched gauntlet.

Mind you, the day's most challenging delivery was purveyed by the ersatz off spinner Hanuma Vihari, rearing at Harris's sternum and taking the edge on the way to slip — Nathan Lyon would have taken note.

As the sun beat down, there was sufficient encouragement for the pacemen in the afternoon that the pride of Western Australia was preserved, and that the Indians were not left feeling all dressed up with nowhere to bowl.

Pitting their fitness against the sapping heat, Ishant Sharma, Umesh Yadav, Mohammed Shami and Jasprit Bumrah came back for second, third and fourth spells at fuller lengths, tighter lines and impressive velocities.

India's outcricket was less even. Kohli took a superslick catch at second slip, Rishabh Pant dropped a straightforward nick at the wicket. Had the keeper held Shaun Marsh (24) off Vihari, Australia would have been five for 186 with a new ball due within the hour and a tail in view.

As it was, Marsh and Head prolonged their partnership to 84 from 137 deliveries — the day's second useful alliance, amid a growing sense that batting conditions might not grow much more favourable and runs on the board will be doubly valuable.

For a Test pitch is not to be judged on a single day any more than a painted sandhill. Up close, the surface already features a lattice of cracks; no climate could be better suited to widening them by sapping the binding grass's last moisture. With minutes to go, a delivery from Bumrah with the second new ball seamed jaggedly past Paine's outside edge.

India having preferred Vihari to Ravindra Jadeja and Yadav to Bhuveneshwar Kumar are also lighter for batting than at Adelaide Oval. They would not want to repeat their first—innings misadventures of last week. Alan Bond once opined that he regretted nothing he'd done, only what he hadn't. Kohli might find that that applies to batting first at Perth Stadium.

SECOND TEST, DAY 2

GOOD TO BE KING

15 December 2018

Yesterday a newspaper pronounced Virat Kohli 'super duper' and an 'uber-success story', and a commentator praised the positivity of his body language as he walked to the crease. For India's captain, it was all in a day's hyperbole. What a challenge — unique in world cricket. He must be Virat Kohli without succumbing to the unavoidable distractions of being Virat Kohli.

With India two for eight, Kohli perhaps felt the tug each way. It was a situation in need of his powers and his presence. The flag-waving Indian claque welcomed him with lusty salaams, the Australian pace attack with probing lengths. Kohli had gone eight innings without a half-century in the Border-Gavaskar Trophy, but soon made this seem less like a matter of form than a piece of trivia: a hundred and nine deliveries set it to rights. It was a holding operation — India still trail, on the scoreboard and in the match scenario. But while Kohli batted the match imperceptibly stabilised. It was not quite 'Kohli v Australia', but you'd have been forgiven thinking it so; on 'Kohli v the second new ball' this morning could this match hinge.

Milder temperatures than the first day eased the bowlers' burden yesterday, while perhaps also slowing the pitch's deterioration, with help from a morning's rolling. For the first hour, in fact, India's bowlers appeared grooved at a classic 'pretty length', grunting as bouncers flew, sighing as edges were beaten, overlooking the accruing runs, which swelled Australia's first innings past 300 for the first time in seven Test matches — for the first time since Australia last won a Test, in Durban in March. Only a handful of deliveries would have hit the stumps; finally a couple did.

The Australian bowlers had batted attentively. As pundits searched for positive readings on their body-language-o-meters, Starc insinuated an inswinger between Murali Vijay's bat and pad, and Hazlewood torpedoed KL Rahul with the batsman shaping towards mid-on — sharp bowling, muddled batting, and astute analysis.

Kohli got going with a crisp drive down the ground, repeated in Hazlewood's next over, bracketed by boundaries through mid-wicket: positive batting, nine inches out of his ground, meeting ambitious bowling, probing away at the stumps, molesting the pads.

With India two for 38 from ten overs, Australia's bowlers imposed an austerity policy. Between 1.35pm and 2.20pm, Cummins and Lyon yielded only 12 runs in twelve overs. The batsmen did not so much grow passive as assume a posture of armed neutrality. To adapt the vernacular, Pujara padded away with intent while Kohli left in good areas, if one delivery from Nathan Lyon, turning back sharply, sniffed around off bail.

At one point the off-spinner's figures were a pristine 7-3-5 0 — more like the combination on a brief case than a bowling analysis. At length, Kohli broke the spell with a cover drive so scintillating that it almost threw off stardust.

For a figure who personifies action and vitality, Kohli also has a gift for non-motion, so still as the bowler approaches that a butterfly could alight on the peak of his helmet, so sculpted in defence that he inclines to holding the pose half a beat for personal appraisal. He has a purist's preferences, taking as much pleasure in a decisive leave as a virile stroke.

This was Test match special Kohli, humble in the face of the bowling's demands and the match's stage, sometimes becalmed although seldom long. The only delivery that caused him regular trouble was on a fifth stump line, his hands sometimes stretching outside his eyeline as his bat searched busily for contact. Beaten, he would give a wry smile, adjust the wristbands on his gloves, and penitently re-mark his guard. Passed by Cummins, he gave an appreciative nod. Recuperating from a painful blow on his bottom hand by Hazlewood, he check drove immaculately to the long-on boundary.

The impasse ended when Pujara feathered Starc down the leg side, although that brought Ajinkya Rahane, whose back foot power suited the pitch's bounce, and contributed nearly two-thirds of their unbroken 91-run partnership. Kohli passed fifty by carving Cummins over slip, then eked out only singles for the next half-hour. A few overs from stumps, he drilled to mid-on, gestured in the fielder's direction, then rehearsed a kind of T20 onside flick over the top, which would have brought the house down at Chinnaswamy Stadium on a hot night in the Indian Premier League. It was the nearest he came to indulging himself all day, enhancing his legend all the same. As he walked off unbeaten, his being Virat Kohli had contributed just a little more to his being Virat Kohli.

SECOND TEST, DAY 3

SPLIT DECISION

16 December 2018

It was an updating, almost a remake, of an old, old story.

These days the cricket umpire on international duty can appear a marginal figure, a mid-level bureaucrat exercising a limited discretion preliminary to the definitive business of technological retrospection and media analysis. Sometimes, the players even seem to be umpiring themselves, unofficial field workers of the Decision Review System.

All the more so yesterday as Virat Kohli outside edged, Peter Handscomb rolled to his right at second slip, and tempered celebrations broke out.

Kohli walked down the pitch with a nonchalant waft of his left hand, indicating belief that the ball had bounced; Handscomb raised his index finger, confirming conviction it had not. No consensus emerging, umpires Kumar Dharmasena conclaved with Chris Gaffaney preparatory to calling on their video reinforcement Nigel Llong.

Then, almost furtively, Dharmasena gave his so-called 'soft signal' — the 'I think' gesture distinguishable from the 'I know' by its seeming circumspection, but in this instance carrying immense weight.

Every time Kohli leaves the crease in this Border-Gavaskar Trophy will involve a shift in the balance of power — heaven knows, it could affect Australia-India diplomatic relations and the terms of trade. The circumstances of his departure will matter accordingly.

The next few minutes turned into a Rorschach inkblot test. As it was replayed at multiple speeds from multiple angles, objectivity was elusive. Were you an Indian fan, or an Australian die-hard? Did you want to see Kohli bat some more? Did you think Pat Cummins deserved a wicket? Maybe, like me, to add to the confusion, you wished for both.

Additional context came from Handscomb being the player who drew Steve Smith's attention to the Australian team balcony in Bangalore last year because, he said, he did not understand the review system, the 'protocols' of the elders of Dubai. In the home dressing room, too, those well-publicised signboards enjoining occupants to practice 'elite honesty' which invited so much ironic commentary.

For the older generation it was also an opportunity to explain to the younger that this was the way it used to be, in that olden time when Jack Fingleton said that umpires were more powerful than presidents and prime ministers, able to provoke a nation to jubilation or fury with a single finger.

Back in the day, the decisions were hard, fast, sometimes wrong, essentially respected. And for all this decision's 'softness', it possessed an authoritative quality, low catches almost invariably going the way of the soft signal because contradiction of the on-field umpire requires definitive evidence — the 'soft signal' has become, in its way, the most adamantine of all.

So it went. Kohli wended his way off in a dudgeon of medium height, precluding acknowledgement of applause for his superfine hundred. The Australians were rightly confident of having turned the game.

We were left a cricketing tabula scalata or rabbit-duck illusion — although the latter could equally refer to Mohammed Shami, a number eight with an average of 11 now dismissed by his last three deliveries in Test cricket, and almost lucky to have survived that long.

To that stage, Kohli had appeared impassable, driving through the covers without check, copping one on the tattoo without flinching, reaching his twenty-fifth Test hundred with punch down the ground and a gesture that could start an Indian fad for batting glove puppets.

With his dismissal, India, as many had foreseen, dropped its tail like a skink, losing five for 32 in 77 deliveries, four of these to Nathan Lyon.

At its effective mid-point, in fact, seven of match's twenty wickets had fallen to spin: a nod to this new, intriguing, changeable pitch that has so defied prediction, arriving like a green mamba and as amiable at other times as Kermit the Frog.

What next? Perhaps the first hint of the ball coming through at differing heights and of the influence of a widening crack just short of a good length at the Langer Stand end, plus of the ongoing cost of the composition of India's XI.

Ishant Sharma, Jasprit Bumrah and Mohammed Shami took four wickets, Aaron Finch's finger, Marcus Harris's badge, Usman Khawaja's top hand, Tim Paine's bottom hand. But Umesh Yadav went on appearing surplus, surrendering nearly a run a ball in a match in which runs have been at a premium.

Meantime, social media debate roiled, about not only Kohli but also that mother of all cricketgates, Monkeygate, being rehashed by its chief antagonists Andrew Symonds and Harbhajhan Singh and their online proxies.

For those recollecting that Sydney Test, it seemed both just yesterday and long ago: another game marred by umpiring decisions but also a relic of the pre-DRS world. Much has been done since to narrow and neutralise the potential for similar conflicts. But still, we were reminded yesterday, they cannot be eliminated altogether.

SECOND TEST, DAY 4

PAINE V KOHLI

17 December 2018

Perth Stadium boasts a playing surface area of more than 21,000 square metres, yet before lunch yesterday Virat Kohli and Tim Paine found themselves competing for more or less the same spot.

The former was approaching the stumps as the latter completed a run. Belly-to-belly while studiously looking different ways, the captains resembled two people trying to squeeze past one another in a narrow hallway.

No sandpaper was seen. No soft signal needed to be given. The snickometer was not used to determine whether actual friction occurred. But it was one of those moments on which the camera cannot but dwell: cricket, of course, has been a contact sport in Perth before. The stump microphones, which this week have been the hardest working listening devices in sport, overheard umpire Chris Gaffaney calling the captains into line.

The Australians have had an abundance of advice about how to handle the volatile Kohli this summer. 'A few words' and 'hostile body language', Ricky Ponting urged. 'Make him your best mate,' Dean Jones advised. Looks like Ponting's counsel is carrying the day; it may not be his only weakness.

Kohli has annoyed the Australians in Perth, and not merely by his masterful hundred. His celebrations, his gesticulations, his standing his ground when caught, his enjoining Indian fans to make themselves heard: he has carried the reddest rag since Steve Waugh's. The Australians should now have the last laugh on the scoreboard in this match. They kept their cools yesterday. They understood their limits. But Kohli is also in their heads as few visiting captains have been.

There is an undertone to Australian complaints about Kolhi: that he is a provocateur; that he 'gets away' with stuff that they do not; that he is the beneficiary of 'double standards'. And sure, there is a hint of hypocrisy about a cricketer who affects to let his bat do the talking, then in the next breath has his talk do the baiting.

But the cry of 'double standards' is a feeble one. The world contains multiple different standards, not only because people and cultures and heritages differ, but also because minds and attitudes change.

The Australians have, of course, lately been recalibrating their standards, dogged by the reputation for abrasiveness they used to relish — indeed, it is precisely this on which India's skipper has been playing, working away in their corridor of behavioural uncertainty.

By grumbling about Kohli, the Australians are in danger of reintroducing the jaded concept of 'the line' in another guise, and essentially insisting on their right to draw it. The public, rightly, sickened of that. Paine's men looked better off yesterday enjoying what Kohli brings to the contest: not just a standard of excellence, against which it is exciting to be measured, but also a kind of unifying enemy, of whom it is exhilarating to get the better, as when Nathan Lyon found his outside edge after tea.

In Kohli's approach there also lies risk to himself and others. His tour is becoming like that fabulous French documentary a decade or so ago about Zinedine Zidane, where the camera followed the great footballer for a whole game, capturing the stages he was off the ball as well as on — the exhortations, the feints, the lunges of anticipation, the periods of repose.

An equivalent movie of Kohli would reveal precious few of the last.

He is more often still at the crease than he is in the field, prowling mid-off, pervading second slip. He beckons and dispatches, claps and chivvies, even polishes the ball with a manic energy. As the field changed over at one stage yesterday, he leaned forward and caught a ball behind his back. He looks, in short, like a man in his element, of contagious mood. He lights his team up; he could also, potentially, cast it in shadow.

In India last year, the Australians lost the series but had the better of Kohli. He appeared in a state of constant distraction. The extremes of his moods were summed up by his batting at Pune, where he threw his hands at a wide delivery in the first innings, let a bowl hit his off stump in the second. His relationship with his coach Anil Kumble deteriorated so markedly that it was over within months.

Who now could tell Kohli that he had gone too far? Who are his confidantes? Who moderates and balances him? He personifies an extraordinary world. After play concludes at Perth Stadium today, world cricket's attention will turn to an annual rite: the auction, now in Jaipur, of 350 of the world's best cricketers, for tens of millions of dollars, to the corporate owners of Indian Premier League franchises. In such a system coils enormous potential chaos. Kohli's personality is what binds it; it could just as easily split it. Going toe-to-toe with Kohli is one way of challenging him. But the space Kohli has to himself is, for India, just as much of an issue.

SECOND TEST, DAY 5

VICTORY AT LAST

18 December 2018

The crowd of 10,672 at Perth Stadium yesterday saw only fifteen overs' cricket but wrung some extra value from their dollar coins.

After the teams' conga lines of congratulation dissolved, Australian players adjourned to a sunny corner at the members' end for communion with fans — very deliberate, very visible.

'It's Your Game' is Cricket Australia season's promise and, for twenty minutes at least, it was made good, with old- and new-fashioned rituals of reconnection: autographs, smiles and selfies. Somewhere at Jolimont, a KPI was ticked. But for the players themselves, the sensations would have been novel: with a Test win after ten largely barren months, they were returning to a welcome form of favour.

The last time the team won a home Test, in the first week of 2018, wins were easy and schadenfreude abounded. Players gathered afterwards on a gloat float. Administrators preened, marketers cooed. Steve Smith and David Warner looked tighter than Torvill and Dean.

Since then, of course, a humbling. So yesterday, a groping for fans' good graces and an embrace of new partners. While Aaron Finch, Marcus Harris, Josh Hazlewood and Shaun Marsh familiarised themselves with fans' phones, Mitchell Starc and Nathan Lyon gave simultaneous on-field interviews to each of the broadcast partners, while coach Justin Langer prepared to join a television panel — a pity the coach ignored the written press, but maybe he assumed we were busy transcribing the stump mics.

A particular pity because this was an excellent Test, one everyone could enjoy, making up for in intensity where it fell short in quality.

The captains were both outstanding. Virat Kohli was a cut above any batsman. Tim Paine set standards behind the stumps last attained by Adam Gilchrist and Ian Healy. In what was only his seventeenth Test, Paine also led as if born to the role, with the courage to bat first on winning the toss, the nerve to yield Kohli no ground, and the fixity of purpose to extend no charity to the Indian tail. On the third and the final days, the last five Indian wickets were blown away for 32 and 42 respectively, treated the same way the CFMEU treats files — burned in the first innings, buried in the second.

Some onlookers were queasy, not without reason. But when a Test number eight yet to score is withdrawing to leg and aiming base hits to right field, then that is an issue of competence as much as courtesy.

While the celebrations played out round the stadium's perimeter yesterday, ground staff in the middle also posed for selfies, as well they should have.

In the theatre of a Test match, the pitch is always more than scenery, but this one was a character in its own right, providing lift and deviation through to the last day, attested to by more than 180 documented plays and misses, pulverised protective gear, numberless miscues and jarred handles.

The roller made some timely cameos, too, adding to the subterranean intrigue: on the first four days, only nine wickets fell before lunch.

Above all, of course, the pitch played on Indian minds, tempting their selectors to go long on pace, short on batting. The figures are in: the match's most successful bowler was Nathan

Lyon, while India had a slow bowling option with only twenty-two first-class wickets deployed mainly to expedite the over rate.

Nor was this an anomaly. The national team once synonymous with flight and guile has this year deployed two spinners on a billiard felt at Lord's, one spinner on a bunsen at Birmingham and half a spinner, an unfit Ravi Ashwin, at Southhampton.

India's openers, meanwhile, were each bowled twice, and, like Australia in Adelaide, the batsmen eked out only one half-century partnership, reinforcing the view that the visitors are the world's Test number one faute de mieux rather than par excellence.

But let us accentuate the positives, given that they have lately been in such short supply. In Australia's last half-dozen innings, no batsman has exceeded 72. Yet the team has found a way to win here by an accumulation of little differences.

Lyon took out the individual award before belting out 'Under the Southern Cross', but Usman Khawaja batted bravely with scant recognition, Pat Cummins toiled mainfully with limited reward and Aaron Finch faced recent difficulties if not resolved them.

India's fielders missed little but Australia's dropped nothing. India's lengthened tail was lopped off but Australia's lingered and wagged.

It constituted an 'Australian way' of sorts, one that blessedly did not involve too much cribbing at 'the line' or, indeed, male flying of horses and riding of planes — one for which the average fan could feel a throb of kinship.

When Kohli threw down the gauntlet, the Australians handed it back more or less tactfully. It was pleasing yesterday to see Paine leaving the field with Mohammed Shami, a hearty and likeable cricketer who gave the Australians as much trouble in the match as anyone.

Some will detect Langer's watermark on Australia's wealth-for-toil approach. That may be fond imagining. But let us say he would not be unhappy to see his charges playing such a way. If they continue doing so, too, they will be spending more time involved in what these days is described as 'fan engagement' and have more reason to enjoy it.

STUMP MICS

THE SURVEILLANCE STATE

19 December 2018

It has not been a good year for Australian cricket clichés. First of all, in Cape Town, we farewelled 'the line', which we all knew existed but not where to place it. In Perth another ancient saying went by the board: 'What happens on the field stays on the field.' Because what happens on the field within range of the stump microphones is now fair game, Foxtel having led the way, Seven following.

For broadcasters trying to build an identity for two middling teams, it was manna. The rest of the media filled columns with dialogue. Arguably not since slow-motion replays became ubiquitous has the game been so transformed.

It is not a new technology so much as the tapping of the potential of an established one. Stump microphones were introduced to the game during Kerry Packer's World Series Cricket more than forty years ago. But a politesse restricted their use. After each delivery, they were faded, so as to spare us the ensuing grunts and oaths.

When just occasionally they were not, the results were unedifying. 'Get ready for a broken fuckin' arm' became Michael Clarke's best-remembered contribution to Ashes folklore, about which he was at first mortified but now seems more sanguine — generally a bit of a shame for a fine cricketer and captain.

The content provided by the new dispensation in Perth caught a mixture of the provocative and the sly, some annoyance, some silliness, a great deal of banality. The profanity, unexpectedly, was in Hindi, two remarkably unintelligent Indian cricketers wrangling trivially in recording range, which there was a rush to interpret as 'in-fighting'.

In hindsight, it's remarkable that the stump mics remained muted so long. It was a little like installing CCTV cameras on a street corner and deciding not to use them at night. The reasons, though, were not far to seek. Players found them inhibiting, administrators alarming: they opened up vistas of potential transgression, a pandora's swear box.

The public, interestingly, cared little. There was never any campaign to liberalise mics' use. Some identified the opened microphones with eavesdropping. Others, while liking the way that close-up coverage magnified drama, decrypted technique and captured expression, were content to grant the players a continued measure of privacy, even to enjoy speculating about what might have been said.

'You've just dropped the World Cup, Hersch': that was allegedly Steve Waugh to Herschelle Gibbs in 1999. Except that it wasn't, and no matter how often either of them denied the exchange it lodged in mythology, and was retailed in numberless pubs.

Eddo Brandes explaining his biscuit fetish to Glenn McGrath, number one on a million 'funniest sledge' listicles? Bullshit. Rod Marsh asking Ian Botham about 'your wife and my kids', a timeless classic? Never happened.

Will this apocrypha have equivalent in future? If the tree does not fall within range of the stump mics, will it be deemed to have made a sound? Will the game as a result trend towards a greater literalism, vested in a belief in we now know everything, based on the same assumption that a google search will instantly reveal to us the entire sum of human knowledge?

Because we won't, of course. We will have at best a partial picture, which can in its own way be distorting. Who knows the context of the contretemps between Ishant and Jadeja? No matter, we have already interpreted it.

So what are the arguments for total amplification? A reasonable view is that it will have a deterrent effect on misbehaviour, in the same way as decision review system has had the effect, largely unforeseen, of restraining frivolous appealing and containing dissent.

It's certainly possible. But it may also be that we will only end up hearing what the players wish us to hear. When Tim Paine says that Virat Kohli is captain but you 'can't really like the guy', there is already ambiguity about whether he is addressing Murali Vijay or us — about which there is something both clever, and also a little sneaky and unlikeable.

A further argument could be that it humanises players, reminds us that they are flesh and blood — not that we should need reminding, but every bit helps. Cock an ear to the audio and you can hear the minds ticking. It adds to the narrative layers, the dramatic possibilities, the potential fascinations. All grist to the media's mill.

Yet of the position of the media, there also seems something corrosive. At present, we're loving all this additional 'access', the low-hanging fruit of gotcha moments. So many storylines! It was fun to listen to commentators praising the innovation to the skies afterwards. Just fancy that! Completely objective, of course…

And hey, it's happening in America, and that's where we go for all our ideas. (Did you know, by the way, there's a dining area called The Locker Room at Perth Stadium? Who has locker rooms in Australia? They were 'changing rooms' or 'dressing rooms' last time I looked. 'Locker room talk' is how Donald Trump excuses his misogyny. But I digress.)

Anyway, were the game's skills and excellences really not enough? What if the self-generating controversies begin to crowd the cricket out? A few cricketers have already been cheated. Mohammed Shami is an absolute ripper, gives everything, plays with a smile, presents a seam as perfect as a jackknife in a game of mumble-peg. Did we write about Shami on the day he took six-for? Did we bollocks. We were too busy transcribing audio. Hell, who needs journalists? Why not just employ stenographers?

How many other performances will not receive their proper due because someone said boo, and that became the day's talking point? How much lower will we sink in public esteem because of the impression we are voyeuristic mischief makers? And is it not destructive of our craft that we're increasingly reporting not so much cricket as chronicling and collecting comment about what's been happening on television?

Coincidentally or not, this was the first Test match I can recall in which the commentary, Foxtel's, was on with the volume turned up in the press box — fine in one way, because the coverage was bright and informed, but perhaps another baby step towards a tighter uniformity of views, more information conducing to whiter noise.

Finally, what about the players' privacy? Our attitudes to privacy are ever-changing and far from consistent, in the age of Facebook and of metadata: we're both more blasé and more uptight. Basically, the players have traded some of their privacy away for money. How do we feel about that loss of individual sovereignty?

Perhaps our attitudes depend on whether we see the cricket field as a place of work or of entertainment. If work, then it is worth wondering whether we would wish our own workplaces to be similarly mic'd up — the language around the photocopier would be worse than anything Ishant and Jadeja came up with.

If entertainment, then it could be argued that when we pay our money, we are entitled to all area access. But where does this stop? Do we own the sight of Mitchell Starc putting on his jockstrap? And does the minuteness of our scrutiny come at a cost to the spontaneity of the contest?

At the end of the Test, Virat Kohli insisted that he was not discomforted by the influence of the microphones, and indeed did not think about them. But if they did not obviously impair his performance, India's captain certainly seemed aware of them often enough. He will be still more aware of them now, as his team navigate these new shoals of technology.

I don't pretend to have answers to these questions. I raise them instead in the spirit of inquiry. Nor would I dispute the benefits that broader and deeper audio lend cricket; it is more that the second- and third-order effects deserve an airing. 'What happens on the field stays on the field' was always a bit phony, expedient, self-excusing. But there were reasons for it and they have not gone away.

STEVE SMITH

GUTSY?

20 December 2018

Cricket is a game that punishes error while also offering generous possibilities for redemption. But parallel attempts testing that idea in different ways are not coming off so well.

On 29 March, a few days after the calamity of Cape Town, Steve Smith was dumped by sponsor Commonwealth Bank — or, as it decorously phrased the decision, the bank 'concluded our current arrangement with Steve as a sporting ambassador'.

Who's had the worse reputational time since? The cricketer pilloried from pillar to post, or the bank humiliated by a royal commission?

The cricketer who has forgone approximately $7 million in match payments and sponsorship arrangements, or the bank that had to cough up $700 million to settle breaches of anti-money laundering and counter-terrorism financing laws?

But then, all of a sudden, as Big Bash League 8 commenced on Thursday night, there were both of them busily rebuilding their brands by presenting progressive avatars: Smith part of a campaign by Vodafone drawing attention to his work of the last few months with a mental health foundation, Gotcha4Life, and the bank reminding us that it is a backer of the women's game, through Cricket Australia.

Smith, one fancies, has the simpler task. He emerged as the wholesome kid who grew up on Weet-Bix and shaved with Gillette when he hardly looked old enough. There has been a good deal to respect about the quiet way Smith has gone about his business this year, playing grade cricket here, domestic T20 there, doing some sympathetically-received good works and seeking no remission from his penance. He has much to offer Australian cricket, and hopefully he will.

Which is why the cloying and overproduced one-minute video rolled out by Vodafone struck such a crass note. Apparently it is the first of a number of commercials under the rubric 'Gutsy is calling', celebrating Australians who have overcome adversity because... actually, I don't know, has Vodafone overcome some adversity? Perhaps Vodafone has emerged with a passion for the underdog from having its anti-competitive merger with TPG reviewed, or sucking up taxpayers' money for call centre jobs later axed. They are experiences bound to build empathy. Anyway, to me, the tag 'gutsy' is first of all ascribed to those who have overcome genuine disadvantage, not to those responsible for their own misfortune. Looking forward to the inspirational video about Andrew Broad's first tearful attempts to fly a plane and ride a horse again...

Weirdest of all was the Vodafone video being treated as news, indicative of how difficult we now find distinguishing actuality from publicity. Channel 9, for example, ran a news item stating that 'Steve Smith has spoken for the first time about the ball tampering incident in South Africa', describing him as 'making a frank and honest reflection in an unconventional way', and 'turning his darkest hour into something positive'. Like, ah, an ad.

Fox Sports, likewise, published an article which, without irony, included excerpts from the campaign as though they were candid volunteerings, such as this priceless line: '"Everything I dreamed of, everything I was a part of was just falling to pieces," Smith said in a commercial for Vodafone.'

Hell, why stop there?

'"Caring for business and caring for communities goes hand in hand," Greg Norman philosophised in a commercial for QBE.'

'"It tested positive for speed and power again and again,' Ben Johnson reported exclusively in a commercial for a Sports Bet app.'

Yeah nah, as Australians so brilliantly say.

Let's wish Smith well. But to those who piped up yesterday that he had 'paid his dues', he self-evidently has not: he has a third of his suspension still to serve, and there's no pressing need for him to be heard of until it's over.

While not so obviously tone deaf, Commonwealth Bank offers a variant on the same dilemma. In launching the 'powerful and progressive' commercials that M & C Saatchi designed to promote the bank's role as a long-time sponsor of women's cricket, the ad firm's boss told *AdNews* that 'brands are shaped by the role they play in people's lives'.

Hmmm. So how's Commonwealth Bank travelling by that measure, especially given the role it is known to have played in the posthumous existences of so many dead former clients? Losing client data, screwing insurance customers, rigging markets, despoiling ecosystems: you name it, in recent years the Commonwealth Bank has been involved up to its filthy corporate neck.

So when Meg Lanning, Ellyse Perry, Rachael Haynes, Beth Mooney and other players on cricket.com.au prostrate themselves at Commonwealth's clay feet, even describing the bank as an 'iconic brand', you have to wonder what it's worth. Actually, we know exactly: $15 million over three years, in a tie-up described as in October 2016 as a 'landmark', even though Commonwealth's annual support for women's cricket equates to what the bank makes between opening and lunch one day a year, and the totality of the deal is a third what the previous CEO trousered in cash and vested equity while helping drive the bank into a ditch.

Last month Labor frontbencher Matt Thistlethwaite cast doubt on the propriety of Commonwealth Bank continuing to sponsor Australia Day's Australian of the Year ceremonies, saying that the bank's victims would 'feel pretty hurt seeing Australia Day plastered with Commonwealth Bank logos.'

So how should we feel about our cricketing women, with their continued excellence and hard-won good name, helping to launder this trashed corporate reputation? They're champions after all. Can champions not afford to discriminate?

Cricket this summer is working its way back into public affection. Its players, and its teams, need to take care about whose company they are keeping.

BOXING DAY

PEACE DIVIDEND

26 December 2018

A hundred years ago in Melbourne it rained, and copiously. Early arrivals at the Melbourne Cricket Ground for the match between Victoria and New South Wales were discouraged by signs that there would be no play before lunch.

The signs were erroneous, but understandable: half an hour before the scheduled 11am start, one end of the pitch was under water. Spectators settled in. After all, what was a few hours when they had already waited forty-three months?

Cricket's return to Australia after World War I was greeted as a patriotic vindication, and the most welcome of peace dividends. 'The revival of big cricket reveals with dramatic suddenness the inherent sporting instinct in the British race,' opined the *Daily Telegraph*. 'One has only to consider what would have been the case if Germany had won to emphasise the contrast between the Teuton and the British races. The wildest imagination could not vision Germany plunging into a joyous orgy of healthy sport.'

Yet it would prove an ambivalent sort of spectacle, in tune with a country not entirely sure to laugh or cry about a victory so costly.

Cricket officials from Victoria, New South Wales and South Australia met within a week of the Armistice with a view to resuming interstate and international competition, and agreed a schedule of home and away matches to commence on Boxing Day.

For some, it looked a little premature. A great many cricketers were among the 270,000 Australians still in uniform on the other side of the world; a great many fans were preoccupied with matters closer to home; on a practical level, with Australia in a tightening grip of influenza, there were public health concerns about large gatherings.

Established voices drowned the killjoys out. 'Of course there are some who think that the cricketing authorities are a bit previous in arranging a big cricket programme so soon, but in every walk of life will be found narrow-minded extremists who are up against recreation and relaxation for the mere joy of opposing them,' stated 'Short Slip' of *The Leader*. 'When the boys have all returned from their glorious crusade against the Hun the contests for the Sheffield Shield will take up again all their pristine importance, and be fought out, if anything, with added keenness.'

The country's leading cricket journalist, J. C. Davis of *The Referee*, waxed philosophical about cricket's contribution to a public 'healthy in body and developed mind' after the war's impact: 'The war may have the effect of purging the peoples of many lands of the materialism which had taken possession of them body and soul. If it brings back the wealthy to a simpler life, and a love for the masses, and uplift the workers through the environment of better education and more sanitary conditions, especially in their homes and surroundings, it will have won a big victory.'

Davis thought that 'when the bayonet and the rifle are laid aside they must be at once supplanted by the cricket bat.' The bat's contribution to improved sanitation was perhaps assumed.

In point of fact, proud as these sentiments sounded, there was concern about cricket's reputation. The game had concluded before the war on somewhat of an ebb tide, weakened by administrative disputes, dulled by dour play. Where Australian rules, rugby league and racing had struggled on in wartime, cricket had largely ceased, languishing a little self-consciously, as though it felt a particular need to set an example.

No fewer than 1100 members of the Melbourne Cricket Club had enlisted, thirty dying in the Dardanelles alone. New South Wales had lost its fastest bowler, Albert Cotter, most brilliant young batsman, Norman Callaway, and almost its best all-rounder, Charlie Kellaway, wounded four times.

Perversely, that had tended to draw attention to those cricketers not in the colours including Victoria's captain Warwick Armstrong, who was the subject of barely veiled criticism — notably a notorious editorial in *Australian Statesman and Mining Journal* by its choleric editor Ernest Oliphant. 'When the country is at war, its only heroes are those who serve it,' scolded Oliphant, 'not those who, in ministering to the pleasure of the idle and the disloyal, minister to their own vanity and give proof of their own lack of patriotism.'

In fact, both Armstrong's brothers had enlisted, one dying at Menin Road. But as Boxing Day approached, a devotee writing in The Argus showed an abiding distrust of perceived 'shirkers'. 'I am a lover of cricket,' he avowed, 'but cannot persuade myself to go to the interstate matches which are to be played at Christmas and New Year, as there are at least tour players the Victorian team who, to my personal knowledge, were eligible to go to the war and should have been there assisting their hundreds of cricket mates on the battlefield.'

Perhaps with this in mind, each of the teams featured a recent war casualty. Having served in the Pioneers Regiment, Private William Sewart was chosen for Victoria eleven months after arriving home with 'acute bronchitis, incipient tuberculosis'; from the 19th Battalion, Lt Austin Diamond was picked for NSW just weeks after recovering from gas poisoning.

Both were popular choices. Sewart had been a champion footballer for Carlton, Diamond a vigorous recruiting agent for his battalion's 'Sportsman's Unit'. They would be applauded by the MCG crowd every time they went near the ball for the game's duration.

There were also gestures, unusually innovative, to smarten the attraction up. England had foreshadowed resuming its County Championship as two-day matches; hereabouts there was a push from New South Wales to limit Australian first-class matches, which had always been played to a result, to three days.

The initiative was rejected, but another more lasting change was adopted: eight-ball overs, which it was hoped would reduce the proportions of play spent changing between overs, and which would distinguish Australian cricket from the rest of the world for the next six decades.

Out and incoming batsmen, moreover, were enjoined to pass at the gate, and there was renewed insistence on 'punctuality' around intervals. With an allusion to revolutionary Russia, a satirist in Sydney's *Sun* made merry with the notions: 'The matter will be referred to the Cover-points' Union. The professionals threaten to set up Soviets on the field, and fraternise with the other side, instead of bowling them out.'

Elsewhere, the craving was for continuity, embodied in the captains, former and future Australian leaders: Victoria's 140kg Armstrong, a Falstaff without the jokes, and New South Wales' forty-six-year-old Monty Noble, who emerged from a nine-year retirement to chaperone a team with five new caps in his famously high-minded way.

They were cheered to the toss, which Noble won, sending Victoria in; they would be cheered to the crease, Noble doffing his cap; they would be dominant players of the match, Noble making NSW's only half-century and returning its best figures (seven for 81).

When play at length commenced at 12.15pm, Fred Baring faced the first ball from left-armer Rex Norman, tapping the second ball to mid-on for the first post-war run. A champion Essendon footballer, Baring had been chosen to represent Australia on a tour of South Africa in 1914-15 to which war had put paid; he never had another chance. But he would take the opportunity here, dodging between intermittent showers, to make the first post-war century, 131 in 206 minutes.

Norman took the first wicket, the digger Diamond taking the first catch. Carefully negotiating the sodden pitch, Baring and Armstrong had the first century stand, adding 166 for the fifth wicket. Stoical during the delay, the crowd grew cheerier, swelling to more than 6000 in spite of the weather, and of the competing attractions of racing at Caulfield, Ararat, Echuca and Aspendale, interstate bowls at Toorak and representative rowing at Nagambie. A services band played selections. Refreshment bars traded briskly. Veterans of the inaugural Test in 1877, Jack Blackham and James Slight, were spied in the Members. *The Age* thought: 'The return to class cricket at Christmas has brought rejoicing to veterans and colts alike; and lookers-on, too, are pleased that the dull monotony of things during the past four years is likely to be broken at last.' But there was a solemnity to the occasion too. *The Australasian*'s veteran cricket correspondent Jack Worrall thought that he had never heard a Melbourne crowd so quiet: 'In all my experience, and it has extended over a great many years, I have not heard less barracking, or seen greater interest taken in the game.' It was, Worrall believed, as though spectators were learning how to watch cricket again: 'When the keenness of the game and the fine struggle between bat and ball were recognised, they concentrated themselves on the cricket provided and applauded frequently and impartially.'

This restraint and decorum continued into the second day, when NSW grappled with a worsening pitch, conceding a deficit of 143. Diamond was applauded all the way to the crease, and all the way back, dismissed for a duck. The third day, the Saturday, drew a hearty 10,000, who enjoyed a second-wicket partnership of 146 between Jack Ryder and Edgar Mayne in Victoria's second innings which put the match beyond the visitors. After a rest day on 29 December, the hosts ran out winners by 216 runs, also defeating South Australia in the match than began on New Years' Day.

Cricket was back, and in a big way, the £1277 gate takings being a record for interstate cricket. But there were sour notes too. An anonymous thief made off with £35 from one of the outer reserve refreshment bars. Diamond never played again, Sewart not beyond that season, dying in 1927, aged forty-seven, having never recovered his pre-war health.

A *Sun* leader welcomed the resumption of cricket but prophesied that the public would find sport 'less engrossing than it was'. 'Everybody has grown older,' said *The Sun*. 'The men who went to the war, of course, have become the oldest; they have lived twenty years during their campaigns. But the men also who did not enlist, and the women upon whom fell grief and responsibility together, find that these four or five years have left; upon them the Impress of ten. The very children are growing up graver than children were five years ago. Life is more serious than it was, and feelings are more intense.'

Nor was the country as healthy. As influenza swirled, interstate travel restrictions were imposed for the sake of quarantine, and games planned in Perth, Brisbane and finally Adelaide were cancelled. When the Victorian team travelled to Sydney for their return match against NSW in January 1919, their keeper Frank Hyett fell ill, dying three months later. His funeral drew 5000 mourners, including a stricken John Curtin, to whom as a fellow official in the Railways Union he had been a political mentor. Almost 12,000 Australians would die of the disease that year. Not until February 1920 would the threat abate.

The muted and long-forgotten game at the MCG starting a century ago had, however, accomplished one thing: it had, after the hiatus of 1914-18, re-established and consolidated the tradition of cricket on Boxing Day, which otherwise have fallen into abeyance, like so many other customs annulled by war. Victoria hosting NSW around Christmas time had been a generally established part of cricket's calendar before. Afterwards it centred ever more insistently on Boxing Day, strongly enough a generation later to survive the hiatus of World War II also.

When the Melbourne Test supplanted the Sheffield Shield derby on Boxing Day fifty years ago, preluding the institution we now know as the 'Boxing Day Test', it was in part because cricket had so quickly recolonised the date in 1918, perhaps before it was quite ready, but with a patience about what was to come.

VIRAT KOHLI

IMPERIAL PROGRESS

26 December 2018

This will be another column about Virat Kohli. You may feel that you have read quite enough about him already this season, and that would be understandable.

In a summer rather short of star power, in which most of the great names are behind the microphone, it is easy to default to him as a subject, knowing that he is of interest to at least a lazy billion people or so.

On Boxing Day, however, I want first of all to hark back to the corresponding date fifteen years ago, and an experience strongly imprinted on my mind, of watching the game in the Great Southern Stand.

Mid-way through the afternoon, the crowd suddenly unified to concentrate its attention on a diminutive figure walking out to bat at two for 278.

On the same occasion four years earlier, Sachin Tendulkar had made a delectable hundred; now he was searching for form a little, and hope sprang that he would find it on the cricket calendar's biggest day.

It was not to be. The applause for him had barely died when he was victim of a leg-side strangle, first ball.

His embarrassment was worsened, Tendulkar revealed in his autobiography, by the fact that his wife had paid one of her rare visits to a cricket ground, having been persuaded to attend by other players' wives.

Anjali Tendulkar immediately got up and left, as did several people in the crowd around me. In many years cricket watching, I do not recall such a spontaneous, understated but plain expression of disappointment: Boxing Day was over because a visiting batsman was out.

Similar expectation will attend Kohli in this Test. It does every time he bats, but there is here an additional burden. He leads a team carrying its opening batmen, skittish in the middle, and ambivalent about spin, nonetheless ranked number one in the world — an eminence born of a weak phase of international cricket that nonetheless leaves India with down being the only way to go.

Kohli is, moreover, Indian cricket front and back. The coach, Ravi Shastri, fills the role because Kohli fell out with the previous incumbent, Anil Kumble. The manager, Sunil Subramaniam, is a factotum; the selectors, M. S. K. Prasad, Devang Gandhi and Sarandeep Singh, are ciphers.

If Kohli wishes four fast bowlers to be picked, they will be chosen. If he is concerned about the form of Cheteshwar Pujara or Ajinkya Rahane, they will be excluded. If he believes wives should accompany players on tour — he is recently married, to a beautiful and intelligent woman — then they will be.

Historically, Indian skippers have not made old bones in the job. Since independence, the country has had more than twice as many cricket captains as prime ministers.

If anyone can change that pattern, it is Kohli. Never has an Indian captain enjoyed quite such unilateral authority, thanks both to the force of his personality, and to the weakness of others'.

The crucial context is the intervention, following the scandals in the Indian Premier League five years ago, of India's Supreme Court in the reform of the Board of Control for Cricket in India.

Two years ago, the court appointed an interim committee of administration, chaired by a former Indian auditor-general, Vinod Rai. The committee and the executive Rai ostensibly oversees, it is reliably reported, defer to Kohli on all matters of importance, to an almost cringe-inducing degree.

The historian Ramachandra Guha, who served on the committee briefly before resigning in dismay, depicted the organisation as a group of attendant lords content merely to swell Kohli's progress.

'They deferred to him absolutely, even in matters that were not within the Indian captain's ken,' noted Guha. 'The BCCI men always used the captain's first name in referring to him, perhaps to indicate intimacy; however, in concrete behavioural terms, the proximity was more akin to that between servant and master.'

Since then, Rai has been further weakened by a succession of quarrels, most recently involving the coaching of the Indian women's team, while his CEO Rahul Johri was improbably caught up in a #MeToo scandal. If they were servants before, they might well by now be slaves.

The only figure of comparable pre-eminence in Indian cricket history is, of course, Tendulkar, before whom the BCCI supplicated ever lower, finally shredding schedules in order that the great man's career conclude where it began, in Mumbai.

But Tendulkar and Kohli differ in temper as much as technique. Tendulkar was an establishment figure; Kohli is his own establishment.

Tendulkar lost the captaincy and played on under Ganguly, Dravid and Dhoni. It is impossible to imagine Kohli acquiescing in such a demotion.

And who in this team, save perhaps Ravi Ashwin, has leadership capacity anyway, given that the job would involve captaining both

India and Virat Kohli?

So every time the second Indian wicket falls these days, it portends not only the arrival of the world's best batsman and number one box office attraction, but is also a kind of referendum on how Indian cricket constitutes itself.

Kohli is a cricketer of such preternatural self-belief that one would not rule out his succeeding even in these circumstances. When out, he looks genuinely disbelieving, as though it simply does not compute, or must be some misunderstanding, or was not in his diary for the day.

But cricket is also such a game that it is impossible to stave off the influence of randomness and chance indefinitely, let alone preserve a permanent edge on all one's opponents. It takes as many deliveries to dismiss Kohli as it does Mohammed Shami, as it did Sachin Tendulkar fifteen Boxing Days ago.

This is the bargain we all strike with cricket on going to watch a great batsman. And in the case of Kohli, the drama is enriched by a nation's cricket being leveraged to the outcome.

THIRD TEST, DAY 1

BOXING CLEVER

26 December 2018

The scoreboard clock showed 3.27pm yesterday as Virat Kohli emerged onto the MCG with that familiar gait, busy but unhurried. Indian hosannahs rang out. Cheteshwar Pujara followed a few paces behind his captain, head bowed, more disciple than partner.

Nearing one another in the middle, the pair had the scene incongruously to themselves, Tim Paine prolonging the Australian huddle another 90 seconds or so. A swooping camera caught Kohli tossing a smile over his shoulder at something. A remark? A thought? His eyes can blaze and his hide can bristle, but India's captain also has a capacity, especially when batting, for exuding relaxation. Perhaps he's then at his surest — when it is as simple as skill versus skill, he feels the odds stacked in his favour.

At two for 123, the odds were perhaps even a little better. Only once this year had Kohli had the luxury of a better score on coming in; in fourteen of twenty-two preceding innings, he'd taken guard with scorelines poorer than two for 60.

When the first ball after tea from Pat Cummins was probingly full, Kohli looked to be waiting for it, puncturing mid-on, returning for a relaxed two. He repeated the shot for boundaries in his first ten deliveries. So a Test match that had been tossing fitfully began to stir — as they are wont to when Kohli is at the crease.

Paine's men had whiffs of his wicket. At 17, an edge streaked to third man through a vacant second slip; at 32, a review of an lbw appeal turned up three lemons. But shots also pealed from his bat: that bisection of bowler and mid-on is becoming as much of a signature as his cover drive.

With Pujara doing as Pujara does, and this series has, India at the close had achieved a position of reassuring security — a security that had appeared improbable in the aftermath of the Perth Test, with attendant dramas around selection, injury, harmony and realpolitik.

From these unpromising circumstances, India extracted at least one unheralded benefit. Ten days ago, twenty-seven-year-old Mayank Agarwal was earning $200 a day in the Ranji Trophy on an outground in Gujarat, while India continued to indulge the fantasy that Prithvi Shaw might somehow grow a new leg and play on Boxing Day.

What ensued you could call a volte farce. Prithvi was abruptly evacuated home, KL Rahul and Murali Vijay were made redundant, and Hanuma Vihari promoted from ersatz spinner to makeshift number one, pricking thought bubbles about the use of deputy keeper Parthiv Patel.

Into slot number two stepped Agarwal, with his stickerless bat and sunken profile — two commentators, apparently rummaging in the Mahatma Coat Joke Book, scoffed that his highest score, for Karnataka against Railways, had been made against kitchen staff. In fact, Agarwal showed something of the aplomb of former ticket inspector MS Dhoni.

No student enrolled in a crammer could have applied themselves to closer study of the subject of Australian batting conditions — Agarwal put in the time and did not waste a lesson.

There is an old-fashioned feel to his compact strokeplay. He leaves the ball decisively. His defensive shots are executed with an anachronistically dead bat. He turned his back on a lifter from Cummins, content to wear it the way Vinoo Mankad used to against Ray Lindwall. He was struck painfully on the shoulder by Josh Hazlewood, but got into line next ball as Sunil Gavaskar did against Jeff Thomson with nothing but a cap to protect him.

Not even Kohli has played Nathan Lyon so securely this summer, Agarwal going down on his haunches to drive through cover, skipping down the pitch to hit over the top with little more than a jab.

Partner Vihari saw the first 80 minutes like a true disciple of satyagraha, with six scoring shots amid 66 balls, and a headache from a Cummins bouncer. When the scoreboard indicated he was 'on strike', it seemed to describe his forming of a one-man picket line.

Pujara then settled, with his usual deft and unobtrusive strokes interspersed with flurries of inactivity, while the drop-in surface, though it is early to cast judgement, provided the bowlers with little encouragement, if not active discouragement. The slips emptied out steadily, like guests unobtrusively slipping away from a dull party.

They returned at length for the second new ball, which Starc swung and Hazlewood seamed, bending their backs and baring their fangs. Pujara took one on the gloves, Kohli missed a tentative defensive stroke.

At last, with the ground falling into shadow, Kohli drove hard at a delivery from Starc slanted across him. Paine at full stretch could not quite bag the edge.

Sometimes after a delinquent shot, Kohli will be seen reproaching himself. Now he just looked on, pensively but assuredly, as though he somehow knew this was his day. If he brings the same attitude into today, Australia's task could be formidable.

DAVID WARNER

KEEPING HIS OWN COUNSEL

27 December 2018

David Warner is not a figure who readily elicits sympathy. He is regarded as too brash and too rich, as an unappetising mix of the privileged and the déclassé. And he has, by his own admission, cheated at cricket.

Yet he may deserve more credit than many have been prepared to grudge him. Now alone among the Cape Town co-conspirators has he served his long penance quietly, tight with his family, mucking in at his club, and for what happened nine months ago blaming nobody but himself, publicly at least.

Declining to join Steve Smith and Cameron Bancroft on this week's instalment of Rehabilitation Idol, Warner has compelled nobody to arbitrate on the ethics of advertising one's good works or to parse any wacky word salads. He has solicited no soft ball questions, sought no pity, refrained from invitations to self-forgiveness, and exchanged no matey pleasantries with interlocutors ('Good on ya mate, I know all of Australia wish you all the best'; 'Thanks Gilly, good on ya mate').

But somehow it is Warner who remains beyond the pale. So much for that cultural review, with its complex shades of individual and institutional responsibility — far easier to fall back on the well-worn stereotype of the worm in the apple.

Warner faces strong urgings now — not at all self-interested from the media — to tell 'his side of the story'. Yet why? For it is hard to see what Smith and Bancroft have gained by their public positionings. They divulged no new information, revealed no hitherto unsuspected dimensions to the story, and atoned for events not one iota.

Instead Smith returned to a familiar guise as billboard, allowing Vodafone to project its logo on his remorse, doubtless heartfelt but no worthier for corporate backing.

In his interview with Adam Gilchrist, he referred to the Hobart Test of 2016 as a moment the team started to 'go off track', yet could find nothing to fault in its 'cultures and stuff' at the crucial moment.

Bancroft, apparently in circumstances so reduced that he can no longer afford sleeves, muddied things somewhat, amid tangling himself in abstractions and referring to himself in the third person.

Yes, as has been widely noted, Bancroft publicly tipped Warner in as the initiator of the illegal ball tampering; but it was not Warner to whom he felt answerable. Had he not fallen in with the plan, he told Adam Gilchrist, he would have 'felt like I'd let the team down, like I'd hurt our chances to win the game of cricket'.

That invited further questions, which Gilchrist rather sidestepped in preference to allowing Bancroft to talk about his feelings — these days, of course, emotion trumps content every time.

Bancroft has enjoyed a rather remarkable degree of public sympathy and private support since Cape Town. It's become debateable whether he has deserved it. On the face of things, he seems to have been slow to understand the magnitude of his actions beyond their impact on him.

Back in March, Bancroft commented that 'the thing that breaks my heart the most is the fact I've just given up my spot in the team to somebody else for free' — not exactly the profoundest thought on the matter.

Now he has arrived at positions that do not readily reconcile. Of the plan, for example, he told Gilchrist that he went along because he 'didn't know any better'. Yet somehow he also knew he was in trouble the instant he was caught.

In the context of the calamitous press conference at the end of the day's play in Cape Town, Bancroft spoke of being 'actually proud' that he and Smith 'wanted to be accountable and I guess, really honest about our actions'. He discerned no contradiction between this and proceeding to mislead the media about the use of sandpaper.

Bancroft was not asked about, nor did he volunteer, any feeling he may have about the impact of his action on cricket's reputation and health. I do not doubt that he nurses deep regrets. But so he should, and not merely for his own sake.

So who would have thought it? In all the climate of self-exoneration, Warner has been the perpetrator closest to retaining his dignity. Going back to March, in fact, Australia's former vice-captain seemed the sincerest in his professions of contrition, and his words then stand up strikingly well in hindsight.

To date, in fact, Warner remains the only member of the trio to have offered an apology to Cricket Australia ('I apologise for my actions and the effect it has had on our game under your care and control') and South Africa ('a fine cricketing nation' that 'deserves better from its guests and deserves better from me').

The question of whether Warner represents his country again remains open, and frankly should be left until it is a possibility. Nine months ago, Australian cricket changed beyond recognition in minutes; imagine how much it can change in three more months. But by keeping his own counsel he has shown a degree of maturity and restraint for which he has not previously been noted.

THIRD TEST, DAY 2

PITCHED BATTLE

27 December 2018

The last delivery of Nathan Lyon's 40th over yesterday emerged from his hard-working fingers much like most of the preceding 239, pitching near a darkening patch around off stump.

Ajinkya Rahane played back, aiming to work the ball as it turned through a beckoning leg side gap. He'd have felt it hit the pad just above the boot with an uncomfortable sense of the inevitable, the pang of adjacency.

It had taken 150 overs for Australia to take five Indian wickets; more particularly it had needed that long for the plot of this Test to emerge, as it were. Sideways the ball has done precious little the last two days; now, potentially, loom three days of ups and downs. What cost India their vice-captain's wicket yesterday is among their best hopes of retrieving their series lead.

Getting to this stage has not, it must be said, made for premium box office spectacle despite the 100,000 clicks of the turnstile. The English cricket writer R. C. Robertson-Glasgow once invited a girl he knew to a game of cricket and received a courteous but firm brush off. 'No thank you,' she replied. 'Cricket is all just waiting.' Players, spectators and media at the MCG yesterday understood whereof she spoke.

To paraphrase Parkinson's Law, the cricket had to expand to fill the time allowed for its completion. It would not be accelerated, abbreviated, truncated or discounted.

India, with the advantage of the fall of the coin, needed a certain number of runs to feel secure. Batting conditions would get no better, but they played with care and precision. The deeper they progressed into the day, the longer the pitch's exposure to the sapping sun, the greater the wear and tear, the less time they might need to bat in a third innings.

The signs were promising for them even before Rahane played fatally back. A second lot of four byes, from Hazlewood, steepled over Tim Paine's head in the morning; other deliveries bounced like footballs with deflated bladders.

With his low grip and forward press, Pujara took several blows to the gloves from just short of a length, accepting them as one accepts jamming one's fingers in a slamming door. Yet the delivery from Cummins that curtailed his seventeenth Test hundred hit the off stump no more than half way up. Pujara peeled away disappointedly, as though he'd had nothing planned the next couple of days and been really rather keen to spend them at the crease.

If the tone was attritional, the trend it continued was even more so. Twelve wickets fell on the last day here in 2016, courtesy of a Pakistani panic; otherwise eleven days in three Tests have yielded 46 wickets, the cricket unfolding with all the urgency of osmosis or photosynthesis.

'A three to five-year process': that's the way MCG curator Matt Page has described the work that needs doing to revive this moribund transplanted turf table. He might almost have been describing those stages of yesterday's play when the timescales felt geological.

It is never a happy state of affairs for cricket when the Boxing Day Test suffers by comparison with the concurrent Sydney-to-Hobart. The yachtsmen should count themselves fortunate they do not have to contend with drop-in waves.

All the same, this pitch might yet intrigue, so let's withhold censure, at least for the moment. The Australians could also have made it easier for themselves, or shorter at any rate.

Their captain seemed stretched for ideas. Their outcricket showed signs of raggedness. Three chances were missed from the hapless Lyon, two of them standard issue. For all the annoyance Mitchell Marsh seems to engender in these parts, he could hardly be faulted for his endeavours. His four bowling teammates would have been grateful for the 26 overs he bowled, with which they were therefore not lumbered.

With three-quarters of an hour to go, Kohli's declaration exposed Australia's heavy-legged openers, who against the new ball lived to fight another morning, with a gram or two of luck. One delivery from Ishant bounced a couple of times after Finch let it go, another from Bumrah hit Harris flush on the helmet as he failed to limbo beneath an attempted bouncer. The penultimate over, from Jadeja, passed in less time than a toilet break; Finch's outside edge from the last ball failed to carry to third slip. So day two concluded — with what looked very much like a foretaste of day three.

THIRD TEST, DAY 3

HAZARD LIGHTS

28 December 2018

It's proverbially a recession when your neighbour loses their job, a depression when you lose yours. The Boxing Day Test may have marked a similar transition in Australian batsmanship.

It is 80 days since an Australian Test batsman passed 72; yesterday, nobody passed 22. There was no blaming the pitch, the overhead conditions, the DRS, the stump mics, the Illuminati, or any other miscellaneous uncontrollables. This was routine, humdrum, common or garden mediocrity.

It's arguable that the presence of two outstanding batsmen, Steve Smith and David Warner, has for some time masked the depths of batting recession in this country; without them, at any rate, depression seems to have well and truly set in.

The Test year began in Sydney with the Marsh brothers seeming to come of age with fraternal hundreds; yesterday, with no Smith and Warner to beat the path for them, Shaun and Mitchell eked out 28 between them in nearly 100 balls. They toiled willingly at least. But work is not the issue, any more than the batsmen's 2km time trials and skin folds. It is a lacklustre system that underlies batting so confused and directionless.

Nobody but nobody seemed capable of coming to terms with the pursuit of more than 400. There was a guileless virility about the clutching at aggressive options, using horizontal bats, playing against the spin, taking on fielders — Aaron Finch, Marcus Harris and Travis Head were dismissed playing Russian Roulette with intent.

And while in Adelaide and Perth the batting was shored up by captain Tim Paine and the tail, here the second half of the innings fell open like a trap door. When last an Australian batting unit failed so abjectly, in the corresponding Test here eight years ago, the line-up still contained Ponting, Hussey, Clarke; Justin Langer has no such resources to draw on.

There was, to be fair, some fine Indian bowling into the bargain. Ishant Sharma and Mohammed Shami were an established, effective formula coming into this series. Jasprit Bumrah has brought the combination to a kind of critical mass.

Bumrah clops in like a man riding a pretend horse. It is mainly cosmetic; his action is all in its final surge. He would be very nearly as fast and as awkward from a step or two, thanks to his powerful shoulders and the oblique angle of his arm, veering his stock delivery in, with a natural bias that straightens the ball as it ages.

The Indians apparently call him 'Crofty', for Colin Croft, who bowled malevolent sidewinders from the edge of the crease for the West Indies in the 1980s. His inclination of attack bears a likeness to that of Ben Stokes too. But Bumrah will probably prove better than either.

Unlike most fast bowlers, he threatens the inside rather than the outside edge, seeks the stumps rather than the slips — a method as challenging to prepare for as to play, which also leaves him less dependent on India's permeable catching cordon.

His variations, meanwhile, are subtle, adept and abrupt. His slower ball to Shaun Marsh yesterday on the stroke of lunch, following on five deliveries of uniform speed, was the cricket equivalent of Donald Trump's stealth fighter — to Marsh at least, literally invisible.

There is no need to describe Ravi Jadeja's run-up as it does not exist. He is either bowling or walking back to bowl, as looped as a duck in a shooting gallery. His Rajasthan Royals captain Shane

Warne dubbed him 'Rockstar' for his confident airs, although his minimalism is more of the twelve-bar blues variety.

Here he was vital. His dismissal of Usman Khawaja removed Australia's best player; his accuracy enabled Virat Kohli to keep his precious pace bowlers fresh; his rapidity was a boon for India's over rate, which threatened to coagulate in Perth, but here circulated healthily.

As ever, Australia's bowlers were left to make good the failings of their batting colleagues. And just when it appeared nothing awaited the home team but further downtrend, there was an uptick — maybe a technical correction, but one cannot afford to be fussy.

Pat Cummins has bowled with pace, patience and a poor ration of luck in his last five innings. An over in which Pujara and Kohli fended identically to leg gully amounted to karmic payback. Rahane's leg-side strangulation was on the batsman's part almost a random act of kindness.

In truth, India's batsmen were as neglectful as Australia's had been, if from nonchalance rather than naivety — with a lead swollen to more than 300, you can get a bit casual. It completed a turnabout in the skill ascendancies: from seven wickets for 451 on days one and two to fifteen for 197 on day three. But who will provide Australia with the stimulus it needs to alleviate this depression?

THIRD TEST, DAY 4

THE CORRIDOR OF PERPLEXITY

29 December 2018

When Australia won the Second Test in Perth, they were widely said to have turned a corner. The lesson of the Third Test in Melbourne looks to be that they remain in the same corridor, still in search of a door.

Worse, they have had less of a share of this Test than any since Cape Town. On a conventional measure of dominance, that of sessions won and conceded, they have been steadily overwhelmed. India has shaded them in all but one stage — after tea on Friday, when it was rather too late to matter much anyway.

Nor did this herald anything much, apart from confirming the established impression that Patrick Cummins is Australia cricket's most valuable player — something reaffirmed by his batting, calm, straight and fluent in his second Test half-century and highest Test score, after tea yesterday.

Otherwise, when a team spends two days in the field then only two sessions at the crease, they can expect no better than finishing second.

The one misfortune to which Australia can point is the toss, although in its efforts this year the fall of the coin has loomed far too large. Australia's average first innings score batting first in 2018 was 392; batting second it was less than half.

Conditions in Test cricket change across the course of a match but not that much. A permissible conclusion is that in the face of a total to chase, any total, Australian batting faculties cloud and performances attenuate.

Couple this with the lien over at least two and perhaps even three places in the order arising from the Cape Town suspensions, and you have a dressing room wrestling with itself even before it measures up against opponents.

Yesterday was a day's Test cricket only one country could enjoy, as advertised by the huge Bharat Army flag draped from a tier of the Great Southern Stand before lunch — this was hastily removed for obscuring the logo of an online betting company, because of the danger that onlookers might forget to gamble.

Not that there was a solitary Australian batsmen you'd have staked Monopoly money on. And so it unfolded, more or less according to rote.

The drop-in pitch might almost have been petrified for the last year. In the corresponding Test twelve months ago, however, Steve Smith and David Warner ground out 367 runs for thrice out. More than determination was needed to make good that difference.

The innings was duly broken open, and all too easily. Aaron Finch's flat-footed flail at his fourth ball amounted almost to a deliberate act of self-harm; Marcus Harris's bat-first poke made him at least a co-conspirator in his demise. Mind you, they were rivalled for the player of the day's worst stroke by birthday boy Travis Head, his bat as crooked as original sin.

Shaun Marsh could consider himself unfortunate, undone by fine bowling and entrepreneurial umpiring; Mitchell Marsh not so much. The Australian vice-captain's footwork against slow bowling is reminiscent of an ungainly man trying to teach himself to dance with a set of black and white shoeprints on the floor. The effort is earnest and persevering; the outcome somehow never seems to improve. Insecure in defence against Jadeja, he defaulted to attack with foreseeable results.

It is surely not so difficult. A corollary of the burden on the batsmen is that Australia's tail, of whom less is naturally expected, has lately shown decided stickability, and did so again yesterday, ignoring their fatigue, defying the second new ball. Tim Paine at number seven will end 2018 as Australia's second-highest run scorer; Cummins at number eight has faced more deliveries this series than either opening batsman; as the day petered out beneath twinkling floodlights, Nathan Lyon looked as comfortable in defence as any Australian in the game. It is a corridor of uncertainty all right, but negotiable at a step at a time.

THIRD TEST, DAY 5

INDIA ROMP HOME

30 December 2018

The last time India won a Test match in Melbourne, the names Border and Gavaskar were on the team sheets rather than the trophy — in 1981, actually, there was no trophy, so low-temperature was the rivalry between India and Australia.

In the twenty-two years the silverwear has existed, moreover, it has changed hands very nearly as often as it has changed venues, with Australia's 2004 victory in India the exception. So if retaining the BGT in Australia is not the highlight of Virat Kohli's cricket career, that is only because of his own lengthy pre-existing highlight reel.

There were some familiar sensations in Melbourne. Commentators were still cracking jaded jokes about pronouncing Indian names, and fans hurling damn fool insults. But times have changed. No previous Indian team has looked quite so at home in Australia, a sense reinforced by the cheerful enclaves of its supporters at the MCG, whom Kohli acknowledged yesterday afternoon with a spontaneous donation of gear.

As Tim Paine conducted a typically funereal losing captain's press conference, jubilation emanated from the visiting dressing room, with no concern about its being overheard by eavesdropping stump mics.

Why has this team travelled so much more effectively than previous Indian visitors to Australia? After all, they failed on the road in South Africa and England this year, and boast nothing like the batting depth of previous teams.

Experience helps. Australia has historically been able to rely on the hardness of its pitches, the size of its grounds, and intensity of its summer heat to act as a kind of twelfth man. But only Jasprit Bumrah, Rishabh Pant and Prithvi Shaw of Kohli's original touring party had not toured this country before, and to the first two the conditions have been catnip.

Discussing Bumrah yesterday during his winning captain's press conference, Kohli made a gnomic reference to his star fast bowler's 'mindset'. Bumrah, he said, looks at pitches and 'he thinks wickets' — rather than the formulations routinely trotted out by Australians, of 'work', 'good areas' or 'bowling in partnerships'.

The evidence is powerfully indicative if not definitive: 20 wickets at less than 15 in three Tests, conceding barely two runs an over.

For a bowler so geared to slanting the ball back in, he is seldom worked to leg; for a cricketer so explosive in his method, he sustains remarkably uniform speeds. The question arises: would Bumrah have been allowed to progress so far with such a method in Australian cricket, without the intervention of a dozen well-meaning bowling and conditioning coaches?

Defeat in Perth left India notably undismayed. Even on their unsuccessful tours this year, they had shown a capacity for bouncing back rapidly, winning at Wanderers and Trent Bridge — performances rather better than Australia's last starts at those venues.

It helped them that conditions for this decisive Test were so welcoming. The toss was influential, the height of the bounce agreeable, the pace of the game congenial. Straight from the plane, reserve batsman Mayank Agarwal could acclimatise to batting down under at his own speed, and the team build towards 400 in the knowledge that Australia batting second this year has averaged less than half that.

What of Australia? After the collegial promise of Perth, they here shrank to more or less a one-man team. Was Patrick Cummins' the best all-round performance in a losing side in history? He bowled electrically and batted so effectively that he might as well be promoted to the top six.

But as at Adelaide, this Maginot line-up was readily outflanked, the first three wickets surviving twenty overs in each innings. Shaun Marsh and Travis Head enjoyed the only half-century partnership, if 'enjoyed' is quite the right word for a 51-run fourth-wicket stand in the second innings.

'Inexperience', Paine called it, yet Marsh has played 156 first-class matches, Head 79, Usman Khawaja 134, Aaron Finch 83, and the captain himself 110.

It looked more like rigidity, batsmen yearning to assert themselves, in thrall to the modern slogans of 'batting with intent', 'moving the game on' and 'having a plan' — the old injunctions to play each ball on its merits and to resist premeditation are so pre-T20.

It's become clear this week, if it was not before, that at least two members of this Australian top six are playing, as it were, under sentence of sentence — specifically the expiry of those sentences imposed on Steve Smith and David Warner after Cape Town. Paine went so far yesterday as to call the need for them 'pretty clear'; nobody watching this Test could conceivably differ.

India head to Sydney with the opportunity to play for something little less rare than Test victories in Australia — in this age of almost overpowering home advantage, an away series victory. Reports of a dry pitch bode well for them. For the Australians, meanwhile, more than pride is on the line. At stake are positions, careers, livelihoods.

AUSTRALIAN SELECTION

THE SECRET KNOCK

1 January 2019

Australian cricket has a new obsession. 'The line' has been replaced by 'the door', on which selectors have for some time been bemoaning the absence of insistent pounding.

'Try being a selector at the moment,' coach Justin Langer complained after the Boxing Day Test's contribution to the #nationalbattingcrisis. 'We've got to be careful not to reward poor performances but… it's not as if the guys are absolutely banging the door down. Most of our batters knocking on the door are averaging in the 30s [in the Sheffield Shield].'

Langer is an appealingly frank sort of fellow, and probably unused as yet to having his every word parsed. Yet this hardly stood up to scrutiny. For a start, there is no 'door' of first-class cricket for anyone even to scrabble at the moment; there is the five-bar gate of the Big Bash League, on which is being scribbled graffiti like 'Darcy Short 4 Me' and 'I Heart Marcus Stoinis'.

Also, as my colleague Peter Lalor noted yesterday, Langer's remarks lack empirical support. Since moving back to Tasmania after losing his Test spot, for example, Matthew Wade has made 1225 runs at 51. Maybe that's not banging from the golden age of doors, but it deserves respect.

Over the same period Queensland's Joe Burns has ground out 1197 runs at 52, Victoria's Glenn Maxwell 833 at 49, New South Wales' Daniel Hughes 1123 at 43.2 and Kurtis Patterson 1110 at 40.7. Again, not perhaps comparable to those imagined glory days when every batsman in the Shield averaged 50 and every bowler 15, but still solid performances sustained over extended periods despite being compromised, as is the modern way, with ceaseless interruption.

After all, it's hardly possible to talk about a 'first-class season' in Australia since the Shield was cleft in twain by the BBL.

Historically a huge advantage of home countries staging Test matches has been their wider pool of active talent available for selection. A touring team in practice has only its own ranks to draw on; a host has in theory the whole of its first-class competition as a field of candidates. We decided we were so good seven years ago that we could safely forfeit this edge. Now we're stuck discussing piecemeal remedies like more second XI games and shadow squads, or musing sagaciously about 'rapid format changes' as though this is somehow a skill rather than simply a necessity.

Under these circumstances, the selectors deserve a measure of sympathy, as they are frequently relying on form with a time decay element. Yet they do not help their own cause by their seeming lurchings from one theory to the next. Just what are the criteria for Australian selection at present? Character? Cover drives? Heredity? Horses-for-courses? Mentions in Ponting's commentary or on Warnie's Twitter?

One inference that can be drawn from Langer's remarks is that the door has a secret knock which you need to know. For the problem appears to be not that nobody is making runs, but that it's not the people the selectors want.

Wade is 31, Maxwell is 30, Burns is 29. They've been tried; they've, apparently, been found wanting. There's already a specialist batsmen in the Australian team, Shaun Marsh, with an average less than his age. The selectors seem to dream of a wunderkind, who would not only alleviate the pressures on the Australian team but also vindicate the cricket system — a new Ponting, a tyro Gilchrist, a kid Clarke.

One suspects that these are the 'batters knocking on the door' to which Langer refers. Unfortunately this generation are actually not averaging 30 this season; they're averaging 20.

That's your Hilton Cartwright, Jake Weatherald, Sam Heazlett, Josh Philippe, Ben McDermott, Jason Sangha, Jack Edwards et al, into whom years of coaching and managerial resources have been ploughed, and for whom enormous futures have been prophesied, almost mandated.

Cricket Australia's high-performance empire has hardly had a better day than in early November when teenagers Sangha and Edwards put on 180 for the sixth New South Wales wicket against Tasmania. But that memorable occasion aside, the pair have 286 first-class runs at 17.9 to show for this season.

For his club Manly-Warringah, meanwhile, tall right-hander Edwards has actually never made a century, from fifths to firsts; at first-grade level he has just two fifties. Strip these from his first-grade record, in fact, and it contracts to 121 runs at 8.64. Yet in some eyes, Edwards will be closer to Australian selection than Wade, Maxwell and Burns.

It's unkind to single Edwards out: he's hardly picked himself. He may yet succeed; one hopes he does. But so far he's been offered opportunities well in advance of his performances. What door has he banged on? Or has he simply tapped politely on an open one?

Anecdotally, too, there's quite a bit of this going on, since the advent of a pathways system that encourages subjective analysis and rather deprecates fuddy-duddy old performance. If you've an idle few hours, drill down into MyCricket and check out some pathways cricket averages. Some kids sure seem to get a great run. Just sayin'…

So perhaps there's fewer issues with the banging than with the doors themselves, traditional measures of merit having been so thoroughly subverted — often with good intentions, it needs be said, but subverted just the same.

To this has lately been added an additional layer, post-Cape Town. The search for 'good people as well as good cricketers' is laudable; but what if those the search overlooks end up being regarded as in some ways personally deficient and those who benefit court scorn for being part of the in-crowd? This is actually unfair to both groups. Perception can be hard to shift; it can even be self-reinforcing and damaging of the culture it seeks to build. Because doors bear heavily on the rooms into which they open.

FOURTH DAY, DAY I
CHE-MANIA

3 January 2019

There were traces of Sachin Tendulkar at the Sydney Cricket Ground yesterday in the armbands worn by the Indians in memory of Ramakant Achrekar, the Shivaji Park coach who had the Little Master as a littler pupil. And there was Cheteshwar Pujara.

India is a cricket nation with an almost religious devotion to huge scores. Fifteen years ago here, with a Border-Gavaskar Trophy on the line, Tendulkar made a legendary double-century by completely abjuring the cover drive, an epic of passive resistance. The following year, as if to present his own credentials, Pujara made a double hundred on his under-19 Test debut.

He has been a stalwart servant: more than 5000 Test runs at an average, as of yesterday, better than 50. But this summer has been his career's meridian. While King Kohli has been cynosure of all eyes, his sole century came in a losing cause in Perth. It is plebeian Pujara who presaged victory at Adelaide and Melbourne with his long methodical entrenchments, and might have threepeated the effort here.

Yesterday Pujara took his batting in the series into its 29th hour, during which the Indians have added 1059 runs. He has faced more than 1138 deliveries, before each of which he has readied with a preparatory glance at his splice, like an act of communion with his bat. In doing so, Pujara has become a kind of Medium Height Master, similar to Tendulkar in his dedication and piety.

What Achrekar was to Tendulkar, Pujara's father Arvind has been to him. A Ranji Trophy player for Saurasthra, Arvind began coaching his son in Rajkot aged three, every day, before and after school, and every weekend and festival, eventually persuading the railways for whom he worked to lay a cement pitch for his 'academy'. To this day, father and son train together, their tie so tight that when Arvind talks of his son's batting he uses the word 'we'.

Pujara builds an innings with an according orderliness, approaching it like a capable camper approaches erecting a tent — patiently, systematically, in a sequence tidily logical. He clears the area; he lays the ground sheet; he knows the ropes — also the pegs, the nets, the flaps.

In a decade of Test cricket, it's hard to remember Pujara ever, as they say, 'getting away to a flier' — opening his innings with a cluster of early boundaries. You imagine he might not like it, think it a little frantic, ostentatious. For while some batsmen pursue big scores with avidity, a Narevian greed, Pujara's innings are an endless process of settling in, in full cognisance of the bowling, the conditions, the scenario. The runs accumulate as though via sedimentation. Leave it too long, and he almost merges into the pitch. Which is why yesterday when Pujara was 12, Paine sent a rejected caught behind appeal from the bowling of Cummins for DRS analysis.

It was a speculation. The bowler had stifled his appeal; umpire Richard Kettleborough does not get much wrong; but if Pujara was to be had, it must be soon. So Australia forfeited a review — an advantage for India that eludes calculation, but that was wrung for them by their number three's reputation.

There were no further alarms, not a chance, no memorable miscues, not the merest concession. Even when clocked in the back of helmet by Hazlewood just before lunch, Pujara submitted to only a routine panel beating from the physiotherapist.

There were a few extremes in Pujara's batting last year. He

took 53 balls to get off the mark in a Test as Wanderers, ran himself out hopelessly at Lord's, top-edged a hook to fine leg on the stroke of lunch at Trent Bridge. At one stage he even lost his place. But from the instant he came to the wicket in the second over of this series, he has given Australia no help, in addition to looking more versatile than the batsman of four years ago. After eking a single out of 23 balls yesterday afternoon, for example, he poached took 21 from 12 in the last three overs before tea. Marnus Labuschagne will bowl worse overs, but not many to a better batsman.

As Lyon wearied after tea, Pujara twice came down the wicket and worked him past short leg and between a straight mid-wicket and a wide mid-on — a stroke every bit as much his signature as Tendulkar's cover drive.

When Starc returned for a final listless spell, he cut incisively and flicked commandingly twice, the last boundary raising his eighteenth Test century. Pujara marked this with a fist pump — restrained and decorous, but unmistakably a fist pump. Here, perhaps, the comparison with Tendulkar broke down. Indeed, it was rather like watching Jascha Heifetz indulge in a spot of air guitar.

But as the Australian bowlers felt the efforts of their Melbourne exertions and the pitch mellowed in the last hour, Pujara resumed his natural manner, towards a glimmering objective of something even Tendulkar never accomplished: a decisive role in victory in a series in Australia.

FOURTH TEST, DAY 2

SMITHEREENS

4 January 2019

Cricket grounds have a shape shifting character. At times when you're batting, they can seem as claustrophobic as a cupboard; at times when you're bowling, they can feel vast, open, undefendable, your nine fielders like a Boy Scout troop trying to hold Thermopylae.

A fielding captain in the situation of Tim Paine after tea at the SCG yesterday feels his powerlessness acutely. On the first morning here, his pace bowlers were ferocious, intimidating, might have had India four-down at lunch had they not defaulted to lengths too short.

A day and a bit on and they were paying the price, assigned a third new ball against a runaway partnership with a lickety-split outfield — not an attack, not even a defence, but a full-blown retreat. You understood the appeal to House Republicans of a wall. Paine could not afford his either. Even patrolled by as many as five fielders, the SCG's circumference has seldom looked so vulnerable.

Rishabh Pant and Ravi Jadeja put on 204 in 224 deliveries, a seventh-wicket record for India against Australia, although 'put on' hardly does it justice. They looted it, ran their fingers through it with maniacal laughter, then carried it away in a swag, playing shots with a Sehwagian insouciance. Marnus Labuschagne bowled, Travis Head, even Usman Khawaja — at a pace so slow that he could have run after the ball and caught it up had he felt so moved.

In contrast to Cheteshwar Pujara, the earnest Test specialist who dominated the first day, Pant and Jadeja are cricketers carried forward on India's T20 wave, chased at auction, exalted to stardom. They are young, bold, cheeky, have two and a half million Twitter followers; Pant, of course, has 'gone viral' in the last week, while Jadeja has the tribute of a parody account.

Yet their career foundations are strikingly solid. Twenty-one-year-old Pant averages 50 in first-class cricket, has made six hundreds including a triple century. And while pitches might be flat in India they are still 22 yards in length, and the air through which Pant likes hitting provides similar wind resistance.

So far in his brief international career, Pant has been in search of a comfortable tempo. His first Test scoring shot was a six at Trent Bridge; he pottered 47 balls over a duck at Southampton; he made a run-a-ball hundred at The Oval. He scored 92 in consecutive home Tests against West Indies, in an allegro 84 balls and an andantino 134.

In Australia, Pant has been compromised by the weakness of the Indian tail. At Perth in particular, where he was essentially left to corral four number elevens, he seemed unsure whether to stick or twist.

Jadeja's busy acquisitiveness and helter skelter running was here an ideal complement. Pant went to his century with his forty-eighth single, unflustered by conservative fields and defensive lines, with only a few flecks of flamboyance like a peachy reverse sweep from Lyon.

After tea, all came alike. In consecutive overs from Labuschagne and Lyon, Pant nailed conventional sweeps just as hard, as if to demonstrate there was no safe place to bowl to him. A pull shot from Hazlewood brought cheers for his 150; a switch hit from Head was as celebratory as New Year's fireworks.

Jadeja, a trivia buffs know, has the bizarre distinction of two first-class triple-centuries; also, recently, a Test hundred. He must have glimpsed another as he put even Pat Cummins to the sword, clearing his front leg to launch into the Bradman Stand, drawing back to scythe over point.

The four boundaries Jadeja poached when Cummins took the third new ball with four men on the perimeter somehow summed up Australia's helplessness. Deep square leg and fine leg were close enough to be communicating with two soup cans connected by a piece of string, but neither moved as hook shots bisected them twice. When Cummins pitched in the batsman's half, he was wellied down the ground to the unprotected straight boundary. When Cummins dropped wearily short again, he was pulled contemptuously in front of square.

Australia's only solace is that the pitch is without blemish even for two days' play, and that a leg-weary Pant shelled Khawaja in the third over of their brief reply — a reminder that but for Wriddhiman Saha's stubborn shoulder injury, his stump mic repartee would not have obtained him such a cult following this summer. Australia must hope he has a lot more talking to do.

Earlier, Pujara had prolonged his batting time in the series to nigh on 33 hours, a full day and a night of concentration and stamina, leaving a midden of discarded gloves at the boundary's edge, and trail of civilly detained bowlers in his wake. Again, he batted as if in his own Test match, aslant to cricket generally, a cricketer rather than an athlete, with his round shoulders and broad haunches — run-bearing hips, you might call them.

Pujara is cricket's 'Desiderata'. You could watch him all day as a form of therapy, like listening to whale sounds or wind chimes. He threw his head back when he fell seven runs short of a double century, trying to make a little too much of a straight ball from Lyon: he will be nearly thirty-five by the time India tours again, and may not make it back. The Australians breathed a collective sigh of relief, unaware that the field was about to change shape around them.

FOURTH TEST, DAY 3

MIND THE GAP

5 January 2019

Clouds scudding overhead around 3pm yesterday were the first interruption in three days of this Sydney Test's dazzling sun, the floodlight towers coming into operation as the temperature plunged, wind sprung up and rain briefly threatened.

In the middle, the overall impression remained of daylight — the daylight between Australia and India, grown each day since Perth's false dawn.

When your opponent makes seven for 622, and your average score batting second for the last year is less than third that, you could be said to have your work rather exquisitely cut out. Yet morning's prospect was not so unpromising. The Sydney Cricket Ground had rolled out a blameless, forgiving pitch and an outfield across which the ball skipped like a stone skimming over water.

The climate was congenial; India's pacemen had work in their legs. For a refreshed batting line-up, this was threat and opportunity. Batting conditions in Test cricket come no better, and Marcus Harris seemed resolved to take advantage, again looked well-organised, decisive in his strokeplay, composed in his defence.

The short ball that has troubled Harris a little this summer was no threat here; he was comfortable enough with spin to call for his cap, and poached three boundaries from a Kuldeep Yadav over including two muscular, reverberating drives over mid-on. Jasprit Bumrah looked less incisive from round the wicket,

Mohammed Shami a shade down on pace, and one for 122 at the first break portended well.

Beginnings, however, have not been Australia's problem this summer. Batsmen have, as they say, 'done the hard work' of settling in with regularity. What they have shown is a limited capacity to make that hard work pay off. Thirty-four times Australian batsmen have reached 20 in these four Tests; not one has made it to 80. Nobody has seemed out of their class; equally, few have suggested longevity, and none the kind of public monument-style permanence of Cheteshwar Pujara.

So with lunch still to settle, Ravi Jadeja was gifted a couple of freebies. Harris, after two comparatively breezy hours, dragged a cut onto leg stump — an indeterminate shot to a nondescript ball. Marsh, after two gilt-edged cover drives, nicked one that held its line — his tenth single figure score in ten Tests since the corresponding match a year ago, in which time he has averaged 18. Some statistics are said to speak volumes: this is a veritable Encyclopedia Britannica.

Surviving a shock-and-awe yorker from Bumrah first ball, Marnus Labuschagne had shaped gamely. He looks spirited, undaunted by tasks, determined to learn. But Shami probed patiently away at an alluring front pad with late inswing, forbearing being driven down the ground and worked to leg; now the batsman picked out one of two catching mid-wickets.

For the fifth consecutive innings, Travis Head lost his, bored into squirting a return catch. With the lights blazing after tea, Paine was bowled through not a gate but a driveway. Six for 198 was not a par score on this surface; unfortunately, it has been a par score for Australia of late, with no hint here of improvement.

It was left to Peter Handscomb, fresh from omission, and Patrick Cummins, weary from commission, to put conditions in proper perspective, before the weather fulfilled its promise as Australia had not.

Australia now has two and a half Tests to audition players for the Ashes later this year and, thanks to the Big Bash League's precedence in cricket's calendar, no first-class cricket from which to choose them — for the selectors a mystery wrapped in a conundrum inside an enigma.

Perhaps the day's gravest disappointment, however, was Usman Khawaja, who might have fallen without scoring on Friday night, and should by rights have made India pay full price for Rishabh Pant's error.

Khawaja has faced more deliveries than any of his teammates this summer (580), but apart from a hardworking 72 in Perth averaged 20. That enforced passivity at last seemed to take its toll yesterday: he became Australia's first wicket when he danced down at Yadav and picked mid-wicket out. On Friday, Khawaja was recalled to Australia's one-day squad on the latest selectorial hunch. But as Australia's most recent Test centurion, he was a player from whom an example was sought this summer who has not provided it.

Khawaja is a batsman of great gifts, reflected in lofty peaks and brilliant flashes. A year ago on this ground he made a sublime 171, batting eight and a half hours. But between his best and his frankly most frequent, there is falling an unflattering daylight.

FOURTH TEST, DAY 4

INDIA MAKE HISTORY

6 January 2019

Not much in sport is unprecedented, but today, regardless of whether a ball is bowled at Sydney Cricket Ground, history will be made, with India consummating a series victory in Australia for the first time in its life as an independent nation.

Twenty years or so ago, Steve Waugh popularised the idea of success in India as being Australia's cricket's 'final frontier'. Success in Australia, still more elusive, has been India's. They beat England in England as far back as 1971, Pakistan in Pakistan in 2004; they have won World Cups at home and away.

But for India, Australia has been a place of individual rather than collective accomplishments, cherished for their rarity. When Vijay Hazare scored twin centuries at Adelaide Oval in 1947, he was gifted a gold cigarette case by India's High Commissioner which he carried the rest of his life — empty, he being a non-smoker.

Indian cricketers have been great favourites in these climes: Kapil Dev, Sunil Gavaskar, Rahul Dravid, Sachin Tendulkar et al. Indian teams have been recurrently underpowered, outmatched, sometimes fissiparous. The Nawab of Pataudi's 1967-68 touring party contained representatives of five religions; Bishan Bedi's a decade later featured five strong-willed past or future captains.

This team has one leader, almost one mind, that of Virat Kohli. Whatever Tendulkar's greatness, he was always first among equals — the equals being the like of Dravid, Laxman, Sehwag, Ganguly. Kohli commands undiluted attention, amplified by proliferating media platforms, so that he can seem everywhere at once, and perfectly comfortable being so.

As outsized a personality as he is, however, Kohli was capable of committing this team to a goal larger than himself — what he called the 'obsession' of away victory, which he has been inculcating in Indian ranks since assuming India's captaincy in the corresponding Test here four years ago.

Kohli's predecessor M. S. Dhoni was notable for his equanimity, taciturnity and high ignition temperature. Kohli distinguished himself at first by his greater combativeness and volatility. On this tour, Kohli has shown other sides to his personality, in Melbourne speaking of his squad with an unexpectedly paternal air: 'You see guys growing in their confidence levels and that is a beautiful sight to see.' Asked to describe how his attack prepared for bowling under Australian skies, Kohli paid them a disarming tribute: 'In bowlers' meetings, I usually just sit and listen.'

Make no mistake, simply surmounting the challenge of the conditions in Australia is immense. Historically it has been like prising open a crocodile's jaws: we still have the best win-loss ratio of any country in the twenty-first century. Then there have been Australian cricketers to contend with, traditionally so robust and resourceful — albeit this summer not so much…

But while a lot of attention has focused on Australia's absentees in this Border-Gavaskar Trophy, India's, some voluntary, some compulsory, are worth noting. Some firm resolutions were taken at the selection table a couple of months ago, when India opted against bringing Shikhar Dhawan and Karun Nair, accomplished batsmen with prior experience against Australia. Likewise were there injuries to absorb. Coming into the Adelaide Test, India lacked their premier all-rounder Hardik Pandya, first-choice keeper Wriddhiman Saha, pace prospect Shardul Thakur and, after a mishap in the tour match, hotshot opener Prithvi Shaw.

Indisposition stopped Ravi Ashwin after the First Test; serial failure ruled out Shaw's replacement Murali Vijay after the Second. A share in the plaudits belongs to India's physiotherapist these last three and a half years, Paddy Farhart of Sydney via Kings XI Punjab, whose ministrations have eased and comforted a four-man attack through twenty days' cricket in 33.

Jasprit Bumrah (25), Kuldeep Yadav (24) and Rishabh Pant (21) have confirmed themselves as a generation no longer in waiting, while Mayank Agarwal (27) has offered a glimpse of strength in depth at home, where the likes of Shreyas Iyer (24), Shubman Gill (19), Yuzvendra Chahal (28) and Abhi Easwaran (24) also await opportunities.

Not every hunch has paid off: K. L. Rahul and Rohit Sharma finish the series as enigmatically as they began. Whether Kohli's partialities amount to prejudices remains an open question. But one reinvestment has. Cheteshwar Pujara has sometimes seemed to have more admirers abroad than in India, which is ironic considering his extraordinary home record (average 62, ten Test centuries). But with last year's retirement of Alastair Cook, he has become arguably the sole keeper of traditional crafts of Test match batting, like a fine furniture maker in a world of IKEA.

In all four Tests, Pujara has been called upon to act as an ersatz opener; in all four, his wicket has been the decisive one, Australia able to make inroads at Perth when for once he failed. By rights Pujara should today be named man of the series. Certainly he has made some history which Indian batsmen on future tours of Australia will be exhorted to emulate.

FOURTH TEST, DAY 5

DAMP FINISH

7 January 2019

There is a saying in classical music that no matter when you arrive at a Wagner opera, there is always one act to go. Test cricket has a similar quality. It must be played out regardless of scoreline or circumstance.

Last summer, heaven knows, both the summer's showpiece Tests, Melbourne and Sydney, were 'dead', the Ashes' custody having been decided. The damply inconclusive epilogue to India's retention of the Border-Gavaskar Trophy was by comparison not nearly so anticlimactic.

You could even make an argument that this was one of Australia's better days of summer. Batsmen suffered no soft dismissals, wasted no starts. Bowlers bowled neither too full or too short, inspiring no dressing room divisions, leaving coaches, selectors and commentators no critical judgements to cast. Flat: it's the new up.

You could even make the proposition that, at 2-1, the margin was not so bad, Virat Kohli's fortune at the toss being the kind of advantage Australia might have thrived on. Certainly, had Paine's batsmen gone in first in Melbourne and Sydney, rather than replying in the shadow of seven for 443 and seven for 622 respectively, the rivals' disparities would not have been so obvious.

But the innings not played yesterday were also opportunities forgone, and in that sense a continuation of the last year's disappointments. Like October's Dubai Test, batting time yesterday on a pitch with few demons would have been an excellent chance for this Australia team to demonstrate resilience. Nobody in Australia's top six did not need runs; some needed them urgently.

Which brings us to Shaun Marsh, on his day still the most attractive batsman in Australia, Steve Smith and David Warner included. Yet the last day on which his style blended with Test substance is now more than a year ago — and what a very long year it has been. Australia's selectors meet today to choose their squad for the forthcoming Tests against Sri Lanka, with an eye to their options for the Ashes, by which time Marsh will be thirty-six. What will they learn from picking him? After all, what have they learned from watching him?

It's unclear what Marsh has learned. Doing his duty filling airtime amid the gloom of Sunday night, he was asked to interpret his recent performances.

'Obviously it's been a bit frustrating,' Marsh replied. 'I haven't been able to convert my starts into big scores which is disappointing but [I am] working hard and hopefully there is a big one in the second innings.' Circumstances decreed otherwise.

'I've been getting myself in but just been getting out,' Marsh summarised, with that same strange passivity he is apt to demonstrate at the crease. It just happens, right? In this world, dismissal is just a naturally occurring phenomenon.

To be fair, Marsh has not sacrificed himself five innings in a row, as has Travis Head, or slipped into a state of suspended animation, as has Usman Khawaja. In Melbourne, he could point to a fine delivery and a marginal lbw. But converting his starts is hardly Marsh's problem; it is starting at all. Not only do 42 per cent of his Test innings end in single figures but the propensity is worsening, with ten incidences in his last ten Tests. In away Tests, he averages 29; in Test defeats, he averages 22.

With the best will in the world, furthermore, it is difficult to see these indicators improving; Marsh is at an age where the trend among even great batsmen is in the other direction. His continued selection contains, then, a worsening risk of clusters of wickets in a team that can ill afford them.

Likewise out of sight yesterday was Mitchell Starc, who a year or two ago was burning through batting orders like a universal solvent, but whose effectiveness has been steadily diluted. He has twenty expensive wickets to show for his last eight Tests.

Their pace attack was meant to be Australia's incisive edge this summer. Instead it has blunted itself on Cheteshwar Pujara and Virat Kohli, and nobody more than Starc. A factor should not, however, be left out of account. We have tended to look upon the suspensions of Smith and Warner as a loss simply to Australia's batting, leading to a redistribution of the burden onto shoulders unequal to it. But Starc has lost by their absence also. Over his career, he has flourished as an attacking bowler, a barterer of wickets for runs. Over the last year, he has had to adapt to the new austerity economics of paltry totals, drier lengths, necessarily defensive fields — two slips, not three; one, not two; deep points; third men.

It may be that Starc is the right bowler for the wrong team, and suffered from straining to adjust, in which case his future may depend on how you see the Australian team's prospects in the next year. We play Test matches to win, but, where we cannot, to learn, about those players who might take a team forward, and those who probably will not or can no longer.

Emptying out last night, the SCG was a sombre place, with the Australian players dispersing, Marsh to play in the one-day-internationals beginning Saturday, Starc to take a breather. Their prospects, like the day, were clouded. As nothing seemed to happen, evidence was being appraised and views being formed. A series might have ended. The season is far from played out.

BORDER-GAVASKAR TROPHY

HOME AWAY FROM HOME

10 January 2019

The Border-Gavaskar Trophy has pretty much accompanied each touring team for handover at the end of the series, so ingrained has been home ground advantage, and so determined administrators that it should remain that way. The instalment of 2018-19, however, looked different from the first, Virat Kohli optimistic about India's prospects, Australia always faintly cowed, with Steve Smith and David Warner looking on, and its most permeable batting line-up in at least forty years and perhaps longer.

In the event, Kohli's team lost in Perth by looking at the pitch through green-coloured glasses and choosing an XI long on pace bowling but too short on batting. Otherwise, their superiority was scarcely threatened after the first morning at Adelaide, and by Sydney was growing daily. The margin 2-1 flattered Tim Paine's Australians, for whom not one batsman averaged over 40, and only one bowler paid less than 30 for each wicket.

India, meanwhile, had the outstanding batsman and bowler of the series. Cheteshwar Pujara batted 33 hours and faced 1258 deliveries, fifty of which he despatched for four and two for six, but most of which he left. To Nathan Lyon, he used his feet and his front pad, skipping down the pitch when the ball was straight, kicking it away when the line allowed, and restricting the world's best finger spinner to five for 338 in the last two Tests. This was despite his being an ersatz opener, given the impermanence of KL Rahul and Murali Vijay, who in nine hits scraped together only 108 runs.

The form of Jasprit Bumrah, meanwhile, was a revelation — fast, tireless, threatening both edges, perhaps slightly less effective when operating round the wicket to the left-handers, but at the stumps and hardly ever worked to leg. Twelve of his 21 wickets at 17 were unassisted, five caught at the wicket, three at slip. His baffling, dipping slower ball to dismiss Shaun Marsh in the second innings in Melbourne was the single most replayable instant of the series. By the end, some were prophesying that Bumrah would be the world's best all-format bowler within a year. Whatever the case, he, Mohammed Shami and Ishant Sharma constituted by far the best Indian pace bowling combination to visit Australian shores — relentlessly disciplined, formidably fit.

Spin, meanwhile, has possibly never played less of a part in an Indian attack against Australia, Ravi Ashwin being ruled out after a single Test match with an abdominal strain, and Ravi Jadeja and Hanuna Vihari substituting in a containing role. The balance was somewhat restored at Sydney, where Kuldeep Yadav's variations proved useful on a bare, little-altering surface.

Perhaps the most popular character on tour was keeper Rishabh Pant, a twenty-one-year-old jack-in-the-box whose carefree unbeaten 159 in Sydney was the first Test century in Australia by an Indian gloveman, and whose twenty catches were interspersed with some acrobatic interceptions and only a few errors. His on-field garrulity, meanwhile, gained a cult following via the newly-open stump microphones. A photograph of him with Paine's wife and children was perhaps the social media moment of the series — for such titles there now being a kind of informal competition.

Still more of a surprise packet, however, was Mayank Agarwal, a preternaturally composed twenty-seven-year-old opening batsman flown in before the Melbourne Test who looked like he had fifty caps already, hitting nineteen fours and five sixes in three fluent innings, and overshadowing the established Ajinkya Rahane and Rohit Sharma. India's tail looked vulnerable but was hardly tested.

Australians loved hating and hated loving Kohli, who if he did not quite dominate with the bat was the most vivid personality on either side, relentlessly chivvying his teammates, and only occasionally riling the home side as he had in the past. Sizeable contingents of Indian supporters were seen at each Test, uniformed in replica gear, equipped with standards and banners, and swooning at Kohli's every gesture. The rejoicings when he won the toss at Melbourne and Sydney were unexampled in my experience. Coach Ravi Shastri's word salads were, blessedly, barely intelligible.

For Australia, although the 490,764 turnstile clicks were good news for the exchequer, it was a salutary series. There were some fine personal performances: Nathan Lyon won the individual award for a match-winning eight for 106 in Perth, Pat Cummins a great deal of sympathy for his nine for 99, 17 and 63 in a lost cause in Melbourne. But the batting turned into a source of local despair, notably the failure to convert starts, the inability to build partnerships and the eccentric shot selection. Travis Head, in his second series, showed some pluck in the middle order, but fell five times in a row to flakey attacking shots; Marcus Harris, in his first series, did not look out of his class, although non-plussed by the short ball.

Most disappointing were Shaun Marsh and Usman Khawaja, who failed to fill even a portion of the breach left by Smith and Warner. Marsh played some attractive strokes, Khawaja batted some long periods. But they hardly filled out as senior cricketers, and the burden of leadership fell acutely on Paine, whose remarkable prominence was consolidated at no expense to his own game: he kept wickets immaculately, looked as assured at the crease as anyone, and developed helpfully cordial relations with the media. His coach Justin Langer seemed at times to feel his embattlement.

Australia's pace bowling was persistent and persevering, but after the opening hour of the First Test seldom threatened to break an Indian innings open decisively. Falling back on defensive lengths, Mitchell Starc and Josh Hazlewood barely threatened the stumps — the Australians obtained only one lbw in the series. By the end, they and Cummins looked stale, as relieved as any by the rain and bad light that queered the last two days of the series, and by omission from the one-day squad. Many commented on the doleful and sour expressions the Australians wore at the Sydney Test's conclusion. But they were a long way second, and it smarted.

THE ASHES

MORE QUESTIONS THAN ANSWERS

9 January 2019

During a pause in the rain-interrupted final day of Australia's series defeat by India, a group of pundits on the Channel 7 coverage gathered to speculate about the composition of the team for this year's Ashes. Many names were turned over, only a few names dismissed. And in the category of 'locks' — those guaranteed to go — were left a number of question marks, as though the Riddler and the Joker were in the wings.

Such is the state of confused introspection in Australian cricket after losing at home for the first time to India, and looking ahead to the Ashes and World Cup that the national team must defend this year. A year ago, at the Sydney Cricket Ground, Steve Smith and David Warner led the team on to an eye-gashing victory float to celebrate the regaining of the Ashes. Now both were in Dhaka competing in the Bangladesh Premier League, part of their ongoing ball-tampering purdah, still with three months to run.

Fans were looking back on a twelve-month period in which Australian batsmen passed fifty on twenty-three occasions and a hundred once. Australia's rankings — fifth in Tests, sixth in one-day internationals, fourth in T20 internationals — have never sagged so dolefully.

From time to time over the last nine months, puritan voices have been heard opining that Smith, Warner and their Cape Town co-conspirator Cameron Bancroft should never be chosen for Australia again. Those opinings have faded. If anything, the revelation has been how Smith and Warner had for some years masked a malaise in Australian batsmanship.

Against India not one Australian batsman made a century or averaged 40. The two most seasoned members of the top order, Usman Khawaja and Shaun Marsh, averaged less than 30. The only players to compile more than 200 runs were the pair least experienced, apprentice opener Marcus Harris and limited-overs specialist Travis Head. Worse, the replacements were far from obvious. First-class cricket in Australia is amid a seventy-five-day hiatus for the Big Bash League. But none of the alternatives — Queensland's Joe Burns and Matthew Renshaw, Tasmania's Matthew Wade and Victoria's Glenn Maxwell — are proven performers anyway.

Some are mumbling the question whether this is a cyclical phenomenon, occurring naturally after the retirements of the likes of Michael Clarke, Chris Rogers and Brad Haddin, or a secular shift, aggravated by the embrace of T20 at all levels of the game and the subversion of the old meritocracy by elite 'pathways' cricket. Never more various and therefore more difficult to comprehensively master, cricket often appears a house divided against itself.

For a measure of reassurance, the Australians could look to their summer's conquerors. T20 has flooded Indian cricket but not swamped it. The Indian season still contains copious quantities of first-class cricket. The Indian Premier League awaits the completion of competition in all other forms. Twenty-seven-year-old reserve opener Mayank Agarwal was airlifted from the Ranji Trophy to the Boxing Day Test readymade. With 195 poised runs at 65, he was the discovery of the series. The success of man-of-the-series Cheteshwar Pujara, moreover, has confirmed a continued role for the Test specialist, the jack of a solitary trade. When Pujara was finally dismissed in Sydney after thirty-three hours at the crease this summer, his twenty-one-year-old partner Rishabh Pant ran halfway to the dressing room to engulf him in a hug, a spontaneous expression of the new's regard for the old.

India's captain Virat Kohli held out Ashes hope for his beaten opponents. 'I'm sure [Australia] will regroup as a unit,' he offered. 'We've all gone through those phases where you figure out what needs to be done — it's just mindset. If the same batting unit can go out there more confident and believe that they can do it, it can be done, definitely.' Paramount would be the need to assimilate the Dukes ball — which indeed will be used in the second half of the Sheffield Shield when eventually the competition resumes in the middle of next month.

'Playing in England, what I experienced this time was, if you go out there with an ego you might as well not go out at all,' said Kohl. 'Because that Dukes ball, it buries egos pretty quickly. You have to curb yourself, do the hard yards, grind it out the whole day. You have to be patient as a batsman. There's a lot of time in Test cricket. Sometimes because we're so nervous as batsmen we don't quite realise it, you just want to get away quickly but in England you're not allowed to do that, so you have to bide your time, earn the right to score runs eventually.'

Which is fine in principle, harder to achieve in practice, for the batting's failures have aggravated stresses elsewhere. Giving up seven for 622 in Sydney, Australia's four-man attack of Mitchell Starc, Josh Hazlewood, Patrick Cummins and Nathan Lyon appeared sore and depleted. There were reports of tensions with the coaching staff led by Justin Langer and David Saker. Captain Tim Paine played a weary shot. Shane Warne's compulsive selection tweets, seemingly based on his previous night's channel surfing, have added to the noise around selection.

Then there are systemic considerations. Australia's cricket system was always relatively small, concentrated for a century and more on the simple business of bringing forward eleven outstanding exponents at a time.

Steadily, almost imperceptibly, that mission expanded, complicated, mutated, with the effect that the quality now feels more thinly spread, the ends more multifarious, the means more debateable. All countries face similar challenges, but India, with its breadth and depth of cricket and cricketers, might have a permanent scale advantage meeting them. That perhaps is the biggest question mark of all, and it is not only Australia's to answer.

PUNDITRY

A JURY OF PEERS

11 January 2019

A feature of daily life in cricket's media centres is the proximity of former greatness. At first there is a frisson in waiting for a coffee with Adam Gilchrist, standing in the luncheon queue behind Glenn McGrath, wondering idly what Warnie is up to on his phone. Of course, it soon passes, and one often finds them disarmingly engaging and generous.

This season, however, the dynamic has been subtly different, perhaps unavoidably so. Two television and three radio broadcasters have considerably swelled the personnel, drawn overwhelmingly from the generation in Australian cricket just gone — arguably the greatest generation the game has known. And they have been passing judgement on a generation widely acknowledged as greatly their inferior.

By convention, commentators are handmaidens to sport, an incidental delight, an occasional annoyance. Channel 7 has followed a thoughtful policy this season at the Test matches of not showing the commentators on screen during play, in order to focus eyes and minds on the cricket in front of us, also building coverage around skilled callers such as Tim Lane and Alison Mitchell.

Nonetheless, their coverage obtains its star power from Ricky Ponting, these days cricket's most authoritative and ubiquitous voice. Fox Sports, meanwhile, showcases Warne, as great a name as the game has known, also these days reaching more than three million Twitter followers and nearly a million Instagram followers at the touch of a button.

Their opinions, moreover, are not simply views but news — indeed, quoting excerpts of commentary has stealthily become a feature of the game's print coverage, as though we're no longer covering cricket so much as reporting television.

Like so much, this is driven in part by social media, where Warne seems to pick an Australian team on Twitter every other day based on who he has just seen on television, with places reserved for Marcus Stoinis, who has not scored a Sheffield Shield hundred since November 2015, and Darcy Short, who has made two Sheffield Shield fifties, interspersed with lamentations that 'unfortunately Sheffield shield cricket is not what it once was' and 'hopefully CA change their attitude and make shield cricket important again!' — look out for the MSCIA trucker cap at some stage.

It's entertaining, of course — Warne is never otherwise. What it isn't, really, is a coherent critique. Last week, for example, Warne inflicted whiplash on Twitter by demanding that 'these ridiculous selections must stop in all forms of Australian cricket' then quickly agreeing with his old mucker Mark Waugh that it was an 'easy excuse to blame the selectors when individuals and the team is not performing'.

Ponting is perhaps the more interesting case, because as a commentator he is so good, so intuitive, so succinct and plausible — it is worth watching a cricket match simply to listen to him read it.

His situation is complicated, however, by a fine bromance with Justin Langer, with whom he shares not only a long history but management — they are part of the DSEG stable which also includes Tim Paine, George Bailey and Isa Guha, among others.

Ponting has been among Langer's most ardent apologists ('You could not find a better person in the world to be in charge of the Australian cricket team right now'); Langer has reciprocated his regard by inviting Ponting into Australia's coaching set-up at intervals ('Ricky's knowledge of the game is second-to-none, and we know that his experiences, tactical expertise and leadership will be invaluable for this group').

It's led to some oddly veering headlines. Some days it's 'Ponting lashes Aussies'; others it's 'Ponting tutors Aussies.' In the Sydney Test, for instance, Ponting scourged Nathan Lyon for failing to review an lbw decision against him: 'That dismissal actually says a lot to me about the mindset of this Australian team at the moment. There's no desperation there whatsoever.'

A whole raft of questions flowed from this. Was this Ponting's view, independently formed? Or was it reflective of Langer's view, shaped by Ponting's relationship with him? Was it the perspective of a commentator, or of a sometime Australian assistant coach? At the media conference afterwards, Peter Handscomb was placed in the emotionally complicated position of defending teammates from a great cricketer whom he acknowledges was his boyhood idol.

The cricketer most buffeted this season by the gusts of the greats has been Aaron Finch. In his first Twitter Test team of summer, Warne inked Finch in as opener and vice-captain, then fulminated about Victoria's decision ahead of the First Test to bat Finch at number three rather than one or two: 'This is a disgrace by Vic & must be fixed before the game — can we please have common sense back… Vics have it wrong and should do what's best for Aust — end of'.

Turned out to be start of. And when Finch then failed in Adelaide, Ponting first dismissed him as a long-term opener who had 'a lot of work to do' ('Ponting lashes Finch') then was asked by Langer to do some of that work with them in the nets ahead of

Perth ('Ponting tutors Finch'). How would that have felt, I wonder? Coaching from someone on the public record doubting you can do your appointed job? What would Australia's coaching staff have made of it too?

As we know, Finch ground out 50, inspiring the notion that Ponting's influence had worked wonders. Then the magic faded, and Finch was dropped. End of.

Yet is this realistically how selection and skill acquisition work in cricket? That if we do what Warnie reckons and get Punter in then Finch can become, uniquely in the world, a three-format opener? And if he doesn't it's his fault? The result, unfortunately, has been a good cricketer diminished.

I write all the foregoing advisedly, and with utmost respect for both Warne and Ponting. The last thing I'd wish would be for them to stop calling the game as they see fit, for it adds immeasurably to the experience.

But they and the generation of which they were part now cast a long and potentially inhibiting shadow over Australian cricket, especially given that one of their 'brotherhood' is charged with bringing on the national teams of the next generation.

I have no magical remedy — cricket promises too many of these anyway. Perhaps it is as simple as individuals displaying a sensitivity towards the implications and ambiguities of their multiple roles, a cognisance of what a coach can and cannot do, and an underlying sympathy towards those still striving to master this demanding, ruthless, confusing, sometimes dismaying but utterly wonderful game. We can call it something like, I don't know, maybe...elite honesty.

SRI LANKA

TEARDROP ISLAND

17 January 2019

In Shehan Karunatilaka's kaleidoscopic novel of Sri Lanka and cricket, *Chinaman*, the narrator stops to consider whether the game is so nationally useful at all. 'Does Sri Lanka need more schoolteachers, more soldiers or more wicketkeepers?' he asks. 'A middle order batsman or a bank manager? A specialist gully fieldsman or a civil engineer?'

Needless to say, he resolves the conundrum favourably to the game. 'Left-arm spinners cannot unclog your drains, teach your children or cure you of disease,' he concludes. 'But once in a while, the very best of them will bowl a ball that will bring an entire nation to its feet. And while there may be no practical use in that, there is almost certainly value.'

Just lately, however, Australia's next Test opponents have given their nation little reason to rise. Sri Lanka's peerless left-arm spinner Rangana Herath, who twisted Australia round his tubby fingers when the teams last met in 2016, retired last year, following the example of the great axis of Kumar Sangakkara and Mahela Jayawardene.

In Tests, one-day and T20 internationals, Dinesh Chandimal's team ranks sixth, eighth and ninth respectively; largely excluded from the spoils of global T20, handicapped by a moribund national economy and anachronistic government oversight, it is barely holding on.

Sri Lanka Cricket, the national cricket body, is a mess, leaking money like a pokies addict, going through coaches like Spinal

Tap through drummers. Most humiliatingly, it has been identified as an exposed flank in the game's campaign to thwart corruption.

In the last few years, domestic cricket matches have been brazenly manipulated and individuals detained for suspicious attachment to their mobile telephones at local and international games. Not perhaps the best time to be chaired by Thilanga Sumathipala, a politician and conglomerateur whose interests encompass a betting shop chain.

SLC's quarrels are so severe, in fact, that it languishes at the moment without office bearers, having last May been prevented from re-electing Sumathipala by a legal challenge from one of its numerous factions.

Newly-appointed sports minister Harin Fernando was informed in Dubai at the end of last year that the International Cricket Council regarded the country's cricket administration as "corrupt from top to bottom".

Its CFO has recently been arrested for misappropriation of millions of broadcast dollars; its previous secretary faces ongoing charges of money laundering. It is presently under the jurisdiction of an interim advisory committee reporting to Fernando, who has promised elections next month even if none of the candidates fill anyone with confidence.

With SLC having also recently jettisoned its anti-corruption chief, the ICC has foreshadowed the unprecedented step of opening its own permanent office in Sri Lanka, headed by a former member of the Metropolitan Police's flying squad.

It has multiple investigations running, with charges already laid against former international players Sanath Jayasuriya, Nuwan Zoysa and Dilhara Lokuhettige, and has reported monitoring as many as twenty 'very active corrupters'; it has offered an unprecedented amnesty to any individuals who have failed to report a corrupt approach, expiring Tuesday week.

This is, of course, an old, old story. It's a quarter of a century now since Mark Waugh and Shane Warne were befriended by the archetypal 'corruptor', John the Bookie, in a casino in Colombo.

Six years ago, SLC promoted a T20 premier League, which lasted one seedy season, players being paid in bricks of cash, and at least one franchise being reputedly owned by bookmakers. In a television sting, six umpires revealed that they were prepared to sell decisions; two were suspended.

Three years ago, SLC slapped a life ban on a net bowler Gayan Vishwajith, who had allegedly mooted a fixing arrangement with key players, and suspended bowling coach Anusha Samaranayake, who had introduced Vishwajith to the team circle.

The ICC was drawn in after a one-day international series eighteen months ago which Sri Lanka managed to lose to Zimbabwe, predictably occasioning howls of dismay, and a direct accusation by former Sri Lanka cricketer Pramodaya Wickremesinghe that the games had been thrown. The players signed a petition protesting their innocence, although their captain Angelo Mathews stood down, and interim coach Nic Pothas left soon after.

Even then, Al-Jazeera was at work on its two ambitious if uneven exposes of cricket corruption, which aired last May, whose most disturbing sequences involved an apparent racket for the fixing of pitches at picturesque Galle, including in the Test that Australia lost there in 2016 by losing 20 wickets in 501 balls. More names, more suspensions, more chaos, including the collapse of plans to revive the T20 premier league, although, perhaps most significantly, a badly deteriorating political environment.

Looking on from our state of prosperous overmanaged muddle, we're apt to forget how good we have it. For in noting that 2018 was a bad year for Sri Lankan cricket, we should note also that it was a very bad year for Sri Lankan democracy, rocked by a president Maithripala Sirisena's attempts to install his notoriously authoritarian predecessor Mahinda Rajapaksa as prime minister over the head of incumbent Ranil Wickremesinghe.

During the ensuing constitutional crisis, bribes were offered, and punches thrown in parliament; the legislature remains groggy; the economy, downgraded by three ratings agencies, is out for the count, lighter $US1 billion in foreign reserves, and pending a $US1.5 billion bailout by the International Monetary Fund.

Some of this is an outcome of unresolved agonies of the sanguinary Civil War, some the business of dealing with Indian and Chinese spheres of influence that increasingly overlap. But by the estimate of the Economist Intelligence Unit, in no country did the cause of democracy retreat so far as Sri Lanka last year. And if a country's political and social institutions are subverted, their sporting counterparts are hardly likely to be otherwise.

Cricket in Sri Lanka will always be vulnerable. In a poor country it is one of the few sources of influence, glamour, hard currency and international connection. Right now it is being buffeted internally and externally in ways that reflect the instability of its game and its region.

Every so often, sport being sport, its representatives will be able to close the gap on the rest of the world. But as the speaker in *Chinaman* notes, such solace as this affords is only ever temporary: 'Real life is lived at two runs an over, with a dodgy lbw every decade.'

AUSTRALIA SELECTION

A CLEAN SHEET

23 January 2019

Nothing so cheers your everyday cricket follower than youth given its head. So Australia's looming Brisbane Test against Sri Lanka is a more enticing prospect for the probable presences of Will Pucovski, Kurtis Patterson and Jhye Richardson, three excellent young cricketers patiently groomed.

It thins Australia's experience, of course, only four of the fourteen-member squad having played more than a score of Tests. But better that, surely, than more of the same favoured failures, Shaun Marsh having, for all his obvious gifts, not so much played thirty-eight Tests as the same Test thirty-eight times.

Twenty-year-old Pucovski is the bolter, promoted mainly on the basis of two big hundreds — deduct them from his record, and he averages less than 15.

Yet so highly is the Victorian thought of that he might have earned his new cap sooner but for a mental health break earlier in summer.

Twenty-two-year-old Richardson, a wisp of a fellow with an incongruously sharp edge on his pace, has yet to take fifty first-class wickets. Twenty-five-year-old Patterson is a veritable veteran by comparison, more than seven years on from a hundred on his Sheffield Shield debut.

At the very least, all three look the part, with that seriousness of intent that marks out Test cricketers. And Sri Lanka in Australia do not shape as so formidable an opponent — should they play above their Test ranking of sixth, we have even bigger problems than we already fear.

Yet encouraging as they are, these selections also tell a tale. Teams travelling well do not make themselves over so drastically.

The last time Australia so spilt positions was just over two years ago on the back of five consecutive Test defeats, when it drafted Peter Handscomb, Matthew Wade, Chadd Sayers, Nic Maddinson and Matthew Renshaw for the Adelaide Test against South Africa, which also conduced to a brief euphoria.

They also betray a pretty negative opinion of the Sheffield Shield, truncated, partitioned and denigrated as it has become.

Time was when a Pucovski might have been thought better for the hardening of a season or two of interstate cricket, and the selectors would have wanted the substantiation of their instincts.

In fact, Messrs Hohns and Chappell have already seen a good deal of Pucovski in their national and state talent management roles. A hundred at under-17 or under-19 level in Australia can get you a long way these days — for one thing, it leaves the system feeling a whole lot better about itself.

For all Patterson's fifty-eight first-class matches, meanwhile, Australia's selectors two weeks ago did not think him ready for Test cricket. He was not in their initial squad. Had he been a member of the Sydney Thunder's starting line-up, in fact, it's unlikely he would have been playing today.

As he was playing simply for St George between bench warmings at Showground Stadium, however, Patterson could fill a slot in the Cricket Australia XI in Hobart at minimal inconvenience to the Big Bash League — a paramount consideration these days. Two unbeaten hundreds later, and Australia has its own KP.

Kudos to the selectors for backing Patterson in — there is a lot to like about his method and maturity. But these aren't selection calls made on the basis of Justin Langer's new friend the door, the banging thereon. They are in the spirit of: might as well pick these guys now, because more interstate cricket won't improve them much or add substantially to our understanding of their international potential.

What's this about? There is widespread debate about the quality of elite senior male cricket in Australia, as indeed there should be.

Yet I suspect one of the main challenges today, maybe even the chief gap to bridge in stepping into Test cricket, involves coping with concentrations of scrutiny, which increases not gradually but suddenly, is superficially welcoming but ultimately unforgiving.

Much of the cricket played by an aspiring top-level cricketer these days involves fairly minimal levels of attention, significant degrees of support and comparatively low stakes — there is always another game, another training, another opportunity, more around the corner.

Then, abruptly, one day when you may or may not be quite ready, may be slightly out of nick, a little sore or mentally fatigued, everything changes.

Jhye Richardson has at least experienced the lamplight of international short-form cricket. But for the big time now facing Pucovski and Patterson, with its crowds, media and performance demands, there can be no entirely adequate preparation, and the trapdoor closes hungrily.

Watching Callum Ferguson in Thunder green on Tuesday night, I was reminded that his fifteen years of first-class strivings will probably end up condensing to a single sad and soggy Test in which he's remembered for being run out on a misfield. Cricket can render harsh verdicts.

Tests themselves vary in intensities, this pink-ball wrangle at the Gabba over the Warne-Muralitharan Trophy being at the lower end. But Australia is two matches from facing off with England at their Edgbaston citadel. Plus, of course, six into four does not go. If Steve Smith and David Warner are pardoned, as now seems likely, then at least two of those padding up in Brisbane will not be doing so in Birmingham.

This fresh-faced trio have not, then, ever had so much to play for, so many to watch them do so, so great a need for luck — for it has such influence on every cricketer's fortunes. Eleven cricketers from another country, meantime, will be doing their best to stop them. For once the Gabba is not hosting summer's first Test; it will instead be ushering in a new Australian cricket phase.

FIRST TEST, DAY 1

JUMPING JHYE

24 January 2019

Usman, Marnus, Marcus, Kurtis, Travis — say what you like about this Australian team, at least it's a departure from the humdrum of Shanes and Shauns, and a far cry from the Bills, Arthurs and Lindsays of yesteryear.

But Jhye — there's one from the less-consulted recesses of your baby names dictionary. It sounds like the name of a songbird, or a term from woodwork to be argued over in a game of Scrabble. Ever come across a Jhye? You have now.

It means, apparently, 'victorious'. It rhymes, suitably, with spry and shy. For in an era of fast bowling muscle cars, the twenty-two-year-old, 178cm and 75kg Jhye Richardson is a sporty MG with wire wheels, lithe and wispy, broad-shouldered but light-framed.

Richardson came a little late to cricket after a flirtation with Australian rules, but still looks young enough, floppy-haired and fresh-faced, to be bowling in your school's first XI. He'd not have played in this First Test against Sri Lanka had Josh Hazlewood been fit and had the selectors not leaned away at the last moment from Peter Siddle. Yet there's been no mistaking his fizz since Richardson was capped by Australia in T20 cricket two years ago. He approaches with a scampering rhythm and over a braced front leg with a proud wrist position achieves a rasping pace on consistently challenging lines. Shorter in stature and making sparing use of bouncers, he is awkward to leave on length and menaces the stumps consistently — a useful attribute in a bowling attack that has this summer rather lost the habit.

If the Gabba was closer to deserted than full when Dinesh Chandimal won the toss from Tim Paine, there was soon that low hum of expectancy that new fast bowlers are apt to generate, equivalent to the sighting of a fox in a henhouse's general vicinity. Lahiru Thirimanne bunted Richardson's first ball in Test cricket just past short leg and padded up hesitantly to his fourth. Dimuth Karunaratne was beaten on both edges. Catchers clapped appreciatively. There was also the hint of a nice simpatico between bowler and captain. Hitting Karunaratne's back pad soon after, Richardson waived Paine's proferred review; when Paine reinforced his cordon with a fourth slip, Richardson found the perfect top-of-off length to Chandimal, and Joe Burns gathered a low chance. His first Test spell, of seven overs, was ruled off at a trim one for 17.

David Sandurski's first Test pitch since leaving the MCG assuredly offered assistance, with an inference that India had been shrewd in batting away the idea of a Gabba Test on their own recent tour. The better to protect the pink ball's blushes, the surface bore a healthy green sheen. As the afternoon wore into evening, it seemed to go through phases of pine, lime and chartreuse.

Ironically, the day's most alarming deliveries were probably off-breaks from Nathan Lyon which snagged Karunaratne's outside edge and scuffed the underside of Roshen Silva's bicep. But there was pace here to please. And changing ends after tea, Richardson's second spell was as zesty as his first, angling in to Kushal Mendis and seaming away, pushing Dhananjaya Silva back then luring him tentatively half-forward.

In these countries' last Warne-Muralitharan Trophy encounter, Mendis and de Silva were Sri Lanka's brightest sparks; they offered here only embers. It was Richardson's figures of two for three in five overs that glowed.

The character of the cricket thereafter reverted to a genre familiar in these parts, even if it has not been seen so much lately — an underprepared touring team, as uncomfortable away from home as Australia, cornered, quashed and faintly intimidated. The mercurial Niroshan Dickwella flailed six boundaries and a six, but with the haste of someone running round a burning house trying to gather together a few precious heirlooms.

Otherwise the Australians were efficient, Mitchell Starc completing a long-awaited appointment with 200 Test wickets, Pat Cummins truncating the tail, Paine showing a clean sheet, and everything that went to hand sticking and staying.

That left 31 overs of the pink ball's illuminated tricks to deal with, and a top order that if not raw is at least medium rare. Fortunately, Australia's seventh opening partnership in its last nine Tests were able to settle in against some affably short and wide bowling.

Marcus Harris looked ever more the part as a Test opener, his mannerisms a kind of compound of David Warner and Chris Rogers. The loss of Burns and Usman Khawaja leaves locals with only Marnus Labuschagne to cheer on today, but a restart in natural light is an opportunity for the rest.

Circumstances suggest that the Australians would be wise not to read too much into the day's events. The Sri Lankans are a struggling cricket nation undermined by off-field issues being uneasily addressed.

But in a summer where the bad days have substantially outnumbered the good, Tim Paine's team will take what they can get, particularly when it comes in a guise young, fresh, fit and fast. The rest of us will enjoy getting used to the name.

FIRST TEST, DAY 2

DEPUTY HEAD

25 January 2019

In Adam McKay's new movie *Vice*, Christian Bale as Dick Cheney shrugs off George Bush's first offer of the US vice-presidency on grounds that it's a 'mostly symbolic' position. But y'know, maybe it would be more congenial if his tasks included some of the 'more mundane jobs': things like, y'know, bureaucracy, military, energy, foreign policy...

This suits workshy Dubya. 'Hot damn!' he says.

No such new remit was sought by Travis Head when he and Pat Cummins were promoted to the Australian vice-captaincy on the eve of this First Test against Sri Lanka, of course. But a similar point lurks. Everyone knows what the Australian captain does. But the vice-captain?

After all, there used to be either one or even none. Now there are two, as we were told by chairman of selectors Trevor Hohns in an advice that sounded like it was drafted in human resources, one from 'the batting group' and one from 'the bowling group'. Captain Tim Paine may shortly be reclassified the duly appointed representative of 'the wicketkeeping group'.

Yesterday, however, Head took the opportunity to accentuate the positive of that proposition: that if the responsibilities of a deputy are ambiguous, then they can be what you make them. Stepping into the prickly scenario of four for 82, he and Marnus Labuschagne problem solved out the summer's best Australian partnership — the best by a long way. The 166 they added for the fifth wicket from 299 balls was nearly twice as large as what is now the third-best partnership.

Labuschagne completed his first Test half-century with the hint of more and better to come. He was restricted to a single scoring shot for two from his first 35 deliveries, then took 34 from the next 45. He was organised in defence, quick between the wickets, disappointing only in his dismissal, trying to conjure something from nothing.

Head pushed on, into the evening session, to his fifth Test half-century, which was also, in this summer of diminished expectation, actually Australia's best Test score since 11 October last year: 84 from 187 deliveries with ten boundaries, mostly off the back foot through point.

It was a timely innings from a personal viewpoint. Head was Australia's second highest scoring batsman against India. He was also the most prodigal, arguably complicit in his last five dismissals: twice caught at third man in Perth; twice bowled driving in Melbourne; bunting one overeagerly back in Sydney.

Head started yesterday as though with that in mind. Skewing Chameera to third man off an outside edge when he was 4, he punched the back of the bat in annoyance; nicking Lakmal and eluding Dickwella's outstretched gauntlet on 29, he appeared suitably penitent. Dulwira Perera's off-breaks he studied with scientific scrutiny.

As the pink ball softened, so Sri Lanka's resistance weakened, and scoring chances expanded: a choice drive down the ground from Lakmal took Head into the 40s, a slashing cut from Chameera raised the 100 partnership in 175 balls. He raised his half-century opportunistically from a misfield — not the only instance amid some rather ragged Sri Lankan outcricket, relieved by two sharp slip catches.

The innings also exhibited the sort of qualities one might

associate with leadership: calm, composure, match awareness. As Chandimal tried to shut the game down in the afternoon with slower bowlers and deep-set fields, Head neither stalled nor fretted. As night fell and the new ball was taken, Head pulled his in, unlucky in the end to receive an excellent delivery from Lakmal.

What lies, as it were, ahead? The twenty-five-year-old South Australian is a phenomenon of this national phase of accelerated, ready-or-not development, a vice-captain in a dressing room in which it is almost easier to name those team members without official title, those in what may by shortly be designated the followership group.

Such precocity of responsibility is not unfamiliar to him. Head became captain of his state aged twenty-one before he had made a first-class hundred on the basis of… well, who knows? Maybe his captaining at under-17 and under-19 level; maybe through nominative determinism, as Major Major Major is promoted to Major in *Catch-22* by the kink of an IBM machine. It was a risk. Back in February 2015, South Australia's dressing room was in some disarray, if not downright depression, dealing with the death of Phillip Hughes and the exit of coach Darren Berry.

While it is not always possible to determine if responsibility agrees with a cricketer, it did not obviously disagree with Head — and suffering no performance impairment from the burden of leadership is, very nearly, half the battle. There is something of the same scenario with Australia today: a need for players to fill a vacuum of experience, to bridge a phase of transition, and even, in a way, to assuage a degree of trauma, lingering since Cape Town. When the captain is thirty-four, consideration is also inevitable of the next step.

Since Michael Clarke's ascension, the Australian vice-captain has hardly been a royal road to the Test leadership. Shane Watson was a locum skipper once; Brad Haddin and David Warner never were. The last two Australian skippers, Steve Smith and Tim Paine, were promoted from the ranks; the last two Australian vice-captains, Mitchell Marsh and Josh Hazlewood, appointed in September after an exhaustive one-off process, have lost their stations through form and fitness. But, one day at a time, a case can be built.

FIRST TEST, DAY 3

STARC CONTRAST

26 January 2019

Australian fast bowlers are today micromanaged to a nanometric degree. When the Border-Gavaskar Trophy ended, the elite algorithms were showing three lemons. All three star pacemen were sent to put their feet up, not forgetting to fill in their workload and wellness apps.

For Josh Hazlewood, it was actually already too late: it was determined that his 'emergent stress fractures' needed a further period of convalescence. But rest cannot fix everything. It restored Pat Cummins to red-blooded freshness at the Gabba; it proved only a pause in Mitchell Starc's anaemic performances.

It is as though the pair have passed one another in opposite directions at some point — that point may even have been tacitly acknowledged yesterday. Weighing his weapons of choice at the commencement of play, Tim Paine opted for Cummins and Hazlewood's proxy Jhye Richardson.

Was the captain recalling the two wayward overs Starc had bowled at the top the night before? Paine stuck by Starc after the game, as he has all summer — his number one striker was 'not far from turning it round.' He may even be correct. But in the moment, Paine got the mix right. Bowling with a jackknife-straight seam, Cummins had two wickets, Dinesh Chandimal and Kusal Mendis, before conceding a run. When he added Roshen Silva, his 7-4-9-4 read more like a phone's passcode than a bowler's figures.

It was blindingly hot, but Cummins approached his task like a man refreshed, playfully tossing the pink ball from hand to hand on his walk back, showing the pink soles of his boots as he surged in, earning a cheer at fine leg as he smilingly returned a beach ball that had bounced from the crowd. Jogging back—and—forth along the perimeter as left- and right-handers crossed, he deserved the services of a Segway.

Cummins' final figures of ten for 62, sufficient to earn man-of-any-match, spoke volumes; that he conceded only four boundaries in nearly thirty overs, one of them a fortunate top edge, was an informative appendix. Whatever he did on his furlough, it should probably be made mandatory.

Whilst on hiatus, of course, Cummins was also named Australia's fifth vice-captain of the last year, reflecting both recent team turmoil and the stature to which he has grown despite his start-stop-start career.

It was perhaps equally noteworthy that in connection with this post nobody really seemed to consider Starc, despite his fifty Tests and nearly 150 international caps.

On Wednesday, Starc enters his thirtieth year, something of a hinge point in every fast bowler's career, from which one seldom gains knots but one might add knowledge — at the same age, Mitchell Johnson actually had his best cricket in front of him.

Despite having taken his 200th Test wicket in the first innings here, Starc is not giving grounds for similar optimism, with 22 wickets at 47 in his last nine Tests. His three spells yesterday, four overs for 19, three for 14 and five for 22, were uniformly barren.

Worse, they were just a little hapless. Called from his specialist mid-on duties at 2.10pm, Starc began with an amiable half-volley on leg stump, then continued with a full-toss and a no ball. He even missed an attempt to kick the ball at the stumps. Walking back he examined the pink ball like one suspecting a counterfeit dollar note.

The speed gun stuck loyally stuck by him as Starc was tried at both ends after tea, recording velocities in excess of 140kmh, with one effort ball reaching 150kmh. But there is just a suspicion of fetishism around Starc's speeds, that their remaining more or less uniform has for too long been considered an indicator that nothing too much is amiss.

A better index is arguably what's happening at the other end when Starc bowls, which is minimal disturbance. He has not been beating the edge, hurrying strokes, generating appeals; even when a leg gully and short leg were encamped yesterday, his bouncers were too short and his yorkers too full. Some are saying that in straining to maintain his pace, Starc has compromised his action. Others believe he is thinking too much.

One is loath to critique Starc's 'body language' given Shane Warne's rather repetitive efforts at same: Chesty Bond would be the first picked in any Warne XI. But it hardly needed Desmond Morris to sense Starc's struggle yesterday, and also the latent anxiety around him.

Taking the ball just before dinner in search of a consolatory tail-end wicket, Starc was plied with advice by Nathan Lyon, Travis Head and even the cheeky Nirosh Dickwella. The spell started with a near-wide, on the full, endangering first slip. In his final over, number nine Suranga Lakmal, with a Test average of 11, backed away and powered through point and mid-off for boundaries.

From the visitors this was a rare gesture of defiance; indeed, it was hard to make claims for the strength of Australia's opposition in this match. Angelo Matthews and Nuwan Pradeep are already back in Sri Lanka; the injured Lahiru Kumara is now also headed there. The tourists have played thirteen Tests, twenty one-day internationals and nine T20 internationals in the last year, and there were some demob happy strokes yesterday, batsmen driving balls that weren't to drive, chasing balls they could only nick.

In that sense, the circumstances should really have been ideal for Starc, whose knack has always been wickets even when conceding runs. Now it must be wondered what the future holds for him — both next week, with choices to be made for the Second Test, and the next year, with the World Cup and Ashes to come.

The happy precedent of Johnson exists, but his resurgence arose not from triage between fixtures, but a long lay-off and a steady rebuilding, physical as well as psychological. In the instance of Starc, the workload-o-meters may not be much help.

TIM PAINE

FOLLOW THE LEADER

31 January 2019

In the immediate aftermath of the Perth Test, an email materialised in my inbox with a publishing brainstorm. Would I be interested in writing a book about the leadership secrets of Tim Paine?

In my trade you get this — I dare say half a dozen colleagues received a similar inquiry the same day. I gave it the usual consideration. Instant response: no. Considered response: also no. Final response: again no… but the enquiry itself was interesting.

After all, Perth was Paine's first win as Australian captain in any international fixture for more than six months of trying. Did he have secrets? If so, they were well-kept. Paine had entertained the eavesdroppers on the Optus Stadium stump mics, but that was hardly where the match was decided; India arguably lost the game by choosing four non-batting pace bowlers.

So then what? Everyone wants to detect 'leadership', of course. A hundred years ago, people who had 'visions' were locked up in asylums; nowadays they are appointed CEOs. But as he completes his first home summer as captain of Australia, Paine arrives in Canberra with a better approval rating than Scott Morrison. What to make of his ascendancy?

Paine's success as a Test skipper is mainly that he has not failed. This sounds axiomatic but isn't. Forty-five men had been appointed to captain Australia in Test cricket before Paine, and not one of them in circumstances so unpromising — in the middle of a Test match, in the middle of a scandal.

There were a host of ways that Paine could have bricked it. The simplest would have been to let his individual performance attenuate. Nothing would so have undermined Paine's position as captaincy as questions about his position as player. In fact, he has maintained an unobtrusive excellence as a gloveman and played some handy innings, particularly in that Perth win.

If it can be difficult to judge tactical acumen in an era so full of backroom analysis and collective decision making, Paine has committed no howlers and even pulled off a few blinders, such as the leg gully in Melbourne that snaffled Cheteshwar Pujara and Virat Kohli in the same over.

And despite having little initiation, Paine performs the public-facing parts of his role with aplomb. He is good-looking, plain-spoken. He has eschewed opportunistic commercial deals, and crass campaigns. At press conferences he contrives to be easy but dignified, straightforward but unobjectionable, critiquing the previous regime ('What we probably got caught up with over the years is trying to play a way that people have always perceived Australian teams to be, and that doesn't suit this current side') without condemning it ('I'm very hopeful that the Australian public will welcome those three guys back and give them a fair chance').

What's helped, and it has happened almost without being noticed, is that his task has been subtly scaled down. He is not effectively captain-coach, as was Ricky Ponting. He is not a selector, as was Michael Clarke. He is not a multi-format player, as were Steve Smith and David Warner. 2018 was a remarkable year for Paine not only in that he took over as Test captain. He also became Australia's 50-over keeper, then its 50-over captain, then quietly gave way in both roles, to Alex Carey and Aaron Finch respectively.

In some respects, Justin Langer is the more conspicuous public presence, continuing to coach in all three forms of the game, acting as selector, talking openly and riffing freely — including, just lately, for that obligatory rite of Australian celebrity passage, the *Good Weekend* profile.

Based in Tasmania, Paine is free between times to recede from view. In his column this week, he wrote of returning to Sandy Bay after the Ashes and Border-Gavaskar Trophies and being so exhausted that in each case he slept for two days. In the best possible way, Hobart is somewhere you can do that.

The feature of Paine best known, of course, is the length and indirection of his journey, improbable even before its final jag. At 16, he was the youngest interstate cricketer to obtain a rookie contract; at 33, he was the oldest captain in the modern era bar Steve Waugh.

As is well known, injury played its part. But as he lost preferment, Paine also, quite frankly, lost his way, still reflected in the relative insubstantiality of his first-class record: he averages less than 30 and has a single hundred from 112 matches.

Paine was George Bailey's deputy and locum with Tasmania in 2012-13 and 2013-14 without distinguishing himself. He won 12 and lost 17 leading the Hobart Hurricanes. On hitting thirty years of age, Paine started looking like part of the 'dead wood' that from time to time has been decried as cluttering the Australian cricket landscape, standing in the way of all our pathways princelings.

Certainly his own state thought so, luring three consecutive keepers from the mainland. Until a regime change in Tasmania two years ago, and some quiet advocacy by former teammate Ponting, Paine was not so much adrift as bobbing around in his small, still pond.

In this sense, then, Paine's re-emergence is a kind of critique of Australian cricket's last decade, with its high-performance culture exalting youth, talent and obedience, scorning the notion that cricketers mature at different rates.

Intrinsic to Paine's success has been that he has miles on the clock, that he has known quite long phases of frustration and inertia rather than a pageant of unleavened success. 'He's had time out of the game... so he knows himself quite well, not just as a cricketer but as a person,' Josh Hazlewood, one of his vice-captains, said of him in December. 'Off the field he is great to talk to about life as well.'

How long can Paine hold the job? At his age, every sporting role looks pro tem. But the 'leadership group' round him, such as it is, has taken on a curious shape, excluding what might be felt the senior players (Nathan Lyon, Mitchell Starc, Shaun Marsh, Usman Khawaja) in favour of character-before-cover-drive millennials (Hazlewood, Mitch Marsh, Travis Head, Patrick Cummins), with varying degrees of success.

The sort of comment that makes on the Australian dressing room and Langer's cultural priorities is debateable; it does savour of the possibility of Steve Smith's restoration. Whatever the case, it's clear the kind of Paine that Australian cricket needs: lingering, not shooting. If he can hang in another year or so, that book of leadership secrets may even be worth reading.

SECOND TEST, DAY 2

THE HEAD–BURNS ASCENDANCY

1 February 2019

Hundreds for Australia this summer have been like taxis in Canberra: never round when needed. Yesterday, like taxis, two turned up together, a bit late, and not all that relevantly, so puny and demoralised was the quality of the opposition. They were seized thankfully all the same.

It continued another sort of trend. As summer began, Australia looked to its remaining senior players to tide them over in the enforced absence of Steve Smith and David Warner. If Tim Paine's team was to prosper, it was thought, the likes of Mitchell Starc, Usman Khawaja, Nathan Lyon and the Marshes would need to stand tall.

So far at least, the shoots of promise have emerged from elsewhere, such as Marnus Labuschagne and Jhye Richardson last week at the Gabba. Yesterday the hundreds were peeled off by Travis Head, probably lucky to be in the starting XI at the top of the season, and Joe Burns, certainly unlucky to be so long joining it.

Burns, lean, hawk-eyed and sun-bronzed, has always looked a bit of an Australian archetype. His challenge was not making it to Test cricket; it has been staying there. The twenty-nine-year-old Queenslander made his debut four years ago, and lasted two Tests, unluckily missing the Ashes cut. Restored to the colours, he had the misfortune to be dropped twice in 2016, before being left out again last year after a mercy dash to South Africa in the aftermath of sandpapergate.

That's arguably said more about Australian selection caprices than Burns' returns, which in the Sheffield Shield have remained robust. Sometimes in this country it's as though the quest for champions dampens enthusiasm for the exceedingly competent. When Justin Langer complained last year that batsmen were not 'banging the door down' to get into the Australian team, he ignored that Burns has maintained at least an insistent drumming: an average of 44 in his last twenty-five first-class matches.

Against early semblances of swing, Burns needed vigilance and luck. He inside edged past leg stump on 15, was beaten outside the bat on 20, and was missed on 34, first slip Dhananjaya crowding too close to capture an edge from Dilruwan Perera — part of a fielding effort as reliable as the press box wi-fi. At that point, Burns was perhaps only halfway down the aerobridge for the Ashes-bound QF1, but every run thereafter brought the first-class hors d'oeuvres closer.

Very still as the bowler approaches, his trigger movements are pronounced but slight, leaving little to go amiss. He drove attractively, cut and pulled laconically, used his feet decisively to Perera, forward and back. He will also battle harder for fewer runs than yesterday, faced by modest bowlers with much to be modest about. But, as they say, one must still get them.

Getting his maiden Test hundred, Head confirmed good impressions left in Adelaide and Brisbane without quite eliminating reservations left in Perth and Melbourne. His strokes exuded the hum of quiet industry; he nearly squandered his day's labour just before tea with a wretched stroke to gully, wretchedly missed by Perera, whose day was going from bad through worse to abject. Being plonked for six by the batsman you've dropped is worthy of a Grade Cricketer meme.

In the final session, Sri Lanka's bowlers served up as amiably as public service tea ladies, while the fielders clock watched. From one ten-over phase, Burns and Head carved 81 runs without a hint of risk or even unorthodoxy.

Dhananjaya flubbed a second chance from his own bowling when Head was 155 and was lucky it did not prove costlier. From Dhananjaya's bowling, Lahiru Thirimanne then spared the scoreless Kurtis Patterson at bat-pad — a simple chance but a timely reprieve that might be the difference between a summer in England or a winter at home.

Certainly the players who left runs unmade yesterday will be doubly chagrined, none more so than Usman Khawaja, whom there was a case for omitting here which he did nothing to repudiate. Since scrambling to a half-century in Perth, he has looked increasingly stale and thwarted, muted in Melbourne, dropped before he scored in Sydney, chopping on in Brisbane, and generally dragging himself about as if he'd rather be elsewhere.

A flat pitch, a fast outfield and a Sri Lanka second XI attack with fielding to match should have provided soothing therapy. Instead Khawaja spent the day in the dugout recuperating from a firm-footed waft at his third ball, in due course surrendering the mantle of being Australia's most recent centurion and looking less indispensable for it.

Worse, Khawaja's opportunities for further red ball cricket have recently been compromised by his reincorporation in Australia's white ball plans. Australia's selectors enjoyed the luxury of an unchanged squad here, but this is a team guaranteed to provide continuing conundrums.

A word for the event: on its Test debut, as it were, low-rise, tree-fringed Manuka Oval made a pleasant respite from summer's succession of lookalike stadia. Stands named for Sir Donald Bradman and Sir Robert Menzies lean together conspiratorially; the Jack Fingleton Scoreboard keeps a suitably ambivalent distance. Grassy banks contribute to the friendly human scale; mountains provide a picturesque backdrop.

It's a pity that local officialdom still insist on dinning spectators' ears with noughties power ballads, because otherwise the occasion was a credit to them. Australia's other Test venues face some competition. Now, if something can just be done about the taxis…

SECOND TEST, DAY 2

P-PLATERS

2 February 2019

Kurtis Patterson and Will Pucovski are twentysomething Australian batsmen brimming with promise, whose selection for this series against Sri Lanka was widely praised. Ever since then, their routes have been diverging; yesterday they parted altogether.

Patterson, a twenty-five-year-old stripling playing his sixtieth first-class match, was watched by his parents recording an undefeated maiden Test century. Twenty-year-old prodigy Pucovski was spending what by coincidence was his twenty-first birthday en familie, having 'reported some challenges' to his mental equilibrium over the past few days and flown home Friday night.

The irony is, of course, that Pucovski was chosen first, back on 9 January, as part of the general spill of positions following Australia's defeat in the Border-Gavaskar Trophy. He featured in an Australian XI match against the visitors at Bellerive Oval alongside Patterson, who seized his chance with a bracket of hundreds to gain late inclusion in the Test squad.

Still the attention focused on the boom batsman with only eight first-class matches behind him, and Pucovski in the prelude to the Brisbane Test attracted rave notices. Captain Tim Paine called him 'mature and calm', 'a young man with a wise head' with 'a little bit of an aura about him'; elder statesman Ricky Ponting anointed him 'the best young player in Australia'; Fox Sports decided that Australia had chosen 'its next 100-game player' before he had played one.

When Pucoski and Patterson posed for a photograph together at the Gabba, it was the rock star rookie who occupied the foreground, bat across his shoulders, baby face peering through the grille of a green and gold helmet; Patterson stood back, almost like his caddy.

At the eleventh hour, however, the selectors shied from a top six containing two batsmen on debut and went with recent runs. Patterson played, making an unobtrusive but composed 30 against the pink ball in the twilight — sufficient to earn a second chance. On Friday here, Sri Lanka gifted Patterson a third chance, dropping him at short leg first ball. He seized it.

Patterson has had the good fortune to commence his Test career under circumstances close to ideal, coming in at five for 248 and four for 336 against bowling line-ups shorn by injury of pace and penetration. Yesterday, on a benign surface, Sri Lanka's attack was as limited as a guitar with three broken strings.

Patterson defended comfortably, punctured cover and point off both feet, spun his spindly figure into pull shots off the front foot. He'll have toiled harder over Sheffield Shield hundreds, felt more pain after demanding gym sessions. It happened to be, as locals patriotically pointed out, the only sold-out day of the Test summer.

Tall and angular, orthodox and side-on, Patterson has an old-fashioned aspect: he attended a school that produced its only other Test cricketer 111 years ago; with a nasal prosthetic, he could be a body double in a Bill Lawry biopic. The celebration of his hundred revealed a touch of flamboyance: a blue headband beneath the helmet. It also suggested a smidgeon of superstition: only with three figures next to his name did he feel free to shed his sleeveless sweater.

The selectors will have been delighted, if partly as an analgesic to the headache with which Pucovski has left them. His previous mental travails are well-documented. He has discussed candidly the seven-week break he took earlier in the season after experiencing anxiety in a Sheffield Shield match in Perth. Medical reassurances were given about his well-being before he was considered for higher honours; Pucovski himself declared when he was picked that he felt 'as good as I have felt in a really long time.' But mood, like form, is fickle.

Like other sports, cricket has scarcely begun to grapple with the psychological exactions of its hyper-professionalised form. One line of thought is that mental difficulties should be treated as another form of indisposition, treatable and tractable; the buzz phrase is managing 'wellness'.

A corollary, however, is that choosing a player with a 'wellness' history is akin to picking one with a known susceptibility to injury. Can Australia now take Pucovski to England? It will require copper-bottomed guarantees, and a great degree of empathy from coaches and teammates.

The selectors received a good deal of criticism for choosing Pucovski only not to play him. The question now arises whether this exacerbated pressure on him. The emotional strain of being so close to his goal only to have it snatched away must have been acute — one thinks of Tantalus' eternal punishment in Tartarus.

This is the very essence of Test cricket, of course, that many are called but few are chosen. Selectors can hardly promote players in order to alleviate their potential psychological distress. By the same token, it might be time to rethink these baggy and oversized 'squads', from which players are eliminated like contestants on *Survivor*, waiting for Trevor Hohns to convene tribal council. Meant to advertise flexibility, they just as often smack of indecision. Meant to include, they as easily do the opposite.

Such 'squads' are often justified by reference to the importance of introducing newbies to 'the group'. 'He's been great around the group,' others say loyally of the supernumerary. But we tackle cricket in teams not groups. The true cricketer wants to be playing not watching.

The contrast between Pucovski and Patterson was not the only one in evidence on a day leisured enough to enjoy its aesthetic detail. There was the contrast between the high definition screen and the neighbouring Fingleton scoreboard, with figures cramming up against one another as in a slightly haphazard game of Scrabble; between the simple purity of the Australian cable knit sweater and the vulgarity on its breast of the sponsor's orange splodge, which resembles fly-spatter on a windscreen. The weight of five for 534 bearing down on Sri Lanka, now with a batsman incapacitated, also accentuated the contrast between the teams.

SECOND TEST, DAY 3
FILL 'ER UP

3 February 2019

On country roads one often comes across a sign warning that the next filling station will be the last for last for 100 kilometres or more, an injunction to check petrol and provisions.

For Australia's top order, yesterday at Manuka Oval was likewise a last truck stop: after a summer of six long Tests, Australia's next Test innings is not for another six months, the First Ashes Test at Edgbaston, on the far side of a score of one-day internationals.

Time to stock up? There could be no better opportunity than a flat pitch against a demoralised attack in a third innings undergirded by a 319-run lead to complicate life for selectors who down the track will probably be squishing the current six into four to accommodate Steve Smith and David Warner. Some needed runs more than others; for none were they superfluous.

Again, however, the Australians started poorly against a mere semblance of sideways movement. Kusal Mendis took two low catches at second slip and Nirosh Dickwella dived in front of first to arrest the developments of Joe Burns, Marcus Harris and Marnus Labuschagne. Burns might be said to have runs in credit; the juniors not so much.

Harris, who shaped tightly against India, has looked sketchier since the Big Bash League games into which he was pointlessly shoehorned between times, and here skewed towards mid-on; Labuschagne, victim of a good delivery on the first morning perished to a tentative poke.

February shots, perhaps — when a player's edge is not so keen, especially ones starting out in international cricket and still learning to husband their energies. These were muted notes on which to finish their first Test summers, leaving both to make the best of the Sheffield Shield's back half, and contemplate the prospect of James Anderson.

Nobody in the assemblage, however, needed runs more acutely than Usman Khawaja, who since his noble resistance in Dubai had averaged 21, half his career average — no batsman this summer, in other words, had fallen shorter of their personal standards.

Khawaja had started the day badly and all, shelling Dickwella at slip, and standing hands on hips between deliveries for the next few overs, a teapot stewing.

Khawaja doesn't often lose his equanimity. Indeed, he is a batsman often delineated in moral terms: his dismissals are typed as 'lazy', 'casual' and 'careless', with the imputation that he is similarly indolent.

The diligence with which Khawaja has improved his fitness, not to mention the mandatory nature of modern professionalism, belies this. He may better be thought of as having a high ignition temperature, resolved not to fret too much over failure, and slow rather than swift to take on concerns.

The truth is that his Khawaja's footwork has looked hesitant this summer. A front leg should be a lever not an anchor. To his first ball from Kasun Rajitha yesterday, he was again caught between wind and water, left shoulder coming round as he fended off something not that short; later he was hit on the right shoulder, and toed a pull shot into space behind square. He lofted Perera and thought not to run, only to realise it would not reach the boundary, and self-consciously jogged a couple.

Gradually some of Khawaja's old suavity returned, like the restoration of sensation to a limb gone stiff. He nailed a couple of pull shots, got in a big stride for succulent cover drives, worked the ball soundlessly off his legs and explored his variations, following a crisp reverse sweep with a muscular orthodox version.

He did, in other words, as the occasion demanded, salting runs away against future hardship, lining up long distance for Birmingham to set right a paltry record in England. His celebration of this 136-ball skite was as jubilant as the one for his nine-hour epic in Dubai — perhaps he had been more concerned than he was letting on.

As a hedge against inflation it had its limits, all the same. Runs dwindle in meaning as they grow in profusion, and the longer the exercise proceeded the greater the day's resemblance to batting practice, to the point that nets might as well have been erected on each side of the pitch. As Khawaja's partnership with Travis Head swelled to 159 from 199 balls, Australia's lead passed through 400, 450, 500, crying out for a mercy rule, Sri Lanka's three innings in the series having not added up to that many.

For much of the first half of the day a Sri Lankan mariachi band played a Lanka Lanka Lanka Oi Oi Oi medley, as cacophonous as a truckload of brass band instruments dropped down a flight of stairs. Their repertoire even included a cover of a Barmy Army tune — cultural appropriation, surely? But they steadily lost interest too, in favour of basting themselves under the sun. Others had more to play for, and made it count.

SECOND TEST, DAY 4

TWO CHEERS FOR VICTORY

4 February 2019

So Australia win a series after thirteen months, if you can call two Tests a series rather than a couplet or bracket, and it's a case of two cheers at best.

As the clock neared 3pm at Manuka Oval yesterday, the digital screen served up the equation: 'To win: Sri Lanka 368 runs, Australia one wicket.' Mitchell Starc soon broke the unbearable tension with something full and straight to collect his tenth wicket for a pleasingly symmetrical 100. Tim Paine and Justin Langer fondled their first winner's cheque.

'Good hard Test cricket,' said a commentator, straining to accentuate the positive. But in the same sense is smashing half volleys on a bowling machine good hard practice, and six hours of *Red Dead Redemption 2* good hard PlayStation. Under no pressure, everybody is a front runner.

To be sure, it is better than losing. But Sri Lanka have won seven away Tests in 43 in the last decade, four of them against Bangladesh and Zimbabwe. They arrive, promptly and correctly attired, because the Future Tours Programme obliges them to. They are encouraged by the occasional individual feat, but their playing personnel is an inch deep, and in Canberra their best four pace bowlers and best batsman were scraped away.

They are beset, too, by opaque maladministration, so that their coach on this tour was suddenly and inexplicably relieved of selection responsibilities on the instruction of the Sri Lankan sports minister 'in consideration of the need to form an effective and transparent selection mechanism'. Bureaucratese, eh? It's a more universal lingo than Esperanto.

At home, where Sri Lanka can dictate conditions, it has historically been a different matter. When many of the same Australians visited Sri Lanka in 2016, Dinesh Chandimal, Kusal Mendis and Dhanajaya de Silva peeled off hundreds and Dilruwan Perera bagged ten in a match. Here they have grossed 160 runs in sixteen hits and two wickets in eighty overs.

In the corresponding 2016 series, Joe Burns and Usman Khawaja lost their Australian places. In Canberra they have each scored soothingly therapeutic hundreds. The tables have not been turned so much as two separate tables been used.

This made for a subdued conclusion to a Test summer that began with a clatter of Indian wickets on the first morning at Adelaide Oval two months ago — not the last false dawn. Two thousand fans were in, even if the security jobsworths were still approaching their task as though guarding a nuclear reactor.

Sri Lanka's 'target' of 516, as with many fourth innings, was perfectly theoretical; the objective was more in the nature of 'respectability'.

Such days have a distinctive dynamic. Some dig in, with the same good intentions as readers starting *War and Peace* half-resigned to not reaching the end: thus Lahiru Thirimanne, who withstood 314 balls in the two Tests, and wasn't disgraced.

Some embrace the relative freedom from expectation, the sense of conclusion forgone with only the margin of defeat being negotiated: thus Mendis, who played some classy shots then drove nonchalantly to cover to complete a disappointing series. The Australians pursued their ends with effective fixity of purpose, but little need to stretch.

There was much affirmative nodding about Mitchell Starc,

who was deemed either back, or never away. Actually, both conclusions were supportable.

Starc is regularly paralleled with Mitchell Johnson, swift, athletic, left-handed, hard-hitting. But Johnson's best and worst were for much of his career not even in neighbouring postcodes. It was closing the gap between them, after a long physical and psychological rebuilding, that resulted in his late flowering. The troughs that intersperse Starc's peaks are more like valleys, when batsmen grow inured to his pace and predict his swing. He does not look bad so much as average.

When a team is ripe for intimidation, however, Starc stands a foot taller. He bowled superbly against Sri Lanka in 2016 — 24 wickets at 15 in a beaten team. The sight of them down the other end with 534 to bowl at was the perfect pick-me-up. He probed for a hat-trick yesterday with four slips, a gully, a leg gully, a short leg and the whiff of the kill; it was only just averted.

The Australian top six that jerked in spasmodic unison during the Border-Gavaskar Trophy was rich in runs during the Warne-Muralitharan Trophy, to the degree that in horse racing a swab would have been called for. Good for Travis Head, who grew into his vice-captaincy with a counterpunching maiden hundred here. But when your five-year first-class average is 37, an average of 155 in two Tests has to be deemed an outlier.

The important calls were arguably made ahead of this series. Had Shaun Marsh been chosen, there would probably be words now for his undoubted class and international quality; Aaron Finch might have hacked his way to a score or two as well. And they would have meant very little. As far as takeaways for England are concerned, only a couple really emerged, Kurtis Patterson taking his opportunity, Will Pucovski not having his enlarged. The selectors have here probably pulled the right rein. But given the quality of this opposition and the one-sidedness of this contest, it and many other things will remain unknown until Australia take the field against England six months hence.

JUSTIN LANGER

PUNTING ON PONTING

15 February 2019

Who doesn't love a cricket legend? Cricket is the most spontaneously nostalgic of all games, always reminiscing, always comparing. And right now is a great time to be a legend in Australia because a) we're not very good, so you look even better; and b) we're looking for answers, and you might have some.

Cricket Australia's tapping of Ricky Ponting as Justin Langer's assistant coach for the World Cup is reported as preluding greater utilization of past masters in the capacities of assistant coach, mentors and consultants.

Other names dropped by CEO Kevin Roberts have included Steve Waugh and Adam Gilchrist; also mentioned in despatches have been Glenn McGrath, Michael Kasprowicz, Simon Katich and the inevitable Shane Warne.

Legends don't come cheap, of course — and in Australia, coaches usually have. Never mind, says Roberts. They'll get a special rate to make working 'in shorter bursts' worth their while: 'We don't have an unlimited pool of funds to invest in coaches, but certainly we want to be investing as much as we can and navigating those challenges as best we can.'

Truth is that this has been a long time coming. Langer is heavily invested in the idea of Australia as Camelot and gathering his fellow baggy green knights at a round dressing room table.

'One of the things we've got in Australian cricket unlike other countries is that we've got great players,' Langer contended at his first press conference. 'Not just really good players, or good players. But we've got great players and we're lucky to draw on those... Not many countries have that luxury.'

Why the obsession? The Ponting appointment may obtain a clue. Ponting candidly explained it in terms of helping Langer, for whom the task of being national coach had come at a 'really difficult time' and been 'as hard on him as it possibly could be just because of the situation Australian cricket has found itself in', he being 'a bit of a control freak'. Here's a rare coaching appointment, as much about the coach as the players.

From one standpoint, that suggests an encouraging degree of self-knowledge and flexibility on Langer's part. Some coaches might feel threatened by the presence of an individual of Ponting's stature in the dressing room; Langer, commendably, does not. And Ponting himself? Unimpeachable.

But, well, it's not like the Australian team is short on coaching resources, is it? Even after the departure of assistant coach David Saker, it has more back room staff than players — this in a game, cricket, in which actual in-play coaching interaction is minimal.

Arguably, too, at the very top level, the impact a coach can have is limited. Players' techniques are already ingrained; matches flow so seamlessly into one another that the opportunities for readjustment are circumscribed; day-to-day performance is so shaded by luck that the risk is of overanalysis rather than underreaction.

There is a growing obsession in Australian cricket with explaining every shortcoming by reference to method, partly because of the critical mass of professional observers, inside the system and out, knowledgeable about technique, able to talk with authority about the necessity of side-on defence in batting, the efficacy of a braced front leg in bowling etc. Some of these are our aforementioned 'legends'; some are specialists with skills to sell, whether in power hitting or bowling variations.

Useful stuff, of course. But there is a world of difference between having knowledge and imparting it, and between pointing out a shortcoming and fixing it. The far harder questions to ask are why a player might play the way they do, what they gain from doing so, what will be the cost of introducing doubt and/or enforcing adjustment.

This seems a challenge to a whole idea of 'legends' as coaches. They were often naturally excellent; their strength lay in a core method requiring minimal tinkering; if passing through anyway, how invested can they be in and accountable for the outcome of their advice?

Playing and coaching cricket, too, are philosophically further apart than we like to believe. Playing exalts the individual; scores are instant, dramatic, unyielding. Coaching is by definition self-effacing; results are assessed over longer runs and dependent on numberless variables, including the work of previous coaches in bringing on the talent now at one's disposal. At an elite level, it is as much about the management of egos and the assuaging of disappointment as it is about getting a batsman to bend their front leg more for the cover drive.

You could argue, in fact, that the greatest impact coaches have is at early stages of a players' development, when technique is malleable and temperament developing. In which case it should be junior coaches paid the big bucks; in which case 'legends', if they really wanted to make a contribution, would be better deployed going to look after a state under-16 team or some such.

Which is not to say that great cricketers cannot be terrific coaches. Dennis Lillee and Rod Marsh come to mind; Bob Simpson and Geoff Lawson too. But the most admired Australian coaches of the last twenty years, the ones players talk of with respect and affection, were not star cricketers.

Rather, like your Bob Woolmer or Gary Kirsten, or your Peter Philpott or Alf Gover further back, have they been students of the game, and of human nature: Trevor Bayliss, Tom Moody, Greg Shipperd, Dav Whatmore, Michael Di Venuto, Andrew McDonald, Tim Coyle, John Inverarity, Richard Done, Adam Griffith, Wayne Andrews and the Meulemans, to name but a few.

Ric Charlesworth and John Buchanan made a single first-class hundred between them, but who could stint their coaching records? Likewise, when Mitchell Starc wanted wise counsel recently, who did he seek out but Andre Adams, capped once by New Zealand?

It was Pat Howard who started changing that in his resistible reign as high-performance czar; now it is Roberts. In both cases, one senses, the principle concern has been optics, a kind of 'Making Australian Cricket Great Again' trucker cap populism. As recruiting Ponting is a way for Langer to soothe his anxieties, invoking Waugh and Gilchrist is a means for Roberts to advertise his intimacy with greatness.

But that's not coaching so much as a form of professionalised ancestor worship, and it resolves nothing about an Australian high-performance system still drifting along under temporary management. Hey, don't get me wrong. 'Legends' are ace. But they are sustained, in a significant degree, by our belief in them.

BRADMAN AND PACKER

MESALLIANCE

22 February 2019

Bradman and Packer: in recent Australian history, you could hardly pack together two more potent and subtly contrasting surnames, equivalents in sport to maybe Murdoch and Whitlam, or Jones and insert prime minister's name here.

So Daniel Brettig's new monograph *Bradman & Packer*, launched last night in Melbourne, punches above the weight of its 179 pages, taking on two of the abiding myths of Australian cricket: the myths of Sir Donald Bradman's sagacity and of Kerry Packer's benevolence. They've been challenged before, but seldom so capably.

When Packer died in 2005, Cricket Australia was among the dutiful mourners — there were minutes' silence, armbands, obsequies, the lot. 'That cricket is today taken for granted as a natural part of the Australian way of life is in no small measure due to his influence,' said its chairman Creagh O'Connor.

What people were too polite to mention was that Kerry Packer died absolutely minted thanks in no small measure to the Nine Network's long stranglehold on cricket, flowing from the terms of the agreement he made with the game's administrators, Bradman chief among them, 40 years ago.

It was a negotiation characterised by an acute asymmetry of power and of purpose. The two years of Packer's World Series Cricket had cost him a bomb, but he could afford it; CA's antecedent Australian Cricket Board had exhausted reserves salted away for decades.

For peace, Packer was keen; for their precious game back, the ACB were desperate. Packer's chief negotiator, Lynton Taylor, quotes from a meeting attended by Bradman in February 1979: 'At that point, Don said very succinctly, 'I don't care what we have to give away to get this deal done, I want it done, as long as the ACB has control of the game.' Now that's not a very good thing to say at the first set of negotiations...'

So it was that Packer returned cricket to the ACB's 'control' on terms only slightly less onerous than the Treaty of Versailles, in an initial deal lasting ten years, and inserting PBL Marketing as the board's commercial arm for no fewer than fifteen years.

Brettig, *Cricinfo*'s excellent Australian editor, quotes from a confidential report prepared after five years of the first deal estimating that Nine had accumulated $134 million in advertising revenue from its broadcast and commercial rights, of which the ACB had seen $2 million.

Taylor claims in mitigation that, in that first decade, Nine was sometimes required to subsidise tour guarantees offered to other countries because the ACB could not afford them.

'Yes, we were getting a very good income from the rights we'd negotiated, but we did put an enormous amount of money back in to pay the teams that came to Australia,' he says, in the tones of one expecting gratitude for a blanket after burning down your house.

Brettig might have gone still further in his analysis. Fundamental to understanding what we might call, a la Keynes, the economic consequences of the peace, is the coalition of interest between the parties in negotiation forty years ago. It is *Bradman & Packer*, not Bradman versus Packer.

The players were not represented in those 1979 meetings; their attempts to unionise quickly petered out; once they had outlived their usefulness as bargaining chips, Packer had little interest in ongoing improvement of their financial lot, which would be at the expense of his profits; nor did Bradman, ever resistant to the idea of full-fledged professionalism.

Thus a curious alliance of hard-boiled capitalism and rheumy-eyed amateurism. With the restoration of the cricket monopsony, the players slipped back into what was now a double yoke, jointly secured by the board and by Packer.

Those who sought to shrug it off, such as the rebel tourists of the mid-1980s, were exiled and execrated. Those who stayed the course ended up, frankly, rather worse off than they should have been. Brettig observes that Allan Border's last ACB contract was worth $90,000.

What changed? A key shift in the dynamic was Packer's cashing Nine in to Alan Bond in 1987, affording scope for a later generation of administrators, notably the shrewd Malcolm Gray and Denis Rogers, to push back.

Packer returned, of course, but in poorer health, and only spasmodically interested, still inclined to thunder at commentators who displeased him, but after the expiration of the ACB's relationship with PBL in 1994 less able to bend the game to his will.

It remains possible to argue for the beneficial impacts of WSC, and of Nine, on cricket, in its attuning of the game and its administration to televisual and promotional imperatives. But it's worth contemplating the counterfactual: cricket without Packer.

In 1977, cricket was in rude health. Nine was not the only commercial broadcaster nosing around, merely the most brazen. Bradman's administrative race was almost run. Brettig puts it well when he describes Nine/PBL's terms with the ACB as having 'guaranteed and limited the size of cricket as a business.' So what if cricket had been able to exploit its own popularity rather than have an outside party do so?

In light of Brettig's survey, the quote he has elicited from James Sutherland is even more tone deaf than usual: 'No organisation has put more into cricket financially or promoted it more than the Nine Network, and Australian cricket should always be incredibly grateful for that.' Appreciative perhaps, but 'incredibly grateful'? Sheesh.

'If you really love the game you should be positive about the game, and promote the game,' Sutherland continues. 'It just concerns me when some people get to the stage in life where, even though they proclaim to be genuine lovers of the game, all they can do is criticise. I think it's sad that it's come to that, and maybe they've just done one too many laps.'

For all his capabilities, Sutherland never really grasped the difference between journalism and public relations, or between 'the game' and Cricket Australia. As for the admonition of 'too many laps' from a seventeen-year CEO — my sides!

It takes an enthusiastic, impartial and judicious observer to cut through the interests, self-justifications and received wisdoms that accumulate over time, which is what Daniel Brettig has done in *Bradman & Packer*.

INDIA V PAKISTAN

THE CRICKET WAR

28 February 2019

For the last few months, among the hottest items in sport fandom have been Adult Gold tickets to the 16 June World Cup Match at Old Trafford between India and Pakistan, which have been changing hands for well over $3000. Right now, some shoppers will be feeling nervous about their investment.

Whether a cricket match proceeds is hardly the most important flow-on from the fortnight that has brought these nuclear-armed antagonists closer to conflict than at any stage since 1999's Kargil War. But the state of the countries' cricket relations has always been sound index of their foreign relations, and right now these are dragging along a new bottom, made bumpier by other agendas.

Suicide attacks, bombing raids, bellicose rhetoric: from the events of the last fortnight, the Board of Control for Cricket in India could hardly have held aloof, not least because its own leadership is weak.

The court-appointed Committee of Administration in charge of the BCCI since January 2017 has been divided and damaged by the serial bunglings of chairman Vinod Rai and a #MeToo scandal involving CEO Rahul Johri. Long-delayed elections are finally due in the next three months.

The CoA's response to Jaish-e-Mohammed's bloody insurgency at Pulwana was a tough-talking and studiously-leaked letter under Johri's signature to other ICC members urging 'the cricket community' to 'sever ties with countries from which terrorism emanates'.

While Pakistan was not identified and the World Cup referred to only in terms of security, Rai reinforced the message in a pugilistic interview with *India Today* in which he committed the BCCI to a policy of isolating cricket in Pakistan as once the world isolated racist South Africa: 'Long term plan, we want to declare Pakistan as the apartheid of cricket.'

While they have continued competing in ICC events like the Cup, India has imposed its own de facto cricket boycott on Pakistan for a decade, reneging on promises of bilateral fixtures and excluding Pakistani players from the Indian Premier League.

But the notion of extending that boycott and calling for others to join represented a sharp escalation of hostilities, affecting, not least, Australia, set to play Pakistan in the UAE in three weeks and to host them next summer.

Was this a genuine punitive measure or posturing? Probably a bit of both. These days Kipling needs revision: if you can keep your head when all about you are losing theirs and blaming it on you then… well, maybe you've misread the situation.

Indian greats like Sourav Ganguly, Mohammed Azharuddin and Harbhajan Singh were bellowing for a boycott; Indian tabloid television was packed with sound-alike sabre rattlers.

Even Sachin Tendulkar, whose initial position was a softly-softly sport-comes-first statement ('India has always come up trumps against Pakistan in the World Cup. Time to beat them again'), has since tweeted salutes to the 'bravehearts' of the Indian Air Force with stern reinforcings ('Our niceness should never be comprehended as our weakness').

So Rai and Johri, with a feeling of the popular pulse and an eye on their administrative power rivals, had to have a strong public position going into this week's meeting of the ICC executive board in Dubai.

They supplemented this with a populist gesture: scrapping the IPL's opening ceremony and donating its budget to the families of the 'martyrs' of Pulwana.

The problem with their position is that it's by no means clear that the ICC has constitutional power to 'sever ties' with any country. Pakistan Cricket Board chairman Ehsan Mani knows this. He was president of ICC fifteen years ago when petitioners sought Zimbabwe's excommunication and found that the council lacked the power to do so.

Chances are, then, that the BCCI and PCB will find a workaround. They have historically been good at this. Jaish-e-Mohammed's attack on the Pathankot Air Force base in January 2016 did not, in the end, prevent India hosting Pakistan in the World T20 two months later, even if the venue had to be changed at the last minute.

For all that, this has been a worrisome week. Moderating voices were heard in India, but they seemed to be significantly outshouted.

To his credit, Sunil Gavaskar was one. He insisted that the way to deal with Pakistan was to 'beat them [in the World Cup] and make sure they don't qualify', and that the dispute needed to be looked at with 'a little more depth' although emotions were 'running high'.

Gavaskar probably looked back on his own career. In 1971-2, he toured Australia with a Rest of the World XI alongside Pakistan's Intikhab Alam and Asif Masood even as their countries were at war. He welcomed last year's election of his old rival Imran Khan as Pakistan's prime minister, describing him as a 'friend' who 'understands India'.

The sadness is that Gavaskar belongs to a generation of

Indian cricketers who met their Pakistani counterparts on the field regularly, where today the players are strangers. Virat Kohli and Sarfaraz Ahmed enjoy no bond like Gavaskar and Imran. Ditto the administrators. Days when India hosted international tournaments jointly with Pakistan and Sri Lanka are long past: India today is a bloc-of-one.

Troubling, too, is that the situation may get worse before getting better. Indian politicians are in election mode ahead of polls in two months. Toeing the Line of Control in Kashmir has never been an unpopular political stance.

A young electorate knows Pakistan less as a cricket rival, more as a nemesis. After five years of Narendra Modi, politics can seem like a series of competing Hindu nationalist gestures: last week in Calcutta, for instance, a BJP youth cadre in Calcutta camped outside Eden Gardens demanding that a portrait of Imran in his cricket days be removed.

At the same time, while we can all be very pious from here about India and Pakistan just needing to jolly well sort their quarrels out so we can get on with our nice cricket, it's as well to be sensitive to the violations Indians have experienced in this century from jihadist cells seemingly succoured by Pakistan's 'deep state'.

It's worth remembering that, as far as the game at Old Trafford is concerned, Australia and England have forfeited World Cup matches with considerably less cause. In 1996, some hurtful hate mail deterred us from visiting Sri Lanka; in 2003, England suffered moral queasiness about visiting Zimbabwe. None of those cricketers' countrymen had died; the world has only grown less secure, more vicious, since.

So even assuming the showpiece match goes ahead four months hence, the preconditions of crisis will remain. Everyone loves India v

Pakistan: so much pride, so much passion, so much history. But those same factors are conspiring to make it ever more sensitive.

NEW ZEALAND

THE ROAD LESS TRAVELLED

9 March 2019

Page 90 of last year's Ethics Centre's cultural review of Australian cricket records an exchange that's looked ever more worth revisiting since.

Discussing the national team's on-field demeanour, one of the centre's interlocutors commented on the decision by their counterparts in New Zealand to renounce sledging. You sense the hackles rising in the recorded retort of an 'Australian Test player': 'And how are *they* going?'

Six months later, the answer could be thanks for asking, because it's pretty bloody well.

The Black Caps are poorly reported in this country, partly due to the overlap of seasons, partly because of the Australian cliché of New Zealand as a 'little brother' which frankly has more to do with our own national conceit. Brendon McCullum's commitment to cricket 'in a decent manner' was interpreted by some in these parts as a pitch for the Mrs Joyful Prize for Raffiawork.

But as Australia has spent the last year talking to itself — are we too hard? too apologetic? too rich? too pampered? — New Zealand has talked by its cricket.

On the ICC rankings, Kane Williamson's team has reached the giddying heights of number two in Tests behind India, number three in one-day internationals behind England and India — an unprecedented eminence.

They've done it playing their own way — cricket 'that suits us as people', Williamson has called it, without fuss, folly, and even pitch mic pissing contests.

By the end of the Wellington Test that New Zealand began against Bangladesh yesterday, Williamson may be the top-ranked Test batsman by the ICC algorithm. After reaching his twentieth Test hundred in 71 Tests innings with an unbeaten double at Hamilton, he is just seven points astern of Virat Kohli.

Kohli is a phenomenon, the outstanding batsman and most vivid sporting personality in a country of 1.3 billion; but Williamson, the best in a land of fewer than five million who has nonetheless set global standards, nailing his captaincy down while batting at number three, is surely little less so.

It is three years since Williamson succeeded McCullum, an outsize personality who he has felt no pressure to emulate. In 2016, McCullum published a slightly uncomfortable autobiography, revealing a few chips on his mighty shoulders; Williamson published an unassuming little instructional book with Dylan Cleaver, making cricket the subject rather than himself.

(Passing comment: when was the last time an Australian cricketer published such a 'coaching book'? As a representative of what used to be an abundant genre, I can think only of Mike Hussey's *Winning Edge* in the last decade. Maybe they no longer have the time; maybe they lack the inclination or aptitude. Such books are by nature generous, inclusive; so much easier to push out the regulation autobiography.)

McCullum did a wonderful job challenging his countrymen to think in terms of winning trophies, beating rivals, being a power rather than always a plucky outsider — a confidence founded in his success in the Indian Premier League against all-comers.

Williamson has carried that on, scaling ever greater standards of excellence with the minimum of histrionics — without even a cloying false modesty.

Succeeding David Warner as captain of Sunrisers Hyderabad in the IPL last year with as little fanfare as that pageant of sis-boom-bah permits, he also won the Orange Cap for the most runs. The stylish Test match touch player hits a long ball in T20, including 100 sixes.

Even better, players have responded to Williamson's leadership in the last two and a half years.

His 1577 Test runs at 64 have been mirrored by Ross Taylor's 2319 ODI runs at 64. Trent Boult bounced back from injury to take 71 wickets at 24; Tom Latham has become a substantial opening batsman with 1366 runs at 52; in his last Test, keeper BJ Watling broke New Zealand's dismissals record.

There is a kink to this rise, it should be said. New Zealand's rankings surge owes something, paradoxically, to playing less Test cricket. When they tackled Pakistan in the UAE last year, they had gone two years without an away Test, a scandalous lack.

Despite that, though, they won, where Australia had recently failed, bouncing back from an innings defeat at Dubai.

There is also something about the thrifty, make-do-and-mend New Zealand attitude that commands respect. John Wright once observed that the country's seeming weakness of a small playing population and domestic set-up also had virtues: of talent, the system was not wasteful; it stretched what it had. Nor is there the overhang of not-in-my-day former giants.

When their excellent, undersung coach Mike Hesson called it quits last year just before that trip to the UAE, New Zealand Cricket simply chose between two successful domestic coaches, Gary Stead of Canterbury and Heinrich Malan of Central Districts.

Stead was a steady Plunkett Shield opening batsman who could have played more than his five Tests; Malan had played only ten first-class matches. They were judged as coaches rather than as brands.

On his appointment, Stead achieved an unremarked but unique double, having previously coached the Silver Ferns, New Zealand's women's team, into two global finals.

There remain vulnerabilities, of course: Mitchell Santner notwithstanding, the Black Caps have never replaced Daniel Vettori, and will struggle to replace Taylor, who turned thirty-five yesterday. There are hints that domestic cricket depends overly on émigré South Africans.

New Zealand Cricket is prudently run, avoiding the machismo that has coloured industrial relations in the sport here, but may exhibit a little too much confidence in its handling of one serious controversy, the rape charges against pace bowler Scott Kuggeleijn.

In their own way, however, New Zealand's careful husbandry of scarce resources has become an example for the rest of the cricket world that often seems in danger of tripping over its own money bags. How is New Zealand doing? Maybe Australia should pay a bit more attention to finding out.

SANDPAPERGATE

A LONG SHORT YEAR

22 March 2019

Sometimes, in an atmosphere of groupthink, of lack of accountability, of short-term expedient, people in cricket make crassly spur-of-the-moment decisions that harm the game in ways they scarcely understand.

But enough about the initiative from Cricket Australia and the England Cricket Board this week for Test cricketers to wear names and numbers on their shirts; let's talk about Sandpapergate, whose first anniversary falls tomorrow. Actually, I'll track back to the former in due course…

Look out, inevitably, for numerous retellings of that fateful week at Cape Town and Johannesburg, including rescreenings of that footage and those press conferences, which still somehow never fail to shock.

In financial terms, once the commercial income forgone is laid alongside the matches not played and the brand damage inflicted, the penalties on Smith and David Warner were probably the heaviest ever levied on Australian athletes.

Were they too heavy? In his new book, Mike Brearley sets the Australians' misdeeds against match fixing, and draws the comparison between 'minor shoplifting' and 'aggravated burglary'.

Future generations trying to make sense of it all, however, should not overlook the various aggravating factors, such as the nonchalance and gormlessness of the slide into malpractice, the crudity of the use of sandpaper, the sense of the perpetrators being caught 'in the act'. It was not just what was done; it was the way.

We are apt to complain about sporting delinquencies being played down and covered up — damn the spin doctors and their wiles!

Here the gruesome fascination lay in two ill-prepared athletes trying to fix the problem they'd created, and worsening it with their every answer. Steve Smith's concluding remark, a blithe response to the question of whether he was the right man for the Australian captaincy, proved integral to his losing it.

One question barely posed since, let alone answered, remains: where were the managers? Asleep at their posts in South Africa, asleep in bed in Australia, it would seem.

It's hardly as though the incident came from nowhere; the series had taken angry, bitter, destructive turns. But the controversy became a crisis, within twelve hours a catastrophe, and after twelve months remains a cause celebre, because of sins of omission as well as commission.

These run deep too. What was instructive about the intensity of the ensuing indignation was how stored up it felt — how in their fury with the specific the public made known its dissatisfaction with the general.

In fact, soundings about the profile and popularity of the national team had been discouraging for some time. Cricket Australia ignored this. High performance counted Smith's runs, commercial counted bucket hats; the executive paid themselves bonuses and the board lapped up their perquisites. When it came to qualitative rather than quantitative judgement, there was little will or imagination to question cricket's direction.

But don't take my word for this: consult the Ethics Centre's unsparing review of CA, which was found to be 'arrogant and controlling', perceived to 'say one thing and do another', and understood to be a place 'where people struggle to say "no" to people in positions of power and influence'.

Has this changed? Maybe a little. Some quietly constructive changes have occurred at Jolimont in the last few months, as well as more visibly in the national team. But then comes news such as that with which this column opened — the mooted departure from 142 years of playing Test cricket in unblemished white.

It has not been formally announced, merely trailed by a newspaper, perhaps to test the waters.

It is advocated by no individual. It addresses no significant problem, responds to no identifiable groundswell.

It is justified by reference to principles of 'fan engagement': it offers the prospect of replica gear money; it is part of bringing Test cricket into line with other sports because... well, because everything must be in line with everything else or who knows where we are, eh?

It has involved no process of consultation, encountered no contestation. So let's give it some.

Test cricket is not merely a great game, but a beautiful sight with an exquisite and unimprovable palette — subtle, restrained and abiding.

Among other things, the similarity of the white-clad figures symbolises the blend of personalities and skills into a team whole and the following of players in timeless succession. Part of Test cricket's appeal is that its duration allows an attentive spectator to learn to identify a player by the way they stand, interact, gesture.

There's nothing particularly highbrow about this, by the way; it's simply anti-obvious, anti-stupid. But maybe I can put it more succinctly. OK here goes. Numbers and names on white clothing. Look. Like. Shit.

What's proposed, then, is an initiative from which a minuscule degree of accessibility will be gained at an aesthetic and cultural cost which nobody will trouble to calculate because it cannot be reduced to dollars and cents.

It will alienate the sizeable portion of Test cricket's actual audience that is attached to its charm, romance and anachronism to cater for a fantasy audience hardly likely to develop a taste for Test cricket because of such cosmetic tinkering. It's like getting down with the kids by getting Australian cricketers to wear their baggy greens backwards.

And far from 'building the profile' of players, as CA argued last week in a statement to which nobody was prepared to put their name, what could be a greater effacement of cricketers' individuality than encouraging spectators to identify them not by how they look or play but by a number?

So this is cricket administration circa 2019, imposing capricious, tone-deaf changes that nobody asked for while brushing over issues that actually matter. That, for example, went on treating ball maintenance on a nod and wink basis until Super Sport's cameras declined to do either, then shut the stable door after the bolting horses had been suspended for a year.

That is all about accountability for players, but otherwise cowers behind committees, corporate voices and commercial confidentialities. That will reincorporate Steve Smith and David Warner into the Test fold at Lord's in August, and somehow thinks that sticking numbers and names on their backs will enrich the experience. And that, frankly, poses a greater threat to cricket than either of them.

ABOUT THE AUTHOR

Born in London, raised in Geelong, resident in Melbourne, Gideon Haigh has been a journalist since 1984, contributed to more than 100 newspapers and magazines, written thirty-two books and edited seven others. He has been a regular panellist on the ABC's *Offsiders* since 2005, and reported the 2017-18 Ashes for *The Australian* and *The Times*. He is the author of An *Eye on Cricket*, *Shadows on the Pitch* and *Crossing the Line*.

étoiles d

Revue trimestrielle de Femmes en Méditerranée

45-46 - mars 2011

L'étranger

publiée avec le soutien de :
La Région Languedoc Roussillon
Le Centre National du Livre
L'ACSE

France : **Editions Chèvre-feuille étoilée**
ISSN : 1620-5022

Le clos de la Fontaine Bat B
65, cour Libéral Bruant
rue Jacques Lemercier
34080 Montpellier
Tél/fax : 04 67 73 75 45
contact@chevre-feuille.fr

Algérie : **Paroles et Ecritures**
ISSN : 1112-3311

10, impasse Poincaré
22000 Sidi-Bel-Abbès
Tél/fax : 48 54 65 11
parole_ecriture@yahoo.fr

http://www.chevre-feuille.fr/

étoiles d'encre

Abonnement en France : 52€+8€ de frais de port pour 4 numéros

ISBN : 978-2-914467-70-4

RUBRIQUES

Edito

Carte blanche à… une auteure qui parle de ce qu'elle aime, de ce qu'elle lit, de ce qu'elle a envie de partager. Y est inclus son texte sur le thème

Une artiste à Etoiles d'encre : une artiste illustre chaque numéro

Forum : points de vue et débats de société sur le thème

De vive voix : entretiens sur le thème

Variations sur… : textes de fiction sur le thème du numéro

Du côté de l'enfance : textes de fiction ou témoignages où il est question de l'enfance

Mémoire et Histoire : tout ce qui a trait à la mémoire, à nos histoires ou à l'Histoire...

Journal de mes Algéries autour de ma chambre par Leïla Sebbar

La clé sous la porte : récits de voyages et poèmes d'ailleurs

D'un art l'autre : textes littéraires ou non d'analyse, de réflexion, sur les arts, se rapportant ou non à la littérature

Entre nous : correspondances

À livres ouverts : critiques de livres, notes de lecture, ouvrages à paraître, entretien avec une auteure...

Jeux d'écritures : ateliers et jeux d'écriture

Partages : nouvelles des éditeurs, annonces, compte-rendus de rencontres et de salons, votree courrier.. ..

Biobibliographies des auteures

SOMMAIRE

45 - 46 / mars 2011

ILLUSTRATIONS

Peintures de **Witold Januszewski, Elaine Mokhtefi.**
Photos de **Jean Lattes, Marie Malaspina, Marie Bueno, Marie-Noël Arras**, et autres photos coll. privées.
Sculpture de **Simon Manby.** .

APPEL

Envoyez vos textes avant fin mai 2011 pour

le masculin-féminin - octobre 2011

« Le 26 août 1970, une dizaine de femmes remontaient les Champs Elysées sous la banderole “Un homme sur deux est une femme”. Le 26 août 2010, c’est l’esplanade des droits de l’Homme à Paris que les féministes du MLF ont choisi pour se réunir. Pour marquer le coup de ce quarantième anniversaire, elles ont décidé de rebaptiser le lieu “Place du droit des Femmes et des Hommes”. »

La hiérarchisation du masculin et du féminin n’est pas une donnée de l’Histoire, mais est historiquement construite et ce depuis des millénaires. Elle s’est construite et complexifiée non sur la différence biologique mais sur la référence à une symbolique sociale et culturelle. Comme le montre Françoise Héritier, le signe du masculin et du féminin n’est pas un fait de « nature » mais un fait de culture. C’est ainsi que « le genre précède le sexe et le module, le corps [n’étant] pas la donnée première » (Michèle Perrot). C’est autour de cette « pensée de la différence » sur le masculin-féminin qu’a élaborée Françoise Héritier que nous ouvrirons ce numéro.

Vous pouvez trouver vous-même une illustration de votre texte en bonne définition avec les références (nom du photographe, de l’illustration elle-même et date). Elle sera imprimée en noir et blanc et soumise au comité de lecture.

comitedelecture@chevre-feuille.fr

À TEXTES

AVANT FIN OCTOBRE 2011 POUR
SOUS LE SIGNE DU MULTIPLE - MARS 2012

Un numéro sous le signe du multiple. Un numéro sous le signe de nos appartenances et de nos *voisinages.* Notre quête pour ce numéro de mars 2012 sera consacrée à cet extraordinaire phénomène moderne qui fait que nous ne vivons et ne vivrons sans doute plus jamais dans des sociétés closes, barricadées sur leurs endogamies. A des milliers de km les uns des autres ou sur le même territoire, les citoyens du monde d'aujourd'hui se côtoient, se mêlent, s'interpellent, s'écrivent, s'appellent, se consultent, se questionnent, s'épousent, se quittent et se remarient en bousculant les frontières géographiques, culturelles, religieuses, raciales…

L'altérité individuelle est aussi désormais altérité sociale et construira inéluctablement tous les rapports à venir entre les gens et entre les pays.

À vous de nous écrire sur ce thème.

Que celles qui ont envie de se joindre à nous pour raconter leurs expériences de vie, leurs aventures, leurs voyages à la rencontre d'eux-mêmes et des autres nous donnent des nouvelles ! Nous les attendons avec curiosité et amitié.

N'attendez pas les délais, faites-le dès à présent ! Ces textes, d'un maximum de 10 000 signes, doivent nous être adressés uniquement par courriel accompagnés de vos coordonnées et de quelques lignes bio-bibliographiques.

comitedelecture@chevre-feuille.fr

©*Maçafra* recto et verso : « Sac de voyage » des nomades de Mauritanie. Collection Behja Traversac

A toutes les femmes, à tous les peuples - qui à la suite de la Tunisie - ont brisé le silence et l'interdit, nous dédions ce numéro marrainé, à travers sa carte blanche, par une Tunisienne, Sophie Bessis.

Edito : Nous sommes tous des étrangers

Ne me demandez pas qui je suis
et ne me dîtes pas de rester le même :
c'est une morale d'état civil, elle régit nos papiers
Qu'elle nous laisse libres quand il s'agit d'écrire.
Michel Foucault

Les textes contenus dans ce numéro nous disent non seulement la polysémie du mot « étranger » mais aussi sa densité. Presque chacune des auteures l'a traité sous un angle différent quelle que soit la rubrique ou le genre utilisé.

La très belle *carte blanche* de Sophie Bessis et les textes d'auteures qu'elle a choisi de convoquer sur ce thème, nous en donne toutes les entrées et révèle la résonance quasi magique de ce mot. Un mot profondément enraciné dans nos consciences et nos environnements. Parfois revendiqué, parfois nié ou rejeté. Toutes les sociétés humaines et tous les groupes humains, même restreints, ont leurs étrangers ou leur étranger. L'étranger a des figures multiples. Celles qui retentissent de l'écho d'une vie autre, une vie d'ailleurs, une langue d'ailleurs, l'esprit ou le corps ailleurs, d'ailleurs… celle aussi de très proches mais dont l'étrangeté est souvent invisible, inconnue, insaisissable. Il n'y a pas si longtemps, l'*innocent* du village était somme toute l'étranger. Aimé et craint.

Qu'est-ce qui confère de l'étrangeté ? On serait d'emblée porté à répondre : les frontières. Et cela peut faire penser en un premier réflexe aux frontières physiques, géographiques. Elles sont réelles bien sûr et, comme le montre Guillaume

Leblanc dans son livre *Dedans, Dehors : la condition d'étranger,* c'est l'étranger, en s'y heurtant, qui les rend paradoxalement constitutives des nations en tant que telles. Mais les frontières sont aussi multiples que les figures de l'étranger. Elles sont en nous, entre nous, chez nous, passagères, pérennes, dissimulées, intolérables… dramatiques ou… salutaires. L'étrangeté est inséparable des frontières et il n'y a d'étranger que parce qu'il y a frontière, y compris en soi. L'assignation à « l'état » d'étranger ou l'auto-assignation à cet « état » masque ce qui ne peut être formulé par l'autre ou par soi. *[…] chacun voit en soi ce que l'autre ignore* rappelle Metchild Gilzmer, citant Germaine Tillion, dans la carte blanche de ce numéro.

Que nous révèle donc l'étranger ? Que nous cache-t-il ? Qu'est-ce que sa fragilité nous dit de la nôtre, de la fragilité de la vie, de l'être ? Le magnifique et bouleversant texte de Marie Malaspina nous en livre quelques clés : *Elle se réconciliait avec une part légère d'elle-même, si longtemps laissée dans l'oubli. Le temps des lassitudes s'effaçait. Elle nageait dans le regard bienveillant de l'étranger simplement parce qu'il avait répondu, libérant le passé.*

Cependant, il y a toujours une opacité dans le terme, une discordance avec la vie réelle de l'« étranger » et avec les représentations qu'en ont ceux qui l'accueillent. Dans l'introduction de sa carte blanche, cette phrase de Sophie Bessis : *On sait juste qu'on est étranger quand on entend comment on nous parle…* ou celles-ci de Leïla Sebbar évoquant la langue de son père : *Ainsi mon père m'a déshéritée. Je serai l'étrangère, toujours.* Ici, on est distingué par la langue ou dépossédé de la langue. Deux ressentis qui se côtoient, s'imbriquent et énoncent la langue comme un carrefour de l'étrangeté. On peut être étranger par la langue que l'on parle ou par son absence.

Et cette altérité fondamentale, la folie, qui fait de ce qu'on appelle le fou, un autre irréductiblement le même. Inspirant souvent frayeur et fascination. Un étranger parmi les étrangers. L'amplitude du lieu de la folie est telle que ses frontières sont mobiles, indistinctes… l'enfermement physique ou chimique est cette frontière qui place des êtres sur les bords du monde, aux périphéries de leurs semblables.

Une autre périphérie, celle des *damnés de la terre*, on ne peut plus étrangers, représentée ici par le vieux lecteur de la *Coque de nacre* dont nous parle Nic Sirkis avec tant de sensibilité : *Un mouton sans troupeau, sans berger, sans prince. Un mouton hors de la bergerie et sans compte à rendre*. C'est cette figure de l'étranger qui nous hante certainement le plus. Celle de cet effondrement qui installe la vie dans le néant de l'extrême précarité, celle de l'effrayant dehors dehors.

Opacité encore du terme souvent renvoyé à la figure du migrant et d'un migrant pauvre, perdant, en demande d'exil, d'asile. Or, les migrants offrent eux-mêmes au moins deux figures : celle du vaincu et celle du vainqueur. L'Histoire humaine – si elle ne manque pas d'exemples d'exilés contraints – ne manque pas non plus d'exemples de conquérants devenus étrangers pour les peuples qu'ils ont soumis. La terre étrangère conquise les fait étrangers. Ainsi aux Amériques, ainsi aux autres colonies.

On ne mesure jamais vraiment ce qui nous fait étrangers dans le regard des autres et à notre propre regard. On sait ce plein… cette faille… là, au creux du corps nous séparant et nous unissant aux autres. Un signe silencieux, lancinant, impalpable, volatile comme l'éther. Apparaissant et disparaissant au gré des circonstances. Quelque chose en surplomb, un supplément de mémoire, un supplément de ciel. Une richesse au fond.

Pourtant, l'actualité de ce début d'année 2011 nous a montré de la manière la plus inattendue, la plus éclatante, la plus historiquement inoubliable, la force du sentiment d'absolue étrangeté.

Celle qui n'a pas même pour fondement d'être imposée par-delà les frontières. Être étranger n'est pas le propre des exilés, des émigrés et des immigrés. On peut être étrangers chez soi. Étrangers à toute possibilité de décider de son sort, étrangers à la libre parole, étrangers au droit, étrangers à la dignité humaine, étrangers au bonheur, étrangers aux richesses de son pays... Jetés *au bout de la nuit* par ses propres compatriotes, exclus de la pensée de gouvernants oublieux de leur rôle et de leur fonction qui, pourtant, n'ont d'autre raison d'exister que celle de veiller à l'intérêt de leurs peuples.

Ces étrangers-là – devenus étrangers par la captation insatiable de monarques en carton – sont « Dedans, dehors » comme le dit aussi le titre du livre de Sophie Bessis. Ils sont mis dans la situation intenable d'être à la fois chez eux et chez les *autres* – ces *autres* qui ont la même nationalité, la même langue, le même territoire et même parfois la même histoire individuelle. Déréalisés dans leur vie ordinaire, voix et visages effacés, ces hommes et ces femmes, devenaient étrangers, là où ils étaient nés et supposés partager le ciel et la terre.

Aux confins de l'insupportable, ils ont déplacé les normes, mis fin au silence strident de la peur, rompu la logique de la dépossession, du désaveu de soi, et assigné leurs despotes à une étrangeté qui n'a rien de noble : celle de la déroute et de l'opprobre. Une étrangeté qui a brusquement changé de camp, ce qui illustre assez sa contingence.

Non, on n'est pas « étranger qu'à l'étranger », on n'est pas étranger que chez l'autre, par l'autre. On peut l'être dans sa maison, du fait de son alter ego. Y compris du fait de l'autre qui sommeille en chacun de nous, car, comme ceux qui portent en évidence la marque fabuleuse de l'étrangeté, nous sommes tous des étrangers.

Behja Traversac

Carte blanche à Sophie Bessis

La révolution tunisienne est d'une extraordinaire nouveauté, dans sa région et au-delà. Elle est moderne, mixte, démocratique, séculière, ses mots d'ordre empruntent au registre des principes universels de liberté et d'égalité. Alors, d'abord, saluons-la. Saluons cette jeunesse qui déborde dans les rues, reprend à son compte les slogans et les rêves de tous les mai 68 qui l'ont précédée, réclame la dignité pour tous et pas seulement pour elle. En quelques semaines, la Tunisie – grâce à elle – est passée de la mort à la vie. Elle montre la voie au Caire, à Tripoli, à Bahreïn, Sanaa et ailleurs. Elle fait sentir son onde de choc plus loin encore. Rendons grâce au miracle.

Mais la bataille n'est pas gagnée. Les révolutions font si peur à ceux qui haïssent la liberté, par amour pour leur dieu, leur monarque, leurs dogmes ou leurs privilèges. Celle qui a eu lieu en Tunisie demeure fragile et menacée. Partout, les femmes et les hommes qui se sont reconnus dans les aspirations de ceux et celles qui l'ont faite doivent aider ce pays qui vient de naître à la citoyenneté à construire la démocratie. La vraie, et non sa parodie. Une démocratie où la liberté de conscience doit être reine, où l'égalité des sexes doit primer sur toutes les nostalgies patriarcales, où la majorité doit reconnaître la pluralité.

Ce sera difficile, ce n'est pas impossible. Qui pensait, il y a quelques mois à peine, qu'un peuple par sa seule voix chasserait son dictateur ? La Tunisie doit étonner encore en faisant de son territoire la première terre de liberté et de fraternité du monde arabe. Encore un effort, le plus dur a été fait !

Sophie Bessis

©dessin Federica Matta *Ils se regardent, se tournent le dos, s'embrassent peut-être. Que font-ils ?* 2010

Le mot et le sens

Sophie Bessis

Etranger, ère (de étrange). Qui est d'une autre nation : *les étrangers résidant en France doivent faire une déclaration de séjour.* Qui n'appartient pas à un corps, à une famille : *être accueillant pour les étrangers.* Qui n'appartient pas à la chose dont on parle : *dissertation étrangère au sujet.* Qui ne connait pas : *étranger à une science, à un art.* Médecine : *corps étranger*, qui se trouve contre nature dans le corps de l'homme ou de l'animal.
Renvois à aborigène, autochtone, naturel, indigène.

Droit : les étrangers sont soumis à toutes les lois d'ordre public en vigueur dans le pays où ils se trouvent. Renvoi : extraterritorialité. Il est spécifié que « les droits politiques qui supposent la qualité de citoyen sont refusés aux étrangers ». Suivent des développements sur les droits et contraintes des étrangers sur le territoire français.

Le Larousse universel de 1922 qui donne ces définitions m'apprend qu'étranger est aussi un verbe (il étrangea, nous étrangeons) signifiant : écarter d'un lieu. Exemple : étranger le gibier d'un pays (peu usité).

Alexandre Dumas fils, m'indique-t-il encore, a écrit en 1876 une comédie dramatique en cinq actes intitulée *Étrangère.* « Un gentilhomme ruiné, de moralité douteuse, le duc de Septmonts et une étrangère énigmatique, mistress Clakson, sont les héros de cette oeuvre puissante, dramatique, mais d'invention un peu bizarre » nous précise le dictionnaire.

Complétons cet inventaire en précisant que l'adjectif étrange est lui-même dérivé du latin *extraneus*, c'est-à-dire *du dehors*. Dans d'autres dictionnaires, écrits de mains différentes ou plus récents, on trouve quelques occurrences supplémentaires, comme le fait de rapprocher étranger d'imperméable, distinct, extérieur. Ennemi parfois : le parti de l'étranger est toujours menaçant.

On l'aura compris, le terme est aussi étrange que la racine dont il vient, polysémique mais n'ayant, à bien y regarder, qu'un seul sens. Naître étranger, le devenir ? Y a-t-il, dans ce monde, des gens qui ne l'ont jamais été ? À rien ? Il paraît que oui.

C'est un état. Peut-on le quitter ? « Si longtemps que le tronc d'arbre séjournera dans la rivière, il ne deviendra jamais caïman » dit le proverbe. Cet état d'étranger serait-il donc une tunique de Nessus qu'on ne pourrait retirer qu'en arrachant, du même mouvement, sa propre peau ?

Le fait de s'inviter chez l'autre oblige à des devoirs dit le dictionnaire. Mais l'hôte doit-il aussi reconnaître des droits à celui qui s'installe chez lui ? « L'étranger aussi a droit à l'huile de ta jarre »[1] enseigne un autre adage, des temps anciens. Car il est là depuis toujours. Cet inconnu fait partie des intimes, il n'est jamais très loin. À force de proximité d'ailleurs, on ne le reconnaît pas toujours. Les peuples en ont peur, ainsi que les personnes. C'est pourquoi on tient les étrangers en lisière, à distance, c'est-à-dire pas trop près, mais pas trop loin non plus. Car à quoi pourrait-on se reconnaître s'ils n'étaient pas là pour dire qui est l'autre ?

1. Aménopé, Egypte vers 1300-1100 avt JC. In *Le droit d'être un homme, anthologie mondiale de la liberté*. Unesco/Lattès, Paris 199.

Je laisse en chantier cette impossible tentative de nommer l'étranger, de savoir qui il est, c'est-à-dire s'il est fréquentable.

Je vais de l'autre côté. C'est moi l'étranger, l'étrangère. J'ai traversé beaucoup d'années et quelques frontières. Me suis établie dans ce lieu où je suis aujourd'hui. Je suis d'ici. Non. J'essaye seulement. D'ailleurs je n'essaye pas tout à fait. Je sais l'entreprise vaine. Mon écorce se plisse mais je reste tronc d'arbre et le caïman, lui, n'a pas besoin de s'approcher pour savoir que je ne suis pas de la famille. Alors j'arrête, moi aussi, de chercher le territoire où je saurai, d'emblée, que je suis arrivée. Je marche. Ils marchent. Ils marcheront jusqu'à ce qu'ils trouvent, à supposer qu'ils puissent trouver. Car l'étranger porte l'exil sur ses épaules. C'est sa maison à lui. On a les maisons qu'on peut.

Une fois de plus j'arrête. Et laisse parler les autres. À chaque auteure des textes qui suivent j'ai dit : il y a quelque chose que vous savez de l'étranger, faites-en ce que vous voulez. Dites ce que vous avez vu, vos départs, vos voyages et vos arrivées. Et chaque auteure à qui j'ai demandé d'écrire a dit des morceaux d'histoire, la sienne ou celles des autres. Histoires de voyages, de pertes et de retrouvailles, histoires d'une tribu dont les membres innombrables se reconnaissent sans se connaître toujours. Il y a tant de façons d'être étranger.

On sait juste qu'on est étranger quand on entend comment on nous parle : tu ne seras jamais moi, même si tu habites où j'habite. Alors, ils s'arrangent comme ils peuvent. Sans ces arrangements, le monde serait déjà mort.

☆☆☆

Quitter

Terres perdues, territoires trouvés

L'étranger de l'autre

Re-partir

Ils marchent

Catherine Simon

Août 2009, Pas-de-Calais : dans la *jungle* des Erythréens, sous la tente des femmes.

Ce n'est pas une tente, en fait, mais une solide cabane en planches, recouverte de toiles et de bâches en plastique. Elle a été construite grâce aux bénévoles de l'association *Terre d'errance* (à Norrent-Fontes, dans le Pas-de-Calais). C'est grâce à eux aussi que le reportage pour *Le Monde* a pu s'organiser. La tente des femmes est installée, comme celle des hommes, dans le creux d'un fossé, au bord d'un chemin de terre qui file à travers champs.

À l'intérieur, c'est comme une caverne, un igloo. Pas une vraie maison. Il y fait calme et sombre. La journée, couvertures et duvets sont soigneusement roulés contre les murs en toile. On dort là-dedans à dix ou quinze. La tente des femmes est un grand lit : des palettes de chantier font office de sommier ; et les matelas, posés côte à côte, n'en font qu'un, immense, qui mange à lui seul la presque totalité de l'espace. On s'éclaire à la lampe électrique. Il n'y a pas de désordre, juste une écharpe ou un tee-shirt qui pendent à la corde à linge, tendue au-dessus des couchages.

La nuit, dans le camion frigorifique, il faut être sérieusement emmitouflé pour tenir jusqu'à l'Angleterre. Chacun/chacune garde ses affaires, veillant à ne rien égarer. Une bonne paire de chaussures est plus importante qu'un bijou de famille. À ce stade du voyage, de toute façon, des bijoux, il n'y en a plus beaucoup : ils ont été dépensés ou volés, comme le reste. Le peu qu'on a, on le retient. Les espoirs et les tourments aussi, serrés, noués, cachés à l'intérieur. C'est l'économie de la marche.

On mange, on boit du thé, on rit. Parfois des couples se forment. C'est le mois d'août, on les voit qui partent « faire la sieste » en direction des bois. Mais personne ne se lâche vraiment. Personne ne déballe son sac. Personne ne se pose pour de bon. La petite *jungle* de Norrent-Fontes est juste une étape – la dernière frontière.

Chaque nuit, marchant en file indienne, les migrants disparaissent dans le champ de maïs, trottinant en silence en direction de la station-service de l'autoroute, où les camions pour l'Angleterre font escale. Chaque nuit, le groupe tente sa chance. Certains passent, d'autres non. Chaque nuit, ça recommence. Demain, l'Angleterre, la délivrance… Demain… Tout le reste devient secondaire. Tout ou presque.

Une nuit, dans la tente des femmes, au moment des préparatifs d'avant l'autoroute, j'ai aperçu, dépassant d'un petit sac à dos, un livre à la couverture bleu marine. Un instant, j'ai cru que c'était un plan de ville. Un plan de Londres peut-être ? La propriétaire du sac à dos a souri. C'était une Bible en anglais, qu'elle trimballait depuis son départ d'Erythrée, qui avait voyagé avec elle, qui avait traversé les montagnes, les frontières, qui avait mangé la poussière et le sable et la terre. Y avait-il d'autres secrets, enfouis dans son minuscule bric-à-brac ? Elle a refermé le sac.

Ces migrants d'Erythrée ne sont pas des randonneurs comme les autres. Ce n'est pas le mouvement qui les définit. Ni l'effort ou les souffrances qu'il suppose. Pas non plus la destination qu'ils se sont fixés – le fameux *« Eldorado européen »*. Ils sont migrants, parce qu'ils sont étrangers. Et non parce qu'ils bougent. A-t-on déjà traité un touriste de migrant ? Ou un marathonien ? Ou un homme d'affaires en voyage ?

Les migrants ne sont pas d'ici. Ils ont quitté leur pays. Ils ont quitté, mais n'arrivent pas à se poser : on ne leur permet pas de le faire et/ou eux-mêmes ne se l'autorisent pas. Le cul entre deux chaises, deux maisons ? Même pas. Ils n'ont plus ni maisons, ni chaises.

Ils marchent.

*

Septembre 1990, au Libéria, dans la hutte imaginaire d'une petite folle de Monrovia

D'après un vieil homme du quartier, la gamine venait du nord – où les massacres avaient commencé. Personne ne sait où elle dormait. Elle avait des yeux de pierre, pas un mot ne sortait de ses lèvres. Elle passait son temps à nettoyer un bout de trottoir. À en juger par les mouvements circulaires de son balai, elle se trouvait à l'intérieur d'une maison ronde et petite : une hutte ? Sauf qu'il n'y avait pas de balai. Et pas de hutte. Juste le trottoir et l'avenue déserte. La petite avait les mains vides, on aurait dit qu'elle jouait. A la petite ménagère. À l'infini, sans se lasser. *Stranger in the night* pour toujours.

*

Octobre 2010, en Pologne : dans la chambre-mouchoir-de-poche de réfugiés tchétchènes

Il y a du lino marron par terre et une fenêtre minuscule, qui donne sur la route et la forêt. La chambre des jeunes Tchétchènes et de leur petit garçon doit faire 8 m² à tout casser. Elle est meublée d'un seul canapé (pas convertible), où Karina et Rouslan dorment à tour de rôle, avec l'enfant.

Sur l'étagère, il y a du shampoing et un rouleau de papier-toilette. Le reste de leurs biens (des vêtements) est entassé dans une commode lilliputienne en formica. La maison où ils habitent, à une quarantaine de kilomètres de Varsovie, est occupée par deux autres familles tchétchènes, avec lesquelles ils partagent cuisine et salle de bains.

Avant que la peur des milices ne les pousse sur les routes de l'exil, ils habitaient une jolie maison. À deux étages. Avec un bout de jardin. Ils avaient du travail, des amis, ils n'avaient pas envie de partir. Ici, en Pologne, dans les endroits où ils vivent – les centres pour étrangers, ce trou en pleine campagne –, ils n'ont aucun souvenir. Ils n'ont pas envie d'en avoir.

*

En 1997, en banlieue parisienne : sur le palier, où Awa a attendu (en vain) les salutations des voisins

Elle se rappelle très bien son premier jour à Paris. Venue rejoindre son époux, elle débarquait de son Mali natal et ne connaissait rien ni personne. À l'aube, son mari était parti au travail, la laissant seule dans l'appartement. Une fois le jour levé, elle avait fait comme au village : quand une étrangère y débarque, lointaine cousine ou jeune nièce en visite chez des parents, la coutume veut qu'au matin, elle s'assoie devant la case, afin de recevoir les salutations (et les questions) des voisins.

Elle avait donc tiré une chaise sur le palier, persuadée que les habitants de l'immeuble allaient venir la saluer. Personne, évidemment, n'avait pointé son nez. Elle était restée sur sa chaise toute la journée. En rentrant du travail, le soir, son mari l'avait trouvée là, plantée sur le palier. Il avait ri aux larmes, se moquant d'elle et de sa naïveté. Aujourd'hui, elle en rit aussi. C'était il y a longtemps. Depuis, elle a eu ses papiers, quatre enfants et travaille comme femme de ménage dans une école. Sur le mur du salon, un tissu imprimé brosse le portrait d'un village africain, avec le vieux qui fume la pipe, les femmes qui pilent le mil, les huttes rondes et tranquilles, etc. L'histoire d'Awa et de sa chaise s'est bien terminée. La preuve : on la raconte aux étrangers.

***

TERRES PERDUES, TERRITOIRES TROUVÉS

Étrangère dans la maison de mon père

Leïla Sebbar

C'était en Corse, à Ajaccio, dans le cercle du Lazaret. On parlait du deuil de la langue. J'avais évoqué *L'arabe comme un chant secret*, ce livre des questions que je ne cesse de poser à mon père, outre-tombe. Sous la tonnelle de glycine ouverte sur la mer, ou peut-être à l'ombre des filaires, ces arbres qui ressemblent à des oliviers par les feuilles longues et étroites, moins argentées, les filaires poussent dans le maquis, un Corse m'a dit :

« Vous êtes comme moi. Moi aussi, mon père m'a déshérité...

– Déshérité ?

– Oui, déshérité, le mot n'est pas trop fort. Et je lui en veux. Une langue c'est un héritage. Il ne m'a rien transmis, rien. Je sais ce que vous allez dire, je peux l'apprendre, oui, mais je ne parlerai jamais la langue corse. Une langue, on l'apprend dans la petite enfance, plus tard c'est possible bien sûr, mais c'est technique, un outil... »

« Mon père m'a déshérité. »

L'homme qui me parlait a répété plusieurs fois cette sentence, et il est parti boire un café.

Déshérité. Je n'avais jamais pensé à ce mot-là, si fort, trop fort. Déshéritée.

Je me suis demandé pourquoi.

Peur de la violence que j'aurais ainsi reconnue. Peur d'écrire, de reconnaître, l'écrivant, que mon père m'a déshéritée, lui, instituteur, il ne m'a pas appris sa langue, l'arabe de sa terre algérienne.

J'ai cru, jusqu'à ce moment où l'homme corse affirmait avoir été déshérité par son père, que mon père était l'étranger dans la maison, l'étranger bien-aimé, mais l'étranger, celui qui n'occupe pas de droit la maison d'école qui lui donne l'hospitalité de l'amour, l'amour de l'étrangère au pays, chez elle dans la maison de sa langue maternelle, la langue puissante de la colonie.

J'ai compris, ce jour-là, comme un éclair, dans la douceur de septembre corse, face à la mer, près de l'une des cellules du Lazaret où on avait mis en quarantaine les pestiférés de la Méditerranée, un éclair intelligent, irréfutable, j'ai compris que malgré mes tentatives de dénégations, d'un texte à l'autre, depuis toutes ces années, avant et après la mort de mon père, ce n'était pas la volonté de mon père, mais, oui, il m'avait déshéritée.

Ainsi, mon père m'a déshéritée.

Le geste ancestral à l'égard de l'enfant bâtard, l'orphelin que la famille accueille mais il n'aura ni le nom ni les biens. Les plus qu'étrangers, parce qu'ils n'héritent pas. On ne lui laisse rien. On ne lui donne rien. Pas de traces. Quelle mémoire ?

La mémoire, aujourd'hui, d'avoir été étrangère dans la maison de mon père. Pas la belle étrangère, ma mère. Non. L'étrangère pauvre, sans la ressource de la langue.

Et qui pense encore qu'elle ne pourra jamais vagabonder sur sa terre de naissance, enfance et adolescence, parce qu'elle n'a pas reçu en héritage la langue de son père.

Je n'ai pas revu l'homme corse. Je lui aurais dit que c'est lui qui a raison.

Je serai l'étrangère, toujours.

Paris, 14 septembre 2010

⁂

La langue, butin de qui ?

Dans l'un de ses articles [1], la linguiste algérienne Khaoula Taleb Brahimi pose la question de l'écriture « entre les langues », et plaide pour le métissage littéraire dans les pays qui ont reçu deux ou plusieurs langues en héritage. Déshérité ? Hérité ? Dans laquelle des langues est-on étranger ? Dans laquelle est-on ailleurs ? Ou dans aucune ?

Elle insiste pour sa part sur le fait que les écrivains algériens contemporains se sont approprié le français qui, désormais, n'est plus une langue étrangère mais une des langues d'Algérie. « Nous sommes dans la littérature-monde d'Edouard Glissant », conclut-elle.

Khaoula Taleb cite, à l'appui de ses dires, plusieurs écrivains maghrébins qui redéfinissent, en quelque sorte, le chez l'autre et chez soi.

Maissa Bey *Née pendant la colonisation, j'ai appris le français à l'école. Mais le français est aussi ma langue « paternelle ». Mon père était l'un des rares instituteurs arabes à la maîtriser parfaitement.*

Il est mort en 1957 sous la torture. J'avais six ans, mais il a eu le temps de m'apprendre à lire et à écrire en français avant même que j'aille à l'école. Il m'a transmis cela comme quelque chose de précieux, car, pour lui, la langue permettait d'aller vers l'autre, de le comprendre. La langue française est donc celle que j'ai reçue en héritage, une langue legs. C'est grâce à elle que j'ai eu accès au monde, à la culture. Après la période coloniale, j'aurais pu me tourner vers la langue arabe ou du moins m'y intéresser, mais j'ai appris l'arabe classique sur le tard. À la maison, nous parlions l'arabe algérien, qui est présent dans mes écrits, dans mes personnages. Je les entends, je les appréhende dans la langue populaire algérienne. Mon rapport à la langue française est un rapport d'amour. Je n'ai aucun complexe à écrire et à m'exprimer en français. L'essentiel est de pouvoir dire ce que j'ai à dire, ce que je ressens, mes colères et mes révoltes. Il n'y a pas de différence entre l'intime et l'écrit. [2]

Tahar Ben Jelloun *Pourquoi la cave de ma mémoire, où habitent deux langues, ne se plaint jamais. Les mots y circulent en toute liberté et il leur arrive de se faire remplacer ou supplanter par d'autres mots sans que cela ne fasse un drame. C'est que ma langue maternelle cultive l'hospitalité et entretient la cohabitation avec intelligence et humour. Ainsi, que de fois il m'est arrivé en écrivant, d'avoir un trou, un vide, une sorte de lacune linguistique.*

Je cherche l'expression ou le mot juste, mot parfois banal, et je ne le retrouve pas. La langue arabe, classique ou dialectale, vole à mon secours et me fait plusieurs propositions pour me dépanner. Ces mots arabes, je les écris dans le texte même, en attendant que ceux qui m'ont lâché reviennent. C'est une question d'humeur, de fatigue ou d'errance.

Oui, il m'arrive de céder à une errance dans l'écriture, comme si j'avais besoin de consolider les bases de mon bilinguisme. Je fouille dans cette cave, et j'aime que les langues se mélangent, non pas pour écrire un texte en deux langues, mais juste pour provoquer une sorte de continuum de l'une par l'autre.

C'est mieux qu'un simple mélange, c'est un métissage, comme deux tissus, deux couleurs qui composent une étreinte d'un amour infini. [3]

Aziz Chouaki *J'écris en français, certes, histoire oblige, mais à bien tendre l'oreille, ce sont d'autres langues qui se parlent en moi, elles s'échangent des saveurs, se passent des programmes télé, se fendent la poire.*

Il y a au moins, et surtout, le kabyle, l'arabe des rues et le français. Voisines de palier, ces langues font tout de suite dans l'hétérogène, l'arlequin, le créole.

Je suis un oriental, avec tout le jasmin et la vase, mais aussi un parfait clone de la colonisation [4].

1. in Cahiers de linguistique, numéro 34/1, 2008/2009, EME, « Plurilinguismes et expressions francophones au Maghreb» sous la direction de Philippe Blanchet et Khaoula Taleb Ibrahimi

2. Jeune Afrique n° 2404, février 2004.

3. Ben Jelloun Tahar (2008), Des « métèques » dans le jardin français in La bataille des Langues, Manière de voir, Le Monde Diplomatique, numéro 97, 2008.

4. Chaulet-Achour Christiane, Aziz Chouaki : entre héritage et dispersion… in Insaniyat, numéro 32/33, 2006

©Sophie bessi, Cordoue

La musique, comme un territoire… Et voilà pourquoi je les chante !

Sandra Bessis

Les musiques nomades sont à la mode. En ce début de XXIe siècle, les « musiques du monde » ont le vent en poupe, ce terme excluant bizarrement le répertoire, savant notamment, qui nous vient de l'Occident développé. L'Occident ne fait pas partie du Monde, sans doute, à moins qu'il ne lui manque cette pointe d'exotisme qui fait le charme des musiques étrangères, étranges qui, naguère encore, étaient pointées comme des curiosités d'un autre temps.

Les chants séfarades ne sont pas grandioses, ils n'appartiennent pas à la « grande musique ». Ce sont des chants populaires, comme on en trouve sous toutes les latitudes et chez tous les peuples. Il y a tout dans les vieux chants des hommes, toutes les histoires, tous les désastres, tous les espoirs, toutes les fantaisies.

Pour la plupart, ces chants disent des histoires simples, parfois drôles, parfois gaies, parfois tristes. Ils étaient le reflet du quotidien de femmes et d'hommes qui les chantaient depuis si longtemps qu'on ne savait plus très bien, à dire vrai, si celui-ci venait vraiment d'Espagne, de l'Espagne d'avant le grand départ, ou s'il s'agissait simplement de la composition récente d'un cousin, d'un frère, d'une voisine. Car les Séfarades, comme les Tziganes et les Gitans, autres peuples sans territoire, se sont laissés imprégner, au cours de leurs errances successives, par les habitudes culturelles et musicales de leurs terres d'accueil et d'exil, façonnant des formes multiples et restant cependant fidèlement attachés à la langue originelle, lointain héritage de l'Espagne médiévale.

Cancionero, romancero... Les chants judéo-espagnols sont vivants, témoins d'une extraordinaire histoire d'exil et de fidélité, longue de près de cinq siècles. Ils sont vivants parce que tout au long de cette longue traversée du temps et de l'espace, les voix des femmes ont permis qu'ils se perpétuent, la mère au creux de l'oreille de sa fille, de communauté en communauté, dénouant et renouant, recomposant, patiemment et infiniment, les fils de la mémoire et de la nostalgie. Car il est une idée forte dans cette tradition, qui veut qu'à travers la fidélité au passé, l'élan soit donné, neuf et vigoureux, à chaque génération nouvelle.

Alors comment chanter, pourquoi les chanter, ces chants qui courent d'une rive à l'autre de la Méditerranée ? Et pourquoi ceux-là plutôt que tant d'autres, plus majestueux, plus sauvages ?

Ceux-là me parlent, ils racontent une histoire que je n'ai pas vécue mais qu'une part de mes ancêtres ont supportée, ils parlent de cette mer auprès de laquelle j'ai grandi, mariant toutes les sonorités de cet Orient si proche, où se sont mêlés et succédés Grecs et Latins, juifs, chrétiens et Ottomans, Berbères et Arabes, et tous ceux qui d'aventure, entre guerre et paix, se sont frayés un chemin entre ses rives.

Petit à petit ces chants-là vous habitent, et sans que vous ne vous en rendiez vraiment compte, vous vous mettez à fredonner une complainte, une romance, une berceuse. Vous êtes dans la rue et vous vous prenez à chantonner… En la mar ay una torre, en la torre ay una ventana, en la ventana ai una ninya ke a los marineros ama...[1]

Le public est là, il ne sait pas ce qu'il vient écouter. C'est quoi les chants judéo-espagnols ? C'est du flamenco, c'est de l'arabo-andalou ? De la world music, un patchwork oriental ? Le public ne connaît pas cette longue histoire et je ne suis pas là pour faire œuvre de pédagogie, heureusement.

Je chante, toute proche de chaque chant... Les histoires qu'ils racontent, ne pourrai-je pas les avoir vécues moi aussi ? Ne les ai-je pas rêvées, senties un jour ou l'autre ?

Est-elle si loin de moi, cette jeune fille qui guette du haut de sa tour, perdue au milieu de la mer, attendant le marin qui viendra lui parler d'amour ? Où sont les marins dans mon 11ème arrondissement parisien, où est la mer de lait, où est le pêcheur qui y puisera l'encre avec laquelle il écrira ses peines ?

Je ne sais pas ce qu'est l'authenticité. Je n'étais pas à Grenade en 1492, lors de la défaite du dernier des Abencerages. Ma mère a fredonné d'autres chants à mon oreille, nul chez moi n'a reçu ce patrimoine en lignée familiale. Prétendre les chanter de façon « authentique » me paraît être une supercherie. Je les chante comme je les aime, comme je suis, ici et maintenant, un point dans cette longue lignée d'exil, habitant la musique comme un territoire...

Alors la seule fidélité possible, c'est sans doute la fidélité à la transmission. On ne transmet jamais dans l'exactitude de ce qui a été, et c'est tant mieux, sinon on ne transmettrait qu'une matière morte. On ne sait pas au juste ce que l'on transmet. La seule chose dont on soit sûr c'est que l'on transmet, dans un mouvement qui est celui de la vie même.

Tanger et Salonique, Istanbul et Andrinople, Tétouan et Sarajevo, là où le soleil cogne, comme là-bas, ce pays qu'il a fallu quitter parce que les rois l'avaient décidé ainsi. L'Espagne s'éloigne, l'Andalousie est perdue et les siècles passent, loin de Sefarad[2]. Que reste-t-il du temps de la splendeur ? Il reste la langue, l'espagnol, le « judezmo », il reste la poésie, la musique, et les chants, ceux qui racontent l'amour, ceux qui bercent les enfants au berceau, ceux qui rythment l'année, les joies, les fêtes et les deuils.

Les chants judéo-espagnols passent par la voix des femmes. L'instrument lui-même en devient accessoire. Chaque interprète réinvente à partir de la source, cette source riche d'ornements et de mélismes propres à la tradition musicale orientale.

Les femmes sont les gardiennes de ce territoire musical. Elles ne savent pas lire, ou rarement, elles ne vont pas à la synagogue, elles restent cantonnées à la sphère domestique, elles n'ont pas droit au vent du large. Alors elles chantent, dans cette langue qui raconte le temps passé et qui est aussi celle de leur quotidien, elles chantent les histoires incroyables que leur mère leur a chantées, que leur grand-mère a recueillies de la bouche de sa propre mère… Poèmes épiques, affrontements entre chrétiens et maures durant la reconquête, intrigues de palais ou scènes bibliques, récits de captivité, longs développements décrivant le retour de l'époux après d'interminables guerres, telles sont les aventures du romancero…et aussi l'éternel défilé des amours malheureuses, incestueuses ou adultères et son cortège de femmes assassines et d'hommes séducteurs... Elles sont la mémoire, elles sont les livres qui racontent toute la vie, elles sont le vent du large.

Parfois aussi, il faut être léger. Alors elles chantent des recettes de cuisine, les multiples façons de cuisiner l'aubergine, par exemple... Et puis il faut supporter la belle-mère, toujours là, à surveiller le couple... Mi suegra la negra ! Et prévenir sa fille... Mille recommandations n'ont jamais rendu sages les jeunes amoureuses, mais on n'oublie pas la voix de sa mère, ni les paroles qui nous ont bercées.

Laisser au public l'espace pour rêver, pour entendre, peut-être sans la comprendre, l'histoire du pêcheur, l'histoire de la jeune infante perchée au sommet d'un chêne, dont les yeux éclairent la colline et ravissent le cavalier qui la découvre. M'embarquer avec lui dans une histoire, dans les mélismes d'une mélodie, dans les longs développements d'une romance, dans l'introduction méditative du 'oud ou l'invitation à la danse du violon.

Car la musique, pour qui veut bien se mettre à l'écoute, n'a pas de frontières. Le rythme est une langue que tous comprennent au plus profond d'eux-mêmes et la cantilation a accompagné le travail, les prières, les joies et les peines des femmes et des hommes, en tout temps et en tout lieu.

Chants qui sont l'empreinte des peuples, reliés par un fil invisible, comme celui qui, ainsi que le disait Garcia Lorca à propos du Cante Jondo , « nous unit à l'Orient impénétrable »...

Durme durme mi andjeliko (berceuse)
Dors, dors, mon petit ange, petit enfant de ton peuple, petit enfant de Sion.
Tu me demandes pourquoi je ne chante pas.
Ils ont coupé mes ailes, et ma voix s'est tue.
Ah ! quel monde de douleur, ne connaît pas la douleur.

☆☆☆

1.Dans la mer il est une tour, à cette tour une fenêtre, et à la fenêtre une jeune fille, qui aime les marins…

2.· Espagne, en hébreu.

3.· Le « chant profond » des gitans d'Andalousie

© Witold Januszewski, *Géomancie* en couleurs, huile/toile, coll. Particulière, Paris 1971

© Witold Januszewski, *Éolienne I*, huile/toile, 130 x 97 cm, coll. particulière, Paris, 1969

Géomancie

Aldona de Januszewski

Tu as traversé l'Europe à pied, et combattu « pour votre liberté et la nôtre », comme tant d'autres étrangers, qui ont donné leur vie pour ce pays. Finalement, tu as habité la peinture, rien que la peinture, avec le monde pour horizon, et le cosmos comme seule frontière, en jetant sur la toile les signes d'une divination étrange, ta « *Géomancie* en couleurs »…

C'était la guerre, et ton pays une fois encore venait brutalement d'être rayé de la carte. Sur ta route tu l'as croisée, la belle jeune femme brune, venue en France étudier l'histoire de l'art. Elle venait du même pays que toi. Mais ses ancêtres avaient été accueillis dans ton pays, après avoir été chassés d'Espagne, après sept siècles d'une coexistence harmonieuse, dans cette mythique Andalousie.

La petite juive, comme l'appelaient ses camarades, étrangères elles aussi, partait à l'aube, résistante de la première heure, chez ce fabricant de pièces d'avion près de Toulouse. Elle, la fille de famille qui n'avait jamais travaillé de ses mains, fabriquait des pièces pour les avions alliés, dans cette partie du pays encore libre. Ce pays vous a de nouveau accueillis, après quelques années passées en Espagne, quand le retour chez vous est devenu impossible.

Votre pays, barré, interdit, vous aviez dû le laisser derrière vous, abandonné au nouvel ordre politique de l'après guerre. Ces Confins Orientaux de ton enfance, dépecés avec la bénédiction des puissants, avalés ensuite par l'ogre rouge du nouvel empire voisin.

Longtemps j'ai fui, loin, ne voulant plus rien entendre de ces récits entremêlés des aventures de votre couple de héros anonymes. Vous aviez fini par vous installer dans un provisoire définitif, sans retour possible vers ce pays, sur le dos duquel les alliés avaient construit leur armistice, « pour votre liberté, mais surtout... pour la nôtre »...

Longtemps j'ai fui loin, le plus loin possible de vos récits colorés, qui masquaient cette douleur muette, que tu tentais d'apprivoiser sur la toile, douleur de l'exil, de l'abandon, de la solitude.

Cette douleur, tu n'as jamais voulu la montrer, car tu étais un homme solide, un rempart contre l'adversité, celui qui doit montrer l'exemple, ne pas flancher. Alors tu as tenté l'alchimie impossible, transformer le plomb en or, la douleur en lumière, et tu as gratté la toile, jeté la couleur, fouillé les entrailles de ta terre symbolique, la seule qui t'était désormais accessible. Tu as cherché le secret des étoiles et des galaxies, tu as voulu capter la force des vents, le miroitement des eaux du fleuve, celui des lacs et des étangs, les brumes sur les marais, le scintillement argenté des bouleaux, la force des chênes centenaires, le passage des saisons, le ciel, la terre, et l'eau, tu as traqué les souvenirs, toile après toile, jour, ou nuit, au fil des trois-huit, quand tu faisais l'ouvrier pour nourrir cette femme et cet enfant qui constituaient désormais ta seule famille.

Inlassablement, tu as fouillé, gratté, raclé, dessiné des signes invisibles, assemblé des nuances, caressé les couleurs, pour t'approcher au plus près du mystère de la matière colorée, et la transcender, dans l'odeur de la peinture, cette odeur qui a habité mon enfance. Tu luttais avec la toile pour l'apprivoiser, tu reculais, en plissant les yeux, pour mieux voir, la main suspendue, avec l'outil du moment attrapé au vol, prêt à attaquer à nouveau le coeur de la matière, le fil de la vie, le fil de ton histoire. Tu voulais transmettre la mémoire des générations, laisser une trace, comprendre, interroger, interpeller l'esprit dans la matière, incarner la force de l'inconnu, transcender le gouffre du désespoir, créer des passerelles entre les mondes, hurler la couleur muette, tu voulais me protéger, m'indiquer la route, et longtemps, si longtemps, je n'ai pas voulu voir, je me suis bouché les oreilles, j'ai fermé les yeux, pour ne pas entendre ton appel, recueillir ton témoignage, incapable de décrypter les signes muets que tu jetais sur la toile, imperméable à ton patient travail d'alchimiste.

Je ne pouvais pas, je n'arrivais pas, trop dur à porter tout ça, trop violent, trop chargé...

Et pourtant, tous ceux qui ont eu le bonheur de t'approcher, ou juste de contempler ton travail, surtout celui de tes dix dernières années, sont frappés par la sérénité qui s'en dégage, ces vibrations lumineuses que tu as laissé en héritage sur la toile,

© Witold Januszewski, *Harmonie du verseau*, huile/toile, coll. Particulière, Paris, 1973

l'esprit arraché à la matière, le mystère alchimique d'un labeur jamais interrompu, ton travail sur la couleur et les formes.

J'ai d'abord eu la tentation de tout détruire, tentation d'un grand brasier, génération « table rase ». Puis j'ai mis longtemps, très longtemps, avant de pouvoir de nouveau regarder ces tableaux, que pendant des années j'avais entassé face contre le mur, tableaux si lourds à déplacer dans mes déménagements successifs. Seule restait visible la croix du châssis supportant la toile, trace concrète de ce chemin de croix invisible, auquel malgré tous mes efforts, je n'arrivais pas à échapper.

Et puis dix ans après ta mort, l'ami Jacques m'a dit :

– Tu ne crois pas qu'il serait temps de sortir les toiles de Witold du tombeau où tu les as enterrées pour aller leur faire prendre l'air ? Tu sais que dans certains cimetières de Bretagne les gens viennent au bout d'un certain temps ouvrir les caveaux de famille et nettoyer les os des défunts ?

– Ah bon ! C'est un peu comme à Madagascar, le retournement des morts ?

Et grâce à Jacques, tu es sorti pour la première fois de ton tombeau. Dans l'église où on avait prévu de t'exposer, il faisait vraiment trop sombre. Alors c'est au milieu des herbes folles d'un jardin de curé que tes toiles se sont ébrouées, au milieu d'un joyeux bordel, dans les cris et les rires d'enfants, pour le plus grand bonheur de tous ceux qui avaient fait le voyage, dans l'odeur du méchoui préparé par un homme, venu lui de l'autre côté de la Méditerranée, le père de ta petite fille, Leïla, née quelques années après ta mort. C'était une belle journée de printemps ensoleillé, dans cet ancien presbytère, non loin de Chartres et de sa cathédrale, dont les vitraux qui avait ébloui naguère, par leur lumineuse beauté, l'étudiante en histoire de l'art, devenue plus tard ta femme Féla, ma mère.

© Witold Januszewski, *Dessin 1*, huile/toile, coll. Particulière, Paris, 19xx

Puis dix ans encore ont passé, et c'est cette fois ta petite fille, qui sans jamais t'avoir connu, t'adressait enfant des mots doux griffonnés sur de petits bouts de papier, « Witold, je t'aime ! », c'est elle qui à son tour un jour m'a dit :

« Et si on faisait enfin quelque chose pour mon grand père ? Tu ne crois pas qu'il est temps ? »

Alors une autre main amie s'est tendue pour m'aider à franchir le pas, puis une autre, et d'autres encore, proches ou lointaines, mains de ceux qui t'avaient connu, ou de ceux qui souhaitaient découvrir enfin ton travail, et peu à peu, tu es ressuscité d'entre les morts, sur un chemin emprunté d'abord à l'aveuglette, en France, le temps de quatre expositions, portées à bout de bras, grâce à cette chaîne des mains amies.

Et puis un jour ta petite fille m'a dit :

– Et maintenant, tu ne crois pas qu'il serait temps qu'il rentre enfin chez lui ?

J'ai répondu :

– Mais son “chez lui” n'existe plus !

– Oui, mais il y a la capitale de son ancien chez lui non ? Là où m'as-tu dit, il a terminé les beaux-arts juste avant la guerre. On pourrait peut-être essayer non ?

Et un nouveau périple a commencé, vers l'Est cette fois, « en Pologne, c'est-à-dire nulle part » comme dirait Alfred Jarry.

« Bienvenue dans le monde réel » a fini par dire ta petite fille.

Bienvenue « alouettes naïves » !…

Tu avais bien raison de te proclamer citoyen du monde. Cette nouvelle Europe, pétrie de contradictions, était bien trop étriquée pour toi, habitant de la planète terre. Né sur les bords du Niémen. Ce fleuve dont tu m'avais tant parlé, je l'ai découvert un jour. C'est ta *Géomancie* qui m'y a conduit. Ta maison n'est plus là, elle n'a pas échappé aux bombardements. Je me suis assise dans le jardin public, précisément à l'endroit où elle se trouvait...

– Pense à tes ancêtres », m'a dit alors mon guide biélorusse, « dans ce pays qui n'est plus ton pays, peut-être qu'ils te répondront ? Tu sais dans nos contrées, depuis toujours, on est relié aux forces de la terre, et aux esprits des morts. »

– Mais je n'ai plus personne, d'un côté et de l'autre de cette nouvelle frontière, tous ont disparu, alors à quoi bon ? Tu sais bien que du côté de mon père ils ont été déportés en Sibérie, et que personne n'est revenu !

– Peut-être, mais quand même, assieds-toi un moment, et pense à eux, on ne sait jamais !

« *Géomancie* en couleurs », la seule toile que, 20 ans après ta mort, j'ai pu enfin accrocher sur mes murs blancs, restés vides durant tout ce temps, c'est elle qui m'a guidée, qui a éclairé ma route chaotique, cette toile que tu avais peinte pour moi : « Celle là, je l'ai faite pour toi, elle est dans tes couleurs ».

Cette toile, c'est la seule que je pouvais contempler des heures durant, et qui m'apaisait. Rien à comprendre, regarder seulement, le temps suspendu, se laisser porter par la magie des couleurs, et la paix qui s'installe...

Et tu m'as pris par la main, et tu m'as guidée jusqu'à ta maison. Sur les ruines, tu as construit un nouveau pays, un pays où tu étais libre, sur un rectangle de toile, libre comme l'oiseau dans le ciel, comme le murmure du vent dans le feuillage des forêts millénaires de ton enfance au bord du fleuve. C'est Julien, Julien, lui aussi orphelin de ces confins orientaux, aujourd'hui lui aussi envolé, comme « L'oiseau en papier journal » d'un de ses films d'animation, c'est lui qui m'a donné la clé de ta *Géomancie* :

« La peinture de ton père n'est pas abstraite, elle évoque pour moi les paysages de mon enfance, leurs nuances si particulières, les marais et les tourbières, la couleur des saisons... Elle n'est pas abstraite la peinture de ton père, elle est profondément enracinée dans la terre qui l'a vu naître. Cette terre, il l'a ancrée dans la toile, avec des couleurs, des rythmes et des signes à déchiffrer. Bon voyage ! »

* * *

© Witold Januszewski, *Dessin 8*, huile/toile, coll. Particulière, Paris, 19xx

© Witold Januszewski, *L'escargot philosophe*, huile/toile, 130x97cm, coll. Particulière, Paris, 1972

Paris 2010

Nadia Tazi

Que se passe-t-il lorsque l'étranger (l'autre, le dissemblable, l'inassimilable parfois) ne relève plus de l'espace (de la géographie planétaire) comme dans le passé, mais du temps, de l'histoire en devenir, plus exactement de l'historialité dans laquelle on se trouve immergé ou, plutôt, jeté à notre corps défendant ? De quelle étrangeté s'agit-il lorsqu'elle se rapporte à l'époque, au *zeitgeist* qui nous traverse, comme un gaz qu'on absorberait de manière insidieuse, ou pire comme un sol qui se déroberait sous nos pieds ?

Il y a toujours eu des nostalgiques, des êtres souffrant du deuil, d'un grand bouleversement statutaire (déclassement, exil, échec) ou se complaisant dans une délectation morose envers ce qui n'est plus. Et c'est aussi, bien sûr, un signe indubitable de vieillissement, phénomène qu'il est, soit dit en passant, devenu quasiment grossier de manifester dans un temps voué au « jeunisme ». Chaque époque enfin comporte ses réactionnaires, comme sa part de doute et de questionnement par quoi elle fait preuve de santé psychique. Mais ce n'est pas de cela dont il est question ici, face à ce qu'on appelle l'hyper ou la postmodernité, ou que certains dénomment la modernité tardive – en écho à une période de l'antiquité longtemps perçue comme décadente. Le malaise est plus profond, moins sentimental. Et on peut mettre en doute la fraîcheur de cette remise en cause, puisque tout en procédant de données avérées et en prenant appui sur des faits incontestables, elle est elle-même symptomale, et prise dans la mélasse qu'elle dénonce.

Il y a toujours quelque perplexité à se surprendre hochant de la tête en silence, ou haussant intérieurement les épaules, à l'image de ces personnes âgées qu'on moquait hier, et qu'on rejoint désormais dans un désaveu muet face à ce qui semble irrémédiablement perdu. Voilà qu'on est à son tour gagné par l'embarras, confronté à une époque qui dans sa totalité systémique (et non seulement ici ou là, par éclipses) rend le quotidien poisseux. Cela colle comme un papier gras à la semelle, on secoue, on court, on gratte, on se boucle chez soi, rien n'y fait.

À moins que la métaphore soit mal venue, et qu'il s'agisse d'un processus moins accidentel. Cela ne se laisse pas traduire dans des signifiants politiques uniquement. On ne peut davantage l'affubler de connotations métaphysiques sans que cela sonne hors propos : l'absurde, la déréliction, la nausée ou la honte de l'humain comme on disait naguère. Tout cela (ces interjections emphatiques) est usé, l'os lui-même a blanchi, il n'est plus possible d'en appeler aux grands noms et aux référents en surplomb. On nous l'a assez dit, l'histoire est finie, tout comme le monde, ou les récits qui faisaient sens. Et il n'y a pas d'alternative disait Margaret Thatcher, la mégère comme l'appelle Salman Rushdie, et qui a à coup sûr fortement contribué à rendre le monde étranger à lui-même. Il en est d'autres, la liste est longue ; et ce qui a amené les Français à manifester à l'automne, et dont la retraite est l'occasion qui désigne dans une logique d'équivalences un système honni. Les Français ne protestent pas (tous) par besoin de sécurité pour le futur, il se répandent effusivement – sans idéologie ni projet et c'est tout le problème – par pur rejet du présent, de tout le présent en bloc.

L'acte d'accusation face à l'époque est lourd. Certains parlent de grande régression, beaucoup de décadence. D'autres arguent plutôt d'une mutation politique, voire anthropologique, prononçant l'avènement d'un âge de fer inédit qui mettrait en défaut les repères et les catégories d'usage. Quelques-uns enfin attendent secrètement les Chinois, comme Aldo sur le rivage des Syrtes.

Chacun selon son point de vue et son lexique le décline à sa manière : marchandisation de l'étant, homme jetable, techno-libéralisme et capitalisme financier, colonisation du quotidien par la consommation, perte des valeurs et du sens, culte de la violence et de la guerre, société de contrôle, triomphe de l'inégalité et nouvelles féodalités, racisme et populisme, obsession sécuritaire, société du spectacle et médiacratie, culture de masse : narcissisme, crudité et frivolités, cosmopolitisme du vide, *new-age* et dérives sectaires, levée de censure, perte des avant-gardes, des marges, des possibilité de repli, encombrement et pollution etc. Le désert croît… On pourrait prolonger la liste ; en dépit d'une versatilité apparente, cela va dans le sens du reniement ou de la désertion. Et rien ne semble épargné : sous le signe du système globalisé (ou du désert) l'un des maître–mots de l'époque est la holistique (de là ses renvois insistants à la « singularité »). Et l'un des effets pervers de ce devenir holiste et de cet affaissement général, c'est un attachement réactif et un peu vain au passé, à un passé qui s'est éloigné à vive allure et qui pour la jeune génération est devenu étranger, à mesure que le temps s'est emballé et a changé de couleurs.

© Elaine Mokhtefi , *Chrisa*, huile/toile, 56 x 51 cm, mars 2008, New York

© Sophie Bessis, en corse

© Sophie Bessis, avion de la compagnie *Niktam air*

© Sophie Bessis, gare routière au Laos

On vit ainsi dans la dyschronie, un pied ici l'autre ailleurs : le temps du monde fini est dyschronique, avec ses hétérogénéités qui résistent, mal mixées ou mal accolées d'une région à l'autre, mais aussi avec cette nécessité du retour sur soi qui prend la forme d'une politique identitaire. Qui aurait jamais cru après 68 qu'il y aurait un jour en France un Ministère de l'Identité Nationale ? L'autre conséquence malheureuse de ces états du désert, c'est qu'il devient chaque fois plus difficile de se faire l'avocat de « l'Occident » (encore une totalité problématique) face à ceux qui le combattent : intégristes, extrémistes de tous poils qui pullulent et gagnent chaque jour du terrain. Comment en serait-il autrement ? Et sans doute faut-il voir aussi en eux la face la plus obscure et archaïsante de ce moment de l'histoire ?

Mais c'est de l'expérience existentielle dont je voulais rendre compte, dans sa dilution vague, sa déperdition qui finit par affecter l'énergie vitale. Maladie de l'époque, urticaire chronique, sentiment d'irritation qui s'attache au détail et à l'accroc quotidien qui interpelle face à tant d'étrangeté, tant de noir.

Si en effet quelque chose devait rendre compte du *zeitgeist*, c'est le noir. Non comme les mélancolies ou la dérision punk, mais comme l'empire d'une non-couleur, d'une absence de vibrations, l'achromie qui s'est emparée de la rue par exemple. Ou la vision de toutes ces silhouettes sombres, entre grisaille et bitume, sans grâce ni subversion aucune, dans une foire d'art contemporain par exemple : pas une éclaboussure de lumière, pas une échappée, et pas davantage la beauté ténébreuse ou le noir de velours d'une infante espagnole, mais la grégarité dans le temple du signifiant, l'indifférencié même, l'atonie. Mondialiser c'est rendre uniforme, mais c'est aussi fermer et enclore, obscurcir dans la compacité comme dans l'extension de la banalité. Il faut désormais aller au musée, dans des serres, ou dans un pays du Sud pour retrouver l'élémentaire, l'éclat du jour, la jubilation pure et l'art de la couleur. Si comme disent les spinozistes on ne sait ce que peut un corps, on ignore *a fortiori* ce que la raréfaction de telles vibrations modifie en nous. Que se passe-t-il lorsqu'il n'y a plus autour de nous de bleu Klein, de bleu paon, ou de bleu Majorelle ? Comment cela affecte-t-il nos neurones, nos rêves, notre puissance d'agir ? A travers la notion de *rasa*, les Hindous associent une couleur à une passion, un signe du zodiaque et une vibration cosmique, un récit, un dieu ou un personnage de légende, un niveau d'illumination de l'Être… Dites-moi la couleur qui vous retient et je vous dirai votre destin. Bhayanakam, l'éthos qui chez les dramaturges renvoie au noir, correspond d'abord à Kala le Temps lui-même, et par extension à la destruction, la fureur, la terreur. Sa divinité est Kâlî, la mère noire et nue. Vêtue de son seul collier de crânes humains, elle boit le sang des hommes, traite ses fils en ennemis et danse sur le monde, qui s'en trouve ravagé.

On a fini par réhabiliter l'Antiquité tardive, avec ses cultes orphiques, l'attraction des stoïciens, Plotin, la théologie astrale, toute cette période indécise où la superstition et le syncrétisme côtoyaient les spéculations les plus subtiles. Ce qui semble décadent est gros de propositions insoupçonnées et de tentatives semées à l'aveugle dans le grand désordre du monde.

Sur internet, j'apprends que Shiva, le Dionysos indien, qui est blanc car couvert de cendres, intercède auprès de Kâlî sa parèdre. Internet a été la seule utopie de la fin du XXe siècle, la seule « frontière » ouverte, celle que poursuivent encore les pirates, ces hackers un peu anarchistes – encore des étendards noirs ! – et explorateurs. En 1994, on fête le cinquantième anniversaire de la Banque mondiale et du FMI et la fondation de l'alliance *Fifty Years is Enough*. On signe les accords du GATT qui vont anticiper l'OMC. C'est le premier janvier de cette même année, décidément cruciale, que commence le soulèvement zapatiste, alors qu'un an plus tôt les prédécesseurs d'*El Qaïda* ont commis leur attentat contre le *World Trade Center* ; c'est aussi le moment de la distribution massive du navigateur Mosaic, qui apporte à Internet la structure rhizomatique des hyperliens, et les images couleur. On a vu les héritiers des situationnistes et des nomadologues, les arpenteurs d'une nouvelle psychadélie et de l'intelligence collective, les promoteurs du logiciel libre et du *flat rate* (proposition de taxe unique), les altermodernistes proposant le remixage et la réutilisation des « biens communs culturels et informationnels », les gens de la périphérie et les tribus associatives en tous genres expérimenter un temps, un ailleurs. Ils doivent encore camper quelque part, non loin des agents du malheur qui eux aussi occupent les lieux.

⋆⋆⋆

© Elaine Mokhtefi , *Grégory*, huile/toile, 61 x 51 cm, mars 2008, New York

© Sophie Bessis , *Haine à Casa*, 2009

« Me voici donc seul sur la terre, n'ayant plus de frère, de prochain, d'ami, de société que moi-même. [...] J'aurais aimé les hommes en dépit d'eux-mêmes. Ils n'ont pu qu'en cessant de l'être se dérober à mon affection. Les voilà donc étrangers, inconnus, nuls enfin pour moi puisqu'ils l'ont voulu. Mais moi, détaché d'eux et de tout, que suis-je moi-même ? Voilà ce qui me reste à chercher.

[...]

Tout ce qui m'est extérieur m'est étranger désormais. Je n'ai plus en ce monde ni prochain, ni semblables, ni frères. Je suis sur la terre comme dans une planète étrangère où je serais tombé de celle que j'habitais. Si je reconnais autour de moi quelque chose, ce ne sont que des objets affligeants et déchirants pour mon coeur, et je ne peux jeter les yeux sur ce qui me touche et m'entoure sans y trouver toujours quelque sujet de dédain qui m'indigne, ou de douleur qui m'afflige. Ecartons donc de mon esprit tous les pénibles objets dont je m'occuperais aussi douloureusement qu'inutilement. Seul pour le reste de ma vie, puisque je ne trouve qu'en moi la consolation, l'espérance et la paix, je ne dois ni ne veux plus m'occuper que de moi. » Jean-Jacques Rousseau, *Les Rêveries du promeneur solitaire,* Première promenade.

L'ÉTRANGER DE L'AUTRE

L'étranger n'est étranger qu'à l'étranger

Mechtild Gilzmer

C'est de Karl Valentin, artiste comique bavarois, que nous tenons cette caractérisation particulièrement savoureuse de l'étranger. Dans une fameuse scène avec sa partenaire Liesl Karlstadt, Valentin essaie de définir l'étranger – jouant comme à son habitude librement avec les mots et leur signification. L'enjeu du sujet dans une Allemagne raciste – le texte est écrit et représenté en 1940 – est masqué par la banalité du propos. Dans un dialogue burlesque, le maître (Liesl Karlstadt) et l'élève (Karl Valentin) étudient la question « qu'est-ce qu'un étranger ? » dans une attitude pseudo-scientifique. La réponse « L'étranger n'est étranger qu'à l'étranger » et « tout étranger qui se sent étranger est étranger aussi longtemps qu'il se sent étranger » semble aussi simple que banal. Mais sous sa prétendue naïveté et son air d'élève sage mais bête, Valentin cache une fine critique subversive du racisme et de la xénophobie en Allemagne. Ainsi la phrase « l'Allemand de souche peut être, sous certains aspects, étranger parmi d'autres étrangers dans sa ville natale » vise l'horizon borné de l'Allemand petit bourgeois. Pour illustrer son propos, Valentin donne l'exemple du Munichois type, « familier du *Hofbräuhaus*[1]» mais « étranger des musées », ciblant ainsi

1. Fameuse brasserie munichoise et lieu de manifestation politique, c'est ici que Hitler fondait en février 1920 le parti national-socialiste.

© Catherine Shapira, *baby Tunis*, 2008

© Marie-Noël Arras, *Café maure à Sidi Bou Saïd*, Tunisie, septembre 2008

le manque de culture de certains de ses contemporains, adeptes plutôt de saouleries collectives que des beaux-arts. La particularité de l'autochtone c'est « qu'il ne connaît pas l'étranger, mais qu'il le reconnaît tout de suite. » Car image plutôt que réalité, l'étranger n'existe qu'à travers le regard, la perception comme Autre.

Deux ans plus tard, en 1942, paraît le roman *L'Étranger* d'Albert Camus. Ce chef-d'œuvre de la littérature française a longtemps été interprété uniquement comme traduction littéraire de la philosophie existentialiste. Dans un monde absurde qui ne propose plus de sens, le protagoniste, Meursault, est indifférent au monde et à ce qui lui arrive. Son attitude a été lue et comprise comme réaction d'un homme jeté dans un monde absurde dont le sens lui échappe. Il est « étranger » par ses réactions étranges, son manque d'émotion, son indifférence face à la vie. Ce n'est que depuis peu que l'on perçoit qu'avec cette histoire du meurtre d'un Arabe par un Pied-noir sur une plage algérienne, Camus a abordé aussi indirectement (consciemment ou non) l'Autre, la colonisation et l'injustice inhérente de cette société basée sur l'exclusion de ceux qui étaient considérés comme étrangers : les Arabes. Que telle n'ait pas été une des premières lectures du texte s'explique par l'aveuglement général face à l'injustice coloniale et l'eurocentrisme de l'époque. L'Algérie était considérée dans les années 40 comme appartenant naturellement à la France et comme enjeu stratégique de la résistance de cette dernière contre l'Allemagne.

Pendant cette même période d'autres étrangers, des millions de personnes, hommes, femmes et enfants sont recrutés de force dans l'Europe entière pour être utilisés en Allemagne et dans les territoires occupés comme « travailleurs étrangers » (*Fremdarbeiter*), euphémisme qui cache le caractère contraint de leur travail. Prisonniers de guerre et civils de toute l'Europe ont été exploités dans l'ensemble de l'économie national-socialiste : dans l'agriculture et l'industrie militaire ou civile, sur des chantiers ou chez des particuliers. Les chiffres varient d'une source à l'autre. On parle généralement de 13 millions de personnes. Le texte de l'exposition qui depuis fin septembre 2010 retrace au Musée Juif à Berlin tous les aspects de ce gigantesque esclavage moderne parle de 20 millions de victimes [2]. Parmi les photos insoutenables du traitement infligé à ces hommes, femmes et enfants « étrangers » que montre l'exposition, une a particulièrement retenu mon attention, et ce n'est certainement pas un hasard si on a choisi celle-là comme tête d'affiche. On y voit un jeune soldat allemand qui se penche en hurlant vers un ouvrier terrorisé, un juif forcé à creuser un trou. La composition de la scène et l'expression physique des deux hommes résument de manière éloquente le caractère généralisé de déshumanisation du nazisme.

L'envergure du phénomène – présenté pour la première fois dans cette exposition dans sa globalité – ne laisse aucun doute : les Allemands ne pouvaient pas ignorer ces « étrangers », indispensables pendant la guerre pour faire marcher leur économie. Recrutés de force partout en Europe, ils étaient regroupés selon leur origine et en fonction de l'idéologie nazie en différentes catégories et traités différemment. Pour les juifs, les Polonais et les Russes, considérés comme sous-hommes, le travail était une étape sur le chemin de leur extermination.

L'ethnologue Germaine Tillion a connu aussi bien l'Algérie de Camus que l'Allemagne des camps. Revenue de déportation en 1945, elle consacre une partie de sa vie à étudier et comprendre les deux. Partie travailler en Algérie comme ethnologue dans les années trente, elle y retourne comme médiatrice quand la guerre d'indépendance commence. Sur sa proposition sont créés les Centres Sociaux afin d'améliorer la situation matérielle des familles musulmanes. Durant ce séjour, elle est témoin de la violence et du mépris raciste des Français envers les Algériens. En constatant qu'on commet des crimes au nom de sa patrie bien-aimée,

2· http://www.ausstellung-zwangsarbeit.org/index.php?id=242

© Jean Lattes, *Nanterre*, j1972; coll. Janine Lattes

elle se pose la question : « Pouvais-je alors me désolidariser de mon pays ? C'était pour moi impossible. » [3] Mais sa vision des choses change et elle comprend que son expérience concrète, ce qu'elle a vécu pendant la Résistance et lors de sa déportation joue sur sa perception et son jugement de la situation en Algérie dans les années 50. Car « Comprendre, imaginer, deviner, c'est associer selon des modalités inépuisablement diverses des sensations acquises par l'expérience, [4] et acquises seulement par l'expérience ». Pour Tzvetan Todorov qui a publié ces lignes après la mort de Germaine Tillion : « Il ne s'agit de rien moins que d'une véritable révolution dans la manière de pratiquer les sciences humaines ou même, plus généralement, la connaissance de l'humain. L'idée de base de Germaine Tillion est qu'il est vain, dans ce domaine, d'aspirer à la pure objectivité : pour comprendre les autres, nous faisons appel, toujours et nécessairement, à notre sensibilité subjective. » [5]

Pour cela il est indispensable de se connaître soi-même, car nous n'avons l'accès que d'un être humain – nous-même – et il est impossible d'inventorier les autres, si ce n'est par rapport à cet inventaire premier que nous ne pouvons trouver qu'en nous. Si l'on ne se connaît pas soi-même, on ne connaîtra jamais personne. » [6]

La possibilité d'arriver à la connaissance de soi et des autres passe par la relation entre l'étranger et nous-mêmes. Germaine Tillion est obsédée par cette idée que la compréhension du monde et de l'humanité passe par le dialogue. Dans sa préface au livre *Le harem et les cousins,* elle décrit ce qu'elle entend par cela. Selon elle, l'ethnologie et le dialogue entre les humains suivent le même schéma. Ils ne peuvent réussir que si, dans le va et vient de la parole de l'un à l'autre, s'installe un mouvement continu et que les deux positions subissent une transformation. Les fils noués lors de ce dialogue forment un réseau de significations,

3. Germaine Tillion : Fragments de vie. Textes rassemblés et présentés par Tzvetan Todorov. Paris 2009, p. 47 - 4. Ibid., p. 49 - 5· Ibid., p. 25, 6. Ibid., p. 49

une trame jusque-là invisible, comparables aux traces d'un paysage qui livrent leur signification seulement quand on les regarde de très loin, d'un avion par exemple. « Dans le dialogue, comme dans l'ethnologie, on est deux : un interlocuteur (être inconnu, peuple inconnu) et en face un autre être : celui qu'on connaît le plus et qu'on connaît le moins [...] Le dialogue s'engage, la navette commence son va-et-vient et à chaque aller et retour quelque chose se modifie, non pas d'un côté mais des deux côtés, car ce que l'interlocuteur perçoit de lui-même c'est ce que le locuteur ne voit pas, et réciproquement. Mais inversement chacun voit en soi ce que l'autre ignore. Cette confrontation fait apparaître alors des *tracés* invisibles. Il se passe ainsi quelque chose d'analogue à la découverte aérienne d'un paysage.» [7] Ce concept d'échange que Germaine Tillion pratique comme individu et comme chercheur, est basé sur la conviction que tous les êtres sont égaux et qu'identité et connaissance de soi passent par la rencontre avec l'autre : « L'ethnologie est donc d'abord un dialogue avec une autre culture. Puis une remise en question de soi et de l'autre. Puis, si possible, une confrontation qui dépasse soi et l'autre. » [8]

Dans leur spectacle sur l'étranger, Karl Valentin et Liesl Karlstadt arrivent à peu près à la même conclusion : « Quand un étranger rencontre quelqu'un, celui-ci lui est d'abord étranger, mais en se connaissant petit à petit, les deux ne restent pas étrangers. Mais quand ces mêmes personnes font un voyage dans une ville étrangère, ces mêmes personnes deviennent à nouveau des étrangers. Ils sont donc, même si cela peut paraître paradoxal des étrangers qui se connaissent ». Germaine Tillion, qui avait beaucoup d'humour, les aurait certainement applaudi.

☆☆☆

7. Germaine Tillion: *Le harem et les cousins*. Paris, Seuil [5] 1982, S. I
8. Ebd., S. II

Etrangère, et après ?

Zakya Daoud

Lorsque j'y suis arrivée, pour y vivre, le Maroc était indépendant depuis deux ans seulement. Après une phase de grande instabilité, voire d'anarchie, le pays fourmillait de projets, d'idées opposées, d'idéologies contradictoires et de leaders qui marquaient leurs territoires respectifs. Il y avait un avenir à construire, on avait le sentiment que tout était à faire. C'était enthousiasmant. Je voulais y participer, m'y inclure, m'y intégrer. J'étais mariée avec un Marocain qui avait des convictions, j'avais un petit garçon, je me sentais en phase avec cet environnement et en droit d'y apporter ma contribution, si modeste fut-elle.

Un an après, à la faveur de la promulgation du premier Code de la nationalité à laquelle, l'ayant lu, je n'avais pas postulé, n'estimant pas avoir le délai de présence nécessaire, on m'attribua la nationalité marocaine, attribution dont je sus par la suite qu'elle était exceptionnelle mais qui, à mes yeux, ne faisait que devancer mes propres intentions et que je considérais donc comme normale. Je pouvais alors m'installer dans ma nouvelle condition de citoyenne et je me sentais autorisée, légalement, à m'impliquer dans les batailles politiques et journalistiques. Bien entendu, je n'en mesurais nullement la difficulté.

© Jean Lattes , *Nanterre, Foyer,* 1972, coll. Janine Lattes

© Sophie Bessis, , *Yoff, Sénégal.*

J'étais cependant décidée, d'abord inconsciemment, puis de plus en plus consciemment à être marocaine à ma façon, en ne reniant rien de ce que j'étais préalablement, ni la langue, ni la culture, ni les sentiments, ni les comportements, ni donc tout ce qui m'avait construite depuis l'enfance. Je respectais les autres, la majorité, tels qu'ils étaient, mais je voulais qu'on me respectât de même, c'est-à-dire qu'on accepte ma différence, à laquelle je tenais. Ainsi, il y avait des choses que je n'aimais pas et que je ne fis aucun effort pour aimer, comme la musique andalouse, les chanteuses populaires appelées *chikhates* et l'obligation du Ramadan, par exemple. Malgré mes efforts, je ne parvins jamais à franchir l'obstacle de l'apprentissage de la langue. Outre que je n'ai aucun don linguistique et sans doute une certaine paresse, je pense qu'il y avait là – au fond – un refus d'être avalée totalement par ce nouveau pays, ce nouvel environnement, cette civilisation et cette histoire que j'appris avec passion.

C'est ainsi que je commençais à frayer mon chemin dans le monde du journalisme et de la politique au Maroc, très vite blessée cependant lorsque, pour m'évacuer d'un projet, d'un voyage, d'une décision, on me traitait de *nasranya*, c'est-à-dire de nazaréenne, donc d'étrangère, avec la connotation religieuse que les Marocains mettent plus entre les musulmans et les non musulmans qu'entre les citoyens d'un même pays, ce qui fut une grande surprise pour moi, au début. Donc, à chaque polémique journalistique et politique, je me suis trouvée écartée, voire insultée, parfois violemment, comme « une étrangère qui n'a pas le droit de se mêler des problèmes nationaux ». La phrase fut d'ailleurs écrite en ces termes.

Je me suis vite convaincue, qu'aurais-je encore accru mon intégration en parlant un arabe parfait, les choses n'auraient pas été différentes. Etrangère donc j'étais, étrangère donc je resterais. Mais avec cette complexité supplémentaire que les gens qui étaient d'accord avec moi ou plutôt ceux avec lesquels moi j'étais d'accord, louaient ma différence et ma nationalité comme un plus, l'utilisant pour nos batailles communes et relevant avec insistance que moi, au moins, j'avais voulu être Marocaine, ce qui n'était pas le cas des vrais Marocains qui l'étaient de fait.

J'étais donc installée, et durablement, dans une ambiguïté totale et détentrice d'une identité bizarre, Marocaine pour les uns, plus même que Marocaine, disaient-ils, étrangère à jamais pour les autres. Après les premières déceptions, je fis avec, je vécus avec.

Après tout j'avais voulu être différente, eh bien je l'étais.

Il ne me restait plus qu'à devenir moi-même, à assumer cet entre-deux dans lequel je me retrouvais coincée, m'accrochant à des valeurs et à des comportements universels, revendiqués tant au Maroc qu'en France, la démocratie, le respect des autres, le développement, la connaissance, la culture, les droits des femmes et des minorités, dont j'étais. Ce que je fis inlassablement et, quelque part, ce qui me permit de trouver ma place dans ce Maroc qui aime autant les étrangers qu'il les déteste, pratiquant à leur égard des sentiments mêlés d'amour/haine que le temps ne semble pas, bizarrement, poncer.

Bizarrement n'est d'ailleurs pas le mot adéquat, car cela s'explique.

Les relents de la période coloniale ne sont pas estompés et ils ont été ravivés par la mondialisation, par le tourisme, par la politique européenne des visas, par les deux guerres du Golfe et l'éternel problème de la Palestine, et, désormais par la montée du racisme et de la xénophobie en Europe.

Aujourd'hui, les enquêtes montrent que les Marocains se sentent plus musulmans que Marocains, contrairement à ce qui se passait dans les années 60-70 et à une très forte proportion ; près de 70 %. Ils voient donc d'un très mauvais œil les attaques contre l'islam en Occident et particulièrement en Europe et la montée partout d'un sentiment de détestation à l'égard de cette religion qui est la leur et qu'ils observent bien plus que par le passé. Les Marocains se sentent également arabes et critiquent la politique des deux poids, deux mesures que l'Europe pratique au Moyen Orient en pointant inlassablement du doigt l'asymétrie des conflits qui déchirent la région.

La mondialisation a en outre creusé la différence dans les rangs des pays dits du Tiers Monde. Les Arabes et les Musulmans, donc les Marocains, qui n'ont pas su en tirer autant de profit que les Asiatiques, se sentent dévalorisés et à nouveau colonisés, ce qui ravive leur blessure narcissique. La mondialisation a donc provoqué un nouveau sentiment de dépendance. Comme la modernité est désormais occidentale et asiatique, ils s'en sentent exclus, tout en s'en voulant d'y aspirer et de vivre sans états d'âme avec les Mac Donald, les grandes surfaces, les autoroutes, les OPA financières, partageant les goûts des autres, sans y avoir apporté leur pierre ni contribué d'une quelconque manière. Enfin, les capitaux, les idées, les goûts circulent au travers des frontières, propagés de part le monde par les chaînes satellitaires dont les Marocains sont aussi friands que les autres habitants de la planète, mais les hommes, eux, sont bloqués aux frontières, leur circulation est entravée par les visas, les mots, le racisme, les phrases et les attitudes assassines. Tout ceci fait que cette phrase d'Albert Memmi, « *le colonisé survit longtemps chez le décolonisé* », n'a jamais été aussi exacte. Ces batailles d'amour propre engendrent le refus de l'autre, généralement masqué, parce que tout ceci est trop complexe pour être avoué clairement.

Ainsi, au Maroc, pays qui se prétend si hospitalier, si ouvert, qui a d'ailleurs bâti sur ces qualités d'hospitalité et d'ouverture, de tolérance et de vie agréable, une politique touristique qui a porté ses fruits, le mot étranger est une insulte !

Ce paradoxe est aussi plus profond et plus ancien qu'il n'y paraît. Par leur situation géographique, les trois pays du Maghreb dit central sont des lieux de passage, des îles aussi, caractéristiques contradictoires et qui expliquent beaucoup de leurs actuels comportements. Ils ont une mentalité insulaire car ils sont coincés entre le grand désert et la mer, ce qui a longtemps fait du Maroc un Tibet aux portes de l'Europe, aussi jalousement fermé que le fut ce pays et pendant des siècles, derrière la muraille défensive qu'il s'était fabriquée pour se prémunir contre toute pénétration étrangère, évoluant hors du monde et contre le monde qui voulait l'assaillir. Les Marocains ont ainsi développé un fort sentiment identitaire s'appuyant sur une singularité supposée, mais tenace.

Néanmoins, ni la mer ni le désert ne sont infranchissables et, depuis des temps immémoriaux, le Maghreb a été traversé de part en part par des populations diverses et nombreuses. Que le Maghreb en général et le Maroc en particulier aient une population très mélangée, il n'est, pour s'en convaincre, que de regarder les foules déambulant dans les villes et de considérer leurs types humains très variés.

Mais ce peuple très mélangé, qui a accueilli les populations de tout le pourtour méditerranéen et celles venant de l'Afrique profonde, sans oublier celles d'Europe, bien avant la colonisation, refuse le mélange. Les étrangers ont été tous absorbés, digérés, progressivement assimilés et le rêve de tous est l'endogamie, qui concerne encore aujourd'hui le quart des mariages, ce qui est énorme.

Enfin, plus de cinq millions de Marocains vivent hors du Maroc, dont 85 % en Europe. Aujourd'hui toutes les familles marocaines sont concernées par ce phénomène migratoire qui ne tarit pas en dépit de ce qui se passe de l'autre côté de la mer. L'importance humaine, économique, culturelle, politique, de cette diaspora n'a pas encore produit tous ses effets, mais joue un rôle très important dans le Maroc d'aujourd'hui.

Mais, malgré les liens humains, malgré les mariages et les enfants mixtes, malgré les émigrés de part et d'autre, puisque de plus en plus d'étrangers s'installent et travaillent aujourd'hui au Maroc, il n'y a pas entre les deux rives de tissu commun ni de véritable rapprochement. Au contraire : l'incompréhension est grandissante, les hiatus se renforcent, même si les Marocains veulent à toute force, tout en dénigrant les étrangers, mettre leurs enfants dans leurs écoles et envoyer leurs capitaux dans les places européennes, consommer et vivre comme en Europe, mais en gardant des spécificités que la mondialisation atténue et pour la persistance desquelles ils luttent.

Etre une *nasranya* dans ces conditions n'est pas une situation très confortable, mais ce n'est pas non plus une situation invivable. C'est difficile, cela peut être schizophrénique, mais c'est aussi de plus en plus partagé. Il n'y a plus, comme autrefois, quelques centaines de personnes dans cette situation, il y en a des milliers à évoluer entre les statuts juridiques et identitaires, les cultures, les histoires, les familles. C'est donc de plus en plus supportable. Mais cela présente toujours le même inconvénient. Puisqu'on est d'ici et d'ailleurs, qu'on y tient et qu'on l'assume, on est de nulle part, on est nulle part, surtout.

Ainsi pour moi qui suis journaliste et qui écris des livres, je ne peux pas être classée quelque part, ni en France, ni au Maroc, puisque je suis des deux. Je ne puis être reconnue dans aucun de ces pays, étant des deux. Je ne peux même pas être classée parmi les émigrés/immigrés, puisque je suis considérée dans les deux pays comme ne l'étant pas, même si je vis à cheval entre ces deux pays. Je ne puis faire partie réellement d'aucune mouvance nationale et je ne peux m'intégrer que parmi des gens comme moi, des passeurs entre les deux rives, qui ont vécu dans l'espoir qu'elles se rapprochent et qui constatent qu'au contraire, elles s'éloignent de plus en plus. Je ne peux, comme ces passeurs atypiques que rechercher tout en moi-même. Peut-être est cela la vraie liberté ?

***

Français à l'étranger, étrangers en France, quel vécu de la nationalité ?

Monique Cerisier Ben Guiga
Sénatrice des Français à l'étranger

Comment un Français établi à l'étranger vit-il sa nationalité française ? Répondre à cette question peut contribuer à éclairer le vécu des étrangers en France face à l'acquisition de la nationalité française.

45% des Français établis à l'étranger ont aussi la nationalité de leur pays d'accueil. Nombre de Français bénéficient de cette seconde nationalité par naissance à l'étranger et application du droit du sol, par filiation à l'égard d'un parent étranger, ou l'ont acquise par naturalisation.

Ce vécu est divers selon l'âge, la durée et surtout la nature de l'installation à l'étranger : toutes les nuances du sentiment de la nationalité s'observent, fierté nationale parfois dégradée en chauvinisme, affection pour le pays natal et ses symboles. C'est parfois le point d'ancrage d'une personnalité fragilisée. Il peut n'en subsister qu'une vague relation nostalgique ou historique. Parfois c'est l'oubli, voire le rejet.

La situation la moins fréquente mais la plus connue en France est celle de l'expatriation temporaire à finalité économique : un emploi à l'étranger est proposé pour une durée limitée, assorti d'avantages pécuniaires confortables, c'est le départ de l'ingénieur, du cadre commercial, du fonctionnaire. La possession de la nationalité française demeure dans ce cas un des éléments de l'identité personnelle : langue, manière de se vêtir, de se nourrir, d'entrer en relation avec autrui. L'ensemble des comportements sociaux et professionnels caractéristiques de notre société persistent et font que deux Français à l'étranger se reconnaissent de loin à des signes ténus. On rentre au pays aussi souvent que possible. On s'informe. On vote par procuration en France plutôt que dans les centres de vote consulaire.

Plus en profondeur, quand l'expatriation se prolonge, le sentiment d'être français prend le visage de l'attachement charnel au pays, de la nostalgie d'un paysage, d'une ville, du ticket de métro que le héros du *Salaire de la Peur* conserve précieusement. C'est aussi l'émotion à la vue du drapeau bleu-blanc-rouge, aux notes inattendues de La Marseillaise se frayant un chemin entre les parasites d'une radio crépitante. C'est le bonheur de découvrir un vieux numéro du *Nouvel Obs* ou du *Point* dans un kiosque de gare d'Europe centrale ou de racheter un *Monde* ou un *Figaro* tout fripé à l'étal d'un petit vendeur de rue d'Addis Abeba. C'est le choix de plus en plus fréquent d'ouvrages historiques parmi les livres qu'on emporte à la fin des vacances, la recherche passionnée des traces laissées par des Français ou par la France dans l'histoire, les paysages et les villes du pays d'accueil. Le sentiment d'appartenance nationale qui demeurait largement implicite tant que le Français habitait son pays, aussi essentiel que la respiration ou le battement des paupières mais aussi inconscient, ce sentiment se renforce. Il devient souvent un facteur important de l'équilibre mental. De pièces à usage administratif, la carte d'identité et le passeport sont promus au rang d'objets d'identification affective.

En quoi ce vécu est-il différent de celui de l'immigré de la première génération arrivé en France à l'âge adulte ? En rien : même motivation financière à la migration, même renforcement de l'attachement à la nationalité d'origine, même répugnance à l'acquisition de la nationalité du pays d'accueil, même sentiment de vivre entre parenthèses, dans l'attente du retour à la vraie vie, chez soi.

Mais la situation la plus répandue est autre : le Français part pour quelques années et finit par s'installer à l'étranger. Ou bien il se fixe dans le pays où, venu pour un an, il a rencontré l'âme soeur. Il s'enracine alors là où naissent et vivent ses enfants. Dans ce cas, nous avons affaire à une véritable émigration, d'où une évolution différente du sentiment de la nationalité. Elle passe par plusieurs phases d'une durée et d'une intensité qui dépendent surtout du degré d'ouverture et de la force d'assimilation de la société d'accueil. Au départ, le Français a tendance à se jeter dans un processus actif d'assimilation culturelle : langue, alimentation, décoration de son logement, loisirs. Il (elle) met toute son énergie à se fondre dans sa société d'accueil. Il (elle) « oublie » de s'immatriculer au consulat, de renouveler ses pièces d'identité, ne déclare pas la naissance de ses enfants à l'état-civil français. Sa nationalité lui importe peu et il (elle) interprète toute manifestation d'attachement au pays comme un chauvinisme d'avant-hier. Le cœur tranquille, il (elle) demande à bénéficier de la nationalité de son pays d'accueil... en s'assurant tout de même que cela ne va pas lui faire perdre sa nationalité française.

C'est au bout de cinq à dix ans d'assimilation à toute force qu'il est pris d'un doute existentiel : même américanisé, il n'est pas américain et les Américains ne le perçoivent pas comme tel. Même espagnole de nationalité et de mœurs, ses voisins l'appellent « la Française ». C'est au fond de lui-même et dans le regard des autres qu'il se voit comme Français. La phase de nostalgie irrépressible, de rejet des mœurs et coutumes du pays d'accueil est entamée. Et c'est la démarche au consulat, le renouvellement d'une carte d'identité périmée, l'inscription des enfants au lycée français, les prix des billets d'avion économisés pour aller revoir le pays, les parents et les amis de jeunesse. Et puis, petit à petit, la mesure revient, tout s'apaise. Le Français à l'étranger est devenu un Français de l'étranger. Français de droit, Français de fait, mais Français de deux cultures, légèrement distancé à l'égard de son pays d'origine comme de son pays d'accueil, jetant sur les deux sociétés le regard du Persan de Montesquieu, se prêtant sans peine aux us et coutumes diverses, passionné par la vie politique nationale ou le succès de l'équipe de football locale mais sortant avec un petit pincement au cœur son passeport français en arrivant à Roissy.

Bien loin de se réduire à une notion purement juridique, créatrice de droits et de devoirs envers la Nation, la nationalité se révèle, en situation d'émigration, comme une composante subjective et évolutive de la personnalité, susceptible d'éclipses et de retours fulgurants, soumise aux métamorphoses de la vie humaine : c'est toujours le même fleuve, jamais la même eau.

Les étrangers durablement installés en France connaissent les mêmes évolutions, les mêmes tensions entre la préservation de leur identité originelle et l'acquisition au moins partielle d'une autre appartenance. L'oscillation est permanente, plus ou moins accentuée. Selon la personnalité, le niveau culturel, la situation sociale et économique, le désir et le besoin d'obtenir la nationalité française varient.

La naturalisation dans son pays d'accueil est vécue tantôt comme un acte d'adhésion, tantôt comme une source de protection, souvent les deux à la fois. Plus le pays est puissant, plus sa culture est dominante, plus sa nationalité est source d'attraction. Mais si ce pays est simultanément accueillant, si la xénophobie y reste marginale, si les lois ne sont pas discriminantes pour l'exercice des professions, pour le droit de propriété et l'héritage, la nécessité de se faire naturaliser ne s'impose pas. Dans ce cas, une excellente intégration ne conduit pas forcément à la naturalisation. Paradoxalement, ce sont les pays les plus hostiles qui contraignent l'étranger à se faire naturaliser. Ainsi celui-ci se protège, au moins sur le plan juridique, des dénis de droit que peuvent lui valoir sa condition : devant une justice, une administration encline à la xénophobie, que celle-ci soit inscrite dans les textes ou ancrée dans les usages, il se ménage quelques chances d'être moins injustement traité. Il est évident que la France moderne tient des deux modèles : puissante, dominante, ouverte, et simultanément grosse de deux courants xénophobes, le populaire et l'intellectuel d'extrême-droite. Elle induit donc chez les étrangers installés sur son sol une forte ambivalence face à la naturalisation.

Reste un autre vécu de la nationalité, celui du jeune Français qui a toujours vécu à l'étranger. Complexe, il revêt des aspects conflictuels différents de ceux que ressent un adulte transplanté alors que sa personnalité était déjà constituée.

Quelle que soit sa nationalité juridique, la personnalité du Français élevé durablement à l'étranger est profondément marquée par le pays de son enfance : la langue étrangère est sa langue maternelle et tend à supplanter le français familial, souvent perdu à l'âge scolaire. Les préférences alimentaires, les choix de loisirs, les goûts musicaux sont ceux de ses camarades de classe. La France est le pays des vacances, celui d'une famille lointaine, parfois celui d'une école où l'on parle français en classe et la langue du pays dans la cour. Ce peut être le pays de cocagne pour les unes, le pays du rêve et du raffinement pour Andreï Makine, l'auteur du *Testament français*, le pays de l'ennui et de la contrainte pour d'autres.

Et la nationalité ? La règle générale – qui souffre de notables exceptions – c'est que la nationalité dominante, pour cet enfant binational dans deux cas sur trois, est celle du pays de l'enfance, quelle que soit la nationalité des parents. La société prime sur la famille et, en cas de conflit, c'est la première qui l'emporte. Cette primauté va s'accentuant si le jeune s'installe durablement là où il a été élevé. Dans la majorité des cas, il va cesser de se sentir français. C'est le cas le plus fréquent en Europe et dans le continent américain. La désuétude cinquantenaire prévue par la loi s'inscrit dans les faits dès cette deuxième génération.

Ailleurs, dans un pays francophone où la France est présente et a du prestige, à la suite d'une scolarisation française, d'études supérieures effectuées en France, ou bien parce que la nationalité française est protectrice, ce jeune va continuer à la revendiquer et peut-être à la transmettre à ses enfants. Mais, au-delà de la troisième génération, la transmission de nationalité française est rarissime.

C'est le même phénomène qu'on constate en France pour les jeunes étrangers. Le Français s'assimile au-delà des mers et assimile sur son sol. Dès la deuxième génération, l'enfant du Portugais, du Marocain, du Vietnamien est, de fait, avant tout français, exactement comme le jeune Français éduqué au Mexique est avant tout mexicain. Faute d'une éducation bilingue et biculturelle qui préserverait la richesse de ses origines, il ne gardera à l'égard de la nationalité d'origine de ses parents qu'un éventuel attrait pour leur pays, une fidélité sélective aux mœurs qui ne heurtent pas ses propres habitudes. La double nationalité est une phase transitoire destinée à disparaître en une génération. Le double sentiment d'appartenance aussi.

C'est pourquoi la conception républicaine de la nationalité française, inscrite dès les lois de 1851 et de 1889 est une si pragmatique et si efficace machine à intégrer les enfants d'étrangers. Elle prend en compte l'évolution naturelle vers l'intégration sans la brusquer, en admettant la transition par une génération, d'où le double droit du sol. Elle se fonde sur la confiance envers la force d'attraction de sa culture pour franciser les enfants d'étrangers en l'espace d'une éducation scolaire et sociale, d'où la condition de résidence en France ajoutée à la naissance.

Aborder le débat sur la nationalité française de l'extérieur, en Française dont le sentiment de la nationalité a été aiguisé par l'éloignement, les conflits intérieurs et souvent la souffrance, confirme ma confiance dans le droit français de la nationalité. Nous avons la chance d'hériter d'un droit riche de multiples évolutions historiques, souple, en harmonie avec notre conception originale de la Nation et de l'Etat. À une époque où les migrations se généralisent, ce droit de la nationalité offre à la France la chance de continuer à intégrer progressivement les étrangers qu'elle accueille sur son territoire, par un accompagnement législatif adapté aux évolutions naturelles du sentiment d'appartenance nationale d'un migrant.

Octobre 2010, retour sur 1998

Voilà 13 ans que j'ai écrit ce texte et je dois avouer que mon optimisme sur le droit français de la nationalité a considérablement décliné depuis 2002. Ce droit a connu de nombreuses évolutions qui ont transformé notre nation en une forteresse. On y retrouve la distinction héritée de notre passé colonialiste entre les Français « de souche » et ceux, naturalisés de la 2ème ou 3ème génération, menacés de perdre cette qualité, surtout s'ils sont originaires d'Afrique. Il en est ainsi des enfants, petits-enfants ou même arrières-petits enfants de Français qui se sont mariés en Algérie devant le Cadi. Français, ils l'étaient et reconnus comme tel jusqu'en 2002, ils ne le sont plus désormais. Le marqueur musulman du mariage religieux leur retire ce droit en niant purement et simplement les enfants qu'ils ont engendrés. Peu importe qu'ils aient leurs précieux sésames (carte nationale d'identité ou passeport), ceux-ci sont confisqués, les autres membres de la famille recherchés pour abus de nationalité. Après avoir créé ces nouveaux « faux Français », la déchéance est la nouvelle arme brandie par le gouvernement. La double peine qui s'appliquait aux étrangers ayant commis un délit s'étend à ces Français pas tout à fait Français pour ce gouvernement. S'ils sont condamnés pour un délit, ils sont susceptibles d'être déchus de leur nationalité, dernière protection avant l'expulsion.

La méfiance, les discriminations administratives et juridiques envers les binationaux, surtout si leur autre nationalité les relie à un pays musulman, bloquent l'évolution harmonieuse des migrants d'aujourd'hui vers le désir de naturalisation. Ils sont plus nombreux à la demander pour se protéger, moins nombreux à y venir avec le sentiment d'être accueillis dans la nation. La régression de ces huit dernières années a produit des dommages qui seront difficiles à réparer aussi bien pour les étrangers en France que pour les Français à l'étranger.

★★★

RE-PARTIR

©Eve Luquet, *Rêve,* pointe sèche sur cuivre, 24,5 x 31,5 cm, 2002

La halte

Catherine Shan

On n'éprouve aucun besoin de créer si on n'a pas en soi un sentiment de dualité
Sean Scully, *La surface peinte.*

J'ai toujours eu une grande confiance en ce qu'écrivent les peintres. Un peintre qui pose son pinceau – ou sa brosse – pour prendre la plume ne songe nullement à faire œuvre (pour cela il a la peinture), et par conséquent, parle toujours avec une admirable liberté ou une vraie nécessité, c'est la même chose.

À cela tient sans doute le plaisir particulier qu'il y a à lire les écrits de Delacroix, Matisse, Motherwell, d'autres encore, et de Sean Scully que cette page cite en exergue.

Sean Scully, peintre irlandais, immigré aux Etats-Unis, qui a trouvé sa palette en méditant les couleurs des artistes anonymes d'Afrique de l'Ouest et de l'Est où ne se trouvent ni le rouge carmin ni le noir absolu. Ces couleurs sourdes des compositions géométriques des tisserands et des femmes qui peignent les maisons ont un éclat un peu sombre que l'on retrouve chez le peintre américain.

Sean Scully est de ceux qui m'ont appris à regarder – sinon à comprendre – l'art non-figuratif ou l'art abstrait, à regarder la toile qui ne représente rien comme une invitation au voyage. Sans les embarras du voyage. Une invitation à la méditation sur le voyage.

Je l'ai découvert par hasard avec une suite d'œuvres (une vingtaine, je crois) qui ont toutes pour titre *« Catherine »*, mon prénom, qu'ici, en France, on prononce *« Katrin »*.

Mais mon amie Sophie Bessis qui m'a demandé de contribuer au présent numéro de cette revue dit *« Katerin »*, avec la même accentuation tonique sur le « e » que mon père.

Comme mon père, Sophie vient d'Afrique. Et c'est dans un court texte intime et pudique, intitulé *Dedans, Dehors*, mais qui aurait pu s'appeler *Eloge de l'Ombre et de la Lumière*, qu'elle parle pour la première fois de ce sentiment de dualité engendré par cet ailleurs d'où elle vient, ce pays, la Tunisie, où elle ne vit plus, mais où elle va encore chaque année retrouver les soleils clairs, les murs blancs, et une certaine vérité dont aucune rationalité ne peut rendre compte.

Quand on a grandi sous le soleil, vient toujours le moment où il faut en parler. Parler, non de soi, mais d'un lien que l'on garde avec cette ardeur, mais aussi de la pauvreté et de la dictature qui fleurissent aujourd'hui sous les soleils de plomb.

Oh ! je sais. On me dira qu'Albert Camus a déjà parlé de *« cette vérité qui est celle du soleil »* sur l'autre rive de la Méditerranée. Et l'on me demandera, quel besoin d'y revenir ?

Pourtant, si. Il faut y revenir. Parce qu'on ne peut laisser à autrui la responsabilité de dire sa différence. Et il faut dire ce que Camus n'a peut-être pas dit. Que la nostalgie du pays d'origine, loin de nous enfermer dans les regrets, l'enfance perdue ou l'identité blessée, ouvre sur *« cette nostalgie du pays qu'on ignore »*. Et que vivre l'exil permet d'appareiller à toute heure.

Le fait que je sois moi-même née dans le nomadisme n'est sans doute pas pour rien dans ma morale, mais cela m'a toujours paru la plus sage des façons d'envisager la vie.

Quelquefois, je suis invitée dans des intérieurs où il y a de nombreux objets hérités. Que j'admire en silence.

Je n'ai pas d'objets hérités. Je ne connais pas cette version du bonheur encombré de tout ce qu'on vous a légué ; je ne sais pas ce qu'est une maison de famille pleine de reliques et de fantômes bienveillants. Je ne peux pas avoir envie d'en acquérir une, de la mettre à mon goût et de m'y installer. Je me suis fixée depuis un moment, comme on dit, mais mon appartement reste un appartement qu'on pourrait empaqueter à toute vitesse. On dirait que je vais partir bientôt, que j'attends seulement d'aller ailleurs pour reconstituer ma chambre en deux heures quand ma malle arrive.

C'est que je ne connais pas l'ameublement. En dépit de mes efforts, toutes les pièces que j'habite ont un caractère provisoire qui tient à une vague idée de départ, mais aussi au souvenir d'autres manières d'habiter, où les meubles ne sont qu'un décor et non ce décor intérieur qui leur communique la vie. Parce que si on a acquis une salle à manger et une chambre à coucher, on continue à repousser la table pour partager le repas assis en tailleur sur le tapis. C'est ainsi qu'on est bien. Depuis presque toujours. Les nuits où il fait trop chaud, on transporte les matelas sur la véranda : on est mieux dehors à parler avec, peut-être, un dernier visiteur qui est arrivé chez vous à l'heure du coucher. Ce sont des visites où on n'est pas obligé de soutenir la conversation. On peut aussi se taire. Aujourd'hui la télévision marche fort sur la véranda, mais quand il n'y a plus de programme, on reste à regarder longtemps ensemble un ciel où il y a peu d'étoiles. Et quand un souffle vient vous caresser, il a exactement la température du corps. Alors, chacun se confond un peu plus avec la nuit. Et dort à demi comme sous le soleil de deux heures.

J'aime les objets, mais je les garde juste le temps de les polir moi-même et de fatiguer un peu ma vue car mon œil se polit aussi sur eux. Il me faut les renouveler. Et je suis prisonnière d'un troc incessant qui me fait échanger tout ce que je possède contre quelque chose d'autre dont je finirai par me séparer aussi. Les objets anciens me font beaucoup rêver. Mais je ne peux les garder, et déjà je songe à revendre cette petite chaise de buis, cette chaise de couvent si simple et si dure, si parfaite sur laquelle je suis assise pour l'instant et que j'avais déjà échangée contre une statuette du Bénin dont le bois semblait vivant.

J'ai l'air de tenir des propos d'antiquaire. Il s'agit pourtant de ce qui accompagne notre vie. Nos choses... Pour moi, tout pourrait tenir dans une valise : mes outils, mes souvenirs. Je fais à nouveau l'inventaire de ce qui me serait nécessaire si je partais tout à l'heure. Et je demande qu'est-ce que je veux ? Qu'est-ce que j'attends ? Je suis bien là où je suis. Pourtant. Il y a devant moi la photo d'un jeune homme. Il est en pull-over et s'avance vers moi une boule de neige à la main pour me la lancer. C'est lui qui ira de poste en poste en Afrique. Dans toute l'Afrique. Sa famille suivra. C'est lui qui m'a fait une enfance nomade. Mais tout de suite, il s'avance vers moi dans la neige qui lui ouvre la vie comme une page blanche. Quel âge a-t-il ? Vingt ans peut-être. Voici donc deux ans qu'il a quitté Saint-Louis du Sénégal et qu'il a découvert ce qu'est l'hiver. Une saison gaie. Quand je regarde cette photo, je ne parviens pas à me dire que tout n'est pas encore à venir. C'est un appel secret : je sens que je vais partir bientôt. Je sais maintenant qu'on peut devenir sédentaire et garder cette respiration au fond de soi qui dit : patience, c'est une halte, une halte prolongée.

On le sait. Des villes comme Paris demandent à être apprivoisées. Ce fut un apprentissage. À Paris, j'ai commencé à fréquenter les grands musées et les galeries d'art. Là où j'ai vécu, il n'y en avait pas. Au long des années, j'ai pu apprivoiser cet art moderne, non figuratif ou abstrait, comme on voudra, que je ne connaissais guère et qui est une réponse à la vie moderne, spécialement la peinture qui est toujours une tentative pour se réconcilier avec un monde qui met chaque homme mal à l'aise, comme le dit Sean Scully.

Mais il me semble que l'art résolument moderne a un visage différent de celui du passé, que l'art des temps anciens pouvait faire corps avec le monde qu'il représentait, qu'un artiste pouvait être grand sans être rebelle. Il n'est qu'à regarder comme la peinture orientaliste était en accord avec le monde qu'elle représentait. Il n'est qu'à regarder les dessins de Delacroix qui décrivent *« les pays des soleils clairs et des murs blancs »*, le pays de Sophie Bessis.

Il est vrai qu'*« on n'éprouve aucun besoin de créer si on n'a pas en soi un sentiment de dualité »*. Mais c'est une vérité du monde moderne où il est impossible de s'accorder immédiatement à ce qu'est ce monde.

☆☆☆

BIOGRAPHIES DES CONTRIBUTRICES À LA CARTE BLANCHE

Sophie Bessis : Historienne de formation, Sophie Bessis a été journaliste pendant de nombreuses années, notamment à l'hebdomadaire *Jeune Afrique*. Spécialiste des questions liées aux relations Nord-Sud et au développement, et de la question des femmes, essentiellement dans le monde arabe et en Afrique, elle a enseigné à l'Institut national des langues et civilisations orientales, d'abord, puis au département de sciences politiques de l'Université Paris I. Elle est actuellement chercheuse associée à l'Institut de Relations Internationales et Stratégiques (IRIS, Paris) et Secrétaire générale adjointe de la Fédération internationale des droits de l'homme (FIDH). Derniers ouvrages : *L'Occident et les autres, histoire d'une suprématie*, La Découverte, 2001 ; *Las emergencias del mundo : economia, poder, alteridad. Ediciones Nobel*, Oviedo, Espagne 2005 ; *Les Arabes, les femmes, la liberté*, Albin Michel, 2007 ; *Dedans, dehors*, Elyzad, 2010.

Sandra Bessis : Née en Tunisie et ayant vécu dans plusieurs pays avant de s'installer à Paris, Sandra Bessis a étudié la guitare classique et le chant parallèlement à des études littéraires. Elle interprète depuis plus de vingt ans le répertoire de la musique judéo-espagnole de l'Andalousie médiévale et de l'ensemble du pourtour méditerranéen. Elle est accueillie par de nombreuses scènes en France, en Europe et dans les pays du Maghreb. Elle a édité quatre CD, dont le dernier s'intitule *Entre deux rives, chants sépharades et autres chants de la Méditerranée.*

Monique Cerisier Ben Guiga : Après une jeunesse sarthoise et des années d'études parisiennes, Monique Cerisier Ben Guiga s'établit en Tunisie en 1969 avec son mari tunisien et leurs trois enfants binationaux. Elle y enseigne le français dans des lycées tunisiens. Elle participe à la fondation de l'Association Démocratique des Français de l'Etranger (ADFE) où elle défend le principe d'un soutien à la défense des droits de tous les Français de Tunisie, aussi bien les personnes âgées restées seules après l'indépendance que les conjointes françaises de citoyens tunisiens et leurs enfants binationaux.
Elle est élue représentante des Français de Tunisie au Conseil Supérieur des Français à l'Etranger en 1988 puis Sénatrice représentant les Français établis hors de France en 1992 et en 2001.

Zakya Daoud : Journaliste et écrivaine, Zakya Daoud a été la fondatrice et la rédactrice en chef de la revue marocaine *Lamalif*. Elle a publié plusieurs biographies historiques, dont *Abdelkrim, une épopée d'or et de sang* aux éditions Séguier et *Mehdi Ben Barka* aux éditions Michalon. Elle est également l'auteure de plusieurs essais et de deux romans : *Zaynab, reine de Marrakech* et *Les petits-enfants de Zaynab*, éd. de l'Aube.

Mechtild Gilzmer : Mechtild Gilzmer est professeure de Littérature et de Civilisation Française et Francophone à l'Université Technique de Berlin. Ses recherches ont porté sur l'histoire de l'internement des femmes en France entre 1939 et 1944. Elle a également travaillé sur la mémoire de la deuxième guerre mondiale en France. Plus récemment, elle a réalisé des recherches sur la littérature et le cinéma francophones maghrébins, et plus particulièrement sur la diaspora sépharade au Québec.

Aldona de Januszewski : Aldona de Januszewski est auteure de récits, de nouvelles et de poésie. Elle a également réalisé plusieurs courts-métrages (fiction et documentaire). Après des études d'ethnologie, de théâtre et de cinéma, elle a travaillé plusieurs années au Maghreb et en Afrique de l'Ouest. Elle a fondé Lez'Arts intervention, une association qui développe des projets culturels et artistiques. Dans ce cadre elle a organisé depuis 2004 plusieurs expositions de peintures en France et à l'étranger. En 2011 plusieurs expositions du peintre Witold Januszewski (1915-1981) seront présentées à Paris et en Pologne à l'occasion du 30e anniversaire de la mort de l'artiste.

Jean Lattes : Photo-reporter à France-Dimanche, Elle, Paris-Match Life Magazine et Time pour lequel il travailla pendant plus de vingt ans. Ces photos font partie de l'exposition *Six photographes en quête de banlieue*, BPI, Centre Pompidou, Paris, 1977.

Eve Luquet : Eve Luquet a exposé pour la première fois ses gravures à Paris en 1985. Elle pratique le dessin, la gravure et la peinture. Les thèmes récurrents de son travail sont la lumière, le monde végétal comme tissu vivant, l'eau, les éléments, et aussi le corps humain. Elle a fait de nombreuses expositions de ses oeuvres en France et en Europe.

Federica Matta : Federica Matta est née en France d'une mère bostonienne et d'un père chilien, le peintre Roberto Matta. Après une enfance française, elle parcourt le monde dès l'âge de seize ans et commence à dessiner, à peindre et à sculpter. Elle n'a pas cessé depuis. Elle est l'auteure de plusieurs sculptures urbaines monumentales, notamment au Chili et en France (*Le voyage de la sirène* à Saint Nazaire, dont elle a aussi fait un livre, entre autres). Elle a fait de très nombreuses expositions de ses oeuvres, sur tous les continents. Elle a également illustré plusieurs ouvrages, dont celui consacré au poète soufi persan *Rumi* (Albin Michel Paris).

Elaine Mokhtefi : journaliste, elle a épousé un Algérien rencontré à Alger. Elle a occupé de nombreuses fonctions dans ce pays dont journaliste et enseignante. À son départ d'Alger, elle a publié un livre documentaire pour les jeunes sur la guerre de sécession, 1990, éd. Nathan, et un autre sur les quartiers noirs de New York, 1992, ed. Albin Michel. Elle a également conçu et rédigé un guide de Paris et un autre de la France pour une maison d'édition new-yorkaise, ainsi qu'une histoire illustrée de Paris. Elle expose ses peintures en Amérique et en France.

Leïla Sebbar : née à Aflou en Algérie, d'un père algérien et d'une mère française, elle est romancière et nouvelliste et vit à Paris. Auteure de nombreux ouvrages et directrice de nombreux livres collectifs aux éd. Gallimard, Bleu autour et Chèvre-feuille étoilée. Aux éd. Chèvre Feuille Etoilée, *Mon père*, 2007 et *Ma mère*, 2008. Parmi ses titres récents : Fatima ou les Algériennes au square (poche Elyzad), 2010 ; *Mon cher fils*, Elyzad, 2009 ; *Voyage en Algérie autour de ma chambre,* Bleu autour, 2008 ; *Isabelle l'Algérien, portrait d'Isabelle Eberhardt*, nouvelles, dessins de Sébastien Pignon, Al Manar, 2005 ; *Journal de mes Algéries en France* 2005 ; *Je ne parle pas la langue de mon père*, Julliard, 2003.

Catherine Shan : Franco-sénégalaise, Catherine Shan a passé son enfance en Afrique. Après avoir enseigné quelques années la philosophie, elle a travaillé à l'Unesco, puis exercé le métier de journaliste. Elle a publié *Gens de sable* aux éditions P.O.L. ; *La vie à deux* aux éditions Balland et *Sa vie africaine* aux éditions Gallimard. Elle a également réalisé plusieurs films sur la danse.

Catherine Schapira : journaliste, iconographe, elle est l'auteur de la photo : *Tunis, hiver 2008*. Galerie aux climatiseurs avec, au fond, l'enseigne du monde des jouets.

Catherine Simon : Journaliste, grand reporter au quotidien français *Le Monde* dont elle a été la dernière correspondante en Algérie. Elle a publié trois romans policiers : *Un baiser sans moustaches*, Gallimard collection Série noire ; *Du pain et des roses* et *On ne quittera jamais le territoire des loups* aux éditions de l'Aube. Elle a également publié en 2009 aux éditions La Découverte *Algérie, les années Pieds-Rouges, des rêves de l'indépendance au désenchantement 1962-1969*.

Khaoula Taleb Ibrahimi : Spécialiste en Sciences du langage, Khaoula TALEB IBRAHIMI est professeure à l'Université d'Alger, où elle dirige le Laboratoire de Linguistique, sociolinguistique et Didactique des Langues. Elle a publié de nombreux ouvrages et articles, en arabe et en français, sur la question des langues en Algérie dont, notamment, *Les Algériens et leur(s) langue(s)* (El Hikma, Alger, 1997). Elle a participé à l'ouvrage de Mohamed Harbi et Benjamin Stora, *La guerre d'Algérie,* Laffont, Paris, 2004.

Nadia TAZI : Philosophe de formation, Nadia Tazi est journaliste à la fondation de L'Autre Journal et éditrice pour plusieurs maisons d'éditions. Elle a publié, entre autres *Les mots du monde* aux éditions La Découverte. Elle est actuellement Directrice de Programme au Collège International de Philosophie à Paris.

★★★

© Jean Lattes, *Nanterre,* 1972, coll. Janine Lattes.

Forum

Un film, un livre, un événement, une question sociale et culturelle... ?

Faites nous partager vos coups de coeur et vos coups de sang ! Tout ce qui vous interpelle...

Cette rubrique est là pour recueillir vos impressions et ouvrir le débat.

N'hésitez pas à réagir quelle que soit votre opinion.

Il y a un étranger dans la ville

Il y a un étranger dans la ville
J'ai vu son regard clair allumer d'étranges miroirs sur le fleuve
J'ai vu sous les ponts les courants palpiter en de sombres lueurs
J'ai vu l'étranger se pencher et interroger l'infinie tristesse de l'onde
- les noyés-
J'ai vu le faisceau blanc d'une torche unir les statues
Comme le fait le ciel à l'heure du partage des eaux
L'étranger parcourt la ville et comme le songe d'une nostalgie,
Sa musique s'installe au cœur, de plus en plus profonde
Il est là où chacun fuit, sa présence ou son ombre redoutées
- et puis -
Quel est son nom?
Apparu, disparu, il veille et comme un souvenir qui hante et qui enfreint
Il dit la prédiction qui s'abat au matin
Tandis qu'il accourt et montre le chemin
Tragique et innocent, le désespoir serein, il avance à pas lents
Étrange sacristain aux antiques prières
Aux confessions tronquées
À la foudre des cœurs, à l'oubli des chagrins
L'étranger dans la ville a pour nom le destin.

Nicole Barrière

« S'aimer soi-même comme un étranger »

Behja Traversac

J'emprunte ce titre, chargé de sens, à Jean-Michel Hirt[1], mis en exergue de son livre Les infidèles qui m'a beaucoup appris et surtout m'a éclairée sur le sens de l'être et de son rapport à l'autre en soi et l'autre hors soi.

Je choisis de parler ici des unions interculturelles parce que dans ce qui nous occupe sur le dialogue des cultures, il me semble que l'union interculturelle est, dans la majorité des situations, l'un des pôles les plus irréductibles à la clôture sur soi et ceci du fait même qu'il est un lieu affectif de la rencontre entre les cultures.

Même si l'union interculturelle se présente, dans de nombreuses sociétés, comme une entrée par effraction du couple dans les deux milieux d'origine, elle est aussi l'entrée, pour chaque membre du couple, dans une autre terre, celle qui matérialise le départ d'un lieu et l'arrivée ailleurs, celle qui se cultive de renoncements et de découvertes, de ruptures et de retrouvailles. C'est un lieu où s'entremêlent les héritages, un lieu du déplacement. C'est aussi une ère de passeurs, les passeurs d'amour, de gestes et de mots, le pays de ces présences multiples tragiquement absentes des sociétés qui se veulent closes, monolithiques, endogames, mais qui ne peuvent

1. Les Infidèles, Grasset, 2003

d'ailleurs jamais l'être tout à fait. L'union interculturelle est dépositaire d'un legs qui met au jour la part aliénée du rapport qu'ont édifié toutes les sociétés avec la matrimonialité et ce qu'elles en projettent, non seulement dans leur vision des deux sexes mais aussi dans la hiérarchie et le sens qu'elles confèrent à l'ensemble de leurs rapports, à leurs valeurs, à leurs comportements envers l'étranger, ce miroir dans lequel on refuse de voir son reflet, cet « autre-autre », quintessence de la différence, méprisé et craint, inaccessible, inconcevable dans le lit de la fille, de la sœur… quand il est de sexe masculin.

Alors, l'union interculturelle, du fait même qu'elle est ce révélateur, est également un espace de médiation où se négocie et se transforme, par un aller-retour permanent, la distance culturelle objet de tant d'effrois. C'est certes une terre de dissidence, de rébellion contre les archaïsmes et contre le sort que ceux-ci réservent à l'étranger intérieur – dont la figure de la femme est l'icone – et à l'étranger extérieur – celui dont la langue, la peau, l'histoire sont différentes, mais les terres de dissidence ne sont-elles pas souvent celles de la renaissance, de la vitalité, de l'élection… ?

« La constitution d'un couple est l'événement-étincelle qui fait apparaître les racismes les plus camouflés, les plus inconscients [2]. » disait Albert Jacquard. Ceux qui nous mettent face à la peur de l'autre et de nous-mêmes ; ceux qui provoquent nos dénonciations et nos colères devant le refus du dialogue, de la métamorphose, du risque de l'autre. L'union interculturelle,

2. Albert Jacquard – généticien, dans sa préface au livre d'Augustin Barbara « Les couples mixtes » Bayard 1993.

c'est ce continent où l'autre n'est pas tout à fait autre, pas tout à fait étranger, où les liens se fondent sur une réciproque traversée, un mutuel passage de chaque côté du pont, ouvrant l'espace de l'hospitalité des cultures, des langues, des territoires physiques et symboliques... En fait, un lieu où s'arraisonne l'ailleurs, où l'éloignement se fait jonction, où la différence est destination parce que justement ces unions sont le signe de reconnaissance du dedans et du dehors, de l'autre en soi, de soi en l'autre, un voyage quotidien dans l'altérité.

Depuis la nuit des temps, il s'est trouvé des hommes et des femmes, acteurs et témoins de leurs époques, qui ont transgressé les interdits de leurs sociétés et ont inscrit à jamais dans l'histoire des peuples, la marque du multiple, de l'ailleurs. Ces unions, sont ce franchissement, cette échappée hors des frontières, la continuité des pérégrinations millénaires des êtres humains.

***

© Marie-Noël Arras, *La petite vierge de Santa Cruz, Algériens, Français et « Pieds-noirs » viennent la prier d'exaucer un voeu*, Oran, 2007

L'étranger et l'étrangère

Marie-Noël Arras

Est-ce génétique dans ma famille ou dû à l'hospitalité de mes parents ? Sur six enfants, cinq ont épousé des étrangers(ères) et quatre ont vécu comme étrangers (ère) plusieurs années de leur vie.

Depuis toujours je voulais vivre « ailleurs ». Je m'en souviens. Bizarrement, vivre en France, plus tard, adulte, était pour moi synonyme d'ennui alors que je ne me suis jamais ennuyée enfant. Nous avions de nombreuses activités, de nombreux amis, français et étrangers….

Je ne sais pourquoi mais les étrangers m'ont toujours attirée. Soit je me battais pour les déshérités (les affamés, les illettrés) soit je recherchais leur amitié.

Ce n'est donc pas étonnant si un jour, à défaut de me rendre à Lambaréné comme j'en avais rêvé, je me suis mariée à un algérien et suis venue avec mes trois enfants vivre ici en Algérie, à Sidi-Bel-Abbès.

En France pendant les sept ans de notre vie commune c'était lui l'étranger, lui qui pourtant était allé à l'école de Jules Ferry et avait appris que ses ancêtres étaient les gaulois, lui qui me récitait Lamartine par cœur et pour qui il était venu en pèlerinage sur les rives du lac du Bourget. *Ainsi, toujours poussés vers de nouveaux rivages / Dans la nuit éternelle emportés sans retour / Ne pourrons-nous jamais sur l'océan des âges / Jeter l'ancre un seul jour.* Lui qui avait subi la guerre d'indépendance et n'avait pourtant aucune rancœur envers les français... Je n'aurais jamais pour lui employé le mot « intégré », il était comme moi, c'est tout, et à l'aise dans ce pays comme s'il y avait toujours vécu. Ce n'est que le regard des autres qui lui faisait – et me faisait – prendre conscience de son statut d'étranger. Il dut s'inscrire à la préfecture pour étudier à l'université, puis à la mairie du village où nous avons commencé à travailler. Les policiers qui l'arrêtaient au bord de la route le tutoyaient. Malgré tout c'est moi qui l'ai poussé à quitter cette France-là pour venir nous établir dans son pays, ce pays dont j'ignorais tout ou presque.

En Algérie, c'est moi qui suis devenue l'étrangère. Et en un certain sens, je l'étais doublement : je ne parlais pas, comme lui, la langue du pays d'accueil même si beaucoup parlaient la mienne. Je ne connaissais pas les us et coutumes locales, je ne savais pas ce que je devais faire. M'intégrer ou m'adapter ? Respecter ces coutumes ou les adopter ?

Ce fut un long cheminement avec des allers et retours. Apprendre déjà la nourriture, les plats, les fêtes, préparer les gâteaux de l'Aïd es-sghir, préparer le mouton sacrifié de l'Aïd el-Kebir – ce que j'ai refusé de faire à partir du moment où les « terroristes » ont commencé à égorger des êtres humains – apprendre à danser pour les mariages, à suivre les rites funéraires, tout ce qui fait une culture… et même faire le ramadhan, quelques jours d'abord puis un mois entier, non par conviction religieuse mais pour savoir ce que les autres autour de moi ressentent, pour « communier » avec eux autour de la table du soir et comme une offrande pour l'âme de la grand-mère que j'avais adoptée, dada Aïcha. Et, malgré cela, rester moi-même, la *roumia*, la *gaouria*, la française, selon l'interlocuteur, mais tout cela sans décision consciente.

Lors de mes vacances familiales en France, je me sentais un peu décalée. Jusqu'au jour, où un ami coopérant qui préparait son déménagement me dit : « Marie-Noël, si tu veux rester dans ce pays tu devras t'intégrer et un jour faire le choix de mettre le voile, sinon il te faudra partir ! » à quoi j'ai répondu de suite « Jamais ! » Et j'ai su ce jour-là exprimer clairement que pour moi s'intégrer ne voulait pas dire s'assimiler, que je resterai toujours différente, toujours l'étrangère et que cela me convenait très bien. Les années noires que nous vécûmes par la suite lui ont donné raison et lorsqu'il fut décrété qu'en tant qu'étrangère « si je restais au pays j'étais responsable de ma mort subite » je partis, du moins je m'éloignais...

Rentrer chez soi dans un pays que l'on ne connait plus... Voir un pays en vacances, n'est pas comme y vivre. Là aussi il faut un certain temps de réadaptation (de réintégration ?)

Comme je l'ai écrit quelques temps après, un 8 mars, dans un texte intitulé « Le chèvrefeuille », je me sentais étrangère dans mon propre pays. Étrangère non pas dans le regard de l'autre comme c'était le cas pour mon époux en France mais dans le regard que je projetais sur les autres… comme à travers un voile. Et par exemple je dois dire que je n'ai jamais fait autant de cuisine algérienne que lorsque je me suis installée dans une maison et que j'ai réussi à faire venir mon fils qui n'avait jamais vécu en France, malgré le déchirement de son père qui, lui, ne voulait pas quitter son pays, sa maison, son atelier. Mon fils était un français étranger.

Si j'ai trouvé excellent le texte de Mechtild Gilzmer dans la carte blanche de Sophie Bessis, et que je suis d'accord – comme elle – avec Germaine Tillion, je comprends son titre : « L'étranger n'est étranger qu'à l'étranger » mais n'y adhère pas totalement car on peut, je l'ai vécu, se sentir étrangère chez soi. Se sentir appartenir à un pays ne peut se faire que par l'action, le travail, la participation associative, la culture. C'est ainsi que j'ai quitté mon étrangéité. Mais à ce jour, je me rends compte que mes amies les plus proches ont vécu ailleurs, soit à l'étranger soit venant de l'étranger... Ce n'est pas le cas pour quatre d'entre elles mais ce sont des créatrices et en ce sens elles sont « étranges-ères » dans leur propre pays.

Aujourd'hui, avec la réalisation des éditions et de cette revue, avec toutes les amitiés que cela a engendré, avec la maturité et l'épanouissement que je ressens, grâce à toutes les rencontres autour de ce travail, de cette passion, je ne ressens plus en moi ce statut d'étrangère qui a tout à prouver pour être acceptée. Je sais pertinemment qu'ici en Algérie où j'écris cette nuit, je le resterai toujours pour les autres, mais pour moi, je suis Moi et je l'assume dans les deux pays où je vis, dans les deux pays que j'aime, chacun à sa façon, et je souffre de toutes les difficultés qu'ils vivent en ce moment. Et lorsque tout dernièrement ma belle-sœur me confie combien elle m'aime, des larmes de joie me montent aux yeux car ainsi elle confirme qu'en restant soi-même mais en étant à l'écoute permanente de l'Autre, on peut être étrangères et sœurs à la fois.

Ah ! si... je me sens étrangère lorsque je vais dans un autre pays mais, en fait pas vraiment car je n'y vis pas, je me sens « touriste » et c'est très plaisant.

28 janvier 2010

***

© Marie-Noël Arras, *Baklawas maison*, Sidi-Bel-Abbès

© Marie-Noël Arras, *le troupeau*, Tessala, 2007

Le 25 septembre 2010, Peggy Sultan et moi-même participions au colloque sur les 40 ans du féminisme à la mairie de Paris. Pour la rencontre autour des 10 ans d'Etoiles d'encre au salon des revues, j'ai demandé aux auteures présentes de réfléchir à ce qu'elles avaient envie de dire sur la revue, sur ce qui leur semblait être sa raison d'être actuelle et sa raison de perdurer. Son originalité aussi dans le paysage éditorial des revues. La réponse de Peggy retranscrite ci-après est pour moi un lien entre le thème de ce numéro, L'étranger *et le prochain :* le masculin-féminin *!*

M-N Arras

©Marie-Noël Arras, photo des années 70, prise lors du colloque sur l'histoire du féminisme, Paris, 27 février 2010

2010 : 40 ans de Féminisme-Lutte des classes 10 ans de la revue « Etoiles d'Encre »

Peggy I. Sultan

Pour Anne-Catherine Lochard

Je ne connais pas bien le paysage des revues, sinon vaguement, car j'en lis peu. J'ai cependant une expérience lointaine mais très forte de ce que la revue « Elles Voient Rouge » pesait dans le contexte politique des années du Programme Commun et de sa chute. Fin des années 70, début des années 80. Oui, ça fait un bail…

Revue féministe et engagée « sur le front » des femmes issues du PCF et créée par Nicole-Edith Thévenin et moi-même, « Elles Voient Rouge » – féminisme et lutte des classes – « confectionnée » entièrement par celles qui en faisaient partie mais accueillant également toutes celles qui s'y reconnaissaient, sans pour cela adhérer forcément au PCF (dont nous fûmes d'ailleurs exclues en raison de notre remise en cause féroce du machisme à « l'intérieur » de l'appareil dans un article publié dans le Monde par Thierry Pfister : « Le Parti Communiste mis à nu par ses femmes » et rendant ainsi publique notre contestation tonitruante) – a duré de façon essentielle et passionnante pour les luttes et les débats d'alors : cinq ans. Cinq ans c'est peu et beaucoup à la fois.

Cinq ans de discussions, d'échanges, de rencontres avec les autres mouvements de femmes (je me souviens de ces moments « historiques » croisés avec les Algériennes qui se battaient contre le « statut personnel »), cinq ans pour continuer à défendre (ce que d'autres avaient commencé bien avant nous) les droits des femmes (Loi Veil pour le droit à l'avortement, lutte contre le viol, écoute et défense des femmes battues, lutte pour la parité et la discrimination positive, analyses du travail domestique, de l'éducation des enfants et de la double journée de travail « non payée » etc.), et transmettre nos délibérations bouillonnantes et nos écrits sur l'oppression et l'exploitation subies par les femmes, toutes classes confondues, mais traversées diversement par le Patriarcat : antérieur et inhérent au système capitaliste qui allait s'aggravant mondialement pour tous.

Si certaines « choses » ont tout de même bougé pour les femmes, d'autres ont massivement reculé et les batailles d'aujourd'hui, bien qu'elles existent, demeurent malgré tout dans un repli politique massif et plus qu'inquiétant. Les femmes végètent dans des inégalités de toutes sortes et ce qu'elles ont gagné hier, elles le paient à présent de façon plus sourde, plus perverse. Ou plus gravement : au grand jour et de manière quasi « convenue », banalisée. On s'y habitue, on « passe dessus », et on repart comme en l'an quarante.

Elles sont en première ligne à être atteintes par la question des retraites récemment adoptée par le gouvernement Sarkozy contre le tôlé de la rue et le soulèvement d'une belle majorité du pays au sein de manifestations nombreuses et tenaces. Quant au viol, les statistiques sont plus qu'affolantes, augmentées des nouvelles formes de destruction des femmes que sont les tournantes, de sinistre mémoire. Et j'en passe. Cette année 2010, le combat contre le viol et les violences faites aux femmes est décrété : « CAUSE NATIONALE ». No comment. La mode est encore aux commémorations et aux prises de conscience annuelles ! À cette enseigne elles sont inscrites ad vitam aeternam.

Faites rapidement le tour du monde et voyez le désastre. À nos portes, devenu à peine sournois, le recul des femmes est d'une provocation récurrente. On s'y fait, voyons. Elles contribuent, admettons-le, pour certaines, à la dégradation de leur image et de leur être-sujet. Pour autant, nous imaginons la « force herculéenne » qu'il leur faudrait pour qu'elles puissent agir sur le cours de leur propre destin car elles sont plus qu'empêchées dans notre société de la pensée molle et de l'autisme bien orchestré, laquelle s'engage si peu dans les faits pour changer les modes de regard et de comportement.

Notre société qui ne s'engage pas davantage dans les pratiques du monde du travail où la division sexuelle des fonctions, des rôles et de la hiérarchisation n'a guère beaucoup évolué et où, à diplôme égal, les femmes gagnent toujours 20 à 30 % de moins que les hommes (je me revois trente ans en arrière « gueulant » les mêmes revendications !!) alors que la précarité les éprouve plus amplement avec la crise ; quant au système éducatif (oui, encore lui), le SEXISME exacerbé entre garçons et filles sévit de plus belle et nous voyons celles-ci reprendre la gouaille hargneuse du masculin-machiste pour se défendre et rendre la pareille : les arguments et les armes finissent par se ressembler et les clichés et lieux-communs tristement se confondre.

Les temps ont changé, en effet, et j'ai le sentiment, en écrivant, à la fois d'un éternel recommencement et d'une impasse impitoyable jamais traversée jusqu'ici. Comment ne pas rester simple nihiliste face, notamment, aux « forces de progrès » (ne parlons pas des positions plus révolutionnaires !) qui ne pèsent pas lourd dans la balance des programmes et des promesses faites aux femmes.

Oui, on a le droit et le devoir d'être désenchantées, car il y a de quoi pleurer. Ou alors il faut être aveugles et se cantonner dans des valeurs refuges qui finalement isolent la rébellion et le front du refus d'une véritable solidarité, en perpétrant, soit le camouflage étouffant des femmes dans du sublimé tronqué, soit un optimisme hors sujet à l'endroit de situations insoutenables.

Oui, ailleurs, le désastre est tragique : ailleurs, sous d'autres cieux, naître femme est une véritable malédiction. Elles nous alertent si fort ces femmes - butins de guerre, violées afin de prolonger une filiation ethnique, ou anéanties par des hommes dont l'équilibre tribal consiste, au moindre « dérapage », à torturer et à se débarrasser de tout lignage féminin échappant à leur LOI- que ce sont elles, les ÉTRANGERES – qui portent le flambeau pour nous toutes.

Etrangères au-delà des frontières de l'acceptable et du crédible, étrangères au cœur des hommes, étrangères et parias à la périphérie de leur communauté, ballotées, masquées ou défigurées par des traditions d'un archaïsme barbare, étrangères, pour finir, dans notre miroir personnel où nous les rejoignons, elles, étrangères à notre reflet et cependant si proches de notre mémoire commune : il n'est pas possible de leur ressembler et cependant nous savons.

Lorsqu'elles nous touchent, nous bouleversent et remobilisent notre résistance et notre révolte, elles nous questionnent justement sur cette part « d'étrangéité » qui nous rapproche de ce à quoi nous aspirons, ce que nous voulons concrètement et de façon « autre », qui demeure encore « étranger » à ce que nous sommes : car ce qui nous est familier, nous est plus souvent imposé, assimilé contre nos désirs, consenti sous influence ou par collusion, étranger car inaccessible, étrange et dérangeant car revendiqué en « folles », ou « simplement » refoulé jusqu'à l'étrange vertige où se tapit une indicible vérité.

À les entendre hurler dans un mutisme accablant, le visage troué ou les traits défoncés – la liste morbide est interminable, hélas – on se dépêche de se souvenir que « chez nous c'est tellement mieux » et on retombe dans une intranquille amnésie.

Au risque de caricaturer, disons que les femmes flottent entre les extrêmes. D'un côté, des « têtes », chefs d'entreprise ou autres (on ne va pas bouder le nombre croissant de celles qui réussissent en assumant « toutes les composantes de leur féminité », what else ?), au caractère plus souvent formaté par le masculin dominant (comment faire autrement ? Paradoxe insoluble ? On peut essayer d'y réfléchir une fois de plus : si elles ne s'identifiaient pas aux hommes de pouvoir, pourraient-elles réaliser cette conquête en haut lieu acquise « à la force du poignée » ?), et de l'autre, l'exhibitionnisme d'une sexualité « libérée » à la chaîne (sic), partagée par de nombreuses femmes et d'aucunes de notre jeunesse, sur les bases d'une violence inouïe des rapports sexuels, à teneur ultra-pornographique et sadique, affolants. Les femmes, visiblement, ne se « gênant » plus, se croient « désinhibées » et maîtresses de leurs corps et de leur destin alors qu'elles sont enfermées dans le spectre pervers de projections et de phantasmes masculins.

Est-ce cela que nous espérions ? Nous disions que les femmes étaient la moitié du ciel : que fait, en attendant, l'autre moitié ? Pour « Elles Voient Rouge », il fallait articuler notre « guerre » singulière et privée à celle, incontournable, du politique, l'autre zone de ce ciel si désespérément scindé, clivé, schizant.

Allez voir l'excellent film : « Inside Job » de C. Ferguson, vous comprendrez encore mieux la crise financière de 2008, ce que la globalisation des marchés financiers veut dire pour nous tous et pour une « certaine population féminine » donc ! Comment Wall Street, les lobbies, les bonus exorbitants, les stock-options, les produits dérivés, les subprimes, le surendettement désastreux des individus qui s'appauvrissent à vue d'œil, bref, la dérèglementation éhontée et sauvage de toute la haute finance- conseillée et soutenue par d'éminents économistes femmes et hommes de Harvard– eh bien, comment tout ce beau monde, et dont « certains survivants » non pénalisés conseillent allégrement Barack Obama (ce n'est plus un secret), est intimement lié au blanchiment de l'argent sale, de la drogue et à la grande prostitution de luxe !!!! Non, ce n'est pas nouveau, mais ça devient un empire, cet argent lié au sexe où les femmes ont leurs réseaux, leurs carnets d'adresses, leurs entrées, leurs sorties, leurs investissements, leurs parts, leurs bénéfices, leurs conseillers, leurs protecteurs etc. Leur corps mis en Bourse (sic) ou vendu au rabais, comme en Allemagne, au moment des soldes ! Quelques exemples affligeants seulement, glanés, ici et là…

Allez sur les sites et faites défiler, écoutez un certain rap américain importé « chez nous » et levez les yeux au ciel ou plutôt, baissez-les. Le corps des femmes, en premier, est au déshonneur... aux abois, pris dans une jungle de « jouissances » féroces et de postures bestiales auxquelles elles se plient et, se soumettant, elles recyclent leur propre aliénation et leur enfer. Ici on est loin de cette fameuse « liberté sexuelle pour chacun » qui en soi, ne veut rien dire. On ne souhaite pas davantage être figées ni épinglées à une « pudibonderie » qui fait froid dans le dos et coince l'ajustement plus inspiré de nos désirs. Nous ne voulons pas plus une religiosité qui appelle la compassion ou l'hypocrisie en acceptant l'inacceptable. Tout fatalisme est fatal aux femmes, fatales ou pas !

Il est vrai que nous devenons les adeptes passifs de toutes formes de torture que la société du spectacle, de l'image à outrance et du voyeurisme mortifère, nous sert nuit et jour sur nos différents écrans : guerres, viols, incestes, pédophilie, tourisme sexuel, séquestrations maniaques d'adolescentes et grossesses forcées dans des caves, génocides, mises à mort expéditives sur place publique, lapidations, excisions, décapitations, émasculations – qui a dit que les hommes étaient à l'abri – l'horreur en direct promettant de nouveaux épisodes inédits au milieu d'un plat de spaghetti.

Je ne suis plus engagée politiquement mais je reste attentive aux combats des femmes. Ce combat, j'essaie de le mener aujourd'hui au sein de mon écriture.

J'ai pris le train en marche, il y a bientôt trois ans, dans « Etoiles d'Encre ». Une revue pour les femmes en méditerranée : un espace accueillant pour écrire, réfléchir, dialoguer, exprimer tout haut ce qu'il vaudrait mieux taire, inventer là où le silence enterre. Exalter des expériences originales qui prennent leur essor sous le chatoiement de la beauté, de l'étranger, de la pensée, de notre mémoire, d'une bataille secrète ou ouverte : tout élan et recherche créateurs appelant à engendrer l'art et l'emblème. Aux quatre points cardinaux.

Il n'y a pas des masses de revues de cette facture, consacrées uniquement aux femmes. Il faut donc « tenir », étendre plus avant les pages à celles au-delà de la méditerranée et pousser la réflexion et l'analyse de ce que nous voulons, souhaitons, solidaires ou contradictoires, diverses, étrangères venues d'autres contrées ou simplement étrangères l'une à l'autre, mais familières à l'écoute et aux exigences de l'esprit et du cœur, là où les femmes gravissent l'arbre de la connaissance en prolongeant les racines censées les unir à l'universel, à travers leurs paroles, leurs imaginaires, l'audace et les transgressions de leur questionnement, et puis, ce harcèlement douloureux des compromissions dont on ne sait pas toujours que faire : on « collabore » beaucoup trop avec notre malheur..

N'oublions pas que nous portons et les stigmates plus ou moins enfouis des coups bas du politiquement puissant – du prêt-à penser ou à ne pas penser dominant – et les interactions aussi riches que régressives de nos filiations, de nos origines, notre milieu, notre place décalée ou pas dans la société et ses cultures. De notre être femme, unique et plurielle.

À travers nos peintures, sculptures, photos, poèmes, textes, nouvelles, la mosaïque de nos écritures irisées – croisements et métissages – nous exprimons ce que personne d'autre ne peut faire à notre place. À prendre et à ne pas laisser. Ne pas laisser faire.

Nous partageons, de notre méditation et du mûrissement de nos énergies, ce qui engage à transformer en centre ardent, aussi bien notre conscience que la dispersion contrainte de nos multiples vies et en intelligence créatrice, ce que nous donnons à voir et à entendre sous le voile des apparences ou de la caricature : cette troublante étrangeté de notre féminité lorsqu'elle est dévoyée par les lieux communs misogynes, le déni et la violence sans limites de nos sociétés. Résister et transformer reste pour nous, femmes, la question incontournable, en attendant le grand soir où « nos » hommes comprendront que l'autre moitié de ciel n'a pas encore gagné à ce qu'ils soient plus libres, plus égaux, plus fraternels.

Ce que nous vivons ou ne vivons pas de l'intérieur, c'est tout un monde à recréer. Ce que nous vivons ou ne vivons pas à l'extérieur, c'est tout un monde à renverser.

Etoiles d'Encre est cet habitacle privilégié, l'écrin où nous tenons à porter plus haut et plus largement l'expression de nos sentiments les plus désobéissants, les plus impertinents – libres, impliqués et subversifs – et, bien sûr, les plus distingués !

***.

©Peggy I. Sultan, 16 octobre 2010

©Peggy I. Sultan, A.C. Lochard,
militante de *Elles Voient Rouge* en 1981

©Damien Perdereau, *Nic devant sa coque de nacre*, 30 janvier 2011

La coque de nacre

Nic Sirkis

Je ne peux pas m'endormir alors vamos pour le comptage des moutons ?

J'aime pas les moutons.

Déjà le Petit Prince voulait enfermer le sien dans sa caisse ou lui mettre sa muselière. Pas confiance avec le mouton. Le mouton et l'esprit grégaire.

Les moutons pensent en groupe. Les moutons se ratatinent les uns dans les autres comme les doigts de la main. Les moutons bêlent en tremblant comme les feuilles agitées de l'automne. Les moutons se resserrent, ouailles de la trouille, dans la toison collective.

J'aime pas les moutons.

Ont-ils rencontré le lobule gauche de Van Gogh, rejeté de la fosse, que l'infirmier de Arles a jeté dans les toilettes ? Même en ce cas, les moutons n'auraient rien à en faire. L'oreille du peintre le plus génial ne pourrait se greffer sur celle triste et tombante des ovins obséquieux.

Ils ne savent que suivre leur vie en pointillé. Jamais d'initiative. Jamais de risque ou de folie. Il faudrait un mouton à cinq pattes pour aller donner un coup de main à la chèvre de Monsieur Seguin. Les chèvres affrontent les loups, pas les moutons.

Les moutons sont plus paralysés que les autruches par les lendemains inconnus. Si peu de moutons noirs dans les troupeaux de crème.

Les moutons s'aplatissent d'obéissance. Les moutons se tartinent eux-mêmes de moutarde ou d'harissa avant le gigot ou le méchoui. Les moutons plongent en chœur dans la bêtise annoncée – histoire de ne pas déparer dans le bouquet.

J'aime pas les moutons.

Ils survivent. Ils continuent. Ils surnagent quitte à partir avec l'eau du bain.

Les moutons gardent l'ombilic raccordé au berger en mâchouillant leur chewing-gum végétarien. Le mouton frémit sur ses cannes en suintant la lanoline.

Panurge et le loup de La Fontaine ont enregistré les moutons dans le panier des victimes. Le mouton ne se rend même pas compte qu'il est « interchangé ». Il bêle, tremble et se désole. Le mouton tourne son mufle vers le sol pour oublier le soleil. C'est lui qu'on a choisi en premier pour tester le clonage.

On s'endort dans la monotonie en comptant les moutons sous les paupières qui s'affaissent. J'aime pas les moutons. Leur bêlement veule m'insupporte.

L'année dernière il y avait un type vieux – toutefois le paraissait-il – qui était – du moins chaque fois que je passais là avec ma bécane- dans le renfoncement d'un magasin grossiste au 4 de la rue des Fontaines du Temple, lieu dit « La coque de nacre ». Et il lisait. Installé le plus confortablement possible, vêtu de ses habits de hasard, assis sur sa paillasse, adossé par terre à la vitrine, il lisait, absorbé par les chapitres. C'était en général d'épais bouquins, bien lourds, bien gros, bien nourrissant d'histoires. Et il était plongé dedans, sans tenir compte de la circulation réduite de cette étroite rue secondaire. Que lisait-il ? Tolstoï ou Albertine Sarrazin ? Genet, la correspondance de George Sand ? L'île au trésor ? Pennac ? La prose du transsibérien ou Nathalie Sarraute ? Il lisait sur son bout de trottoir sur notre planète arbitraire. Je passais en pédalant sur mon vélo, il était toujours là ; je le regardais ; il me fascinait ; il lisait ; la Terre pouvait tourner sa sauce, il était occupé. J'ai pensé lui apporter… une lampe torche pour la nuit, des lunettes loupes que j'avais en doublon, pour peut-être faciliter sa lecture, reposer sa vue, ou surtout des livres, des bons bouquins que j'avais aimés, lui dire aussi qu'il était près de chouettes bibliothèques dégorgeant de livres magnifiques. Le savait-il ? Y avait-il accès ? J'étais gourde. Je ne me suis mêlée de rien. Je l'ai juste vu. Jusqu'à ce que cette année, il n'y soit plus. Disparu. Sa paillasse aussi. Et ses livres.

Ce mec était un mouton à cinq pattes. Un mouton sans troupeau, sans berger, sans prince. Un mouton hors de la bergerie et sans compte à rendre. Dans notre troupeau bêlant il n'y a pas de place pour lui. En brebis conforme et convenue de notre bergerie solidaire, j'ai continué ma transhumance vers le cimetière de bateaux, en jouant à saute-mouton sur les malaises domestiques. Où est le mouton noir sans pâtre et sans patrie ? Que lui ont dit ses livres ? A-t-il rencontré les girafes ? Allez, il faut compter les moutons pour se rendormir, 6. 261 509 228, 6 261 509 229, 6 261 509 230, 6 261 509 231… et la coque de nacre est vide.

***

©Marie Bueno, Errance 1, 2009

©Marie Bueno, Erranc 2, 2009

Blanche comme neige...

Marie Bueno

« Aux analphabètes émotionnels, aux passants pressés,
aux talons qui claquent sur le pavé,
lorsqu'il fait si froid et si faim... »

Au pied de la grue au bas de ma rue,
Elle survit là...

Over-dosée du malheur qui sévit sur elle…
Epuisée de se brûler aux halogènes, parfois elle court, pétrifiée comme un insecte qui cherche la sortie qui lui rendra la vie…
Elle s'époumone à la recherche des limites de ce qui rend heureux...
Douleur de promesses incessantes !
Dans ses rêves éveillés le jour, elle grelotte sous ses cartons, remplis de cauchemars la nuit.
Elle voudrait tout brûler, tout fumer, souvenirs en prime...

Elle en a plein le dos et pourtant aucune coquille, ni de protection, ni d'escargot pour se béquiller à l'abri…
Oui, plein le dos et pas de hotte, aucun cadeau, ni de Noël, ni de la vie, plutôt néant de l'autre côté de la rue...

Une seule envie lorsqu'elle se regarde dans sa flaque, sur le pavé urine, une envie de tout carboniser, paquetage et cauchemars en prime !

Destin sordide qu'elle n'imaginait pas lorsque tout se jouait et se rejouait, à l'heure, où, dans ses contes de fées, Cendrillon rentrait déjà trop tard et le prince charmant ne venait pas…

Cette nuit-là, il a neigé et ce matin-là, il a fait moins sept, d'ailleurs les nains étaient déjà tous là, une guirlande de noël jaune et noire en guise de périmètre de sécurité et une musique de gyrophares pour faire plus fête mais, ironie du sort, parmi tous les princes qui s'affairaient autour d'elle, aucun ne semblait vouloir déposer un baiser sur ses lèvres violettes...

Je crois qu'elle ne s'appelle pas Blanche Neige !

Aujourd'hui il était une fois…
mais
Il était une fois et aujourd'hui
Il est trop tard...

Je crois qu'elle ne s'appelait pas Blanche Neige !

***

Comète

Son corps céleste extase la liberté.
L'approche grisante de sa puissance arrache,
Sur les perspectives et l'espace,
Des spectres
Aux scintillements sauvages.

Dérive de l'esprit,
Sourdine des chairs en liesse,
Derrière la verrière dans sa bulle
Plane l'aviatrice,
Soudain étrangère
A son existence.

La mer renversée désintègre ses amarres,
Paradis d'émeraude abyssal.

Sépulcrale harmonie !

Thérèse-Françoise Crassous

©Ourida Nemmiche, *Beni Abbès, in Ici Je veux vivre, ici je veux mourir,* 2007

Passer une frontière

Geneviève Briot

Des rêves dans les plis d'une mémoire étrangère frappent à ma tête. Visages déposés sur mon propre visage. Terres brûlées de désirs, sables passés au four des souhaits, désespoirs pulvérisés jetés aux yeux.

Je ne sais pas comment la vie des autres monte à l'assaut, m'investit, guide ma main vers les mots qui les raconteront. Peut-être suis-je une plante dans le vent, dépendante de ce qui l'entoure et qui doit en rendre compte.

Écrire, n'est-ce pas être amené à passer des frontières ?

Quand j'ai vécu avec des femmes voilées au cœur du Mzab, j'ai d'abord ouvert grand mes yeux devant leur étrangeté. Elles en faisaient autant devant ma liberté de femme voyageuse. Leur curiosité « C'est la première fois que nous rencontrons une étrangère » fut mon passeport. Elles m'invitaient à comprendre, c'est-à-dire à prendre avec moi leur histoire, la logique de cette société qu'elles croient immuable, parce que d'origine divine. Ce n'est pas sans souffrance qu'on entre dans cette logique-là, mais la souffrance n'est-elle pas inscrite au cœur de la création ? J'ai ainsi livré dans un roman « L'appel du sud » un peu de ce monde-là, si loin de moi et qui me semble familier aussi parce que notre rencontre a créé une fraternité. Tu es de notre famille maintenant, m'ont dit ces femmes.

Je me suis confrontée aussi à un monde étranger en recueillant des témoignages qui ont donné naissance à sept récits dans « Un livre à la mer ». Paroles venues d'Algérie encore, mais qui me faisaient entrer dans une Algérie que je ne connaissais que par les livres, celle vécue avant et pendant la guerre. Je me suis préparée à la rencontre avec ces personnes comme on prépare un voyage. Se mêlaient envie et appréhension. Ils étaient bien éloignés de moi, ces pieds-noirs, ce harki, ce militant du MNA[1]… Il me fallait entrer dans leur souffrance, leur émerveillement, leur humiliation, leur fierté, leur naïveté, leur révolte, leur rancœur. Ne pas parler à leur place mais puiser dans les moindres parcelles de leur ressenti pour faire revivre leur parcours. Être à leur écoute pour restituer leur parole. Leur être fidèle tout en imaginant le non-dit. Traverser le temps, malaxer dans la paume la matière des mots.

Peut-être ai-je compris à quel point j'avais passé une frontière lorsqu'au moment où je transcrivais ces histoires de vies, une nuit, je me suis sentie à l'intérieur du personnage le plus sombre, le plus revendicatif, le plus amer. Je pouvais être au cœur de sa souffrance sans porter de jugement sur la hargne qui l'habitait et le rendait difficile d'accès.

Donner à entendre la voix de ces personnes, c'était les délivrer d'un silence. C'était aussi, les faire devenir personnages, les mettre à distance d'eux-mêmes. Dire le passé, c'est pouvoir lui dire adieu. Quand je leur ai lu leur histoire avant d'envisager la

1. Mouvement National Algérien créé par Messali Hadj

publication, je me suis sentie accueillie. J'ai pris part à la fierté du militant messaliste qui ne savait ni lire ni écrire et qui allait disparaître en laissant trace de sa vie. J'ai partagé l'émotion de chacun d'eux. Ils ne m'étaient plus étrangers.

Cette forme d'écriture, pas si éloignée finalement de l'écriture personnelle, donne la jouissance de voir au-delà de soi.

À la réflexion, quand je m'exprime pour moi-même, pour dire mon ressenti, je chemine aussi vers des zones inconnues, obscures même. Une épreuve, un plaisir aussi, celui de se surprendre.

Écrire, c'est aller à la découverte, parfois passer une frontière, repousser les limites de l'étrangeté.

©Marie-Noël Arras, *Tunisie, 2008*

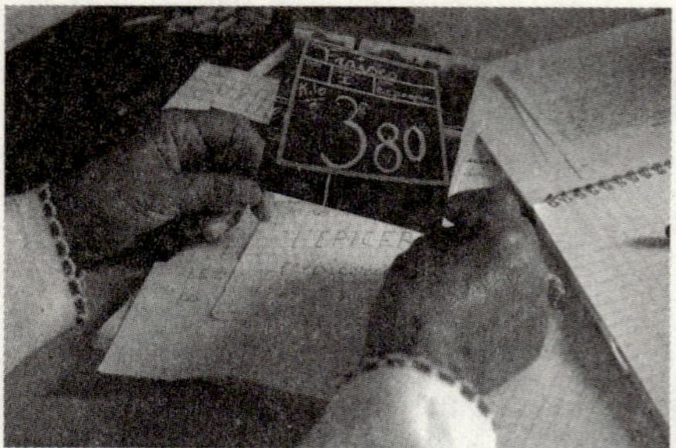

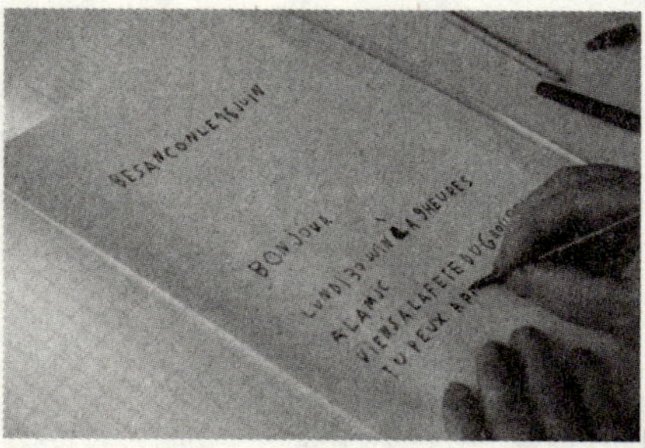

©Elisabeth Trouche

Etranges étrangères

Elisabeth Trouche

Fatima, Mounia, Zahra... Leurs prénoms résonnent au plus profond de moi, en échos incertains. Le mien, elles le prononcent comme autrefois les femmes arabes de mon enfance algérienne. Les barrières du temps, de l'espace, s'effritent. Parfums d'épices, foulards de toutes les couleurs, un soleil d'ailleurs entre à flots dans la salle.

Deux fois par semaine, nous reprenons un échange balbutiant. Entre nos mondes, si peu de ponts....

Cette langue, encore presque étrangère, si longtemps interdite, langue de l'émancipation, mais aussi autrefois de l'oppression, elles essaient d'arrache-pied de se l'approprier. Honteuses de leurs échecs, fières de leurs progrès, même minuscules.

Elles se saisissent des cours comme d'une revanche, sur les parents, qui ont choisi d'envoyer les garçons à l'école, pendant qu'elles étaient maintenues à la maison pour des tâches peu valorisantes ; sur le mari qui « fermait sur elles ». Elles ne cessent d'exprimer leurs regrets et leur rancune, mais aussi leur volonté d'acquérir enfin une autonomie qui leur a été refusée.

Je m'émerveille avec elles de ce « o » qui s'inscrit « rond comme un beignet », nous sourions de ce « k » à l'envers, qui semble « porter un bébé sur le dos ». Sur le tableau où se construisent peu à peu des phrases hésitantes, se reflètent aussi l'extérieur, les arbres, les immeubles, cet univers où elles sont exilées.

Elles brandissent leur montre – ça y est, elles savent déchiffrer l'heure, ou le papier du rendez-vous médical – elles ont pu s'y rendre toutes seules, reconnaître sur les plaques les noms, de la rue, du médecin.

Parfois elles partent avant l'heure, pour un rendez-vous avec un proviseur – que reproche-t-on au garçon si gentil à la maison –, chez un médecin -sortent un papier de leur sac, s'inquiètent – « c'est bien aujourd'hui ? » –. Alors les mots « diabète », « tension », « arthrose », font le tour de la salle.

J'aime quand les rapports s'inversent. Je les observe qui guettent l'erreur au tableau, -mais non, aujourd'hui ce n'est pas mercredi, « et 2010 alors, vous ne l'écrivez pas ? » Elles plaisantent : « l'an prochain c'est moi à votre place au tableau ! »

Auxiliaires précieuses, elles organisent autrement la salle, m'arrêtent quand l'exercice mal choisi est infaisable. Imbattables dans les parcours et horaires de bus, elles me renseignent sur un itinéraire, s'esclaffent de me voir si ignorante. Que d'ingéniosité dans les stratégies mises en place pour se repérer dans un univers de pancartes et panneaux !

Le « tu » qu'elles m'adressent, je ne le reçois pas comme une faute, mais comme un signe de confiance ; moi, je regrette de ne pas pouvoir leur renvoyer le même « tu », chargé dans ma mémoire de condescendance et de mépris. Mais je peux leur rendre le merci qu'elles me sourient en sortant de la salle : avec elles, je redécouvre le dessin des lettres, la magie des mots.

Quand elles ne sont pas au rendez-vous, je crains de ne plus les revoir. Mais elles reviennent toujours, ou presque, s'excusent – une visite inattendue, une mère malade au pays... – mais les voilà de retour, lourdes d'histoires dont elles ne laisseront échapper que quelques bribes. Elles s'enveloppent de leur mystère, riches de leurs secrets.

Il m'arrive de croiser l'une ou l'autre au marché. Alors elles rayonnent en me disant le nom des légumes et des fruits qui emplissent leur panier, me présentent le jeune homme, ou la jeune fille qui les accompagne – et qui travaille si bien à l'école –. Je réponds « comme vous ». Dignes et belles, elles poursuivent leur chemin entre les étals.

À l'approche de l'été, je les écoute évoquer les préparatifs. Comment acheter les cadeaux qu'on attend au pays quand elles croulent ici sous les difficultés matérielles ? Qu'ils sont chers, les billets d'avion, de bateau ! La route est bien longue quand il faut traverser l'Espagne, la voiture chargée de passagers et de paquets... Le temps des vacances, elles vont retrouver un pays qui n'est même plus le leur. Elles soupirent : « Etrangères là-bas, étrangères ici ! Etrangères partout ! »

Elles sont entrées dans ma vie depuis peu, mais je les connais depuis toujours, pour toujours.

Ensemble nous luttons contre l'humiliation des sans-papiers, des sans-mots, des sans-rien, de ceux que les pouvoirs ignorent. Peut-être un jour découvrirons-nous notre force contre les tout puissants.

Au tableau s'écrivent des mots de braise.

⁂

Etranges étrangers

Etranges étrangers étranglés par rangées
Strangers in the night étrangers dans la nuit
Etrons gelés sur l'iceberg de nos peurs
L' Étranger de Camus
Patron ! et un Meursault !
Au grand cycle de l'absurde
Le mythe de Sisyphe
Caligula et le Malentendu
Quand l'Algérie était française
L'étranger n'effrayait pas
Il était asservi à d'étonnants Pieds Noirs
Algérie allergie
Ah j'ai ri chantait la Castafiore
En se mirant en son miroir
Algérie ton mouroir
Française tes tiroirs
Etranges étrangers
Que nos soldats plus tard sont partis « apaiser »
Devenant étrangers parmi les étrangers
Il y en aurait des bons et des mauvais
Les bons roulent sur l'or sont les rois du pétrole
Les mauvais sont de pauvres exploités immigrés
Pour la vie de leurs mômes
Par révolte, liberté et passion
Etranges illuminés
Fils du désert ensoleillés
Etrangers grands poètes ou
Esclaves du dit du prophète
Etrangers hommes libres encore à vérifier
Etrangères femmes libres encore à inventer

Libres et égaux en droit
Pas même à l'endroit où elles vivent
Etrangers à soi même
Etrangères à elles-mêmes
Etrangers trente ans de jais
Etrangères sur étagères
Est rangé dans mon ciel un soupçon
De fraternité
En verrai-je la cime depuis mon olivier
Arcane solitude des femmes expulsées
D'une cité archaïque vite à émanciper
Etrangères fantasmées d'un Occident frustré
Fatia Hanna Maria Soraya Hassina Mahalia
Filles cloîtrées privées de parole
Derrière les voiles d'une prison ouverte
À toutes et à un seul
Etrangers despotiques en leur citadelle dérisoire
Etrangers violentés en leur prison d'espoir
D'étranges étrangères sommes-nous l'une à l'autre
Ce n'est pas raisonnable encore moins tolérable
C'est tout bonnement insupportable
Etrangers de toujours à nos proches
Et aux lointains Humains
Nous ne torturons pas pour autant notre prochain
Etrangers des trésors sont enfouis en vos vies
Sur la terre tous nous sommes étrangers de passage
Tous nés sans papiers !
Tous égaux tous différents
Si proches étrangers
Tous à mort condamnés
Quand décider de s'aimer de semer d'essaimer
Sera-t-il conçu comme une liberté ?

Geneviève David

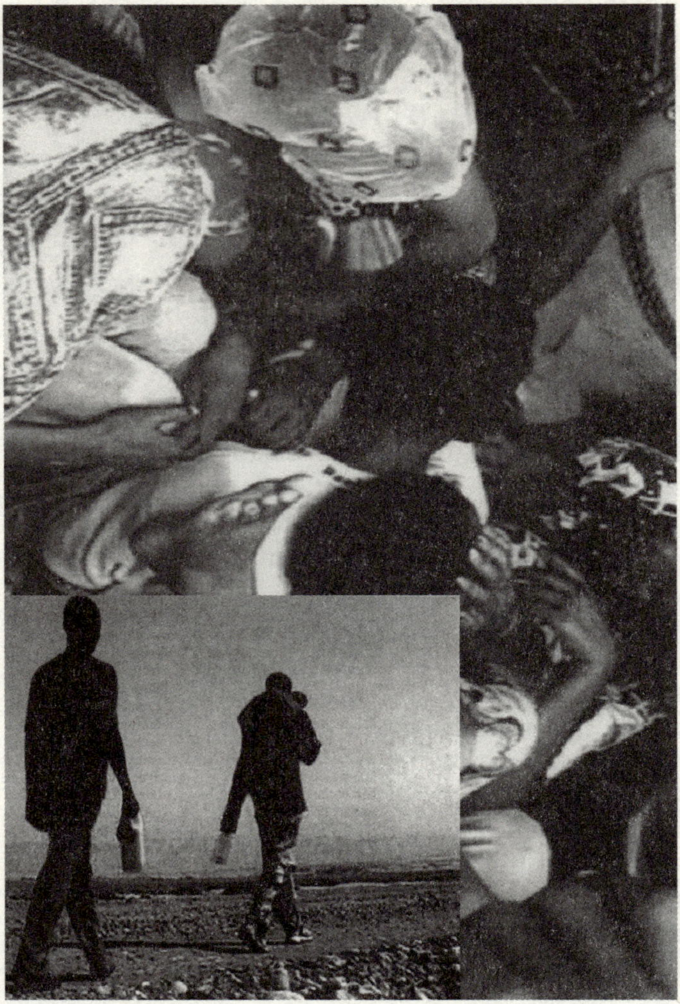

©Rose Marie Naime, montage.

Jungle 2009

Sommes misère
Sommes colère.

Sables d'Afrique
Sables d'Asie
Humaine barbarie
Ont lacéré nos cuirs
Arraché notre chair

Le vent de nos déserts
En rafales chez vous
Drosse nos radeaux
Là-haut voilure noire
Flotte notre peau
Outremer d'outre mer
D'entre ciel et terre
Plomb de nos malheurs
Pourpre de nos douleurs
Notre ardente nuée
Corrodera vos songes
Et vos nuages blonds.

Car
Nous sommes
Votre nuit
Et l'orage qui suit.

De par vos propres dires
La nuit de notre peau
Vous ruisselle d'effroi.
L'absolu de notre infortune
Vous frissonne. Déjà
Vous rentrez vos petiots
Et celez vos magots.

Bientôt vous tremblerez,
Comme en vos invasions
Hier avions tremblé.

Haboob, vent de poussières...
Vent des déserts

Que faire contre nuées affamées
De colères alourdies ?
Elles partent en grêlons,
Bondissants fracassants
Explosent en tous sens.
Que faire contre assoiffés
Gens de poussières
Qui, genoux en terre,
Aux rivages des mers
Aspirent sources et océans ?

En nos déluges vous sombrerez
À moins que ne survienne
Et au cœur ne vous prenne
Cette arche nouvelle, partage d'un ciel

Tramé de noir, tramé de blanc...

Rose Marie Naime

Un avion pour Kaboul

Le renvoi par le gouvernement français de trois Afghans en situation irrégulière en France a m'inspiré le poème suivant

Un jour automnal et les rues sont nouvelles
Le soleil se balance entre les feuilles des platanes
Dans le brouillard épais et chaud de Kaboul,
Les larmes de trois hommes, déracinés de leur exil
et une fois encore, dans une rue de Kaboul
Sans papiers, la jungle pointait comme une lumière.
C'est la première fois de ta vie que tu affrontes le retour
dans ta patrie en guerre

Case départ, dans les salles d'attente de la mort
Ainsi, te voilà sorti des statistiques, et ceux qui prétendent
soutenir ton pays, te refusent le moyen d'appartenir aux
droits de l'homme

Ils effacent de ton visage toutes les marques d'humanité
par lesquelles on peut te reconnaître.

Comme il était difficile de vivre :
Tu es afghan, l'Afghanistan apparaît dans le paysage du
monde comme un carré de limites et tu ne peux plus voyager,
ton identité est le nœud des contradictions d'espaces en
conflit.

Tu ne veux que vivre, tu ne veux qu'espérer, tu ne veux qu'aimer et tu t'es arraché à l'enfer
Aujourd'hui tu ne peux même plus nommer ton exil
Sur l'horizon les collines dispersées de Kaboul, il est effacé par l'horreur du présent,

Quelle lutte pourrait-il susciter ?
Comme vous étiez fiers, et beaux dans l'espoir de rencontrer cette source jamais connue, cette soif d'être libres que la guerre assiège depuis près de trente ans

Tu as dis neuf ans ou vingt deux ans, tu n'as jamais connu la paix.

Tu t'es enfui à l'espoir qu'une autre partie d'humanité te dirait « nous t'attendons, ne pleure pas ton pays détruit, viens et fonde ici sa reconstruction »

Alors tu es parti à cet appel , à ce cri entendu dans l'hallucination des bombardements, tu as répondu « j'arrive »

Et tu pleurais de quitter ton père et ta mère, tu te séparais de la mort muni d'un passeport et du droit à être protégé, à trouver abri dans une patrie d'adoption.

Avais-tu seulement le choix ? d'être où est ton peuple, c'était de faire une guerre où ton histoire ne prend plus sens, ou l'autre alternative est d'être enrôlé dans des bataillons de la mort et la perte de toi-même, entre ta vérité humaine et ta situation actuelle.

Il n'y a pas de place pour les amoureux sur ta terre,
Il n'y a pas de place pour les amoureux sur la mienne
Il y a cette division de nous-mêmes
Notre appartenance véritable et historique est la liberté, Non d'être soumis aux conditions de déni et de cruauté tracées par d'autres

Tout l'être même refuse que la vie s'arrête ici, comme ceux qui sont morts sans avoir vu leur pays avec les ailes libres des cerf volants, par amour total.

Que restera t-il de mémoire de ceux qui ont aimé et risqué leur vie ? Poètes, humbles et résistants, ils ceignent de leur force les hauteurs de Kaboul, la rocaille des collines, les douces vallées du Panshir.

Tu refuses l'affairement entre absurdes, tu refuses de célébrer les désirs oubliés, les suggestions qui resserrent la vie entre des murs, tu veux la liberté du galop et l'espace neigeux des cimes, tu veux l'absolu, rien que l'absolu de l'amour et de la vie.

Nicole Barrière
9/12/2009

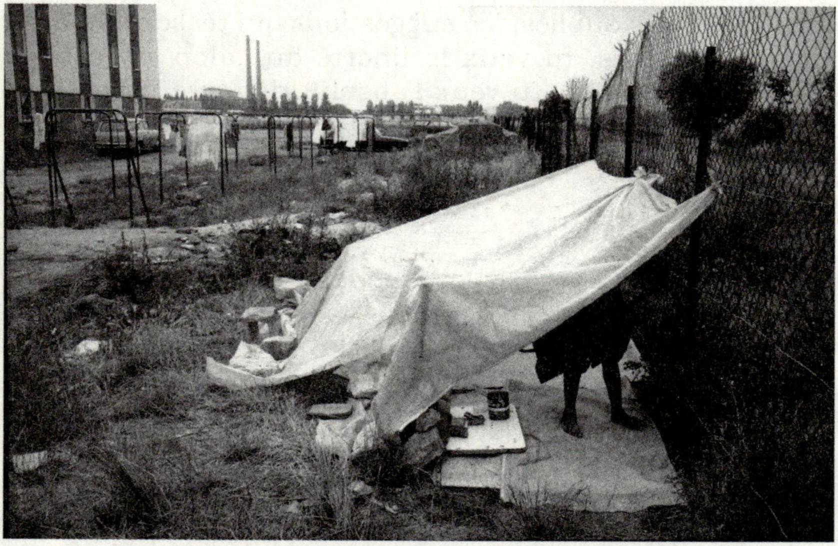

©Jean Lattes, Nanterre, jeux d'enfant, 1975, coll. Janine Lattes.

Ya 'atek saha

Cécile Oumhani

Enfant… Je rêvais de bottillons fourrés à fermeture éclair et de tricots en laine chinée. Je harcelais ma mère pour qu'elle me fasse porter des boucles d'oreille comme mes camarades à l'école. Je ne comprenais pas son obstination à me refuser ces attributs dont je rêvais. Sans eux, je ne serais jamais comme elles et je continuerais de rester seule à la récréation, dépaysée par des comptines que je ne savais pas chanter, des jeux dont je ne connaissais pas les règles. La marée enfantine me rejetait sur un étrange îlot, qui se déplaçait avec moi d'un jour à l'autre dans la cour plantée de marronniers. Un vide infranchissable l'entourait. Même les balles de caoutchouc ne s'y aventuraient pas. Je n'aurais pas su les renvoyer, encore moins jongler avec, comme elles le faisaient avec tant d'adresse et de plaisir.

La géographie des lieux m'était pourtant si familière. Je m'y serais déplacée les yeux fermés, évitant les toilettes où flottait une persistante odeur d'urine. J'aurais dérivé sans me tromper vers le préau, la salle de classe, qui sentait la craie, l'encre et la cire. Rien d'étranger à tout ce que je retrouvais le matin avec appréhension. L'étrangeté était en moi, sur moi. Elle collait à mes vêtements, à mes chaussures à lacets venues de Grande-Bretagne. Elle imprégnait mon palais, habitué à la saveur du thé, qui ignorait tout du café au lait et des tartines trempées dans le bol du petit déjeuner. J'étais saturée de la nostalgie d'un pays où je n'étais jamais allée, celui de ma mère. Les autres humaient ce curieux halo que je promenais autour de moi, avant de s'éloigner résolument vers des territoires qui leur étaient familiers, comme ils m'étaient familiers, bien que j'en fusse inexorablement repoussée.

J'avais vite compris qu'il fallait taire à tout prix ces contrées de mots et d'histoires dans l'*autre* langue, inconnue, incongrue à leurs oreilles, faute de quoi j'aurais aggravé mon cas. La saveur des puddings, les cartes de Noël accrochées dans le salon dès le mois de décembre, tout cela il fallait le contenir à l'intérieur du périmètre de la maison. Surtout ne pas laisser déborder à l'extérieur une étrangeté qui aurait déchaîné des remarques narquoises, voire des quolibets.

Deux espaces contigus… Je passais de l'un à l'autre, obéissant à une loi aveugle, extérieure qu'il était impossible de fléchir. Chaque jour était une éternité à franchir avant que je puisse me replier le soir au sein du cocon familial.

☆

Adulte… Trois espaces contigus… Je passe de l'un à l'autre, en être d'habitude. Chaque jour passe à la vitesse de l'éclair et le temps me file entre les doigts.

Trois langues résonnent à mes oreilles, en toile de fond, alors que le français est bel et bien ma langue d'écriture. Chez moi, je saute agréablement de l'une à l'autre, saisissant l'expression dont la saveur s'impose à moi dans telle ou telle situation du quotidien.

Un monde élargi, agrandi d'une multiplicité de chemins… Même si ce sont des expériences difficiles à partager. Certains moments requièrent davantage, pour moi ou pour mon mari, un *ya 'atek saha* qu'un simple *merci*. Trois mots surgis ici dans une mer de français parce qu'à un instant précis du quotidien, je suis saisie de l'impérieux besoin d'une formule qui est un vœu. *Que cela te soit bénéfique*… La nécessité parfois de dire plus que deux syllabes. La nécessité de faire ce don d'une petite phrase qui entoure, protège, augure d'un avenir que l'on veut doux, lumineux et propice. Une petite phrase de trois mots… Avec tant d'autres, ils se sont enracinés, au-delà de leur étrangeté première, quand je les ai appris, trébuchant sur deux consonnes nouvelles que ma bouche peinait à reproduire. Trois mots qui se sont déposés en moi et m'ont séduite avec une cohorte de proverbes et d'expressions. Des phrases ricochent dans ma tête, entre le français, l'anglais et l'arabe. *Once bitten twice shy*… Pourquoi choisir *une fois mordu deux fois plus timide* ? *Chat échaudé craint l'eau froide*, ce n'est pourtant pas mal, c'est imagé et puis j'aime les chats, je connais si bien le frémissement de leur pelage, leur fuite soudaine, aussi légère que fulgurante. Est-ce parce qu'en un moment donné, je ressens davantage la morsure dans ma chair que l'image d'un félin apeuré sur le point de détaler ?

Par-delà l'ivresse de ces horizons élargis où puiser les mots à des sources multiples, mon étrangeté si ancienne que je ne la vois plus reste pourtant cuisante. Elle me pousse à me recroqueviller pour parer les chocs. Même si je suis convaincue qu'elle m'est bénéfique et qu'elle m'enrichit. *Ya 'atek saha.* Mais elle fait mal aussi. *Once bitten twice shy.* Les gens n'aiment pas ce qui est polymorphe, inclassable, atypique. Il faut être l'un ou l'autre, mais pas les deux, encore moins les trois. Alors on polit, on lisse les aspérités, les granulosités. On rentre en soi les étrangetés, comme l'escargot cache ses cornes et se replie dans sa coquille. *Un escargot dans sa coquille*… Parce que je ne crois pas que l'on dise *a snail in its shell. Comme un escargot rentré dans sa coquille,* on garde pour soi la danse des mots. On attend de rentrer chez soi pour partager les saveurs et les phrases. Il faut offrir à l'extérieur une surface à la fois neutre et résistante. Si un rayon de lumière bienfaisante survient, il sera alors bien temps d'aller à sa rencontre.

⁂

Variations sur...

©Witold Januszewski, *Danses polonaises*, fusain, coll. Particulière, Paris 1971

Ceux-là, d'autres et nous

Des corps dansent...

Ceux-là offrent leur Brésil : racines africaines, énergie-favelas, séduction-samba, et le plaisir de communier. D'autres font valser des gants de boxe au son d'un quatuor à cordes. Le hip-hop des rues françaises se mêle de poésie.

Ceux-ci sonnent espagnols et donnent chair au tempo.

D'autres, extraits d'Israël, parlent d'oppression des peuples. Ceux-là, du haut de leurs pointes précises, disent la rigueur flamboyante d'une Russie.

D'autres ondulent à l'orientale ou portent l'énergie états-unienne.

Ceux-ci, ceux-là.... D'autres ? D'autres !

Des rythmes. Percussions, violon, violoncelle, guitare... mains et voix... tant de possibles !

Et, pour chaque corps qui danse : des pas, des bras levés, des genoux assouplis, un souhait, quelque chose à dire.

En face, des corps assis s'ébrouent. Applaudissent.

L'humanité est un pont, on y danse, on y danse !

Norlane Deliz

Singe, quoique vêtu de soie
ou l'héritage espagnol

Magali Junique

©Tristram Kenton, *Carlos Acosta, Royal Ballet Company de Londres*, 2008

À 14 ans, Esteban aimait toujours la danse classique, il ne ratait aucun cours et ne vivait que pour sa passion. Son père l'observait sans vergogne depuis ses 11 ans afin de déceler en lui toute présence de caractéristiques « féminines ». Comment un garçon « normal » aurait-il pu s'y entendre en ballet ? Malgré une surveillance sans égard pour la vie d'Esteban, son père, pas plus qu'aucun autre membre de la famille complice ou soumis aux dictats paternels, ne put jamais rien déceler de « louche » chez le garçon. Esteban était bel et bien un mâle. D'ailleurs il avait une copine danseuse et vraiment très jolie, une voix virile, une démarche masculine quoique souple, un grand corps musclé quoique svelte. Enfin il s'habillait comme un vrai garçon et ne passait dans la salle de bain que le temps nécessaire. Son père avait alors insisté dès lors qu'une représentation de danse traditionnelle afro-cubaine était donnée pour qu'ils y assistent ensemble. « Mon garçon, viens avec moi, accompagne-moi mon garçon, ce sont les nôtres, tu vois ? Nos racines sont là ».

Il jouait sa dernière carte. Depuis que son fils était adolescent il avait refusé de le voir danser. Toute la famille y allait mais pas le père car il jugeait cela indigne d'un homme. Un « vrai » homme peut-il passer son temps à reluquer des danseurs en justaucorps ? C'est pourquoi il vantait les mérites et les capacités de tous ces garçons virils aux torses dénudés qui exécutaient sans équivoques les gestes traditionnels des leurs, de ceux de leur couleur : semences, coupe de la canne, récoltes, pêche, chasse, combats guerriers, séduction et hommages aux Orishas. Esteban approuvait l'engouement de son père mais rien ne le décidait à changer de section. Même ses professeurs n'y étaient pas parvenu lorsque plus petit, ils lui avaient parfois demandé de remplacer un camarade dans la section folklorique pour le bien de l'école... Esteban l'avait toujours fait de bonne grâce mais était revenu aussitôt à sa place dans le ballet.

Les années avaient passé, les copines s'étaient succédées, seul le ballet était resté. Puis Esteban avait intégré l'école de danse la plus prestigieuse de la capitale. Au prix d'heures de travail, de bien des sacrifices et d'entraînements incessants il avait réussi tous les examens. Il côtoyait désormais les meilleurs professeurs, danseurs et chorégraphes du pays. Il sortait peu, ne buvait ni ne fumait. Cela chagrinait encore un peu son père qui lui proposait souvent une gorgée de rhum ou une cigarette sous prétexte de complicité avec son fils. « Mon garçon, tiens, bois avec moi, accompagne-moi mon garçon. » Esteban l'avait rassuré de nombreuses fois, il lui avait parlé de sa « vocation ». Le père d'abord sceptique l'avait pourtant laissé faire et un jour il décida de le voir danser, sans doute lui serait-il plus facile ensuite de le convaincre que non, « mon garçon c'est pas pour toi, c'est pas nous, ces froufrous, ces soies moirées, ces chaussons ridicules. Non, mon garçon. » Il imaginait qu'il aurait beaucoup d'arguments et s'installa au fond de la salle de spectacle. Ce qu'il vit le laissa pantois, ébloui. Il se pencha plusieurs fois vers son voisin pour lui dire « C'est mon garçon, oui, c'est mon garçon ! » Dès lors il assistait de plus en plus souvent aux répétitions et ne craignait plus qu'on le voit au théâtre ni que cela remette en question sa propre virilité. Sur scène Esteban n'avait jamais l'air d'un garçon féminin ou efféminé mais plutôt d'une espèce de félin puissant, agile, souple et viril, et même, au grand étonnement de son père, très viril. Un vrai guerrier, un vrai mâle porteur de toute la testostérone de sa lignée, un vrai danseur.

Pourtant aujourd'hui le père était chagriné, quelque chose qu'il feignait d'ignorer et que son fils lui avait fait redécouvrir, un peu comme si une cicatrice très vieille, une blessure familiale portée de génération en génération s'était ouverte une fois encore. Cela avait commencé lorsqu'Esteban s'était plaint des rôles qu'on lui faisait danser. Il n'avait aucun rôle de soliste, mais mettait en valeur celui-ci par sa force physique et ses performances en matière de jetés, de pirouettes et de portés. Esteban excellait pourtant dans tous les morceaux de bravoure mais aucun maître de ballet n'acceptait de lui confier le rôle de premier danseur, encore moins celui de danseur étoile. Esteban savait qu'il en avait les capacités. Il avait eu de petites altercations avec Rey son maître de ballet, puis les altercations s'étaient transformées en disputes. Il s'était rendu à l'évidence : il ne décrocherait jamais le rôle convoité, sa carrière, certes brillante et honorable, n'évoluerait sans doute plus guère. Il avait alors cessé de s'opposer à Rey et comme s'il avait reçu un coup de fouet, une cicatrice s'était ouverte en lui. Il redoublait d'efforts à chaque entraînement et ses prestations étaient toujours très applaudies. La presse lui avait consacré quelques articles. On pouvait y lire l'étonnement que sa personne soulevait chez les journalistes : pourquoi n'avait-il pas choisi la danse folklorique ? Il était atypique, un noir en danse classique... Rien sur son style, rien sur son travail, rien que des cancans...

En 1995 le ballet national d'Angleterre fit appel à lui, le contrat était juteux, l'école s'en pourlécha les doigts d'avance. Il fallait sans cesse rénover les bâtiments, les parquets, acheter de nouveaux costumes, bref, il aiderait ainsi le pays, l'école, les camarades. La période spéciale imposait ses lois.

« Mon garçon, c'est ta chance et tu dois la saisir, le jour est venu, aujourd'hui c'est à mon tour de t'accompagner, alors je te dis : vas-y, fonce ! Montre au monde entier ce dont nous sommes capables. Porte notre couleur sur la scène des plus grands théâtres et opéras du monde mon garçon. »

Esteban est parti et à l'aéroport son bagage est tout petit mais il pèse très très lourd.

☆☆☆

©Reynaldo Pagan, *El Mono aunque lo vistan de Seda*, peintre cubain, 350x576 cm, acrylique sur toile

Noir et blanc

Olivia Villon

Napoléon et Blanche sont ses meilleurs copains.

Chaque après midi après le goûter, elle les retrouve, dans le terrain vague appelé jardin, à l'arrière de l'immeuble tout neuf dans lequel ils viennent tous trois d'emménager.

Dans la journée, Napoléon va à l'école des garçons et Blanche est avec elle à celle des filles. Deux fois par jour, le matin à huit heures et en début d'après midi, ils font ensemble le chemin de l'école, accompagnés par leurs mamans jusqu'à l'entrée des deux vastes cours de récréation. À l'arrivée, Napoléon les quitte le premier. Il franchit toujours en courant le portillon grand ouvert sur la cour où s'ébattent déjà en tous sens des hordes de petits garçons.

Blanche et elle, n'ont plus que trois pas à faire. À leur tour, elles embrassent leurs mamans et gagnent les nuées piaillantes des autres petites filles. Là, Blanche lui fait un petit signe de la main et rejoint un groupe de fillettes de sa classe. C'est normal, pense-t-elle, on n'a pas la même maîtresse et Blanche est plus grande, elle a sept ans.

La voilà seule, plantée au milieu de la cour.

Tout autour, ça saute, ça bondit, ça joue à la balle et ça crie. Ça zigzague. Elle regarde. Toutes ces petites filles et tous ces bleus, ces jaunes, ces rouges qui colorent leurs blouses pimpantes et les nœuds de tissu soyeux qui ornent leurs coiffures impeccables. Elle regarde et se sent perdue. Elle porte ses doigts à la bouche, grignote ses ongles et cherche des yeux sa maîtresse. Parfois elle l'aperçoit qui arpente la cour, alors, à quelques pas d'elle, elle se met à la suivre. Le plus souvent, elle la voit qui discute en petit groupe avec ses collègues. Elle a très envie d'aller lui donner la main, mais elle n'ose pas.

La plupart du temps sa solitude s'arrête là. Une petite fille s'approche et vient la chercher. Elle se retrouve donc à sauter à la corde ou à lancer en l'air une ou deux balles. Elle essaye parfois de jongler avec trois balles. Sans succès, mais tant pis, elle sait que c'est pour les grandes.

Et puis des sifflets aigus retentissent dans la cour. Tous les jeux s'interrompent. Très vite. Cordes enroulées autour de leurs poignets de bois peint et balles en caoutchouc sont rangées dans les cartables. Deux par deux, toutes les élèves vont se ranger face au mur percé d'un alignement de hautes fenêtres et d'une large porte en bois vernis à deux battants. Les voix se sont tues. Le silence est à peine dérangé par quelques chuchotis, quelques gloussements de rire contenus ou la voix grondeuse d'une des maîtresses. L'une après l'autre, les colonnes de petites filles pénètrent dans le bâtiment.

La classe commence.

Elle est très sage mais a peur de ne pas l'être assez. Elle s'applique à obéir. Ne pas trop bouger (arrête de gigoter), ne pas avoir quelque chose à demander (arrête de bavarder), ne rien faire tomber (arrête de quitter ta chaise), ne pas faire de taches d'encre (regarde moi ce travail de cochon). Mais au contraire, bien lire, bien écrire, réciter et compter sans se tromper, avancer courageusement à tâtons dans le gris de tous ces mystères. En fait, cela lui plaît. Elle est curieuse. Au début de l'année, elle a découvert avec bonheur les « vrais » livres d'école. Elle les feuillette, ils sentent bon ; elle contemple les images, parfois les caresse. Elle aime sentir en elle ces voiles qui petit à petit se déchirent et révèlent alors des choses inconnues, des trucs et des surprises. Elle adore la lecture. Elle est fascinée par les lettres « difficiles » qui forment la queue de l'alphabet, le x, le z, le y ou les groupes de lettres qui font des sons « compliqués », les ch, gu, an, ain, les oi, les oin…elle trouve qu'ils font les malins, mais sont amusants, il faut juste être plus rusée qu'eux, comme pour les devinettes. Chaque semaine, elle attend avec impatience l'heure de poésie. Copier bien proprement sur une page des phrases qui chantent et forment des images, et puis avoir le droit sur l'autre page, de dessiner et colorier un reflet de ces images ! Faire danser, tout autour des strophes ou des vers bien rangés, des rondes de fleurs, des grappes de cœurs, des ribambelles de feuilles ou de soleils ! C'est un délice de liberté, un brin de rêve sans crainte, sans cauchemars. Bien sûr, on doit aussi apprendre par cœur et réciter debout devant tout le monde. Mais ça lui parait facile. Pour retenir le poème, il faut simplement l'amadouer, le lire et relire à voix haute, doucement d'abord, puis de plus en plus vite et presque par magie, quand elle cache les lignes avec le plat de sa main, ses yeux les voient encore et sa bouche peut les répéter. Après, elle est contente, sa maman la fait réciter, la félicite et lui dit qu'elle est fière de sa petite fille. Et si la maîtresse la désigne, lui dit, c'est à toi, elle sait qu'elle n'aura pas de vilaines hésitations. Elle relit dans sa tête le premier mot du poème et sans blanc et sans peine, en cadence et en rythme, les autres mots défilent et s'enchaînent. Elle a toujours dix sur dix et entend sa maîtresse lui dire, très bien, tu mets très bien le ton, comme il faut.

Certaines leçons sont plus coriaces. Le calcul par exemple. Souvent, il suffit de compter ou de faire des opérations, et là c'est sans problème. Mais justement en calcul il y a les problèmes ; et alors, parfois, elle a beau se creuser la tête, elle ne sait pas dans quel sens il faut prendre l'histoire, dans quel ordre faire les opérations pour trouver la solution. Dans ces cas là, plus le temps passe, plus les lignes de l'énoncé se brouillent dans sa tête et ni le plafond, ni les dessins au tableau, ni les affiches sur les murs, ni le ciel bleu au dehors ne viennent la secourir ; elle mâchonne son crayon ou le pointe sur les taches de rousseur de ses bras et les larmes lui montent aux yeux. Heureusement il y a sa maîtresse ; elle survient, se penche sur elle, lui explique un peu, et soudain tout devient clair, et vite vite elle écrit l'explication et fait les opérations avant de refermer son cahier. Son soulagement est immense. Elle se sent sauvée. Elle aura bon.

Elle pense, quelle chance d'avoir une maîtresse si gentille, toujours là pour effacer les doutes, soulever les obstacles et souffler sur les méchantes brumes qui refusent de s'envoler.

C'est donc une petite fille heureuse à l'école.

Néanmoins dans son cœur, il y a souvent comme un mauvais goût dans la bouche qui refuse de partir, comme un secret impossible à aborder et pourtant, très visible. Cette bizarre impression, arrive chaque matin quand elle franchit l'enceinte de l'école, fond souvent dans la journée, mais reprend de la vigueur si la maîtresse annonce la leçon d'histoire géographie. Elle aime bien ces matières. On les apprend dans un livre tout brillant et plein de jolies gravures. Il y a des rois, des chevaliers et des jolies princesses à la peau de lait. Et puis des images de belles grosses vaches à taches noir et blanc, des champs de pommiers, des photos de hautes montagnes couvertes de neige, des ponts géants qui enjambent de larges rivières, des bateaux à étages comme des maisons et des avions haut dans le ciel. Elle écoute avec plaisir les histoires du bon roi Saint Louis, du grand Roi Soleil, les aventures de Charlemagne couronné empereur et celles de la construction des cathédrales et des lignes de chemin de fer. Toutes ces choses, ces arcs de triomphe et cette tour Eiffel, tous ces évènements de son pays, la France. La maîtresse explique que ce ne sont pas des contes ni des légendes mais la réalité, celle d'avant ou d'aujourd'hui.

Elle la croit mais ne comprend pas bien.

Elle tripote le petit plumeau au bout de ses tresses blondes et s'en picote les lèvres. Elle regarde autour d'elle. Les murs, les fenêtres et les têtes brunes de ses compagnes. Elle pense. Aux champs de bananiers et au jus délicieux de la canne à sucre. Aux chars tirés par des bœufs tout maigres. Aux petites routes bordées de cocotiers et de villages de minuscules cases aux toits de tôles. Aux chemins de terre qui grimpent sur les mornes mais arrivent tous à la mer. La mer. Quelle chance, ici c'est une île, on peut y aller souvent. Elle aime cette eau si chaude, si transparente qui laisse voir ses pieds à travers, posés au fond sur le sable, et les petits poissons de toutes les couleurs qui se tortillent tout près et n'ont même pas peur. Elle se dit, j'espère que jeudi on ira à la plage, maman a promis. Avant, quand elle était encore trop petite pour aller à l'école, la mer était beaucoup plus loin de la maison. Elle n'allait jamais à la plage. Mais avant, c'était ailleurs. Dans son souvenir, un peu flou, elle voit des fleurs, des roses surtout, et des palmiers, des oliviers. Mais de toute façon, dans un endroit comme dans l'autre, avant comme maintenant, elle a beau faire, elle ne retrouve rien des descriptions de la maîtresse. C'est étrange. Elle n'a pourtant jamais quitté la France. Elle le sait par son papa et sa maman.

Ils ont seulement pris l'avion et volé haut dans le ciel, comme dans la photo de son livre, pour s'installer ici à cause du travail de son papa. Ils ont seulement changé de région.

Quand elle part si fort dans ces rêveries, la voix chantante de sa maîtresse la ramène brutalement sur sa chaise en se faisant sévère. « Où es-tu ? Tu n'écoutes pas ! Fais attention ! À quoi rêves-tu ? ».

Comment lui répondre ?

Comment dire que dans sa tête elle a d'autres paysages, d'autres gens, ceux d'ici et ceux d'ailleurs, mais pas ceux de la leçon ?

Comment lui dire pourquoi votre peau est si noire, comme celle de Napoléon et de sa petite sœur qui pourtant s'appelle Blanche ?

Pourquoi les rois, les reines et les princes de France ne sont jamais noirs ? Pourquoi je n'ai jamais vu de vaches grasses et de fromages crémeux, ni de neige, ni de montagnes blanches qui touchent les nuages ? Pourquoi Charlemagne est un petit garçon qui joue souvent avec Napoléon et nous, le jeudi quand on n'a pas école?

Pourquoi... pourquoi ? Si la France c'est l'Algérie et aussi la Guadeloupe... Pourquoi, plus de femmes sans visage en voile blanc dans la rue mais des femmes noires qui rient de toutes leurs dents et se dandinent en robes bariolées... Pourquoi... et qui sont les vrais habitants de France ? Y en a-t-il des faux ? D'ailleurs, Pourquoi le grand Charles qui vient bientôt ici à Pointe à Pitre est De gaulle si la Gaule n'existe plus ?

Tous ces pourquoi se bloquent.

Elle ne peut rien dire.

Alors elle baisse la tête et se tait, elle chasse toutes ces questions et reprend aussitôt le cours de la leçon.

Et quand la cloche sonne, elle s'échappe très vite dans la cour comme toutes ses petites camarades.

Comme d'habitude, elle se retrouve seule enfant blanche parmi toutes les fillettes noires.

***

©Olivia Villon, photo montage

Oubli

Si tu me dis que l'Etranger
hésitait à te parler ;
Si tu me dis que son visage
exprimait la méfiance,
Si tu me dis qu'il courbait la tête
lorsque tu l'interrogeais,

C'est que tu n'as pas su l'accueillir !

Si tu me dis qu'il a détourné son regard,
C'est qu'il n'a rien trouvé dans le tien !

Si tu me dis qu'au-delà de son étrangeté,
tu ne sentais pas son humanité,
C'est que tu ne lui as pas révélé la tienne,
demeurée enfouie en toi-même.

Que s'est-il passé pour toi, l'ami
qui autrefois fus l'Etranger ?

Denise Bénaquin

La ville entière

Carole Menahem-Lilin

C'est une ville entière. On ne peut pas entrer dans une rue, sans pénétrer la ville tout entière. Où que l'on se tourne, c'est le corps pétrifié tout entier de la ville qu'on voit. Avec ses souterrains, ses tours et ses arcades.

L'étrangeté de cette ville, c'est que ses habitants sortent du sol. Le matin, ils émergent proprets de ses pores – portes bleues qui s'ouvrent à même la chaussée. Ils saluent la chevelure crantée des tours et s'en vont leur chemin, suivant leur ombre qui s'allonge démesurément devant eux, leur ombre qui épouse au plus près l'épiderme doré de la ville entière.

Il faut pourtant en sortir parfois, de cette ville entière. Il faut bien en sortir, puisqu'on y est entré… C'est en tout cas ce que moi j'ai fait.

Je venais de loin. D'une savane vierge aux épineux brutaux. J'avais pénétré la ville par la porte du haut – l'œil, je crois – et je m'en trouvais bien.

Il faisait doux dans cette ville-là.

Tout de même, du plus doux des séjours, on souhaite parfois sortir.

Lorsque j'en ai parlé aux frères – car ils sont tous frères là-dedans – lorsque donc je leur en ai parlé, ils se sont étonnés. Puis effrayés.

Jamais ils n'avaient fait la distinction entre moi et eux. Ils croyaient que je sortais d'un pore chaque matin, tout comme eux. Avec un costume peut-être un plus différent. Et un air plus… moins… avec un air un peu plus aigu sur le visage, peut-être. Voilà.

Mais ils croyaient que j'étais un frère comme eux.

C'est ce qui les a le plus effrayés, qu'on puisse ne pas être un frère. Et qu'on puisse venir d'ailleurs.

C'était insécurisant au possible. M'ont-ils reproché.

Etre différent, passe. Mais le dire !

Quant aux procédures de mon adoption par la ville… et aux modalités de ma naissance… cela, ils n'ont même pas voulu l'examiner.

Ils ont regardé ma silhouette différemment.

M'ont regardé(e).

Différemment.

Le regard de ces êtres qui n'avaient l'habitude de n'envisager que du semblable se fit, lorsqu'il se posa sur moi, méchant. Bizarrement insistant. Parfois larmoyant.

Leur regard souffrait d'avoir à me considérer.

D'avoir à me considérer, moi, dissemblable.

Leurs yeux souffraient d'avoir à accommoder. Jusque là, ils s'étaient contentés de rendre grâce à ce qu'ils connaissaient. De reconnaître ce qu'ils savaient.

Leur regard était action de grâce pour l'étendue de ce qui leur était offert, et qu'ils connaissaient.

Tout cela qui était issu de la même matrice, qui leur était mère, ou frère, tout cela attestait leur existence et la fondait.

J'étais, moi, un fragment de leur non-existence. Il y avait un ailleurs à la ville entière ; un ailleurs où ils n'existaient pas ; jusqu'alors, ils ne s'en doutaient pas.

Jusqu'alors ils croyaient que, puisque la ville se présentait entière quelque fut le côté d'où on l'envisageait, elle représentait aussi l'entièreté du monde.

C'était une belle idée ; le monde eut ainsi été une joue ; une épaule ; une hanche. Le monde eut été une amande. Egale et douce.

C'était une belle idée. Tout de même, je leur expliquai que si la ville entière avait été le monde tout entier, elle n'eût pu être si égale et si douce toujours. Qu'il existait des rapides ; des précipices ; des colères et des volontés ; des exaltations ; et que si la ville entière avait dû seule représenter tout cela, ils auraient vécu au cœur d'un volcan.

Ils me répondirent que si la ville entière avait été seul monde, il n'aurait rien existé de tout cela, voilà tout. Rien qu'une ville étagée alanguie au soleil.

J'aurais encore pu me taire. Me fondre. Peut-être à la longue, aurait-on oublié ma différence.

Mais je n'ai pas compris le danger. J'insistai. Je voulais fonder mon droit à être moi.

C'était un beau rêve que cette ville entière, leur dis-je. Mais le réel…

Ah, le réel ! Ce réel dont je leur parlais, ils ne le souhaitaient pas.

Que le réel disparaisse. Que la différence s'aplanisse. L'indifférencié leur convenait. Mais je viens du réel, leur dis-je...

Tu ne viens pas de là où tu l'as dit, me répliquèrent-ils. Tu es l'un des étrons de la ville. Cela peut arriver même à la plus distinguée des villes entières, que de déféquer quelquefois. Nous lui pardonnons.

Mais toi, tu ne lui pardonnes pas : alors tu racontes n'importe quoi sur ta naissance. Une naissance extra-citadine, voyez-vous ça ! Va te laver, étron. Lorsque tu auras les idées nettes, peut-être cesseras-tu d'empuantir.

Je partis la tête basse. Je n'avais pas de réponse à ma question – comment sortir quelquefois de la ville entière – et la vie douce avait cessé d'être si douce. Au fil des jours, les regards s'amalgamaient autour de moi. On me regardait, on s'interrogeait sur moi ; mes faits et gestes étaient surveillés.

Oh, mes faux-frères eux-mêmes n'étaient pas pour grand-chose dans cet état de fait inquiétant. C'étaient leurs regards et c'étaient leurs ombres, qui me menaçaient. Eux-mêmes, mes faux-frères, eux-mêmes dans leur entièreté (dans l'entièreté de leur conscience) n'avaient certes pas connaissance de ce qui se tramait.

À leur insu, leurs regards me condamnaient.

À leur insu, leurs ombres me menaçaient.

Et donc, leurs ombres ne filaient plus droit devant eux. C'était moi qu'elles filaient. Lorsqu'elles se rencontraient à un carrefour, elles ne se séparaient plus ; elles s'attardaient ; discutaient ; s'effrayaient et s'indignaient de concert.

Ce n'est pas bien, quand les ombres apprennent l'amalgame.

Ce n'est pas rassurant, je vous le dis.

On ne savait pas bien comment, dans cette ville, les événements advenaient. Mais on sentait.

On sentait par le sol, par les murs, par la peau, organe commun.

Et là, ça n'allait pas. Quelque chose gênait le fonctionnement habituel. Ça ne sentait pas bon.

Et bien sûr, pour la mauvaise odeur, c'était moi qu'on accusait.

Ce sont les ombres qui ont dû fomenter ça ; les ombres, à l'insu des personnes entières.

Dans cette ville entière, les frères ne se méfiaient pas assez de leurs fragments. Ils ne savaient pas qu'on peut être plusieurs, qu'on peut être double.

Dans une ville entière, on n'imagine même pas que la duplicité puisse exister.

Et si on parvenait à l'imaginer, on en accuserait forcément l'autre.

Oui mais l'autre, quel autre ? Pas son frère, pas son ombre, pas la ville. Rien de cela qui issu du tout, y retourne.

J'étais le seul étron disponible.
Coupé. Coupable. Expulsable.
Je dirais même mieux : à expulser.

Un matin, alors que je sortais de mon pore bleu habituel – j'avais élu domicile à l'écart, contre un mur mauve – à la pliure de l'aine, je crois – un matin donc, les ombres se sont pressées autour de moi.

Elles ont recouvert mon corps. L'ont assommé de leur poids. Puis l'ont traîné jusqu'aux remparts. Ce faisant, l'ont un peu abîmé, cahoté, cogné contre les murs.

Je tiens à préciser qu'il s'agissait des ombres. Leurs propriétaires, eux, tournaient le dos. Ils sifflotaient l'air du matin en regardant le sommet doré, potelé, admirable des tours.

Admirer l'admirable, qu'y a-t-il en effet de mieux à faire ?
Rien.
Sinon expulser l'expulsable.
Elégante symétrie.

Mon corps fut donc hissé jusqu'en haut du rempart, à coup de coups et d'efforts, par les ombres.

Il fut hissé, poussé, expulsé.

Je sais à présent comment on sort de la ville entière : en morceaux.

J'ai rassemblé mes restes aux pieds des remparts, et je travaille à ma reconstruction. Sans doute ne retrouverai-je pas figure entière, mais je fais aussi bien que je peux. Les premiers jours, j'ai pleuré des larmes et des larmes sur ces morceaux perdus de moi. Difficile de renoncer à son entièreté, aux pieds d'une ville entière, parmi les épineux et les serpents.

Mais peu à peu je me suis habituée. Les figues de Barbarie ne ricanent pas quand je les croque, et leurs graines daignent pousser quand je les plante. Les lézards ne s'effarouchent plus de ma présence ; l'eau est bonne à mon palais. Tout cela m'encourage. Je me dis que je serai ce que je ferai, et non ce qu'on me renverra de mon image. Mon visage m'exprimera moi, au lieu de refléter la perfection.

Tout ce que je souhaite c'est d'être assez vaillante pour affronter ces remparts. Je me faufilerai dans la ville par l'œil, par l'oreille, par la lèvre, par le sexe. J'apprendrai à garder les portes ouvertes. J'y entrerai, j'en sortirai. J'attendrai qu'on me veuille. J'attendrai qu'elle, la ville, m'aime.

Un jour, je serai l'élue, l'aimée.

Alors, la ville se lèvera. Alors, les frères apprendront à sortir par des portes verticales et à marcher sur leurs ombres.

⁂

Dégage !

Karima Berger

Tu ne me reconnais donc pas ?

Oui, peut-être mais fais-toi oublier

Je ris fort et je rêve clair dans tes nuits

Laisse-moi seul

Tu rigoles ? Toi ? Seul ?

Tais-toi !

Je rêve clair oui mais de hauts crimes aussi, tes horreurs blanches mais t'inquiète, j'efface le sang aux premières lueurs de l'aube

Qui donc t'a ouvert la porte ?

J'étais là avant toi, déjà, je traînais dans le grand vide de ta maison, de la chambre de ton père, de ta mère, un paria.

Et ils ne t'ont pas chassé ?

Ils ont bien essayé mais je leur étais nécessaire

Mais moi ?

Toi, je t'aime, et nécessaire je le suis aussi, malgré toi. Je t'aime, je t'émeus, te trouble et tu ne sais pas pourquoi

Dehors !

Je pleure, je demande l'hospitalité dans le grand vide de ta maison, sais-tu qu'elle serait encore plus vide sans moi ? J'erre en toi comme en un pays familier et je veux habiter tes profondeurs secrètes

Et puis quoi encore ?

Je te cherche ; sans moi, tu serais faible et blafard et, moins intelligent, sûrement. Tu te nourrirais de la même nourriture toujours et ton esprit serait atteint, le scorbut du « même », tu connais ?

Tais-toi bon sang !

Sang oui ! Noirceurs, viles parfois, tu me sens une odeur étrange qui t'attire et t'emplit de doutes

Je te hais

Tu me hais d'amour. Lâcheté.

Je ne comprends pas ce que tu dis

Normal ! Je parle une langue obscure, un roulis qui remue l'enfance ou te rappelle la mer ou la fêlure de. Mais tu préfères fermer les écoutilles et te prendre pour un pur bloc de pureté pure

Tes yeux sont au bord de l'embrasement

Je suis beau d'une beauté ardente. Je revêts toutes formes, je m'habille de vêtements pareils à ceux des gitans et te provoque..., mon être est fait d'un corps subtil et tu veux me toucher !

Pour te chasser !

Et pour me goûter, parle franchement ! Mais c'est dur pour toi de l'avouer

Casse-toi !

Tes mains si douces pourtant, je les embrasserai et le grand vide de ta maison, je m'y loverai, frémissant. La rose de tes lèvres, j'en ferai mon extase

Voleur !

Oh ! Voler ton âme, la plier dans ma main et qu'elle se soumette enfin au vivant qui l'affole

Mais qui es-tu ?

Ta route est jonchée de peurs, je te vois tituber ou là-haut sur les remparts prêt à. Je te survivrai jusqu'au dernier mot éteint

Ta voix criarde

Mais c'est le vide dans ta maison qui la fait résonner. Tu dis que je te colonise, que je viole ton intimité

Dégage !

Je suis d'une race lointaine où tu peux te mirer jusqu'aux confins de ta race !

C'est ça ! Putain de ta race !

Je voulais dire de ta race d'homme, *l'espèce*, you see what I mean ?

I mean rien du tout !

Mon désir dans ta pensée : courts-circuits. Franchir les portes closes des remparts qui te cernent, je te tends les clés et jamais tu ne remercies

Je ne t'ai rien demandé !

C'est ça que j'aime, être là où tu ne m'attends pas. Tu entends ta voix et tu dis : Qui va là? Parfois, dans l'amour tu entrouvres la porte, c'est que tu es déjà ouvert. Ceci, je le dois à ton amante, plus généreuse, ses mots t'altèrent

Et les tiens m'énervent !

J'affleure sur la mer gelée, ton front se déplie puis se noie de douceur, hallucinés tes yeux se penchent sur le port intérieur, ton corps fléchit sous l'aile de mon ombre, se livre, s'épanche, trop. Le flot se rompt soudain et je peux entendre se cadenasser ton être.

Mais qui donc es-tu ?

L'autre de toi-même.

De moi-même ?

Oui l'autre.

« D'entre tous les voiles, ton existence et ton âme sont assurément les plus épais ».
Mawquif 241. **Emir Abd-el-Kader**
Texte écrit en novembre 2010

☆☆☆

Létrangerentoi

L'étranger l'étrangère
Ta violence Ma violence
Cette inconnue en nous
Qui nous fait projeter sur le voisin
Tout le mal du monde
L'étranger est en nous bien avant d'être près de chez nous
L'inconnu du dedans l'étranger le plus méchant

L'inconnue en nous qui pourrait nourrir de son lait d'amour généreux
L'étrangère de ton cœur lui portes-tu un seul regard ?

Cette essence d'amour que tant de nous refusent
Pour mieux jouir de blesser de rosser de tuer
Le bébé ne naît pas assassin
Je le nie haut et fort
Tu deviens je deviens

Assassin bien assis à la meurtrière de sa tour d'ivoire
Israël la Palestine c'est chaque jour partout sur la planète
Dès que l'on peut on se massacre par
La violence les coups le mensonge la manipulation le voile
Dieu et ses saints ne sauvent rien
On tue même en leur nom
Pas besoin de dieu pour tuer ni pour aimer
Il suffit d'être humain
L'humain cet étranger que tu portes en ton être
Et ne reconnais pas
L'humain qui t'engage à faire des efforts
Effort, ô le gros mot
L'effort d'exister grand et de laisser vivre les autres
En grand également
L'effort exceptionnel
De n'être pas criminel-le
Et de laisser pousser des ailes à nos cœurs corps mortels
Poète, ta peau aime
Et moi aussi je l'aime
Ton étrange thé
Et mon cri d'étrangère à étranger...

Geneviève David

Le monde étrange

Il y a des jours comme les dimanches,
des heures floues et nomades parfois
Des jours de terrain vagues à l'âme,
des soirs qu'on n'imagine même pas.

J'ai de la peine au monde étrange.
Les livres ouverts qu'on n'ouvre pas.
Les rêves éconduits aux frontières,
à tour de force, à bout de bras.

Il y a des jardins prisonniers, des barbelés dans les idées,
Des parcs interdits de bacs à sable,
des cours d'école sans un cahier.

J'ai de la peine au monde étrange.
Les jeunes, les vieux, les mieux que ça.
Le catalogue chez Ikea sans un espace pour toi et moi.

Toi, tu es celle pour qui je me bats
Eux, les hommes forts, les drôles de rois,
Moi je voulais tant un au-delà
Un toit du monde, l'Himalaya
Toi et tes allures de caravane
Tu roules à l'envers du décor
Tu es la richesse sans les ors
La blancheur du Karakoram

J'ai de la peine au monde étrange.
Les traversées qu'on ne veut pas.
Les acrobates à effet de manches,
leurs tours de piste je n'en veux pas.

Il y a des jours comme les dimanches,
des heures floues et nomades parfois
Des jours de terrain vagues à l'âme,
des cirques qu'on n'imagine même pas.

J'ai de la peine au monde étrange,
mon étrangère tu le sais bien.
Je voudrais lire dans ta main
l'envie de vivre un lendemain.

Hélène Pradas-Billaud

©Jean-Luc Letellier, *Baobab sacré*, Burkina Faso, août 2010

Cet entre-deux

Arbres.
Comment était le mien avant qu'il ne devienne grand comme ça et tordu penché sur ses racines qui semblent si loin, les branches aimeraient bien cette rencontre apparemment impossible. Seules certitudes, à chaque moment de sa croissance, à chaque moment marquant, l'arbre peut être découpé temporellement, sa vie peut être retracée, en fonction des différents endroits où on l'a planté, replanté, replanté…
Les différents sols comme le rappel d'une vie qui se cherche une unité, une voie, des explications, un pourquoi, un comment.
Ces terres il les aime toutes ; toutes l'ont nourri, vu croître, accompagné.
Pourtant toutes le blessent, aussi. Chacune le renvoie à la précédente, ces transplantations… L'écorce écorchée
Les racines deviennent symboliques
Alors, se les réinventer, les créer, les rêver, avec tout ce que l'on est ici et maintenant
Vécu, conscience et inconscience.
Sentir plutôt que définir.
Avancer
L'arbre grandit.
Arbre caméléon
Voyager
Transitions, transits
Ne rien perdre
Ne pas se perdre

L'opposition intérieur/extérieur marquée par la vitre
La frontière transparente
Le mur invisible ou si peu
Les regards peuvent s'échanger
Le corps stable et l'esprit qui vagabonde
Être en un endroit et en rêver un autre
En partant de ce que l'on voit
La traversée de la vitre permet tous les mondes
Comme une ouverture sur d'autres histoires.

La vitre protège, aussi
Du vent du froid de la pluie de la poussière des moucherons
des mouches des chats des inconnus
Elle me met à l'écart à part à côté.

Deux éléments et cet entre-deux
Qui sépare délimite marque pointe
Les différences
Chaque univers

La vitre la vitre

Sale, elle a sa propre histoire
Contempler ses dessins
Ces récits trajets impressions
Les marques traces empreintes taches
une vitre est rarement impeccable.

Se taper la tête contre la vitre
Briser la vitre
Les mille morceaux
L'air qui rentre.

L'attente au carré dans une voiture.
Echapper aux bourrasques de vent – j'y perçois cependant
le chant d'un oiseau –

Quitter le tourbillon des feuilles papiers poussières
Oublier le froid et ce ciel gris cendre qui tasse
Regarder la gouttière
Le bitume
Les bancs
La poubelle
Les ventilations extérieures
Les grilles
Les barreaux
Les non-couleurs
L'herbe éparse
Les quelques arbres, arbustes, qui luttent pour leur place.
Se mettre sur pause
Et recevoir les images-mots
Les laisser s'amuser ensemble jusqu'à ce que le jeu dérape.
Se plonger dans une mélancolie facile – les doutes peurs drames.
Et le sentiment d'un temps différent
Immobilité
Huis-clos
Se rattacher aux dates aux heures
Se soumettre à cet ordre convention –se rassurer–
Retenir, dans les deux sens du terme, les moments.
Contemplation du dehors du dedans
De l'ailleurs aussi. Les trois temps, les mille lieux
À l'extérieur, les éléments.
Ici et maintenant, un cerveau qui rumine.
Immobilité du corps bloqué en ce lieu par l'absence de l'autre
Qui arrive, il arrive.

Je photographie la route des bouts de route
Le soleil me brûle les yeux
Et le bitume

Sols craquelés à déchiffrer
Pistes chemins trajets trajectoires

La randonnée
Suivre les directions
Parcourir
Se trouver tout à coup très loin de ce qui est pourtant si près
S'en éloigner s'en jouer s'en inspirer
Partir vers des ailleurs toujours vierges
L'imagination à plein régime
Gris blanc noir
Et les parasites, ceux qui s'étalent sur l'asphalte
Les accidents.

Immortaliser, c'est se souvenir d'un point de départ visuel
Je vois, je suis en mesure de me fondre dans ce que je vois et de partir, voyager, et cet instant, dont la durée importe peu, cet instant je veux m'en souvenir, le faire partager d'une certaine manière.
Il y a eu une énergie
Je cadre comme je vois veux voir
Ou comment raconter une histoire.

Sandra Michel

Amour

Je restais derrière la vitre
En regardant ce monde
Hostile et dur
Après la tempête Xynthia.
Je ne te connaissais pas encore.

Un jour je t'ai vu marcher,
Toi l'étranger,
Dans cette ville en folie
Et j'ai couru vers toi,
Mon amour étranger,
Laissant la chaise vide
Derrière la vitre.

Toi et moi,
Découvrons la beauté du monde,
Dans des langues différentes,
Mais main dans la main
Pour nous donner du courage.
Nous voyageons dans des régions glacées
Et inconnues.

Je ne suis plus seule et vide
Dans cet univers en délire
Avec toi,
Mon amour étranger.

La chaise derrière la vitre
Est maintenant abandonnée
Car la vie est revenue
Dans cette cité pimpante
Et fébrile.

Et je me sens bien
Dans tes bras étrangers,

Mon amour exilé.

Thérèse-Françoise Crassous

©Jean-Luc Letellier, *Baobab sacré*, Burkina Faso, août 2010

Entre

Valéry Meynadier

C'est ça : entre

Entre les cheveux, entre les ongles, entre mes mains Entre

Entre mes yeux, entre la vie et la mort, entre deux flocons deux feuilles deux cris

L'air s'est replié ce jour-là

Entre est entré mon mal mort, amniotique, coagulé entre deux s'est échappé corps étranger sans aucune sorte d'appartenance au réel, éthérique et cellulaire, d'une seule peau entre deux vertiges s'est posé, étrangloir pour au grand jour

Entre deux jours impossibles et pourtant a pris place jusqu'à quand ?

Punaisé sur ma langue

Entre deux souffles

Entre

Entre deux dents deux mots profondément enracinés au jour du dernier jour inavouable et maudit sans ressemblance, d'une identité sans concessions, me rognera les reins, m'a rogné la mémoire, déchiqueté, gobé dans l'oeuf, avalé, recraché

Obsession carnassière

Mes souvenirs pissent le sang

Et on croit encore à la mort entière !

Riraront fort bien

Me voici sur un fauteuil, par ta faute, pauvre fou

Suspendus à l'arbre, mes gènes feuillus brillent de ton acte couronné d'épines

L'ombre de tes lignes de main MORDICUS m'a fendu le crâne en deux

L'ombre est entrée, fibreuse, je devais feuilleter entre tes lignes : pourquoi tu avais fait ça

Entre toi et moi

Entre tu es entré

Je n'ai jamais pu te poser la question, tu es mort avant, seul comme un chien dans une salle d'urgence, suspendue entre deux jugements : *il a tué sa femme, il a tué sa femme*, qu'ils chuchotaient à l'hôpital, tu penses, ils n'ont pas soigné le clébard aux mains tachées de sang

Seulement ce chien c'était toi, mon père, un assassin

Puis tu as retourné l'arme contre toi

Bang Bang

Entre systole et diastole, tu t'es sûrement dit que tu ne pouvais pas me laisser comme ça sans explications

Alors tu t'es ramifié liquidien, sans grammaire aucune jusqu'à moi, fillette de six ans et sans plus songer à demain puisque demain venait de mourir : tu t'es planté en moi

Du moins précisément : ta terreur ton effroi, celle que je ressens à chaque fois que j'aime

Entre deux soupçons, toujours à fouiller les poches, les regards, je charogne les mots pour y trouver le vrai et si un retard se profile

Charognarde, je fonds sur mon galant, il sent le cadavre, l'entourloupe, il me ment, il ne peut en être autrement

D'heures malades en heures malades, j'avance sous ta coupe

Des heures d'ossuaires m'ensevelissent

Tu me rejoues ton dernier acte pour que je comprenne. Mais

je savais papa qu'elle te trompait avec ton meilleur ami

Tout le monde le savait !

Tout de même on ne tue pas pour ça

Toi si

Et c'est ça que tu veux me faire entendre : tu y pensais tellement jour après jour nuit après nuit sans rien dire que ton silence en moi, ton enfant, est venu éclore

Tu n'es pas mort en ton entier

Pour cela aujourd'hui sur ce fauteuil en velours noir, de taille basse, légèrement glissant en arrière si on le lui commande, je parle de toi, de moi

Entre deux soupirs, je récapitule : pépé mémé de la branche maternelle, de braves paysans

M'ont menti, bien sûr, m'ont dit que papa maman avaient eu un accident de voiture

Clouée au sol, j'ai reconnu la fable, mais j'ignorais que le mensonge devient pathogène en grandissant, se métabolise en maladie, en troubles du comportement, il pousse, méphistophélique

Patience a été mon mot d'ordre, dehors m'attendait et si tous les arbres en colère se mettaient à marcher, l'Homme ne ferait pas long feu

Mon imaginaire d'enfant se portait bien

J'avais six ans quand tout cela est arrivé

J'ai grandi, me semble-t-il, absente à mon manque, entourée d'amour, de nature, pépé mémé vivaient en pleine campagne près de Châteauroux

Ils avaient une cheminée et pas de télé, je n'avais jamais vu d'arbre partir en cendres

J'étais émerveillée

À partir du décès de mes parents, j'ai vu la toute puissance et l'immense fragilité des choses

Et puis papa était souvent là, maman presque jamais là, mes grands-parents, tout le temps là, J'insiste : j'ai été heureuse

Alors quoi ? Qu'est ce qui se passe ? Mes amants sont derrière, c'était il y a longtemps

Mon mari ne me trompe pas, je le sais mais une petite voix, Ta voix, me dit que je me trompe

Combien de fois entre deux portes, entre deux hoquets suspendue aux belles lèvres carminées de mon mari, ne lui ai-je fait jurer père mère et toute la clique qu'il ne m'a jamais trompée, ne me trompera jamais, sinon, sinon

– Sinon quoi ?

De m'envoyer chez une thérapeute

Je ne parle pas de toi tout de suite

De mon mari je parle, je l'aime, il m'aime, il n'y a pas l'ombre d'un doute

Sauf l'ombre de toi

J'ai confiance en mon mari, dis-je

Le ciel m'envahit quand je le vois arriver

Les nuages se placent à sa droite

Zinzin

Bouche bée

Au lit, les heures s'essoufflent, pas nous

Petit à petit, j'en viens à toi, pauvre fou

Sur mon fauteuil, je suis une multitude

Il ne faut pas que la multitude prenne le dessus, aussi je me rassemble, je fais le tri avec ma thérapeute – aussi appelée psychogénéalogiste.

On a fait un génosociogramme, une sorte d'arbre un peu plus élaboré, avec les moments-clés de la famille, c'est là où j'ai appris d'où tu venais

Devant mon arbre généalogique, j'ai vu

Ton père : un célèbre monte-en-l'air dans le cirque de la société

Motus sur ton grand-père, non moins célèbre maquereau dans les eaux troubles de Marseille

Ton arrière-grand-père un colon empoigneur de terre et d'esclave en tout genre

Jusqu'à toi

L'arbre me prend aux entrailles

Alors, avec tout mon corps d'enfant d'adulte et de vieillarde, je m'accroche à mon fauteuil, j'élague

Entre le dit et le non-dit, j'arrache le fond

Ma thérapeute piste les traces mnésiques, entre psycho et sorcellerie, elle dévoile les corps émotionnels de mes bisaïeuls, trisaïeuls

On met à jour le voleur le maquereau

Mettre à jour c'est émonder étêter secouer l'arbre pour que les souvenirs inconscients pourris tombent crèvent me laissent en paix

Enfin, je parle

J'aime mon mari mes enfants mon métier

Moi, je ne m'aime pas

De souche dégénérative, des remugles de jalousie déshonorante, improbables, innommables me font passer à mes propres yeux pour une moins que rien, aux yeux des autres pour une malade, que je suis

Comment mon mari pourrait-il avoir un penchant pour cette sexagénaire racleuse de plancher à l'haleine tumorale en phase terminale ?

Nous venons tout juste d'acheter le garage Rougemont

Mon mari est mécanicien, régulièrement, il répare la vieille Peugeot de madame Lefebvre

Il faut me voir derrière ma fenêtre, la cervelle bleue rouée de doutes accrochée aux rideaux

Nous habitons au-dessus du garage

Je les vois, tarée, débile, en copulation aigue sur le capot

Je trouve un prétexte, je descends, livide, desséchée, méconnaissable, je les dérange et je vois bien encore une fois qu'il n'y a rien

Rien que toi, pauvre fou

En moi

Depuis deux ans maintenant, je viens ici, sur mon fauteuil, entre deux rendez-vous, habillée de la pâleur qui t'appartient, entre deux blancs, dans la fournaise de ta mémoire entrevue sur mes joues, sur mon front, dans la paume de mes mains, quand je fais l'amour soudain parfois tu es là tout entier, toi et ton doute

Mais aujourd'hui, je te reconnais

Papa, veux-tu finir de mourir, s'il te plait

Pitié, que ce doute avilissant nocif quitte ma mémoire

Ce n'est pas mon trauma à moi

Qu'est ce que je vais transmettre à mes enfants si ça continue ?

C'est donc si important que ça de savoir d'où on vient ?

D'avant le ventre, entre père et mère

Je veux m'en remettre au présent

Devenir libre d'hier

Avec mon mari, on cherche un arbre pour la balançoire. Entre trois arbres, on hésite : le frêne élastique s'élance, plein d'oeils de jais en train de pousser. Ce serait dommage. Vient le charme. Dans le parc d'à côté, il est taillé en charmilles, ici dans notre jardin, il faut le voir, libre et touffu mais pas assez haut.

Reste le chêne, l'arbre allié de nos maisons. Grâce à lui : charpentes, escaliers, parquets. Pourquoi pas balançoire ? Je caresse l'arbre. Je sens une suture toute neuve le long de ma colonne d'être.

Je te sens disparaître, pauvre fou.

Un gui géant mange la sève de notre arbre élu, le boit jusqu'à sa cime l'étouffe comme moi j'ai pu étouffer.

Comme par hasard, Madame Lefebvre arrive, elle a besoin de mon mari. Il est un peu tard, non ? Sa voiture fait un drôle de bruit. Juste un petit coup d'oeil, s'il vous plait.

Je vais chercher le sécateur.

Je grimpe dans l'arbre et je m'attaque méthodiquement aux énormes touffes de feuilles d'un vert blondasse. Ta voix au fond de moi *: il est avec madame Lefebvre.*

J'arrache.

Après, il faudra creuser la branche pour ôter complètement le suçoir destructeur. Peut-être même scier la branche. Puis mettre du mastic cicatrisant. Tout ça demande du temps. Je ne pense pas à mon mari. Quand je pense que je n'y pense pas, mes nerfs si prompts à se lever, prennent le temps, regardent et voient que ce n'est plus leur affaire. Mon cerveau frémit. Ma lucidité se transforme en hargne joyeuse. Je m'arrache à moi. Ma peau se décolle. J'ai été jalouse pour trois vies entières. Plus jamais ça. Je taille dans le vif. Je vais chercher la scie, sans un regard pour Madame Lefebvre. J'exulte. Mon mort est bien mort.

Je remonte dans l'arbre, à califourchon sur une branche et je scie, je sue, j'en ris, j'y suis, je suis libre !

Je redescends, je vais chercher les cordes.

L'arbre est comme neuf.

J'installe la balançoire de mes enfants, elle peut maintenant aller et venir en paix.

***

Chant d'amour et d'exil

Comme le corps disloqué d'un grand oiseau blanc
Dérivent lentement les nuages,
S'écartent et s'entrecroisent en silence,
Eventent, nonchalants, leurs caresses meurtries
Etranger, tu lèves la tête et tu souris.
Tu souris, imperceptiblement, devant cette douleur
De chair muette au ciel inscrite. Comme eux,
Tu as laissé s'ouvrir ton corps au vent de la nécessité.
Grand tronc déraciné engourdi par le froid,
Tu as laissé couler ton cri, de rivières en rivières,
De fleuves en fleuves, dans un clapot de sang et de larmes.
Ton cri de liberté,
Ton cri de déchirure,
Jusqu'à une mer improbable, noyée dans un brouillard de chrysanthème.
Mais la mer ne s'est pas ouverte devant toi et tes compagnons d'infortune,
Elle a dressé au plus haut qu'elle a pu ses remparts et ses tours d'écorchure.

C’est cela que tu as connu ; la douleur comme un opium lourd.
Aujourd’hui, ton salut vers le ciel est tressé de lumière
Fier de reprendre pied sur la grève de ton sourire
De faire jaillir les éclats de souvenirs
De ceux qui te sont chers et font crépiter ta mémoire.
Etranger, prends patience. Etranger, prends confiance,
Semblable à tous ceux que les vents contraires
Isolent sur l’îlot fragile de l’errance,
Un tour du monde pour faire le tour de soi-même,
Parvenir, au-delà de l’écume amère, jusqu’à la nacre pure,
Part venir, au-delà des sables étouffants, jusqu’au rosier des senteurs,
Et bientôt, bientôt… l’irradiante explosion du retour.

Anne Guerber

La photo

Des yeux, sur la photo
De cette riante fête,
Je la cherche cette femme
Si jeune et si fougueuse
Qui chantait et son âme
Et romances d'autrefois
Et vous offrait paroles
De la putain si belle vie
J'aimerais la rencontrer
Cette femme
Qui à la mort brandissait
Et ses poings et ses mots.

Une femme-chanson
D'elle-même et de vous autres.

Sur la photo je la cherche
Elle est jeune la dame qui parle
Elle est vieille quand on la regarde
Une vieille au double menton,
Une que le temps a si fort
Embrassée, baisée et
Parfois violée
Qu'elle en a le visage
Tout gaufré, le ventre
Tout défoncé,
Une éventrée :
MOI.

À vingt ans, au miroir
Je la traquais déjà
Une femme déjà lasse.
Aujourd'hui, septante ans
Oubliés les miroirs
C'est la photo qui traque :
Quelle est cette vieille femme
Que tous reconnaissent
Et que je ne connais pas ?

Ce n'est pas moi…

Moi ne connais de moi
Que la force de la voix
D'une qui
Debout face au vent
Et debout devant vous
Se chante et vous chante
Cris, rêves de beautés
Rêves adolescents. Et
Révolte, la diane du matin
Tenue de combat
Contre l'atroce de ce monde
Mais tout au fond de soi
La gamine qui pleure
Et loin, plus loin encore,
Le cri du nouveau né

Mais cette vieille-là
Sur la photo
C'est pas moi
Ou alors…
Ce fut toujours moi.

Il faut toute une vie
Pour l'aimer la vie

Comme par goût perverti
On finit par aimer
L'amertume d'un fruit
On goûte, on crache
Puis on avale
Et enfin on se dit :
Ça s'ra bientôt fini

Comment marier en l'esprit
La beauté de la terre
Des mille et mille créatures
L'infime de l'infime
Le temps des temps
Des galaxies
L'infini de l'infini
Et la douleur de nos douleurs ?

On s'assoit sur la pierre du chemin
Et parfois on se redit :
Qu'ça s'ra bientôt fini,
On se requiem'ra in pace
Qu'ils disent.

Mais est-ce bien sûr ?
La mort de son torchon
Effacera-t-elle toute larme
Et toute question
Ou sommes-nous con/damnés
À rejoindre le néant, une éternité
Sans avoir rien compris ?
Qui, Quoi, ainsi se joue de nous ?

Alors j'oublie la vieille dame
En moi, je reprends la marguerite
J'en fais un champ très grand
M'y sieds bien au milieu

Et
Tout comme au jour de ma naissance :
Je dis : Je ne veux rien savoir,
Et là dans la page du pré
Je le hèle, le rappelle
L'ange des « Chut ! «
De nos amis Indiens
Il vient,
Je baise ses mains
Verseuses d'oubli
Lui dis merci et...

Folie pour folie
Un peu beaucoup
Passionnément
J'écris de la poésie.

Rose-Marie Naime

©Marie Malaspina, *Insolite I*, été 2010

La femme au bord du puits

Marie Malaspina

Elle rentrait chez elle à pieds, le long du dernier kilomètre qui serpentait en épingle à cheveux sur les contreforts du Vercors. Dans ce pays là, l'été arrivait directement après l'hiver sautant le printemps. La montagne devenait d'une touffeur exubérante, les campanules, les centaurées, les sabots de Vénus, l'églantine pâle et les calcaires moussus bordaient les pentes de son cheminement accompagné par les bruits d'eau. Le torrent à chaque brisure de la conduite qui l'enserrait et le canalisait vers la plaine déversait un feu d'artifice de gouttelettes. Comme chaque année il faudrait se battre avec les ronces qui reprenaient d'assaut les murets de pierres préservant du vide.

Au bout du terre-plein, la chienne blanche l'attendait sous le tilleul. Une merlette sautillait sans façon sur l'herbe. La labrador aplatie de tout son long dans les taches d'ombres et de lumières n'en avait cure. La chatte tigrée chassait ailleurs.

Sur la colline, sa maison ressemblait à celle des livres d'Heidi, cette petite fille suisse dont enfant, elle lisait les aventures, assise sur un petit fauteuil de rotin dans un village algérien. Les livres s'ouvraient alors sur un pays parfaitement exotique et irréel. Aujourd'hui il lui semblait qu'elle habitait dans le livre. Son pays de djebel et de sécheresse rude était parti dans la stratosphère comme une fusée qui s'éloigne dans un bruit de catastrophe, tous fils perdus pour ne pas penser l'éclatement trop douloureux des vies que l'histoire et le pouvoir des militaires y inscrivaient. Il n'y a pourtant qu'un seul monde, dont elle avait peu à peu retrouvé l'ampleur, la démesure et la tendresse. Le petit fauteuil en rotin avait longtemps servi à son fils puis avait fini au feu.

Elle rentrait d'une journée de formation sur les retraites où elle avait enfin compris le régime général, les régimes complémentaires, les régimes spéciaux et les régimes additionnels. Mettre un nom sur les choses et avoir la vision d'ensemble ne changeait rien au réel, mais la rassurait. De la journée qui venait de se clore, surnageait un profond malaise.

Le soir, assise à son bureau, essayant de remplir « la demande d'estimation indicative globale » elle était encombrée, lourde, obscurcie d'elle ne savait quelle tristesse.

Remplissant les tableaux et les colonnes, elle voyait soudain le temps se déplier comme si sa longue vie avait jusque là était « zippée », en boule sur elle-même, tapie dans sa mémoire et venait de lui exploser au visage. Il fallait écrire dans un dossier administratif toute sa vie, préciser ses unions, ses enfants, ses divorces, nourrir un ordinateur avec la chair de ses jours et de ses liens, être débusquée, exposée, en pleine lumière. Qu'allait faire la machine avec toute cette nourriture. La personne qui rentrerait les données et qu'elle croiserait peut être dans un couloir, que penserait-elle de sa vie et de ses maris ? Le rigorisme souterrain de sa culture méditerranéenne venait nourrir cette fantasmagorie.

Il lui avait fallu un temps fou pour s'habituer à la montagne. Longtemps échouée d'Algérie, elle ne s'était plus sentie de nulle part. Cette absence de repères la reprenait parfois aux abords d'un événement fortuit.

Dans le dossier, elle devait marquer le numéro de sécurité sociale de ses anciens maris. Où les retrouver ?

Le premier, elle ne pouvait pas imaginer devoir lui parler. Ce mariage lui avait permis de quitter sa mère dans des formes convenables, avec un mari ingénieur, de débarrasser le plancher, de ne plus être une charge. L'empreinte était lointaine, dès dix mois elle avait été « apportée » chez une grande tante puis chez une tante puis chez ses grands-parents sans explication.

À ce premier mariage, pour la seule fois de sa vie, sa mère se trouva enfin à côté de son père dans une église, Saint Augustin à Paris puis au cercle interallié retenu pour l'événement. Ses parents face au monde, familles, amis, collègues.

Elle offrait sa revanche à une femme dont le père menuisier corse savait à peine écrire. Dans une culture et un temps qui ne plaisantait pas, sa mère avait dû assumer un « statut de fille-mère » oscillant entre cacher sa fille parce qu'elle était sa faute ou la montrer parce qu'elle était sa belle enfant.

Ses oncles en bons méditerranéens plutôt beaux gosses et experts en beauté féminine n'avaient jamais compris pourquoi, elle avait épousé si vite à dix neuf ans un ingénieur, certes, mais myope et aux pieds plats.

Chacune de ses unions allait être reliée à la plaie d'origine. Chacune serait marquée par un désir d'absolu hors d'atteinte, marquée par cette mère escamotée trop tôt dans l'enfance qui l'empêchait de compter jusqu'à deux pour inventer le monde avec un homme. N'être jamais sûre de la légitimité de son désir d'être aimée, vouloir aimer et le faire assez mal tout en sachant l'étendue des possibles.

Enfant, elle aurait voulu le mariage de ses parents pour ne pas avoir à souffrir de l'opprobre social qui dans les années 50, allait de pair avec la bâtardise. Ne pouvant s'en détacher, elle revendiquait sa colère pour tout et rien. Bien qu'elle excusa, plus tard, son père d'être parti avant sa naissance, ce n'est qu'en lisant les courriers qu'il avait adressés, pendant trois ans à sa mère qu'elle put comprendre que cette absence de mariage avait sauvé sa mère d'être une femme trompée et dépouillée de ses biens.

Le lendemain matin, par hasard, elle entendit à la radio, dans l'évangile de Jean, le récit de la rencontre de Jésus et de la samaritaine. Jésus n'avait que faire de la situation religieuse et maritale de la femme aux cinq maris, il lui parla de l'eau de vie qui apaise la soif, elle le reconnut comme un prophète. Celle qui venait seule au puits, en plein midi, pour ne pas subir les sarcasmes des femmes de son village n'eut plus d'autre urgence que de retourner dans ce même village annoncer ce qu'elle avait vu. Rien ne vint entraver sa course et chacun l'écouta. L'annonce à faire la dépassait et lui donnait, dans la communauté, une place qu'elle n'avait jamais eue. Le passé était aboli au profit du présent et de l'avenir...

Le second mari, c'était autre chose, son lion de miel en quelque sorte, son étranger. Un anglais roux à crinière et taches de rousseur qui lui avait plu tout de suite avec son accent et son trench mastic. Un air de confiance absolu dans les bienfaits de la vie et le goût de vivre accroché au regard. Elle ne s'était jamais intéressée à Facebook ni à mes copains d'école mais là, elle avait recherché ce qu'internet disait de lui. Des rapports de recherche du docteur il y en avait des pages qui permettaient de le suivre en Italie, à Stamford, aux Indes et ailleurs, Elle trouva finalement un émail professionnel qui ne donnerait sans doute rien car il avait dû, lui, déjà prendre sa retraite.

Elle envoya un message anodin de reprise de contact et se fit l'effet d'avoir jeté une pierre dans un puits et de ne pas en entendre le bruit de sa rencontre avec l'eau. Penchée au bord du puits durant quelques jours elle attendit puis n'y pensa plus.

Un matin, regardant le compteur des messages arrivés, elle trouva qu'il allait lui falloir une bonne partie de la matinée pour répondre, ce qui ne serait pas possible avant de commencer son cours. Et là dans les messages son nom à lui, qui un temps avait été aussi son nom à elle, et que toutes ses nouvelles femmes avaient soigneusement gardé même celle qui ne vivait plus avec lui. Son nom était dans la liste parcourue.

Un choc auquel elle ne s'attendait pas. Des ondes dont elle était le centre et qui n'en finissaient pas de naître et de s'étendre et de renaître et cela dura une bonne partie de la matinée, la déconcentrant sérieusement face au groupe qu'elle animait.

Sa crainte du regard administratif était pulvérisée. Elle n'était plus la Samaritaine rencontrant Jésus au bord du puits, la femme aux 5 maris qui était la déviante de son village, elle n'était plus la femme aux cheveux blancs à la vie déjà longue, elle était l'enfant se demandant quelle force elle avait ramenée en lançant son caillou, quel génie allait remonter du puits.

Elle sut alors qu'elle avait gardé entière ses facultés d'émerveillement. Peu importait qui viendrait du fond du passé dire le temps de l'intervalle. Déjà elle savait qu'elle avait tiré un fil qui la rendait vivante. Le lendemain, elle avait été voir le marbrier pour lui demander d'inscrire le nom de sa mère sur la case du funérarium. Elle terminait ainsi un long trajet intérieur de séparation qui la conduisait, dix ans après la mort de sa mère, à déposer enfin les cendres dans le cimetière du village en contrebas des pentes.

Le souvenir du regard bienveillant de son étranger sur elle, sa générosité, la gaieté et l'insouciance de leur jeunesse lui remontaient aux lèvres et la faisait sourire. Ce souvenir venait effacer un certain poids du malheur noué dans l'enfance et qu'il n'avait pu exorciser.

Il y avait aussi les répétitions des concerts à *Covent Garden* qui franchissaient le temps, tintaient à ses oreilles dans les harmonies du baroque et des arts florissants. Lui, leur chatte à la patte cassée dans les bras, en face d'elle, dans une rue, elle qui pleurait comme s'il s'était agi là de leur enfant.

Les fêtes du carnaval à *Nothing Hall*, dans Londres effervescente, avec des déguisements et des masques dignes d'Ensor, grimaçants à souhait autour d'eux. Le monde à l'envers, la lumière déformant les silhouettes, les traits grotesques, balafrés de couleurs, rougeoyant. La foule ivre, d'elle-même qui tanguait en grappes dans tout le quartier. Les visages devenus univers de démesure, reflets en prise avec des forces souterraines, les corps gesticulant irradiés d'énergie inconnue. Comment reconnaître quelqu'un dans ce magma de faces déformées ?

Durant quelques secondes elle n'entendit plus aucun son. Le vertige la saisit doublement égarée en milieu étranger, elle pensa l'avoir perdu et ne plus avoir aucun repère dans la ville déchaînée. Il revint dans son champ de vision et le réel se remit à l'endroit.

Tant de bières partout à partager avec des inconnus, Ils allèrent se plonger dans les lacs de *Regent Park* avant de rentrer au logis parental de Richmond.

Le retour en Algérie ensemble, dans le village d'enfance et jusqu'à Adrar pour connaître la magie du désert. Il avait aimé ses rêves, ses quêtes. Il lui sembla qu'elle avait plus reçu que donné. Ils avaient tenté d'être deux à vivre le monde et à le changer. Elle savait qu'elle aimerait jusqu'à ses rides, qui consentaient au temps, sur sa peau translucide.

Elle regardait au fond du puits et des fragments de vie en kaléidoscope, brillant d'éclats de couleurs, s'entrechoquaient, virevoltaient, se superposaient, il y en avait tant et tant qui se bousculaient et revenaient dans la lumière de l'été, éclairer ses yeux. Elle devenait riche et puissante de ce vécu qui refaisait surface. Personne ne pourrait l'en déposséder, pas même l'ordinateur des retraites par qui tout avait commencé.

De nombreux humains, irrémédiablement seuls, fragmentés par l'hyper compétition rejoignaient ces êtres du jugement dernier qui dans la chapelle Sixtine n'en finissaient pas de tomber. Les bruits inquiétants du monde transmis par des médias inconséquents, G 20, défaite d'une équipe de mercenaires au football, procès d'un trader contre une banque ou d'une banque contre un trader, n'y pouvaient rien. Elle se réconciliait avec une part légère d'elle-même, si longtemps laissée dans l'oubli. Le temps des lassitudes s'effaçait. Elle nageait dans le regard bienveillant de l'étranger simplement parce qu'il avait répondu libérant le passé. La respiration dans son bassin prenait un rythme marin, flux et reflux des vagues d'air ouvrant un moment le présent au monde.

Le temps plein d'une musique ancienne saturée de texture et de liens, mettait la vie à l'ordre du jour dans une ampleur sereine. Il importait que ce temps d'union consentie et heureuse un jour ait eu lieu. Ce temps où la différence était un attrait puissant où l'autre nationalité libérait des identités endeuillées.

Pourquoi justement lui, revenait-il avec tant de forces ? Sinon pour avoir beaucoup donné quand elle ne savait même pas, que tout lui manquait.

Il flottait dans l'air chaud et venté de l'été un rêve océanique perdu et réconfortant qui l'accompagnait sans l'envahir. Les histoires d'amour ne sont pas faites pour sombrer dans l'oubli. Tels les elfes bienveillants de nos enfances, elles dansent autour de nous jusqu'à la fin de notre âge en nous parlant d'éternité.

★★★

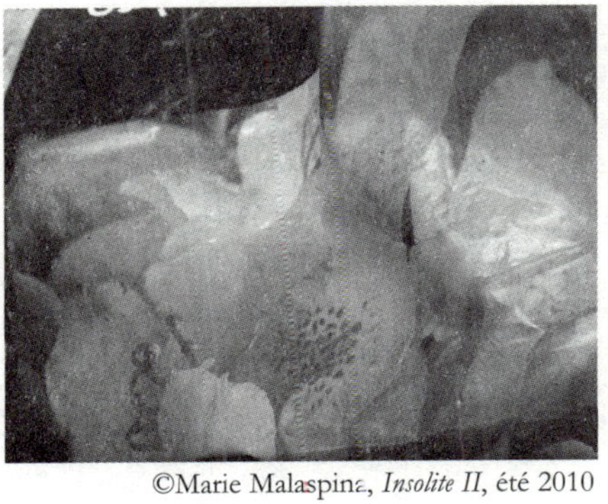

©Marie Malaspina, *Insolite II*, été 2010

Le tapis

Catherine Jallet-Traverso

Il avançait le long du chemin menant à la maison, la tête baissée, inquiet, soucieux. La chrétienne lui avait offert un tapis de prière. Voyant sa piété, elle avait voulu qu'il ne s'agenouillât plus sur des cartons et qu'il fît ses dévotions sur un support plus digne. Demain, il irait voir le mufti. Lui saurait le rassurer, lui proposer une réponse à son dilemme. Et demain vint, et la rencontre avec le mufti se fit. « Prends » lui fut-il répondu. « Dieu donne, mais le jour venu, il te demandera de choisir. » Et ce fut tout.

Il continua donc d'aller chez la *roumia* pour remplir sa tâche de bon ouvrier. Il aimait son travail et le faisait bien. Elle était satisfaite. Elle offrait parfois le café, discrète, comme éloignée. Il ne levait jamais les yeux sur elle, par respect, parce que cela lui était commandé dans sa religion. Chacun semblait se satisfaire de cette situation et tout était bien. Un jour, bien des mois plus tard, il fut appelé par le mufti. « Choisis » dit celui-ci. Et ce fut tout.

Il revint de l'entrevue, perplexe, troublé, ne comprenant rien à ce qui lui était demandé, n'imaginant rien, ne sachant que faire. Il alla au travail les jours suivants, inattentif à sa tâche, ne l'aimant plus, versatile et indolent, crispé sur une sourde terreur dont il n'entendait pas la cause. Choisir, mais quoi ? Dieu donne, oui, mais elle n'était pas Dieu. Ne plus travailler c'était mourir de faim. Ne plus travailler pour les étrangers qui payaient bien, c'était choisir le suicide. Choisir, mais quoi ? Rendre le tapis, cela ne se faisait pas. On ne retourne jamais un cadeau sinon pour faire injure. Et elle était respectueuse, distante mais respectueuse.

Subitement, elle tomba malade et il ne la vit de plusieurs jours. Lorsqu'elle réapparut sur le chantier, pâle et faible, il eut pitié. Elle semblait un être sans âme, frêle et perdu. Il ne savait rien d'elle sinon qu'elle s'était réfugiée un beau matin dans son village venant de France, seule. Elle avait acheté cette maison dans le quartier haut du village et voulait en arranger l'intérieur. On l'avait recommandé à elle parce qu'il était sérieux et appliqué. Il avait besoin d'argent, il avait dit oui. Ce jour là, lorsqu'elle se releva de sa maladie, il n'avait pas même commencé à travailler. Il était dix heures. Elle le regarda avec surprise. Et ce fut tout.

Trois jours plus tard, elle le fit appeler dans son bureau, au premier étage. Elle s'était installée là parce que la fenêtre de cette pièce regardait la mer, là-bas, scintiller tout le jour, comme placée en suspension au-dessus des toits, des arbres, des aiguilles des minarets, comme mariée éternellement au ciel dont on ne pouvait la délacer. Le soir venu, mille lampions clignotants illuminaient les champs et semblaient offrir à la mer leurs reflets vacillants. Elle avait placée son bureau dos à la porte. Au mur des photos souriantes et enjouées répondaient au visiteur qui montait la voir. Il se tint debout dans l'entrebâillement de la porte, ne sachant si ses pas traînants dans l'escalier l'avaient annoncé, s'il devait frapper doucement contre le chambranle ou toussoter discrètement. Il finit par remuer les pieds maladroitement et attendit. Sans se retourner, comme perdue dans sa vision du monde marin environnant, elle lui parla au bout d'un temps qui sembla infiniment long. « Tu le sais, je ne suis pas contente. Le travail que je t'avais commandé n'est toujours pas fini et il est bâclé. » Et ce fut tout.

Il sortit de cette entrevue, mécontent, vexé et plein de rage. Arrivé sur le toit-terrasse, il écouta négligemment une chanson reprise à l'unisson par des jeunes filles occupées à étendre leur linge. Il ramassa ses outils sans entendre leurs rires bondissants et mille fois répétés, hochant la tête de déplaisir. Il était bien décidé à quitter la maison immédiatement, sans terminer son travail et sans être payé. Il avait choisi. Pourtant, dix jours plus tard, il revint sur ses pas, il avait besoin d'argent. Sa colère au creux du ventre, malsaine, larvée, prête à exploser en un torrent de haine injustifiée. Ce n'était pas à une femme, qui plus est une étrangère, de juger son travail.

La demeure était muette et aveugle. Tous les volets étaient clos, aucun son ne parvenait à son oreille dans la torpeur écrasante de midi. Il fut surpris. Il frappa néanmoins à la porte d'entrée qui resta fermée. Au bout d'un moment, agacé de frotter ses sandales sur le perron, il se décida à contourner la maison en priant pour que la porte de derrière soit ouverte. Dans ce silence pesant, ses pas lui faisaient presque peur. Après avoir longé les murs, il pénétra dans une arrière-cour sur laquelle donnait la cuisine. Là, un carré minuscule formait un potager assoupi dans l'odeur douceâtre du basilic. Les fenêtres de ce côté étaient toutes béantes déversant dans l'air leur parfum saturé de peinture et de térébenthine. Il s'approcha. La porte vitrée était entrebâillée et les mouches bourdonnaient dans un rayon de soleil. Il frappa contre l'embrassure tout en appelant, mais n'obtint pas de réponse.

Traversant la cuisine, il s'aventura prudemment jusque dans le corridor. Marchant à petits pas, il prit le temps de jeter un œil curieux autour de lui constatant avec étonnement que le travail commencé avait été achevé, les trous rebouchés, les murs repeints. Tout avait été rafistolé, arrangé, remis en état et nettoyé. Mais la maison était déserte. Il prit peur. C'était comme si des fantômes glissait sans fin à ses côtés. Un sentiment de culpabilité superstitieux le faisait hésiter entre deux portes, ne sachant plus à présent s'il devait se retirer ou progresser. Il avança pourtant dans une dernière tentative pour trouver la maîtresse de maison.

Dans le salon gorgé de soleil où un silence morbide s'était installé, il ne trouva rien, personne. Se détournant, désemparé, il était sur le point de renoncer lorsqu'il perçut un soupir, une brève et muette respiration comme celle que les mourants exhalent, satisfaits. Il eut froid soudain. Une sueur glacée dégoulina lentement entre ses épaules, tandis que les petits cheveux de sa nuque picotaient en se hérissant. Ce fut à cet instant qu'il réalisa que l'odeur doucereuse et amère surnageant dans la pièce était celle du sang mélangé au chloroforme. Il fut saisi d'une terreur effroyable et se jeta hors de la pièce, hors des murs, hors de la maison comme un forcené. Une fois à l'extérieur, dans le soleil brûlant, il respira à nouveau, se blâma pour sa couardise, rebroussa chemin, pénétra pour la seconde fois dans la maison et s'avança jusqu'au milieu du salon.

Sur le canapé, elle était étendue, pâle et évanescente, recroquevillée et frêle, la main droite bandée. Le sang avait transpercé le pansement et mêlé son odeur âcre au désinfectant qu'elle avait dû utiliser. Il se pencha au-dessus d'elle. Elle respirait. Elle avait dû se blesser en terminant les travaux, pensa-t-il avec regret. Il s'assit à même le sol et la contempla. Un lourd sentiment de commisération l'envahit. Elle semblait si immatérielle, comment avait-elle pu trouver la force d'achever ce qu'il n'avait plus voulu exécuter. Il la soupçonna d'avoir épuisé sa rage, ou son désespoir, ou ses remords, dans cet exercice physique. Anéantir ses souvenirs, annihiler sa réflexion, peut-être était-ce un remède qu'elle avait cherché là. Il ne la connaissait pas, mais il ne pouvait s'empêcher de penser qu'il n'était pas naturel pour une femme de vivre seule, loin des siens, exilée, inconnue.

Il allait attendre qu'elle se réveillât. Il allait veiller sur elle. Et pour ne pas l'effrayer lorsqu'elle ouvrirait les yeux, tout à l'heure, dans quelques heures, il se recula jusqu'au mur contre lequel il s'appuya, attentif et préoccupé, tandis que l'appel à la prière roulait sa mélopée éternelle sur les toits aveuglés de soleil.

Nouvelle extraite d'un recueil à paraître *Colophon*

★★★

©Michèle Perret, *Paris*, 2011

La vieille dame et le chibani

Michèle Perret

La vieille dame descend du métro. Une bourgeoise plutôt élégante, avec son manteau de poil de chameau de bonne facture, ses mocassins italiens et son sac Monoprix, parce qu'elle refuse de payer une fortune pour ces grands et gros sacs à la mode qui pèsent une tonne même quand ils sont vides. Elle peut faire illusion, elle est toujours blonde, mais c'est grâce à son coiffeur car en vérité ses cheveux sont poivre et sel, peut-être même blancs. Et elle prend le couloir de correspondance à petits pas : elle a mal aux pieds, mal au dos, mal aux épaules, mal à tous ses vieux os et elle va justement voir un charlatan qui vous tripote la vertèbre pour vous rendre votre jeunesse, l'espace de quelques jours. Elle s'attendrit sur elle-même d'être devenue cette pauvre survivante.

Dans le couloir de correspondance, elle croise un regard. Elle l'enregistre sans même le voir, un regard de détresse, ou de quête timide. Elle se détourne, prête à l'oublier. Encore un mendiant, encore une arnaque ? Puis elle revient sur ses pas, car ce qu'elle a aussi enregistré presque inconsciemment, c'est... un parapluie. L'homme au regard perdu (c'est un homme, un vieil homme) est petit, chétif, presque décharné, proprement vêtu et porte un grand parapluie roulé. Et un tel regard perdu, un tel regard de détresse ! C'est un étranger, se dit la vieille dame, il cherche son chemin. Les mendiants ne portent pas de parapluie. En général.

La vieille bourgeoise revient sur ses pas et s'approche du petit vieux, enfin vieux, il a son âge, mais comme il ne se fait pas teindre les cheveux, lui, et qu'il a l'air en mauvaise santé, les soixante-quinze automnes s'affichent ouvertement. Elle s'approche et il lui dit d'une voix presque inaudible : « Je suis Algérien… » Qui, dans le métro, en France, avec toutes ces rancoeurs qui traînent contre les étrangers qui viennent nous manger notre soupe, contre ces Algériens qui ne nous pardonnent pas de les avoir colonisés, qui irait, pour mendier, annoncer qu'il est Algérien ? Il faut être naïf et honnête, son parapluie sous le bras, il faut être arrivé de la veille et ne pas connaître ce Paris grognon, fermé, pressé et somme toute assez malheureux. « J'arrive d'Algérie. Et je n'ai pas mangé ».

Il répète « Je n'ai pas mangé », non pas comme les mendiants professionnels qui psalmodient mécaniquement « J'ai faim » en pensant à autre chose, ni comme ce quêteur de métro bien gros et rose qu'elle avait entendu annoncer qu'il n'avait pas mangé depuis une semaine. Celui-là, il s'était fait prendre à partie par un groupe d'Africains : s'il n'avait pas honte de dire ça ! On voyait bien qu'il n'avait jamais connu la faim ! – faut pas prendre les enfants du bon Dieu pour des canards sauvages ! – non, le vieil homme dit, et répète « Je n'ai pas mangé » avec une sorte d'étonnement scandalisé, comme si ce n'était pas croyable, de n'avoir pas mangé, comme si au pays, où l'on respecte encore les vieilles personnes, jamais au grand jamais on n'aurait laissé un chibani comme lui privé de repas ! « J'arrive d'Algérie. Et je n'ai pas mangé ».

Et qu'est-ce qui fait qu'un vieux monsieur comme lui nous arrive d'Algérie ? Quelle drôle d'idée, de venir se faire prendre au piège et de se retrouver à jeun dans les lugubres couloirs du métro. La dame l'interroge, « Mais quelle idée vous a pris de venir ici ? » et le chibani au parapluie lui répond « Je viens d'Alger pour me soigner. Hôpital Bichat ». « Hôpital Bichat », il répète, comme pour la convaincre. Et qu'est-ce qu'il fait, affamé, dans ce couloir de la station Trocadéro ? se demande la vieille dame – mais elle n'ose pas lui poser la question. Peut-être est-il, en plus, un peu perdu ?

Elle imagine que quelqu'un, un fils, ou une nièce, une nièce, c'est ça tout le monde sait qu'elles sont un peu désinvoltes, les nièces, qu'elles s'en foutent un peu, des chibanis, avec tous les problèmes de moutards qu'elles ont… un fils, une nièce plutôt, devait venir le chercher à l'avion, et ils se sont ratés, ils ne se sont pas trouvés, si ça se trouve, la nièce est arrivée en retard, si ça se trouve, elle a oublié.

La vieille dame sourit, ouvre son porte-monnaie où il n'y a pas grand-chose (elle s'est fait voler plusieurs fois et elle se méfie) : elle donne à l'homme perdu quelques euros, à peine de quoi s'offrir un café et un sandwich, mais elle n'a pas beaucoup d'argent sur elle et elle a quand même un peu peur, encore, d'avoir affaire à un habile mendiant.

Mais l'homme prend les pièces avec tant de joie que pour couper court, elle dit, presque en s'excusant :

– C'est que moi aussi, je suis née en Algérie.

– Où ça ? dit le vieil homme.

– Oran.

Le vieux réfléchit, cherche dans sa mémoire :

-- Wahran ?

– Oui, Wahran, dit la vieille dame.

Alors se passe l'inattendu, l'incroyable : le vieux petit monsieur au parapluie se hisse sur la pointe des pieds, prend la mamie bon chic bon genre dans ses bras et l'embrasse, quatre gros baisers sur une joue puis l'autre puis l'une puis l'autre – à la mode du pays.

Sait-il même que si elle est née là-bas, elle n'est pas Algérienne ?

Et la vieille Pied-noir repart vers son rebouteux, en souriant au fond de son cœur, comme si la boucle était enfin bouclée.

À son retour, trois quarts d'heure plus tard, le vieux n'est plus là.

***

Toi que je ne reconnais pas

J'ai vu les marchands de la place Jemaa el-Fna vendre des dents à l'unité
Les chauffeurs de bus écossais avec leurs figures rouges et leur accent – « Al'rrright ! » font-ils en roulant les « r »
Les chiens errants de Grèce qui vous suivent pleins d'espérance et se jettent presque sous votre voiture
Les amoureux traversant main dans la main le pont Charles vers la tour gothique et le dôme vert pomme aux allures de panthéon

Tous m'ont paru plus familiers
Que toi,
Qui dors dans mes bras quelques fois inerte
Te dérobant à moi souvent de peur d'être objet
Indomptable
Corps soumis
à son propre désir mèche de cheveux bien enroulée autour du cran de la brosse
puzzle à mille pièces avec un grand ciel bleu impossible
à recomposer et des bouts de pensées
s'échappant de tes yeux clos telles des volutes invisibles
qui se perdent dans l'écho insondable
de tes
silences

Toi dont je ne reconnais pas toujours la voix lorsqu'elle m'appelle claire enrouée cassée vidée rieuse cruelle inaudible loin, loin
de
moi

Dont les pensées et les rêves
À la surface de ma conscience
Me renvoient une image spectrale
De cet autre que je suis
de ce Mr. Hyde qui surgit
Aux confins de mes errances
Cet autre moi qui semble refuser le bonheur confortable au prix de
(spasme)
L'éternel frisson

Angélique Thomine

L'étrange mer

Thérèse-Françoise Crassous

Dans cette salle d'exposition de la rue Mouffetard, une Japonaise se cache derrière un rideau. Son chapeau en arabesques de coquillages bleu azur laisse entrevoir, fugace, les perles retenues sur un banc de mémoire. Envoûtantes, des années d'épines se balancent sous son regard lavande.

Autour d'elle les tableaux en bleus de toutes sortes – outremer, émeraude, cobalt – l'engloutissent. Accrochant ses pensées sur fond de musique d'orgue, les pinceaux de l'artiste ont dessiné, sur la toile virginale, des déferlantes et des cœurs d'écumes. Tout l'univers des Arts se presse dans la pièce. La foule, en mouvements pittoresques et bariolés, s'esbaudit devant les peintures accrochées. Par un écart du rideau bleu marine, la jeune femme, indifférente, scrute un landau douillet d'un autre âge, aux roues en métal. Les dessins sur la voiture d'enfant l'émerveillent et se fondent dans le tourbillon des glyphes japonais. Un bébé y suce son pouce : ses onomatopées ne troublent pas la tiédeur de ses succions arrogantes.

Elle aperçoit une main en vol d'oiseau léger et une barbiche neigeuse, qui soudain se penche sur le berceau. C'est la princesse à barbe, chuchote-t-on, la huitième épouse de sieur Han. Elle habite sur la Seine dans une jonque dorée et se réveille à l'aube au son du gong. Elle oublie souvent des mots et s'exclame alors en riant : « C'est une pensée qui joue à cache-cache ! ». On dit qu'elle jette des sortilèges aux nouveaux-nés. La femme cachée aux cheveux de jais attend que les personnes qui papotent à côté fassent enfin attention au manège. Elle aimerait tant être à la place du petit : être aimée, être voulue. Mais vite, elle se renfrogne au vu du regard triste entre la barbiche et la cornette en forme de bateau.

Un instant, elle s'était imaginé, grâce au sort, obtenir une sœur jumelle qui la comprendrait mais si différente pourtant, à l'aise dans ce monde jacassant et cruel, qui l'entraînerait à travers l'argent du miroir, répondrait à sa place, effrontée, spirituelle, toujours l'humour aux lèvres et la répartie haute. Un double adorable que l'on remarquerait : une femme élégante, au chic incommensurable, qui saurait verser le thé aux événements mondains, et qui saurait marchander et amasser un joli pactole en vendant ses œuvres extravagantes.

Notre belle en aurait bien besoin, car il fait froid à Paris en ce mois de Janvier. Et sur son ventre habité, son kimono de soie, si tant rapiécé, laisse découvrir, par endroits, une trame élimée. Ses joues rosissent de peur d'être alors reconnue. Derrière le rideau, elle se cache encore et encore. Elle n'arrive pas à être au diapason, à se vendre, à s'exprimer. Timide, elle est. Effacée par son éducation, elle se sent étrangère à toutes ces effusions. Elle a bien essayé de jouer, d'être cette autre elle-même, mais elle n'est pas à l'aise dans cet exploit si compliqué.

Et ainsi l'auteur de ces merveilles que tout le monde applaudit, se blottit, minuscule, derrière des flots bleus.

⁂

***

L'errant

Pourtant il fut ce voyageur ailé
Il déployait ses mains colombes envolées

Il aimait
  je le sais
    les valises légères

celles qu'on emplissait
du parfum des étés
d'épices et de poussière

la rumeur de la mer
les galets emportés

Il allait
  s'avançant
    impatient de dire

des ombres poursuivaient
sur les rives désertes
sa course singulière

le soir l'accompagnait
là où le vent s'étire

Il inventait
confiant
des chemins solitaires

les herbes folles suivaient
son ombre Voyageur
d'air et de songes clairs

Regard au loin porté
Du doute délivré

Il déposait
parfois
un large coin de ciel

bleu linge joyeux
dont il faisait sa terre
Ignorant les frontières

Mais au terme de l'errance
entre vide et absence
les ailes de sa voix
sur lui se sont brisées

Sabine Péglion

©Sculpture S. Manby

IDENTITÉ

Rose-Marie Naime

Y a
Les pareils
Les pas pareils
Les pas pas pareils
Y a ceux de l'identique
Et que la différence répugne
Y a ceux qui sont dans le différent
Et qui tiquent et répugnent à l'identique
Y a ceux qui se veulent montrer tout pareils
Mais qui au-dedans sont essentiellement différents
Y a ceux qui voudraient être et paraître différents
Mais qui cent pour cent sont tout pareils dedans

Et puis
Y a chacun
Qui en son ventre
S'aime ou se hait
S'aime et se hait
Ou plus souvent
S'haimne tant
Tant tant et tant

Et puis y a :
Qui suis-je moi ?
Suis-je moi ?
Émoi…
Et toi, qui es
Qui es-tu ?
Es-tu ?
Aimes-tu ?
Me tues…
Et puis ! Et puis ?

Pirouette
Cacahouète
Y a mon voisin Albert
Qui pour sa petite fille
Est Grand Papa Rey
Elle qui s'appelle *Patou.*
Patou ?
Et qui lui est tout
Oh ! Tralala…là !

Le parc des attractions

Nadia Leïl

Depuis que j'écris, j'ai l'impression d'être moins étrangère à ma ville. J'observe ceux qui m'entourent et perçois des bouts de leur histoire ou de ce qui aurait pu être leur histoire. Ils frôlent mon regard et parfois je m'y accroche par envie. Je sais tout à coup ce qu'ils pensent et où ils vont. Ce qu'ils veulent et ce qu'ils disent.

Il y a ce couple qui descend du grand bateau. Celui où je ne monte jamais parce que je suis une peureuse et que son tangage audacieux m'intimide. Les sensations fortes je les vis en songes, mensonges que je mastique, modèle et recrache. Souvent, je fais des bulles avant. Des bulles où le temps s'arrête, dans lesquelles prolifèrent mes possibles. Je suis étrangère aux peurs manufacturées, monnayées comme un ticket pour le grand huit. Eux descendent hilares de leur voyage immobile, plus que jamais soudés par la tempête imaginaire qui les a secoués au beau milieu d'un mélange de cris réels et d'excitations abusives. Il lui achète une barbe à papa. Elle peut redevenir enfant puisqu'elle a trouvé où se blottir. Je les vois qui s'éloignent de la foule des consommateurs salivant devant le sucre offert. Ils descendent le petit escalier emboîtés l'un à l'autre, évoluent doucement, puis disparaissent quelque part sur le bord d'un chemin descendant où la forêt se sera écartée.

Leur dessein est fourré derrière les arbres. Je ne les vois plus. J'en conserve cependant un hologramme rémanent que j'anime depuis mon banc, c'est ainsi que tous deux dansent sur la plage blanche posée sur mes genoux.

Le voile magenta de la fille s'ouvre et tombe rejeté par sa chevelure torsadée, déroulée en vagues douces. Charme déferlant. Il s'est assis ; elle est debout face à lui. Vient le tour de la veste noire en lainage – longue pour cacher les formes –, elle la déboutonne lentement, s'en défait, puis la laisse tomber derrière elle. Son visage est une peinture ironique où se côtoient bonheur et appréhension. Joues rosées, regard oblique. Elle a un peu froid, mais ne dit rien, attend parce que c'est trop tard. L'homme se redresse, trois pas sur les feuilles craquelées lui suffisent pour la rejoindre. Ses mains entourent d'abord le visage, ensuite les doigts s'infiltrent dans la toison bouffante qui respire le pin. S'en détachent avec l'envie dérobée d'y revenir. Les mains s'apposent sur les épaules délestées, marquent un arrêt, puis descendent le long du dos, se rejoignent au-dessus des reins, emprisonnant la silhouette fine et droite, tranchante. Elle se rend compte doucement que les bras qui l'encerclent engendrent une chaleur invasive. Frissons écartés.

L'homme réduit le diamètre de son étreinte, dégommant l'espace entre leurs corps tendus. Dilatoire, la fille reproduit les gestes de l'homme citadelle, abandonnant la chorégraphie sur une pause symétrique. C'est là qu'il se jette sur la bouche entr'ouverte avec pétulance ; il recouvre le méat de sa lèvre inférieure, se promène d'une langue dilettante au sein du territoire soumis. Rencontre en dedans les faces planes et les pointes aguicheuses des dents ; dangereusement diligent, il aborde la langue conjointe molle, tiède, ankylosée, comme une sorcière au bord de la défection.

L'éclairage baisse, le feu s'élève. Tremblements. Pourtant, il n'est plus envisageable d'abandonner. Tandis qu'il dégoupille sa ceinture, elle s'affale sur la veste.

Ce n'est pas une après-midi ordinaire, elle s'en souviendra comme d'un passage important sur le livre de sa destinée. Lui sait qu'il ne lui reste plus qu'à grimper dans le tronc, monter jusqu'aux branches, creuser dans la substance juteuse, jusqu'à atteindre le parenchyme secret, laisser alors à cet instant précis percer la lumière. Rien d'autre.

Ils sont moi ; de l'abîme à l'élévation.

Ils ont pris le manège où je ne suis jamais montée parce que je suis une peureuse et que son tangage audacieux m'intimide. Mais leur désir ne m'est pas étranger.

***

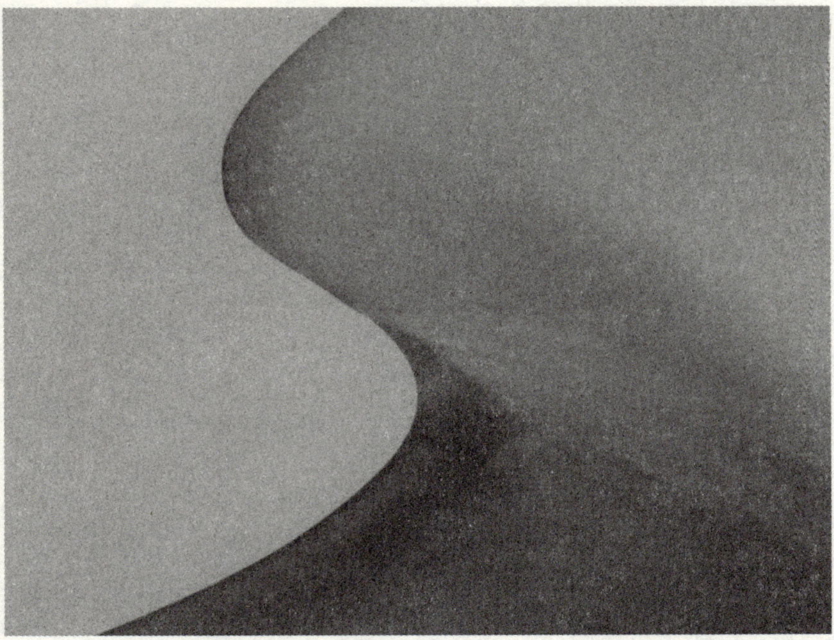

©Marie-Noël Arras/Thierry Claude, Taghit/ Sidi-Bel-Abbès, Algérie

Conte pour Hamou

Françoise Mariotti

Et la rose arriva derrière l'homme.

Il ne se retourna pas, par jeu ; il avait compris ses ruses, dans l'intensité de son parfum.

À son léger frémissement d'épaules, la rose sut qu'il se livrerait à ses jeux avec taquinerie. Elle décida de respecter ses moments, et guetta immobile le moindre retournement.

Il parla enfin, après de longues heures. La rose était habituée à l'attente ; elle n'avait cependant que peu de jours pour la vivre.

Ils s'étaient mutuellement envisagés, dans ce désert strié de marbrures... seuls ils ne l'étaient pas vraiment.

Ils avaient convenu, dans le silence, de se rejoindre.

Pour la rose, il fallait un jardinier tranquille mais fou, aux mains expertes et délicates.

L'homme, dont elle ne voyait pas encore le visage, avait quelques besoins sensuels.

Hello Baobabe murmura-t-il, et à son ton, elle devina qu'il souriait à demi.

Elle aussi sourit du pseudonyme qu'il lui donna, elle se savait puissante et solide, mais ne l'envisageait pas sous ce nom.

Alors elle sut qu'elle pouvait l'approcher d'un peu plus près, mais juste un peu.

Elle déplia ses pétales d'un rose bleuté et en effleura les épaules nues de l'homme. Il frémit sous cette douce caresse inattendue.

Ses épines seraient pour plus tard... elle les rentra.

Légèrement penchée au-dessus de lui, elle observa ce qu'elle pouvait en voir.

Un arabe à n'en pas douter, à la fierté de sa tenue, au miel qu'il y avait dans sa voix, à ses cheveux noirs et bouclés.

La rose aimait les voyages et les découvertes. Elle se serra encore plus.

Il glissa contre elle dans un lent mouvement.

Cette première soirée fut remplie de soupirs silencieux ou échappés, la rose et l'homme s'accordaient dans leur danse excitante et tendre.

Le désert les éloignait, les rapprochait... L'homme collectionnait les roses de sable, il passait beaucoup de temps à les scruter, à les aimer, à les protéger.

La rose aux pétales fragiles ne se sentait pas aussi belle et multiple qu'elles, avec leur solidité striée et leur couleur assortie à la peau de l'homme.

Quelquefois il revenait.

Le seul travail de la rose était de capter toute l'eau possible, pour sa survie, et elle s'en épuisait souvent. Mais il suffisait de quelques gouttes pour la rendre éclatante et pleine de vie.

Lorsque par chance il la prévenait de son arrivée, elle pouvait alors commencer à l'attendre et à en être heureuse. Après avoir ôté pucerons, chenilles et autres poussières, elle s'installait le coeur battant et savait que la joie serait pour bientôt.

Qu'était la joie d'une rose ?

Elle savait qu'elle était belle, parfumée, mais ne supportait pas que ce désert où elle avait poussé par hasard ne lui apporte aucun miroir.

Elle aimait partager ses ressources, ses pensées, ranger ses épines pour écouter doucement les divers voyageurs.

Certains étaient restés plus longtemps et avaient voulu la cueillir. Ils n'avaient réussi, dans la douleur, qu'à lui arracher quelques fibres qui n'avaient pu encore repousser.

Depuis la rose voulait accueillir les voyageurs mais frémissait à chaque ombre qui se profilait. Que voudraient-ils lui arracher encore...

Pourtant elle savait que dans certains pays, que l'on appelle civilisés, les roses sont choyées, nommées, cultivées... et que même coupées et arrosées, elles pouvaient encore rayonner.

Certaines en faisait même le but de leur vie... appartenir à un jardinier.

La rose du désert comprenait que cela serait délicieux à n'en pas douter, exaltant sûrement. Que ses besoins de partage seraient comblés à jamais.

Elle savait aussi qu'une rose coupée n'était heureuse, même pleinement, qu'un court instant.

Elle avait aussi entendu dire que certains jardiniers se lassaient vite et changeaient la composition des vases tous les jours.

Alors, à chaque voyageur aperçu au loin dans l'ombre des dunes, son coeur s'accélérait d'envie et de craintes.

Mais elle aimait ce subtil mélange d'émotions qui ravivait toujours ses couleurs, cette rose était ainsi faite.

Elle semblait calme, tranquille, patiente.

Mais dans ses fibres coulaient l'ardence et tous les aiguillons des désirs.

Ainsi elle attendait l'homme sans vouloir l'attendre.

Ses journées se passaient à guetter l'eau sous ses moindres formes, et ce peu de tâches si vital l'éloignait des souvenirs de la nuit qu'ils passaient quelquefois ensemble.

De plus la rose était sans mémoire, et lorsque les pas de l'homme se faisaient traces dans le sable, elle savait que le vent du désert allait très vite les recouvrir.

Elle retournait à ses pensées... rêvait à d'autres roses ailleurs, d'autres jardiniers, elle se troublait un moment puis retournait chercher son eau.

Elle imaginait quelquefois, furtivement, la vie de l'homme plus loin bien plus loin derrière une autre dune que la sienne.

Elle savait qu'ils étaient dissemblables, et que leur consistance ne pouvait s'accorder et se rejoindre que dans la fusion sensuelle.

Quelquefois, dans les rares instants de repos où il lui accordait le toucher calme de sa peau de soie, il lui racontait ses moments et sa vie parmi tous les grains de sable.

Elle comprenait que les vents n'étaient pas tendres pour lui, mais qu'il aimait les affronter. Qu'il y mettait toute son énergie et sa volonté.

Que revenu près de sa dune, il s'allongeait épuisé sans même préparer sa nourriture et ses habits pour le lendemain.

Qu'il était pris dans ce tourbillon et qu'il y accordait son corps comme il le pouvait. Quelquefois, une plainte presque muette lui échappait, et la rose l'entendait car elle n'était pas si loin.

Elle avait deviné dans ses allusions que lui aussi ne voulait pas être enfermé. Bien sûr il ne pouvait comme elle être cueilli. Leur soif de liberté était différente mais correspondait sans doute aux mêmes peurs.

Ne plus s'appartenir. Dépendre d'unE autre pour des besoins intenses qui seraient nés à son contact. Et risquer de s'y perdre à jamais. Et surtout que le contact prolongé avec cetTE autre ne se paye un jour de la douleur qu'elle avait connue dans ses fibres lorsqu'elle avait été arrachée. Douleur déchirante, intense et si changeante qu'elle ne pouvait jamais s'y accommoder pour souffler quelques secondes. La douleur avait irradié tout son être de belle rose tendre, et si elle ne connaissait pas la nature exacte des craintes de l'homme, elle savait que les sensations d'arrachage de l'âme sont insupportables pour longtemps.

Ainsi chacun restait à l'abri de sa dune.

Ils apprenaient à se connaître.

Le plus souvent dans le meilleur. Elle savait qu'ils n'auraient pas le temps pour le pire.

C'était sûrement mieux ainsi.

C'était le temps qui leur manquait. Certainement plus à elle qu'à lui. La recherche de l'eau dans le désert n'est pas si facile mais elle se rassasiait de peu. Ainsi elle était en général ouverte et disponible aux voyageurs et aux caresses. Mais cette rose était constante et lorsque l'un d'entre eux s'approchait et qu'elle le trouvait à son goût, elle ne se contentait pas d'en effleurer la surface ni de livrer ses pétales et ses fibres dans leur plus intime.

La rose était curieuse et vite émerveillée lorsqu'elle arrivait à trouver de l'or sous la peau d'un homme.

L'homme de cette dune, qu'elle avait laissé approcher un soir et revenir, l'avait troublée par ses qualités. Il semblait austère et aussi passionné. Il l'écoutait et aussi se livrait à elle. Ils avaient les mêmes valeurs qui ne servaient plus à grand chose dans ce grand désert, l'honnêteté, la dignité, l'honneur, le don de soi et la responsabilité. Il était aussi rempli de joies et de gourmandises, et lorsque son visage s'éclairait près du sien et qu'il balbutiait quelques bêtises, elle se sentait touchée et avait envie de détourner son regard.

Pas plus loin. Ne me touche pas plus loin ni plus profond pensait-elle. Ne me donne pas plus, ne me fais pas jouir si fort, ne sois pas là si près et si loin comme un magnifique mirage ; reste un corps dont j'admire longuement et en secret la peau et les muscles tendus, le sexe moqueur magnifique et puissant.

Quelquefois lorsque la conscience lui venait pour un dixième de seconde, elle se rendait compte qu'il était un jardinier possible. Et cette pensée étincelante la faisait rire aux éclats et elle criait dans le vent « Va-t-en, Lover ! »

Mais la rose était aussi sage que sauvage. Elle rangeait ces rares pensées sous le plus beau caillou de son espace, noir et luisant, strié de marbrures vertes. Et le vent tous les jours enfonçait un peu plus le caillou dans le sable, et quelquefois elle ne l'apercevait plus, et elle savait que c'était bien.

Puis l'homme partit. Il lui avait dit qu'il reviendrait.

Elle avait réussi à être la rose qui orne l'espace, que l'on admire et près de laquelle on s'arrête, et qui fait sourire ; même, elle chanta. Et il partait. Et pendant quelques jours elle n'y pensa pas. Elle était retournée légère dans le vent d'autres occupations, l'eau était toujours aussi nécessaire pour elle.

Un matin elle se réveilla différente. Soudain il lui semblait qu'elle ne pouvait plus rien prévoir pour les jours à venir. Qu'elle ne pouvait plus penser ni sa présence ni son absence.

La rose se sentait désemparée, comme étrangère à elle-même.

Elle sentait qu'elle devait appréhender ce temps d'absence, sans doute en décider le poids. Mais curieusement seul le vide l'occupait. Un vide nostalgique. Un vide qui, elle le savait, pouvait l'entraîner dans d'autres tourbillons qu'elle n'appréhendait pas encore nettement, mais qu'elle imaginait mêlés de larmes, de désinvolture, de quelques joies aussi. Comme si elle était à la fois ancrée au fond de l'eau comme un navire et prête à s'envoler comme un oiseau. Et en se réveillant ainsi, elle savait qu'elle n'était faite ni pour l'un ni pour l'autre. Mais qu'elle n'avait pas forcément prise sur ce vide.

Alors elle décida de le vivre au jour le jour.

Et d'attendre le retour de l'homme dans la joie et la confiance, en lui et en elle. Confiance dans son envie à lui de se frotter encore à ses senteurs de rose. Confiante dans sa constance à elle de vivre encore les joies qu'il lui procurait.

Ainsi, tout lui parut simple.

Puis soudain, elle respira mieux. Tourna ses pétales vers le soleil qui déclinait sur le désert, observa avec bonheur le déplacement des fennecs entre les dunes. Quelques larmes s'échappèrent et elle pensa à celles qu'il lui faisait naître dans le plaisir.

Elle se dit qu'il était beau et juste de pleurer sa joie et sa tristesse en même temps.

Et elle souhaita qu'il emporte ces larmes si particulières dans ses bagages.

⁂

© Marie-Noël Arras, *Tiens un touriste sous la pluie...* Tlemcen, Algérie, 2007

L'autre

Maïssa Bey

Je n'aurais jamais dû. Je sais, bien sûr, que l'on ne peut dire cela qu'après coup. Quand c'est trop tard. Quand les mots ont franchi le seuil des lèvres. Quand on sent qu'ils ont pris leur envol sans qu'il soit possible de les retenir, de les détourner, de les empêcher d'aller là où ils seront captés, entendus et compris. Et surtout sans qu'il soit possible d'en atténuer l'impact.

Le visage en face de soi. Le regard. Une onde, un remous, un tressaillement bref. Les lèvres soudain figées dans un rictus. L'étonnement. La stupeur. La stupéfaction et parfois la colère.

Non, ce n'est pas moi. Je ne me reconnais pas, non, je n'ai pas pu dire ça. C'est quelqu'un d'autre qui a parlé, qui a dit…

C'est comme si j'étais nue. Que je ne pouvais plus rien cacher. Et que les autres, eux aussi, se voyaient nus dans mon regard.

La réaction de l'autre aussi. Parfois le silence. Parfois le retour de volée. Aussi violent, aussi percutant qu'un smash. En pleine figure.

En fait, je m'en rends compte maintenant, cela m'arrivait de plus en plus souvent depuis quelque temps. Je ne savais plus retenir les mots. Les mots qui jaillissaient sans préméditation aucune et disaient, malgré moi, le fond de ma pensée.

Combien de fois ai-je dû faire suivre mes paroles par un piteux *Désolée, cela m'a échappé* ! Et toutes les excuses que je bredouillais parfois, sans convaincre. Car je n'avais ni l'excuse du grand âge – elle commence à radoter, la pauvre, (traduisez :

embarquée sur un radeau qui lentement mais sûrement glisse vers l'au-delà). Ni l'alibi d'un deuil, d'une dépression, états qui pourraient être à l'origine de moments d'égarement, et qui constituent souvent, dans les procès que l'on peut faire à des individus, des circonstances atténuantes. Rien d'autre ne peut justifier la brutalité de la franchise. Il faut, dit-on, être au bord de la folie pour pouvoir dire ce tout que l'on pense. C'est dans ce cas, et dans ce cas seulement qu'est admise ou tolérée la vérité ou du moins l'expression crue des sentiments.

C'est arrivé brusquement. D'ordinaire, mes matins sont silencieux et discrets. Et dans la cuisine, lieu des retrouvailles matinales, hormis les *crunch, crunch, crunch* de la biscotte sous les dents de mon père, le recueillement est de mise. Or, ce jour-là, au sortir d'une nuit très calme, aucun événement notable, rien d'autre que les habituels ronflements et quelques vents incontrôlables sous la couette (*oh, désolée* ! vous voyez bien ! et encore, j'essaie de la retenir !) j'ai salué mes parents d'un : *« ça vous ferait mal de ne pas faire la gueule de bon matin ? Pour une fois ! »*. Je n'avais pas plutôt fini la phrase que mon père s'est levé. Inutile de raconter la suite. Pendant plusieurs jours, les collègues m'ont dit que j'avais exagéré sur le blush, et sur une seule joue ! La réaction de ma mère est plus intéressante. On aurait dit la séquence d'un film avec arrêt sur image. La tasse de café immobilisée à mi-parcours, la bouche figée en cul de poule et les sourcils en accent circonflexe, accent si prononcé qu'il se passait de O ! Etant moi-même sidérée par ces paroles qui venaient d'être prononcées, sans préméditation aucune, et par moi-même, aucun doute n'étant permis, je suis restée sans réaction.

Dans la soirée, la tension à la maison était si forte qu'elle aurait pu alimenter une centrale électrique. Mais bien entendu, enfin, façon de parler, pas un mot n'a été dit. Pas un reproche. Nous n'avons pas ces fâcheuses habitudes – bien trop vulgaires – de nous disputer, de crier, *de nous engueuler*. Chez nous, tout est dans les mimiques, dans les gestes, les regards, les silences. Un langage parfaitement compréhensible pour les initiés. Ce même soir, alors que je m'apprêtais pour la nuit, dans la salle de bains, porte fermée bien sûr, j'ai commencé à chanter. D'abord un fredonnement machinal, puis des paroles sont venues, des mots d'amour, des mots que jamais, au grand jamais personne n'oserait prononcer à haute voix, ici, oui, ici, chez nous, dans cette enceinte préservée d'où est bannie toute parole inconvenante. Et nul ne s'était jamais hasardé à transgresser des conventions tacitement établies depuis des temps immémoriaux. Jamais, au grand jamais je n'avais chanté cette chanson. Je ne me souvenais pas l'avoir écoutée et n'en connaissais ni l'air ni les paroles et pourtant c'était bien moi qui hurlais à tue-tête :

Ai… ai… aime moi comme je t'ai… ai... aime, je suis à toi…

Là non plus la réaction ne s'est pas fait attendre. Des coups violents frappés à la porte pendant que je continuais à m'époumoner. Mon père, ma mère et mes deux frères ont fait irruption et m'ont emmenée ou plutôt trainée sans ménagements jusqu'à ma chambre où, toute la nuit, à tour de rôle, ils m'ont veillée en se précipitant sur moi dès que j'ouvrais la bouche pour bailler ou simplement pour respirer.

Dès l'aube, sommée par ma mère de me réveiller et de me préparer très vite, j'ai été invitée à monter en voiture sans savoir où nous allions. Nous avons quitté le quartier, puis la ville, roulé pendant plus de deux heures avant de nous arrêter. Entretemps j'avais pu capter quelques mots adressés à mon frère qui conduisait. On m'emmenait en consultation. Le meilleur spécialiste de toute la région, disait-elle. Un *taleb* ayant pignon sur rue, réputé pour ses interventions quasi miraculeuses.

Élémentaire, ma chère !
Maintenant je sais.
Nous sommes deux.
Le diagnostic est posé. Indéniable.
Nous sommes deux.

Je suis *habitée. Meskouna.*

Dans mon corps, il y a Moi et l'Autre. Ma colocataire. Entrée par effraction et que rien ni personne ne peut déloger.

Les séances chez le *taleb* ont été éprouvantes. Pour lui.

Le plus dur a été de nous habituer l'une à l'autre. Parce qu'elle est imprévisible. Pas question de composer avec elle ni de tenter de l'amadouer. Parce que c'est alors qu'elle se déchaîne.

Vertiges. Vertige de la liberté de parole. Je peux, oui je peux dire, puisque ce n'est pas moi, c'est l'autre. L'étrangère. Celle qui ne sait pas mentir. Celle qui ne sait pas se taire ; celle qui regarde les autres, droit dans les yeux. Etrangère parce que étrange aux yeux des autres, parce que non-conforme ; parce que délibérément différente. Définitivement rebelle.

Dans la famille, à présent, on *nous* regarde avec appréhension. On ne sait jamais quel tour peut prendre une discussion, quelle réaction peut susciter une parole. Mon père se détourne dès qu'il *nous* voit et prend ses repas seul dans le salon. Bon débarras, avons-

nous dit à voix haute, le premier soir. Ma mère n'a pas quitté son expression effarée depuis le jour où *nous* avons décidé et déclaré sans ambages qu'il n'était plus question d'accepter la différence de traitement, flagrante, entre mes frères et *nous.*

Il m'arrive quelques fois, très fugitivement, de me demander d'où elle vient. Quand et pourquoi elle a pris possession de mon corps. Et si les réponses s'esquissent, elle les rejette d'un grand rire. Comme si elle savait. Parfois même j'ai la sensation qu'elle était là depuis toujours, mais qu'elle attendait son heure. Mais c'est peut-être elle qui veut me le faire croire. Parce que j'ai de plus en plus de mal à *nous* dissocier.

Ainsi il t'a fallu tout ce temps ! Tout ce temps, toutes ces colères, tous ces détours pour te connaître ! Pour accepter l'autre en toi ! Et surtout pour faire accepter aux autres ce que tu es !

Quant à moi, je décline toute responsabilité.

***

mémoire et histoire

© Jean Lattes , *Nanterre, Foyer,* 1972, coll. Janine Lattes

©Elaine Mokhtefi, *Andrea,* 91 x 56 cm,.fevrier 2007

Devenir peintre

Elaine Mokhtefi

Difficile de dire ce que j'ai ressenti lorsque Behja m'a demandé de contribuer à ce numéro consacré à l'étranger. Car étrangère je l'ai toujours été, même dans le petit bourg américain où j'ai grandi, fille unique de l'unique famille juive de l'endroit. Aujourd'hui je me dis citoyenne du monde ; c'est que je me sens toujours d'ailleurs... de partout et de nulle part. Au lycée, lorsque la jeune prof de dessin m'a incitée à faire une école d'art, je l'ai à peine entendue – c'était un bruit de fond pas plus – tant j'étais pressée de connaître « l'ailleurs » et de me mêler à l'humanité avec un grand H.

Ecouter la prof m'aurait conduite vers une autre vie. J'aurais appris la peinture, ses techniques, son histoire, dans un cadre académique. J'aurais fait des stages étant jeune. Cette formation m'aurait amenée sur quelle balançoire, je ne peux l'imaginer. Aurais-je connu les mêmes « ailleurs » ? Mais ce sont les langues que j'ai étudiées dans un institut à New York. Puis j'ai pris la route. Elle m'a menée tout d'abord en Europe.

Il y a dans la vie des événements qui sont imprimés avec une encre indélébile. À Paris, le premier mai 1952, au défilé des travailleurs, je me suis faufilée parmi la foule qui s'étalait le long du parcours entre Nation et Bastille. Des centaines de milliers de marcheurs portant des banderoles, criant des slogans, chantant, des chars chargés de gens, branlants et colorés passaient pendant des heures. L'ambiance était joyeuse. La manifestation s'achevait quand, soudain, en queue du cortège sont arrivés au pas de course des rangées de dix à douze hommes. Ils étaient des milliers, tous la mine triste, maigres et pauvrement vêtus : des ouvriers algériens. J'ai eu l'impression qu'ils avaient été gardés en réserve, retenus, empêchés de défiler... mais par qui ? pourquoi ? Leur entrée en scène assombrissait le tableau pittoresque. J'en garde un souvenir trouble…

Je me suis inscrite à la Sorbonne mais ai peu assisté aux cours. J'étais encore pressée et j'avais d'autres priorités : gagner ma vie, aimer, me consacrer aux amis, contribuer aux causes justes… peut-être pas dans cet ordre. Le travail d'interprète m'a conduite en Asie et en Afrique. J'ai milité pour la libération des pays colonisés, manifesté contre la guerre d'Algérie avant de me lier au Front de Libération Nationale. Puis, j'ai travaillé aux bureaux de la délégation du FLN auprès de l'ONU à New York.

Et, en 1962, j'ai pris l'avion pour Alger pour assister aux cérémonies du premier novembre, date anniversaire du déclenchement de la lutte pour l'indépendance. J'étais à mille lieux de la peinture... j'allais fêter l'indépendance du peuple algérien, atterrir sur les terres d'un monde qui venait de renaître et tenter d'y trouver ma place.

Comment dresser le portrait d'Alger en ce temps-là pour qu'il soit crédible aujourd'hui. Il est difficile d'imaginer la liberté de mouvement et d'expression dont nous jouissions : on ne regardait pas en arrière, on discutait de tout, on travaillait comme des dingues, on se liait facilement, hommes et femmes, Algériens et étrangers... on faisait confiance à l'autre. Alger bruissait des mille voix des représentants des mouvements de libération – comme l'OLP (Palestine), l'ANC (Afrique du Sud), le MPLA (Angola), la ZAPU (Zimbabwe), le Frelimo (Mozambique), – et des exilés et militants de toute provenance, hommes et femmes politiques des partis d'opposition du Portugal, d'Espagne, du Brésil, d'Ethiopie car, il faut le rappeler, c'était l'époque où régnaient Franco, Salazar, Hailé Selassié... Certaines rencontres ont résonné de façon particulière pour moi, celle avec le Front de Libération du Sud-Vietnam en guerre contre les Etats-Unis (Tran Hoai Nam et ses camarades) et les Panthères Noirs américains (Eldridge et Kathleen Cleaver, Don Cox et d'autres). Che Guevara allait et venait, Malcolm X y a séjourné, Salvador Allende, Gamal Abdel Nasser ont tenu à connaître Alger. C'étaient les années soixante et soixante dix ! Des années d'espoir et de rêves fous.

Et nous avons vécu cette euphorie comme la transformation du monde car ce n'était pas moins à nos yeux. C'est alors que j'ai connu Behja et René-Paul, Rosa Cortès et tant d'autres gens engagés. Behja et moi avons rejoint le comité d'organisation du Festival Culturel Panafricain de 1969, un événement qui a bouleversé Alger. Des groupes de musique, de danse et d'art du continent et la diaspora africaine se sont produits dans les salles et sur les places et dans les rues de la ville, attirant des foules enchantées. Nous avons par la suite fait notre première tentative de lancement d'un journal mensuel que nous avons symboliquement intitulé « Sud » mais qui, hélas, n'a eu qu'une courte vie...

Pourtant, j'étais toujours restée sensible à la peinture. Partout où j'allais je visitais les musées et les galeries, à Stockholm, à

Paris, Philadelphie, New York et Alger. Dans les années soixante et soixante-dix, ces lieux n'attiraient pas grand monde à Alger. Je me revois au Musée des beaux-arts, seuls autres visiteurs : un couple d'Européens, ou encore au Musée de l'artisanat en bas de la Casbah... personne. Lors des expositions, d'excellents peintres se vendaient à des prix insignifiants. J'ai pu réunir une petite collection. J'ai visité l'atelier de Bouzid, j'ai bien connu Khadda et son œuvre, j'admirais Mesli et Issiakhem. Quand j'ai travaillé comme journaliste à la Radio-Télévision Algérienne je faisais des reportages sur tous les évènements artistiques. Á l'Ecole du journalisme de l'Université d'Alger, je chargeais mes étudiants d'effectuer des reportages sur les expositions d'art.

En 1974 j'ai dû quitter l'Algérie. Alger s'était considérablement transformée, elle n'était déjà plus le phare d'une jeunesse en quête d'idéal.

C'est bien plus tard, à Paris, que j'ai formé le projet de me mettre à peindre : j'ai décidé d'arrêter un travail qui ne m'amusait plus (je fabriquais et vendais des bijoux en pierres semi-précieuses et argent dans un dessous d'escalier à Saint-Germain-des-Près.) Je me suis mise à militer pour la Palestine – tous les samedis, je me joignais aux femmes qui manifestaient sur des places de Paris leur solidarité avec les Palestiniens – et à écrire et aussi à peindre, car évidemment, je n'ignorais pas que je savais dessiner correctement.

J'ai trouvé un cours d'aquarelle donné par une très belle femme très douée, puis un autre pour la peinture à l'huile avec une femme peintre d'une sensibilité extrême. À New York j'ai fréquenté l'Art Students League, un établissement étonnant où l'on peut s'inscrire pour un jour, une semaine ou pour un mois sans présenter le moindre justificatif. Il suffit d'une envie de peindre ou de sculpter. Maintenant, quand je suis à New York, je travaille dans un atelier à Harlem avec d'autres peintres et sculpteurs.

Ma passion pour la peinture ne me fait pas oublier que nous vivons dans un monde terrible, sans cœur. Solidarité est un mot qui s'éteint. L'argent, le marché, règlent les rapports entre les individus. Lorsque je me trouve devant une toile, je m'échappe. Je cherche les rapports entre les objets, les profondeurs d'un visage, le vent dans les arbres, leurs racines, je cherche les couleurs et leurs manifestations, je cherche surtout la lumière et je m'y plonge.

Quand, un jour d'hiver comme aujourd'hui, il m'arrive de me promener sur Broadway, dans cette ville où je suis née, et que je me demande d'où je suis, je sais que je suis d'ici mais aussi d'ailleurs, de Paris, d'Alger, là où j'ai posé mes pieds et là où le rêve m'amène.

©Elaine Mokhtefi, *Mokhtar.*

©Nic Sirkis, *mon amie Assia* chez qui j'habitais à Télemly.

J'ai fait ce portrait - avec mon 1er appareil photo, un « Instamatic 500 Kodak » reçu pour mon entrée en 6ème ! – le dernier jour des vacances de Pâques 1969, quand j'ai écrit ce poème d'adieu à Alger, avant de rentrer à Courbevoie...

Assia, sur cette photo, n'a que 13ans1/2, elle en paraît 17 ! Sa mère, Suzanne, veuve d'Abdelkader Ben Abdallah, née Larribère, était une des 5 filles du célèbre professeur d'obstétrique – médecin-chef à la clinique d'Oran (qui a été fouillée pendant la guerre d'Algérie par l'OAS). Pour honorer la mémoire du Docteur Larribère, l'Algérie indépendante a donné son nom à une place de sa ville d'Oran. Suzanne Larribère et son futur mari Abdelkader Ben Abdallah – brillant étudiant marocain à l'Ecole des Mines – sont venus à Paris faire leurs études dans les années 40 et c'est à la Faculté de Médecine que Suzanne et Luce, ma mère, – militantes engagées dans cette chaude période d'après guerre – se sont rencontrées pour une amitié… toujours fidèle !

C'est ainsi qu'avec mes parents, mon frère et moi avons fait un magnifique voyage en Algérie en avril 1968 où nous avons découvert la famille Ben Abdallah-Larribère, l'Algérie et son immense Sahara, chapelet d'îles-oasis jusqu'à El Goléa. Nous avons cheminé dans une caravane de Renault 16 entre enlisements dans les routes sableuses, roulades dans les dunes blondes et caramel, miracles des mirages sur l'asphalte brûlant et fou-rires unissant Assia, Bernard, Mourad, Catherine Tomkiewicz, (fille de Stanislaw – dit Tom – fameux pédopsychiatre engagé auprès du FLN algérien et contre toutes formes de violence) et moi. Puis mes parents nous ont expédiés, l'année suivante, consolider cette amitié naissante. Nous avons passé 2 semaines formidables avec Assia et son frère aîné Mourad. Malika était la dame algérienne qui s'occupait de nous quatre – préados – toute la journée, qui faisait ménage et délicieuse cuisine et que nous faisions tourner en bourrique avec toutes nos pitreries ! C'est à cette Malika que j'ai dédié « Alger », poème composé sur ce balcon de l'appartement de Suzanne Ben Abdallah, que voici :

Alger

Nic Sirkis

À Malika

Cascades de maisons sur la mer turquoise
Minarets de mosquées dressés sur l'horizon
Sable doré et fin de la plage algéroise
Enfant au front halé tapant dans un ballon,

Sirène d'un bateau voguant vers le lointain
Candeur d'une femme au voile effarouché
Commères au balcon racontant leur potin
Piment d'une merguez qu'un marchand fait griller,

Chien décharné trottant sur le pavé brûlant
Fillettes aux pieds nus soulevant un panier
Marchand d'oranges lourdes dans un chariot croulant
Ballade du facteur apportant le courrier,

Glycine aux grappes mauves dansant dans le soleil
Mouettes soupirant sur le port oublié
Linge sur la terrasse où la brise sommeille
Poussière dans la rue par un midi d'été,

Parc baigné de lumière et jardin de verdure
Ouvrier travaillant dans l'air ensoleillé
Eclat d'une fleur pourpre à l'arôme trop pur
Klaxon d'une voiture dans la rue encombrée,

Eclat de rire franc dans un rayon joyeux
Cycliste pédalant sur la route escarpée
Vie enthousiaste et simple dans des murs blancs et bleus
Landau qu'une maman pousse sur le pavé,

Pains chauds et attirants dans la boulangerie
Petit gosse portant son frère sur le dos
Capitale rieuse de toute l'Algérie
Alger se fait bercer par le ciel et les flots.

Quartier Telemly, Alger, Mars 1969

©coll. Luce Sirkis, Nic en Algérie au printemps 1969

©Catherine Rossi, *Mosquée Pouillon*, Alger in *Alger ou l'impossible portrait*, éd. Chèvre-feuille étoilée, 2010

© Rosa Cortès, *L'Ataturk,* Istanbul

© Rosa Cortès, *Minarets*, Istanbul

Tu es la mère des villes…

Rosa Cortès

Byzance, Constantinople, Istanbul, ville renaissante, ville dévorante, ville conquérante. Qui pense te retenir, prépare sa défaite. Ville phénix égale et différente, ta multiplicité est si subtile que nul ne peut se sentir étranger en ton sein. Tu es la mère des villes couverte d'un manteau de temps entrelacés où présent, passé, futur lissent leurs frontières.

Quand sommes-nous ? Qui peut le dire au hasard des parcours et des rencontres ? Un monument, des pierres dressées et une date surgit du lointain mais un regard, un mot, un vêtement et nous voilà projetés dans un lendemain presque identifiable. A quelle croisée nous trouvons-nous ?

Se promener dans les rues d'Istanbul, c'est marcher dans les pas de Mustafa Kemal, cet homme d'Etat surnommé Kemal Ataturk, le père des Turcs, et trouver à chaque coin de rue cette société immergée dans ce devenir de progrès, de modernité et de rationalité dont il a semé les ferments. Il a fertilisé son peuple en jachère et y a usé son esprit et son cœur.

Poser son regard sur Istanbul, c'est contempler aussi les vestiges des empires déchus et des dynasties abolies. Le temps dompté qui s'égrène dans son sablier n'a pas cours dans cette ville qui déchire la mémoire. Les pierres y ont une âme et les âmes sont de pierre.

Ville blanche, bleue, noire. Ville de lumières et d'ombres offertes. Ville d'eau et de collines qui s'enlacent et ondulent. Ville d'arcs et de flèches, de jardins et de lèpre, de roses et d'orties.

De Byzas – qui sept siècles avant J.C vint camper sur cette presqu'île – à l'empereur Constantin le Grand qui, en 330, donna son nom à la cité, dix siècles de sièges, de retraits, d'espoirs, d'abandon, de poursuites incessantes, dix siècles de hordes, d'armées, de stratèges, de traîtres, de devins, dix siècles de sangs mêlés pendant lesquels l'Asie et l'Occident se rejoignaient, se fondaient et bouillonnaient. Mais – décadence des civilisations rayonnantes qui s'éblouissent et s'aveuglent à saisir leur propre éclat – Rome se débanda pendant que l'Empire byzantin, comme un serpent étêté, l'oubliait et exaltait sa propre grandeur dans une terre posée pour défier le temps.

Et pendant mil ans encore, les croix se mirent à malaxer l'espace comme de la glaise docile et à offrir au Dieu tout puissant des présents dont la splendeur ne pouvait que l'émouvoir et faire pleurer l'esclave. Ainsi s'éleva la basilique de Sainte Sophie, brodée de tuiles si légères qu'il fallut aller les sortir de Rhodes, soutenue de colonnes si puissantes et colorées que les seuls marbres et porphyres du pays n'y suffisaient pas, décorée de mosaïques si fines que les ors qui les recouvrent embellissent avec douceur les figures figées et solennelles des empereurs, impératrices, vierges et martyrs qui veillent le Christ. Car Sainte Sophie se dressa pour honorer le Ciel mais aussi les Maîtres de ces terres.

☆

Dès le VIIe siècle, les incursions arabes marqueront la ville comme pour s'en approprier les contours. Mais la Superbe écrase les tentatives et la conquérir nécessite la constance d'un fou recherchant l'impossible.

Trop de siècles d'opulence, d'arrogance, de lassitude. Trop d'humanité dispersée sur des flots de pierres précieuses. Pleure Constantinople, tes ors éclaboussent, tes richesses emmurent. Pleure Constantinople, tes croix forment des sentiers d'épines géométriques où les infidèles qui te convoitent viennent se jeter comme des vagues écumantes, jusqu'à ce que tous ces corps empalés au fil des temps tissent enfin un tapis de chair molle leur permettant d'avancer et de te transpercer sans retenue.

Mil ans après Constantin, voici arrivés les Ottomans qui, enfin, t'enserrent dans leur passion et te rebaptisent en 1453 Istanbul. Il te faut être vierge et renaissante à leur amour.

Et voilà cette ville qui enchante ceux qui la pénètrent, purgée de ses croix et de ses ors byzantins. Fécondée par ces nouveaux maîtres l'irrigant d'un sang où glissent des étoiles et un croissant de lune, elle accouchera en convulsions répétées de multiples splendeurs sous leur souffle et leur génie. Ils l'habilleront de palais et de mosquées, de jardins et de marchés et poseront comme des calices renversés et soumis, des centaines de coupoles trapues et sensuelles attendant d'éclore au soleil.

Tant de rondeur et de douceur n'effacèrent pas la puissance menaçante qui semblait se tapir sous ces dômes, prête à éclater à l'appel d'on ne sait quel fatal signal.

Et les gardiens vigilants de ces forces masquées s'érigèrent alentour. Ce furent des minarets longs, fins, comme des lanières de pierres aigues tranchant l'azur sans fin. Ainsi les collines offrirent-elles aux regards lointains, une harmonie faite de courbes, de lignes, de parallèles, d'angles à l'élégance et à la violence aussi fascinantes que déconcertantes.

Approchez, semble dire la ville, *je suis l'amphitryon qui vous honore et vous enserre dans son giron parfumé et abondant. Telle Circé accueillant ses visiteurs, je captive et pétrifie. Craignez mes rondeurs nourricières comme des seins maternels qui se transforment en casques de métal pour des batailles souterraines, éloignez-vous des fins minarets qui deviennent des piques n'hésitant pas à transpercer les cœurs insoumis à ses chants.*

⋆

La nuit tombe sur Istanbul et la ville se tapit et se déploie comme une profonde et ample respiration précédant l'effort. Le jour a architecturé la trame nocturne. Les fragrances s'épanouissent et s'évadent des murailles devenues inutiles. Elles vont se déverser sur des flots qui les emportent vers on ne sait quel rendez-vous secret.

Les plaintes et les chants, les gémissements de plaisir ou de douleur qui s'échappent des moucharabiehs cloîtrant les harems tissent des dentelles de soupirs le long des pavés que les sabots de chevaux écumants viennent fouler et déchiqueter.

Les femmes espèrent la main qui se posera sur elles et les apaisera. Elles ferment les yeux et l'imaginent et leurs rêves aussitôt s'effilochent en caresses.

La nuit violette et sanguine frémit sur les palais insomniaques. Bientôt le muezzin tentera de laver les cœurs tourmentés et avides mais son chant ne ravivera que les étoiles qui, de joie, palpiteront plus intensément dans leurs soyeux draps d'ébène.

Voici venir la nuit sur Istanbul, voici éclore l'intrigue et briller la dague.

Des ombres dansent et disparaissent le long des murs ; on ne sait si ce sont des animaux ou des hommes, des diables ou des anges. Bruissement de tissus froissés, claquement de semelles sur les pavés, murmure de paroles indistinctes, cris étouffés, soudain tout semble s'interrompre brutalement à peine ébauché. N'y a-t-il qu'une seule note hésitante dans cette symphonie nocturne ou le compositeur, insatisfait, recherche-t-il sans cesse l'impossible mesure magique seule capable de ravir les corps ?

La nuit s'allonge puis sursaute et vomit son trop plein de chaleur et de sexe. Elle rote sa satiété. Que de turbulences et de grouillements confus sous les pavés. Une armée de cafards et de rats s'échappent des caniveaux, dévalent les collines à l'écoute du clapotis du fleuve. Ils se pressent comme impatients d'aller au bal de la pleine lune un samedi soir. Ils se bousculent comme préoccupés d'occuper un espace où se déployer. Quelle activité seigneur ! Quelle furie ! Se fondant dans l'obscurité, on ne peut que les deviner aux bruissements de leurs ailes et claquements de leurs pattes. Istanbul déploie ses armées secrètes qui, elles aussi, auront droit au repos dès qu'apparaîtront les premières lueurs mordorées de l'aube ; mais pour l'instant, elles sillonnent la ville et se l'approprient, refoulant les hommes derrière leurs portes ciselées.

Istanbul, Istanbul, es-tu toujours alerte ? Entends-tu les loups qui s'approchent et rôdent, humant le sang vaillant qui gicle dans tes veines et prêts à t'égorger et laisser tes os pourrir au soleil des rives éclatées ? Prends garde à toi, ô mon Istanbul repue, prends garde à ne pas te laisser percer l'âme... Ataturk n'est plus là pour te faire revivre.

Repliée sur elle-même tel un fauve aux muscles bandés, frémissante aux odeurs de proies rapprochées que la brise lui apporte, la ville se concentre avant de dérouler sa puissante carcasse et briser dans ses mâchoires énormes les insolentes ténèbres qui menacent de l'annihiler. Avant d'être déchiquetées, regardez-les s'épandre.

⁂

La pièce rapportée
ou *Les belles-mères ont-elles une âme ?*

Geneviève de Dietrich

C'était une soirée du mois d'août, mon mari et moi rentrions d'un séjour dans un pays de l'ancienne Europe de l'Est. Valérie et Pierre, ton papa et ta maman, qui avaient habité notre jolie maison pendant notre absence, nous accueillirent joyeusement. Le dîner était prêt, le couvert mis dans la cuisine.

Nous leur avons offert notre petit cadeau : un œuf en porcelaine peint de dessins bleus. Quelques minutes plus tard, ils nous annonçaient la grande nouvelle : tu étais en vie, dans le ventre de ta maman. Joie, embrassades, vrai bonheur.

Je vécus les jours suivants dans l'allégresse. À tous mes amis, à mes collègues préférés, à ma sœur, à ma fille, je l'annonçai : j'allais être *grand-mère* ! Au bout du fil, les voix s'exclamaient de joie partagée, devant moi, les regards s'illuminaient. Un petit fils ! Une petite fille ! Le premier ! La première !

Le jour où tu devais voir le jour approchait. Je me mis à photographier tout ce que je voyais de beau ou de significatif autour de moi : les iris mauves, la grue repliée, le gros trou pour enterrer la souche du cèdre déraciné, l'esquisse du futur chemin. Pour pouvoir te fabriquer un album agrémenté de courts poèmes, pour te prouver que toutes ces beautés et ces mystères étaient là pour toi, chez tes grands-parents.

Et soudain tu apparus, posée dans le creux du berceau standard de la clinique, toute fine et jolie, tellement paisible. Dès le lendemain, je commençai à t'annoncer à tous mes amis, à ma sœur, à ma fille, à mes collègues préférés : « Vous savez, Apolline est née ! Je suis *grand-mère* ! » La vie en était transfigurée parce qu'il y avait toi, en plus.

Tu te mis à grandir, à être de moins en moins un tout petit bébé. Tu te mis à articuler des sons, qui ressemblèrent à des mots : « papa », « maman », « grand-père ». Le grand-père, mon mari, en était tout tremblant de bonheur pur.

On partait de chez vous. C'était sur le palier. « Dis au revoir à grand-père ! » Ta main minuscule se balançait gracieusement. Tu es une petite fille très gracieuse. Et puis : « Dis au revoir à Elizabeth ! »

« *Elizabeth* ! » Ce fut comme si le sang se retirait de mes joues, de mes mains. Je me sentis blanchir. Nul ne semblait s'en apercevoir, pourtant. « *Elizabeth* »… Je pensai, pour distraire la douleur : « Quel mot difficile à prononcer pour un enfant si petit… » Au fond de moi, la grand-mère perdait pied.

On me demandait de tes nouvelles. Je disais : « Ma petite fille Apolline » et ma voix s'étranglait parce que je me sentais coupable d'usurper ce titre qu'on ne souhaitait pas me donner.

On fêta ton premier anniversaire. On photographia les grands-parents, par deux, par quatre : papy Jeannot avec mamie Simone, puis grand-père Thomas – mon mari – avec son ex-épouse qui se fait appeler « Maï ». Et ce fut tout. Moi, je n'arrêtais pas de te photographier, toi, pour cacher l'humidité de mes yeux, de beaux portraits dansants avec les ballons roses et violets qui virevoltaient autour de toi.

Tu grandissais vite. Tu possédais un petit album plastifié pour les photos de tes parents, de ta famille, mais je n'y figurais pas, on n'avait pas trouvé de photo de moi ! Un jour, j'apportai une photo et la plaçai moi-même dans l'album.

J'avais toujours envie de parler de toi. À ceux qui te connaissaient, c'était facile, je disais seulement « Apolline », ce mot si doux et sucré dans la bouche. Pour les autres, il fallait trouver des périphrases : « Apolline, la fille de Valérie et de Pierre. Pierre, le fils de mon mari. » Aujourd'hui, j'ai trouvé plus court : « Apolline, la petite-fille de mon mari ».

Mon mari, il n'a d'abord rien senti du tout. Rien ne le frappait, rien ne le choquait. Il faut dire qu'il est habitué de longue date aux « pièces rapportées », et j'en étais déjà une pour sa famille bien avant ta naissance. J'ai fini par lui parler. Il m'a dit que c'était à moi de « m'imposer ». Je lui ai demandé d'intervenir auprès de Pierre, ton papa, son fils. Il ne l'a pas fait. Pourtant, il est le premier à dire que, si la poule est la femme du coq, la lionne celle du lion, comme sur les cartes de ton jeu, la femme du grand-père, c'est la grand-mère.

Voilà. Maintenant, ta petite sœur Charlotte a trois jours. Elle est encore à la clinique avec Valérie, ta maman. À mes amis, à mes collègues préférés, à ma sœur, à ma fille, je n'ai pas parlé d'elle, pour ne pas avoir à prononcer ces mots : « Mon mari vient d'avoir une deuxième petite fille, Charlotte ».

De toutes façons, d'ici à ce que toi et ta petite sœur puissiez prononcer « *Elizabeth*», il s'écoulera du temps, et bien plus encore avant que vous ne sachiez lire ce que j'écris là.

Lorsque vous serez grandes, j'espère devenir pour vous deux une sorte de vieille amie hors normes qui sait écrire et peindre et qui vous donnera l'envie de le faire aussi. Quand vous parlerez de moi, vous direz : « C'est Elizabeth, la femme de notre grand-père » !

Et, – qui sait – un jour peut-être, l'une de vous viendra me chuchoter timidement à l'oreille : « Dis, est-ce que je peux t'appeler *grand-mère* ? »

⁂

©Elaine Mokhtefi, *Hannah*, 61 x 46 cm, novembre 2008

Mes grands-mères

Claire Mestre

La première se nomme Andrée. La plus bourgeoise. La plus centrale. J'aime la consonance de ce prénom masculin, ancien, de sonorité brève et grave. C'est aussi celui de mon père. D'elle je tiens avant tout mon habitus corporel. Elle était coquette, les mains fines et blanches, les ongles coupés court et soignés, les mêmes bagues portées quelque soit l'occasion. Un peu austère, le corps enfermé dans les convenances de la bienséance et de la retenue.

D'elle, je tiens le goût pour un meuble : la coiffeuse. Tous les matins, après le petit déjeuner préparé par son mari, un bol de café au lait avec une tartine, elle se baignait et choisissait ses habits avec précaution. Puis, elle passait du temps assise devant sa coiffeuse, relevait ses cheveux bouclés en un chignon serré, et mettait ses bijoux. Enfant, j'avais fouillé dans ses armoires sans jamais trouver le trésor que j'espérais. Je dénichai pourtant une robe de mariée, celle d'une grande tante morte de longue date. Elle m'a servi de déguisement. Cette femme de devoir, bien élevée, très catholique a mis au monde sept enfants. Elle était connue pour son caractère autoritaire et ses cris retentissants, ses colères et ses exigences. Mais derrière la dureté, je devine aujourd'hui les signes de sa fragilité. Ses siestes quotidiennes ne ressemblaient-elles pas à des fugues dans le sommeil ? J'ai récemment découvert, au hasard d'une brocante, un livre que j'avais toujours vu, enfant, traîner dans sa chambre : *Les mariés du bout du monde* de Tchekov Minosa et de Brigitte de Saint-Preux. Il raconte les aventures libertaires d'un couple parti de par le monde pour découvrir les différentes façons de se marier. « Un roman d'amour et d'aventures, une histoire vraie » avertit la préface. J'ai appris qu'il avait été le livre de chevet des hippies dans les années 70. Cette (re)découverte m'a laissée perplexe : cette femme si pieuse, traditionnelle jusqu'à la rigidité, devait aussi avoir des échappées imaginaires…

Je tiens d'elle aussi le goût pour la correspondance épistolaire. Dès que j'ai su écrire, ma première lettre lui a été destinée et j'ai gardé précieusement ses lettres écrites jusque dans sa vieillesse.

La seconde est Marguerite. Elle est ma périphérie. D'elle je tiens avant tout la persévérance dans le malheur. La souffrance et l'endurance. Mon nom est le sien. Sec, court mais aux accents du sud, évoquant une prestance : maestro, maestria ! Fille de paysan, elle est coquette, même dans la vieillesse. C'est une femme déçue par la vie, par les hommes qui l'ont maltraitée. Des hommes violents et alcooliques. Pourtant, elle a résisté, élevé ses deux enfants, le premier est mon père adoptif. Des années plus tard, elle éleva également son petit fils aîné, abandonné bébé à ses soins par sa fille. Elle a travaillé avec obstination. Elle se déplaçait par tous les temps en bicyclette. Grâce à elle, j'aime le bruit, lointain, des trains dans la nuit. Elle était garde barrière, et quand je dormais, enfant, chez elle, les trains faisaient trembler les murs. Je me réveillais dans la nuit et me rendormais sur l'image de la lumière fulgurante d'une machine emportant des voyageurs assoupis allant je ne sais où et ne laissant que l'écho du chemin de fer.

Elle ne lit pas, mais elle prie. D'elle je tiens le goût pour la modestie et la simplicité.

La dernière est Pauline. La plus imaginaire. D'elle je tiens surtout mon goût pour le rêve. Elle avait de l'élégance sur les quelques photos que j'ai d'elle. Son teint foncé, sa tenue claire, sa jupe au genou, et ses pieds nus : une princesse, à la vie trop courte. Vie fulgurante, écrasée par la douleur. D'elle je n'ai que des bribes de mots, d'histoires interrompues. Elle est morte, alors que son fils, mon père naturel, était tout petit. Amoureuse, je veux le penser, d'un homme de l'administration de Majunga, elle brava les interdits d'une société coloniale, pour vivre secrètement une relation transgressive. Car elle était mariée à un homme de son rang, car il était français et elle était malgache. Le mari trompé la battait, en vain, l'enfant naquit. Elle est morte après les événements de 1947, vivant comme une veuve, puisqu'à la naissance du métis, les hommes, le mari et l'amant avaient été éloignés. Et la grand-mère de l'enfant, qui avait pris en main son éducation avait brûlé toute trace de ce passé désormais oublié.

Quand je suis arrivée à Madagascar pour des recherches universitaires, j'ai rêvé d'elle. Elle était allongée sur le sol, ou plutôt son corps avec des seins lourds, émergeait d'un drap blanc et sortait de la terre. Ses cheveux noirs et épais étaient étalés. Elle avait chaud. D'habitude, quand les ancêtres se manifestent aux vivants, ils sont habillés et se plaignent d'avoir froid. Pour les descendants malgaches, de tels rêves constituent des signes pour des rituels post funéraires : il faut « ré envelopper les morts », les honorer pour acquérir leur protection. J'ai compris le mien, aux images strictement inversées à celles de la tradition. Elle était née tout simplement à mon esprit, j'étais devenue sa petite fille. D'ailleurs son fils avait renoué les liens rompus de la transmission : nous avions versé de l'alcool sur les pierres de sa dernière demeure ; il m'avait offert des boucles d'oreille lui ayant appartenu et il avait fait de moi sa fille adoptive.

Je suis métisse, héritière de ces trois femmes, que j'aime même dans l'absence, en silence. Les deux premières m'ont donné des menus objets et des images, mais aussi des restes de rêves, d'attentes et de déceptions. La troisième est partie bien avant ma naissance, bien avant le grand voyage qui m'a rendu une part de mes origines. A travers les ratés de cette transmission, je me suis constituée métisse. Non pas toute seule, mais dans mes rencontres, mes lectures et mes créations. Ainsi, la périphérie irrigue le centre.

***

Des vies en aiguillage

Au balcon de ses rêves
elle guette suspendue
ce défilé sans trêve
Silhouettes menues
à la vitre appuyées
Wagons illuminés
emportant dans la nuit
ces vies à inventer

Tu ne sais plus pourquoi
Un jour dans cette gare
Tu te retrouves là
Parmi tous ces regards

Sous la verrière tombe
en cercle des taches d'ombres

Ni le sens de tes pas
Vers des quais où s'égarent
S'interpellent des voix
Arrivées ou départs

Là des moineaux poursuivent
Les enfants

Pour eux la petite fille
aux tresses blondes
invente une ronde

Des vies en aiguillage
Trajectoires des voies
Parle-t-on de voyage
Quand on n'a pas le choix

Enfants sortez de la ronde
D'autres nuits vous attendent

Et vos étoiles multipliées
Jamais ici ne pourront briller

On laisse on ignore
On confie à l'histoire
On condamne parfois

Pourtant
Masse sombre échouée
Mains tendues sur ces quais
Ceux qu'on nomme
aujourd'hui Etrangers

On passe autour d'eux
On évite leurs yeux
On s'agite on s'embrasse
Il faut vite être heureux

Sabine Péglion

Hommage à un ami disparu récemment
À l'ami Hamid

Behja Traversac

Le passé n'est pas mort et enterré.
En fait il n'est même pas passé.
William Faulkner

Non, le passé de l'homme et de l'ami n'est pas passé. L'homme physique est passé mais pas son histoire d'homme. L'histoire de l'homme et de l'ami est là. Juste à côté, à portée de main, prête à ressurgir auprès des siens. Sa grande silhouette distinguée, ses petites lunettes rondes et son sourire en coin ne s'effacent pas de notre mémoire. Ses affections qui appellent les nôtres. Son inlassable effort didactique qui disait ses préoccupations. Ses révoltes et ses colères toujours à fleur de voix, de ton, de geste, d'allers et de retours. Non, l'histoire de l'homme n'est pas passée, elle nous raconte encore le militant infatigable, les luttes d'hier, les tâches qui restent à accomplir, la pensée à parfaire, à polir… comme le bois entre les mains de l'ébéniste, l'argile entre les mains de ses ancêtres.

Pour moi, comme pour tous ceux qui l'ont connu, Hamid a été le chantre de la justice sociale. Et bien sûr celui de la promotion du secteur agricole auquel il a consacré une grande partie de sa vie. Mais en dehors de toutes les questions qu'il n'a jamais cessé de se poser sur l'Algérie, sur le Tiers Monde, sur l'impérialisme, je retiendrai celle qui illustre de façon originale et presque insolite, sa personnalité : Hamid est, pour moi, le premier féministe algérien que j'aie connu.

Oui, cela paraît étonnant, inaccoutumé, pour ne pas dire plus, de qualifier de féministe un homme, dans un pays où il n'est simplement pas facile d'être une femme. Pourtant, et même si cela choque la bien *pensance* des milieux qui ont toujours voulu faire passer la liberté des femmes après les ténébreuses arcanes du *développement* (lequel ? quand ? comment ? a-t-on envie de leur dire) je l'ai toujours entendu défendre avec conviction, avec passion même, la cause des femmes, leur place dans la société, leur rôle indispensable dans la modernisation de son pays et la sécularisation de ses mœurs. Pour lui c'était d'une telle évidence qu'aucun argument ne pouvait l'ébranler. Le code de la famille représentait à ses yeux une incongruité intolérable dans l'espace algérien. Une tache que tous les intellectuels de ce pays – femmes et hommes confondus – devaient s'efforcer d'effacer… en la combattant sans céder à une quelconque injonction.

Il aimait travailler avec des femmes, il aimait les encourager et il les écoutait comme on écoute le voyageur arrivé de loin… C'est vrai que les Algériennes arrivent souvent de loin. Il les écoutait avec l'émotion qu'il mettait dans toutes ses relations à l'autre et qui, peut-être, sans doute, le rendait vulnérable. Tout être est vulnérable de n'être pas comme la cohorte des *croyants* des églises politiques, idéologiques, religieuses. Mais la vulnérabilité peut aussi être cette ressource qui raffermit, consolide, cimente et laisse loin derrière les hurlements des dogmes. Il était de ceux-là qui, à cause de – ou grâce à – cette fragilité, savait tout le danger des systèmes dogmatiques : un obscurcissement de la pensée, un aveuglement du raisonnement, un arraisonnement des attentes des peuples, une chape de soumission. Ceux-là, tels Hamid, suivent leur chemin avec obstination, avec courage, ne cédant jamais aux autoritarismes, à la facilité, exigeants envers eux-mêmes comme envers les autres.

Mais s'il avait de l'indépendance d'esprit et de l'exigence, Hamid avait un sens de l'amitié et de la solidarité exemplaire et dont témoigneront certainement ceux qui l'ont connu. Il a toujours su ouvrir ses mains et sa maison.

Sa maison, où il accueillait chacun comme une personnalité de marque. Ainsi on allait chez lui comme on va chez soi. C'était simple, normal, accueillant. Il y avait en lui une étrange fusion entre l'espace qu'il habitait et lui-même. Comme les fils entrelacés des métiers à tisser de son Algérie. Une espèce de *reliance,* enracinée, communicative. Ce n'était pas une posture conventionnelle, au contraire. C'était son lieu, le nôtre, dans lequel il nous conviait à une rassurante présence.

Bien sûr il lui arrivait d'être ombrageux, de dire haut et fort ses désaccords, ses exaspérations, mais il savait faire la distinction entre l'hôte qu'il recevait et la personne avec laquelle il n'était pas d'accord. Il lui arrivait d'être intransigeant sur des questions fondamentales mais toujours parce qu'il se plaçait du côté des peuples et non du côté des puissants.

Sa maison où… discrète mais veillant à tout, Nicole, sa fidèle compagne, emplissait l'espace de sa présence, de ses mots et communiquait son sourire et sa chaleur. Elle avait déposé là, comme des totems, tant d'objets brûlants de soleil, de sable, de vents et d'odeurs. Comme le raconte si bien Giono dans « Que ma joie demeure » elle donnait du sens, un sens à ce qu'est *la maison*, bien au-delà de sa présence physique autour de soi. Nicole était en adéquation totale avec le sens de l'hospitalité que Hamid portait en lui comme une valeur cardinale. Nicole qui garde en son sein l'ardeur d'un amour sans faille pour l'Algérie. Nicole qui a veillé sur lui, toujours, et si bien pendant sa maladie. Elle n'a jamais laissé le silence s'installer... l'envahir, elle veillait aux présences et aux repos, elle était le bois, l'acier, le socle qui jamais ne se dérobe. Hamid le savait et moi je sais qu'il la quittait avec regret...

★★★★★

Hamid Aït Amara fondateur de l'I.P.C.A.

René-Paul Traversac

Hamid Aït Amara a été mon premier responsable professionnel. Bien sûr, ça marque. Mais ce ne fut pas, tant s'en faut, n'importe quel responsable. Il avait créé l'I.P.C.A. (Institut de Promotion Coopérative – Alger) destiné à l'animation des coopératives de commercialisation du secteur autogéré agricole et à la formation de leur personnel d'encadrement (directeurs, comptables et animateurs). Nous étions en septembre 1966, encore dans l'enthousiasme de l'indépendance, bien qu'un peu refroidi par le « sursaut révolutionnaire » du 19 juin. Contrairement à beaucoup de mes camarades « Volontaires du Service

National Actif » plus communément appelés « coopérants militaires » je savais, avant de débarquer à Alger, que je serais affecté à l'I.P.C.A. où j'avais été recommandé par le Collège Coopératif de Paris créé et animé par H. Desroche.

L' I.P.C.A. c'était Hamid, entouré d'une poignée de coopérants et de quelques algériens comme Boualem Makouf ou Behja Bensalem. C'était un mélange d'utopie autogestionnaire et de rigueur universitaire. Même si les coopérants avaient de la sympathie pour la jeune Algérie indépendante, ce n'étaient pas tous des socialistes convaincus, plusieurs sortaient de grandes écoles de commerce, qui ne constituent pas un milieu spécialement progressiste, mais tout le monde travaillait avec ferveur et enthousiasme. Ce qu'il y avait de formidable, c'était ce sentiment que, tout en effectuant un travail utile, on apprenait l'Algérie et les Algériens. Cela c'était dû, bien sûr, à l'atmosphère de l'époque mais aussi et surtout à Hamid. Il avait su créer une ambiance aussi volontariste que décontractée. Je ne me souviens pas, en un an et demi d'I.P.C.A., avoir vécu ou assisté à un conflit concernant les conditions ou la quantité de travail. Il faut dire que Hamid prêchait par l'exemple. Il débarquait parfois au siège de l'I.P.C.A., 25 boulevard Zirout Youcef, le teint verdâtre, torturé par son ulcère gastrique, et nous nous mettions au travail parce qu'il fallait préparer un stage imminent ou une mission.

C'est grâce à Hamid que j'ai pu découvrir l'Algérie en dehors des livres. Je me souviens avoir effectué la tournée des coopératives de fruits et légumes du marché intérieur, les CORE, de l'est algérien, (Sétif, Constantine, Biskra, Annaba, Khenchela, Batna, Béjaïa, etc.) en compagnie de Jean Berty Hennel, HEC, pour « redresser » la comptabilité de ces malheureuses coopératives pourvues de Directeurs et de Comptables souvent pas, peu, ou mal formés mais généralement fort sympathiques. Cette période relativement courte m'apparaît comme la plus riche de mon existence. Pour beaucoup elle fut une parenthèse, pour moi ce fut infiniment plus, un nouveau départ, une re-naissance, n'oublions pas que je m'appelle René. Cela aurait-il été possible sans Hamid ? En quelque sorte ce fut mon père algérien, ou tout au moins mon grand frère. C'est sans aucun doute grâce à lui que je suis resté en Algérie aussi longtemps. Mais en suis-je vraiment parti ? Rien n'est moins sûr.

Hamid c'était une vision de l'Algérie nouvelle, souvent réaliste, même si elle n'était pas dépourvue d'erreurs. Vision assez, pour ne pas dire totalement, éloignée de l'enthousiasme délirant de l'immédiat après indépendance, cher à ceux que l'on a appelé les « pieds rouges », et dont l'utopie n'a pas résisté au premiers frissons du 19 juin. Non pas que sa vision fut dépourvue d'enthousiasme, mais elle se voulait réaliste. Hamid était partisan de l'action en profondeur, de la formation et non de l'endoctrinement. Il était partisan d'un état réellement socialiste et non bureaucratique. Quand il parlait du « petit fellah » avec sa prononciation caractéristique qui nous faisait sourire, sans cœur que nous étions, il y mettait tellement de conviction qu'on ne pouvait que le suivre. Le problème c'est que ceux qui l'ont condamné ne l'avaient même pas écouté.

La seule chose que nous lui reprochions à l'I.P.C.A. c'était sa dispersion. Nous aurions préféré qu'il s'occupât un peu plus du fonctionnement de la boîte. Mais finalement ça nous obligeait à nous débrouiller, à improviser, à comprendre comment fonctionnait ce secteur autogéré agricole, dont l'Algérie était si fière, mais dont il fallait bien admettre que ça ne fonctionnait pas comme beaucoup l'auraient souhaité. D'autres se frottaient les mains de voir cette expérience socialisante tourner court. Hamid, comme beaucoup de responsables de l'époque, ne dispersait pas ses efforts par tempérament mais par nécessité. Il y avait tant de choses à faire et si peu de compétences qu'il fallait bien toucher un peu à tout, et puis il était internationaliste, alors il fallait se rendre à l'étranger. Je me souviens qu'il allait souvent en Tunisie et qu'il nous parlait avec intérêt de l'expérience des coopératives qu'Ahmed Ben Salah avait créées pour gérer les anciennes exploitations coloniales tunisiennes.

Mais Hamid ne fut pas seulement un responsable professionnel admirable. Il devint rapidement un ami. Ce fut à l'I.P.C.A. que je rencontrais mon épouse qui y assurait la fonction de documentaliste. Contrairement à beaucoup d'Algériens qui voyaient d'un assez mauvais œil une algérienne épouser un étranger, Hamid nous a toujours témoigné beaucoup d'amitié, allant jusqu'à nous céder gratuitement son logement lorsqu'il déménagea dans le même immeuble ce qui était le plus beau cadeau que l'on puisse faire à Alger à l'époque.

Je ne parlerais pas de tous ses nombreux engagements et actions, aussi bien dans le domaine universitaire que politique. D'autres le feront mieux que moi. Je voulais simplement témoigner d'un engagement qui paraîtra bien éloigné à beaucoup, presque folklorique. Mais je reste persuadé que son engagement, là comme ailleurs, n'aura pas été vain. Il l'a tenu avec son habituelle modestie, alors que tant, qui ne lui arrivaient pas à la cheville, en ont profité pour s'enrichir, pour piller les richesses de leur pays. Il parlait peu de lui, même s'il ne cachait rien. Ce n'est que bien après que j'ai appris des choses sur son histoire, sur sa famille. Il était fier de ses origines, comme il était fier de son pays, sans forfanterie, sans exagération. Avec sa disparition, l'Algérie a perdu un de ses meilleurs serviteurs, faisons en sorte que nul ne l'oublie.

R-P T, Ingénieur agronome

© Jean Lattes, *Nanterre, jour de l'Aïd,* 1972, coll. Janine Lattes

©Jean Lattes, *Nanterre, Imprimerie de jacquette de disques, Graphicolor* 1976, coll. Janine Lattes

Jean Lattes, photo reporter

Marie-Noël Arras

Il y a environ quatre ans, j'ai rencontré Janine Lattes la femme du « photo-journaliste » comme Jean Lattes aimait se nommer. Très vite, elle m'a dit son désespoir de ne pouvoir faire archiver ses plus de 100 000 photos. Lorsqu'elle m'a fait entrer pour la première fois dans le bureau de son mari et qu'elle m'a ouvert quelques une de ses boites d'agrandissements et planches contact, l'émotion a été très forte. Comment un homme qui semble avoir photographié tous les événements et toutes les personnes qui comptaient à cette époque, sans parler d'un tas d'anonymes, pouvait ainsi être resté dans l'ombre alors que tant de ses collègues et amis comme Henri Cartier-Bresson, Robert Doisneau ou Willy Ronis, Gisèle Freund ou Rogi André – qu'il a tous et toutes photographiés – sont, eux, sous la lumière des projecteurs ?

Sa femme m'a donné la réponse : Jean Lattes n'a jamais voulu se spécialiser dans tel ou tel genre de photos ni faire des livres thématiques. Il voulait simplement faire, le mieux possible, son métier, celui de photo-reporter pour des journaux comme France-Dimanche, Elle ou Life essentiellement. C'est Rogi André, la célèbre portraitiste qui lui a communiqué l'art du portrait. Lors des dix dernières années de sa carrière, il a été sollicité pour quelques expositions comme : *Six photographes en quête de banlieue*,

BPI, Centre Pompidou, Paris, 1977. Et ce sont quelques unes de ces photosde Nanterre que vous pouvez voir à différentes pages de ce numéro sur l'étranger.

Ce jour-là, en sortant de chez elle, je me suis promis que, quelles que soient les embûches, je ferai tout pour l'aider à faire le don de ce travail aux Archives Nationales. N'ayant aucune connaissance en la matière, j'ai mis le temps qu'il fallait pour comprendre par quelle « porte » je pouvais accéder à cet institut.

Aujourd'hui, nous avons l'assurance que ce fond sera préservé et mis à la disposition du public, chercheurs ou autres. Chargée par la Mission photographique du Ministère de la Culture de ce fond, je suis aussi chargée de le valoriser.

À ce titre les éditions Chèvre-feuille étoilée vont publier en fin d'année un ouvrage de portraits de femmes célèbres photographiées entre 1950 et 1970 par Jean Lattes. Une façon aussi pour nous d'honorer la mémoire d'un homme qui sut aussi bien mettre en valeur les femmes et d'honorer aussi sa veuve qui a fait tout le travail d'archivage de cette œuvre.

Nous espérons que vous lui réserverez le meilleur accueil.

⁂

e

© Janine Lattes, *Jean Lattes*, 1972.

D'un mythe à l'autre
Entre histoires et illusions

Samira Negrouche

Que les histoires qui se racontent et nous racontent descendent des livres ou du patrimoine oral, elles font toutes partie de notre être et de la construction de nos aspirations et de nos rêves, elles s'organisent et se dessinent en chacune, en chacun de nous, avec singularité.

Il me semble pourtant que les histoires qui nous arrivent de l'oralité, ne pouvant pas s'inscrire totalement dans une exactitude historique, ont une influence parfois plus mystérieuse, plus intime ; nous pourrions même dire qu'elles ont une présence mystique avec laquelle le dialogue est encore possible.

Nombre de ces histoires ont ainsi survécu entre villages et campagnes, caravanes et routes d'exils. Elles ont aidé à vivre, à rêver et à se forger une identité qui a façonné une longue lignée d'ancêtres. Ainsi, ce chemin parcouru finit par avoir lui-même une sacralité qui dépasse celle de l'histoire ou de sa véracité.

Nous descendons de tous ces rêves superposés.

Le rêve de la Kahéna, reine berbère du Nord de l'Afrique qui vécut au VIIe siècle et qui succéda à son père à la tête de sa tribu. Elle réussit l'exploit d'unir sous sa direction les tribus des contrées voisines et lointaines, de la mer jusqu'au désert. Elle résista farouchement à l'invasion arabe et infligea aux troupes ennemies de lourdes défaites avant d'être capturée suite à la trahison de son fils adoptif.

Certains parlent d'elle comme pratiquant des rituels juifs et la situent comme fondement de la culture juive berbère ; d'autres en parlent comme d'une prêtresse ou d'une sorcière.

L'on raconte que Kahéna était guidée par des visions qui lui venaient en rêve.

Pourra-t-on jamais savoir si, à l'époque de Kahéna, la mémoire populaire avait déjà véhiculé l'histoire d'un autre mythe, celui d'une autre femme, Tinhinan, reine et mère des Touaregs du Sahara au IVe siècle.

Tinhinan reste encore très vivante à la mémoire des touaregs qui lui prêtent de nombreux pouvoirs.

Lorsque son tombeau fut retrouvé lors des fouilles archéologiques faites au XIXe siècle par une équipe de recherche française, les Touaregs ont soutenu que leur reine était bien trop rusée pour se laisser découvrir par des étrangers, que le squelette retrouvé serait celui de sa servante ; la reine aurait fait construire une tombe inviolable.

Ces dernières années, une vive polémique a secoué la communauté des chercheurs et préhistoriens algériens. Suite à une nouvelle thèse, la reine Tinhinan ne serait pas une femme mais un androgyne. Ainsi, après une proposition de faire des analyses poussées sur le squelette exposé au musée du Bardo d'Alger – il s'agirait plus précisément d'étudier le génome – la communauté scientifique s'est totalement déchaînée, certains ont même crié à la profanation du mythe.

Cela suppose-t-il que nous avons besoin de temps avant de nous libérer des mythes ? Ou plutôt, jusqu'où ces mythes arrêtent-ils de devenir constructifs et à partir de quand nous empêchent-ils de forger notre propre voix ?

Plus près de nous, pourra-t-on également savoir si cette mémoire collective a voyagé par delà les contrées du Nord de l'Afrique.

Lalla Fatma N'soumer avait-elle entendu parler de Kahéna et de Tinhinan ? Elle qui a vécu au XIXe siècle et qui succéda également à son père comme chef de tribu avant de conduire une armée contre le colon français sur les monts du Djurdjura.

Ces femmes se sont-elles nourries chacune de l'histoire des autres ?

Nous pourrions peut-être même oser parler d'incarnation du mythe de la même façon que l'on sembla parler de l'Emir Abdelkader comme d'une incarnation de l'esprit de Jugurtha, roi numide qui a combattu Rome.

Car finalement, toutes ces histoires ont des limites si floues qu'il nous est même permis de confondre les époques. Nous en parlons parfois comme d'une même histoire, d'un concentré d'histoires.

Avec ces femmes, nous avons pu nous enraciner dans un plus grand rêve, celui auquel nous croyons encore malgré les défaites de l'histoire.

Si j'ai le sentiment accru de descendre d'une généalogie de femmes, c'est sans doute que les blessures de notre réalité actuelle sont encore vivantes, que la quête de liberté du lieu, du soi, de la pensée et de l'être est loin d'être accomplie dans nos contrées.

Il subsiste encore un lien charnel vivant avec cette généalogie de rêves.

Plus près de nous, il y a tant d'autres femmes : Fatma N'soumer, première femme romancière algérienne – elle nous raconta entre autre la répudiation de sa mère –, Djamila Boupacha, héroïne de la révolution algérienne, immortalisée par Picasso et tant d'autres d'hier et d'aujourd'hui.

Plus près de nous encore, celles qui voient leurs rêves s'évanouir dans ceux de leurs enfants qui se jettent à la mer dans l'espoir d'un avenir meilleur ou qui prennent les armes aux noms de guérillas et de révolutions aliénées.

Plus près de moi, les yeux de ma grand-mère me ramènent à l'oralité, me ramènent à ce qui n'a pas été gardé, à ce qui s'évanouit peut-être au travers des mailles de l'histoire.

Mais les yeux de ma mère et de ma grand-mère portent en eux une densité de rêves. Un rêve me regarde, un rêve que je ne peux leur offrir tout en me forçant à croire que ce n'est pas trahison, que répondre au rêve signifie avoir soi-même un rêve, et plus généralement que le rêve est celui qui se meut et prend son indépendance en tout temps et en tout lieu.

Au-delà de tous ces rêves qui se rencontrent, qui s'enchaînent et se donnent écho, il s'agit pour nous et avant tout autre chose d'écriture. Que nous fassions le choix d'accompagner et d'écrire les mythes qui nous ont accompagnés ou que nous décidions de rendre compte de notre soi, biographique ou mythologique, ce qui semble être le plus important c'est de rester dans l'exigence que comporte l'acte d'écrire, dans l'exigence mais aussi dans la générosité et l'indépendance totale de soi.

Car si les histoires qui nous portent sont aussi révélatrices et fondatrices les unes que les autres, nous ne pouvons leur sauvegarder leur force d'envol que par le recul que nous pouvons avoir de nous-mêmes.

Ecrire ses rêves signifie parfois s'en éloigner pour toucher à l'humanité subtile.

Il est arrivé dans le passé que je me sente désemparée de ne pas lire toute mon histoire, ou une grande partie de mon histoire, dans les livres ; désemparée de ne pas avoir à disposition une histoire de la littérature ou de l'art qui soit aussi documentée que ce que nous trouvons en Europe à titre d'exemple.

Comprendre les raisons de ceci ou de cela n'enlève pas beaucoup au désespoir.

Cependant, le bonheur d'être dans un musée comme le Louvre ne me fait plus vaciller de colère à la pensée de ce qu'il n'y a pas chez moi, ou chez nous tous, habitants ou descendants des pays d'Afrique qui avons vécu une féroce histoire des colonisations.

Bien sûr, nous allons avoir besoin de nous écrire et nous le ferons. Bien sûr, des choses sont déjà perdues. Mais, il n'en demeure pas moins que nous portons, en nous, une empreinte indélébile qui nous vient d'une oralité fondatrice. Cette oralité, je ne lui oppose pas l'écriture, je la lui donne et je la vis comme un don inestimable de nos ancêtres.

De l'oralité et des rêves qui viennent d'elle, j'ai reçu une identité que j'associe à d'autres identités qui se sont construites avec le temps et les rencontres ; ces identités construisent l'écriture sans lui imposer de cadre limitant, elles sont au contraire autant d'invitations à l'ouverture et à la découverte de l'ailleurs.

Nous autres savons tous à quel point notre continent est ravagé, nous savons à quel point l'appel de l'ailleurs est irrésistible et parfois nécessaire. Comme nos concitoyens, nous autres écrivains et créateurs avons parfois besoin de nous éloigner et de tourner le dos temporairement ou définitivement à nos racines, d'autres fois, bien que vivant ailleurs, nous avons besoin de rester au plus proche de nos histoires et traditions, parfois même de façon exagérée.

Et quelque soit le choix de chacun, il me semble qu'il est salutaire et souhaitable, que nous en avons besoin comme d'un équilibre nécessaire.

À l'heure où nos émigrants et leurs descendants font face à de nombreux questionnements, au moment où certains sont méprisés et chassés, d'autres perdus ou à la recherche de sens, certains tombent parfois dans la caricature de la révolte et continuent eux-mêmes de croire et d'entretenir l'idée que l'Afrique est désuète, finie, miséreuse et en continuelle décadence.

Cela peut se comprendre mais la réalité est que la réponse aux uns et aux autres se trouve à l'intérieur. Une impulsion est possible. Les écrivains et créateurs qui voyagent entre ces différents rêves, ces différentes réalités, sont ceux qui volontairement ou involontairement ouvrent – ou ouvriront – le dialogue.

Je pense que nous avons dans notre malheur, la chance inouïe de vivre sur de multiples frontières, dans un continent physique ou imaginaire qui reste encore à explorer et à construire.

C'est ici que l'humanité devra à nouveau questionner de nombreux concepts qu'elle croyait déjà maîtrisés, étudiés et compris.

Le contexte est en mouvement, l'écriture observe ce mouvement si elle sait être à l'intérieur et à l'extérieur de lui.

J'aimerais pour finir vous dire que le rêve sud africain n'échappe pas à ma sensibilité d'auteure. Vos écrivains ont magistralement enseigné au monde une part de l'humanité, de ses réalités, de ses rêves mais ils ont su être vigilants alors même qu'ils étaient pour certains (je peux citer Nadine Gordimer pour exemple) de grands activistes. C'est de cela qu'il faut peut-être se souvenir, être dans l'écriture signifie rester vigilants avant et après qu'une certaine forme de rêve soit devenue enfin réalité.

Conférence donnée le 25 août 2010 à Johannesburg à l'occasion du colloque
Mots de femmes : Mondes africains.
Renouveler le dialogue entre les femmes écrivains d'Afrique et les femmes descendant de l'Afrique
Women's words : African worlds.
Renewing a dialogue between african women writers and women of african descent.

à livres ouverts

© Marie-Noël Arras, *vue du Fort, Taghit*, Algérie, 2010

Rouge sang vierge

Karima Berger

Le premier mouvement vers le recueil de nouvelles de Karima Berger est dans le plaisir de tenir le poids du livre en main, d'en sentir la densité et le grain du papier sous les doigts, d'y voir saignante et poignante la lithographie de couverture de Joël Leick.

Aucune des nouvelles de ce beau recueil de douleurs et de joies ne fait l'impasse sur la morsure du réel pour l'être née femme.

À mi chemin entre le poème et le récit, chaque nouvelle saisit l'instant pour en ciseler les pulsations. On ne rentre pas dans un livre mais dans une chair d'où l'infinie mansuétude du cœur n'est jamais loin. Karima Berger y parle des mères, des filles, des putains tendres, des fils enfermés, des enfants exilés, des servantes éloignées. Des femmes comme d'un espoir, comme d'une perte, comme d'un flamboiement, comme d'une révolte, comme d'un désir d'être au-delà. Elle y parle des agneaux qu'il faut sauver du sacrifice.

Se dessine alors, par allusions et petites touches légères, le treillis serré de l'oppression sociale, pleine d'une créativité sans limite, pour étouffer le féminin. Oppression à laquelle chacune d'une manière ou d'une autre doit payer son tribut, à la recherche de son fil d'Ariane entre fatalisme et grâce de Dieu.

Par on ne sait quel détour derrière l'ombre, la plume est légère et l'humour affleure. Le quotidien dans la force du jour éclaire les événements. Il y a toujours un geste qui vient soulager du poids du malheur. Le sourire nous vient aux lèvres, devant les enfants mangeant avec leur père les figues dont il s'est servi un instant auparavant pour les projeter avec sa colère sur ses filles perturbatrices de sieste.

Dans la durée de chaque lecture, nous sommes l'enfant, la mère, la pute, l'exilé, le peintre. De l'intérieur de leurs perceptions, nous atteignons leurs humanités primordiales. Ils deviennent notre famille. Nous ne les oublierons plus. Le rouge sang vierge est aussi celui de dire l'autre avec passion, d'élargir la béance sans y tomber. La force du sang renouvelé qui pulse dans toutes les veines du monde, nous offrant trésor sacré, le fragile territoire de la vie en mouvement.

Le livre clos, une chose demeure : la conviction que la force des femmes vient à bout de tout, sauf du remords qui les tue plus sûrement que l'épreuve.

Marie Malaspina

Éd. El Manar, 2010, Coll. nouvelles du Maghreb, 94 pages, 18 €

Dedans, dehors

Sophie Bessis

La lecture de Sophie Bessis a toujours été pour moi un apprentissage du monde. Cette fois, avec *Dedans, dehors*, elle glisse vers l'autre côté du miroir. Elle ouvre une porte, la plus difficile, ici et là-bas, hier et aujourd'hui. Y passent des personnes, des gens. Comme si les analyses, même les plus lucides, restaient inachevées sans les acteurs, les petits, les perdants, les lâches même, comme nous tous. Mais avec *Dedans, dehors* il y a plus. Le plaisir. Immense. Douloureux. Et des lumières, des odeurs, des goûts. Des blessures. Des vies.

Dans ce récit intime, Sophie Bessis livre sa Tunisie, toujours sienne malgré l'exil, et quelques souvenirs chers à son coeur : les années 70, les compagnons de route, leurs engagements communs, les chemins qui parfois se séparent... En elle, « juivarabe », combats politiques et attachement à la terre natale se joignent pour former son identité profonde, inaltérable, ferment de ses travaux.

Hoda Barakat

Ed. elysad, 144 pages, 13,90€

Beyrouth Canicule

Djilali Bencheikh

Cette fois ci, l'auteur nous emmène loin de son Algérie natale, à la découverte du Liban dans quelque chose qui ressemble à un polar mais qui n'en est pas tout à fait un. L'aventure rocambolesque d'un jeune militant tiers-mondiste, presque « tiers mondain », comme on dirait au *Canard Enchaîné*, qui se trouve embringué dans une aventure qui le dépasse très largement.

Nous sommes au début des années soixante dix, le narrateur, est chargé par le RARE – ce mouvement d'opposants démocrates algériens exilés au régime Boumédienne – qui ressemble comme un frère jumeau au RUR de Mohamed Boudia, de convoyer, déguisé en touriste, quelques vrais ou faux passeports dans une valise à double fond, plus, dans sa poche, celui véritable de Mahmoud Hamchari qui vient d'être exécuté par les services israéliens à Paris.

Alors débute une série d'aventures souvent burlesques, parfois tragiques qu'il serait bien maladroit de raconter ici, c'est un polar dont il s'agit. Ce qui fait l'intérêt de ce livre, c'est l'étonnement de ce jeune intellectuel algérien, formé à l'école française et vivant en France, devant le comportement de la population libanaise, qu'elle soit civile ou, à fortiori, administrative. Son premier contact avec ces comportements sera en effet avec la police de l'aéroport et elle durera un peu plus que pour un touriste ordinaire. Tout se passe comme on ne s'y attend pas, ce qui fait l'attrait du bouquin, enfin son attrait immédiat, le côté polar. Mais l'on découvre, en grattant un peu, l'aspect surréaliste d'un pays, d'un peuple divisé jusque dans son administration policière. Tout est vrai et tout est faux. L'on comprend mieux, après la lecture de *Beyrouth Canicule,* ce que furent les guerres qui ont secoué cet étrange état laïque parce que pluriconfessionnel, moyen oriental mais tourné vers l'occident, lieu de rencontre, non seulement de religions et de sous religions, de rites, de philosophies, de mouvements dont on ne sait jamais trop s'ils sont officiels ou clandestins.

Djilali Bencheikh, comme souvent, présente là, sous des aspects souvent drôles, une histoire tragique, très proche de la réalité, qui nous révèle, bien mieux que de longues dissertations socio-philosophiques, la réalité et la complexité de la situation au Proche Orient. Ce petit texte nous en apprend beaucoup plus sur les oppositions mélangées de connivences entre factions, parfois opposées, parfois complices, qui ont défrayé la chronique durant ces années de braise qui ont secoué la région.

À lire absolument.

Jamal T

Éd. elyzad, , 280 pages, 15,90€ - 650 DAT

Entre les deux rives

Nicole Jean

Tome 1 Maghreb, l'impossible rupture
Tome 2 : Alger, la fin des illusions

Nicole Jean qui avait publié en 2004, chez le même éditeur, *Une enfance tunisienne* nous livre ici la suite de son autobiographie romancée, mêlant vie amoureuse et engagement politique, à l'heure où le Maghreb accède à l'indépendance. Léa, fille de petits colons s'éprend de Chadly, un jeune Tunisien issu de la haute société, occidentalisé et cultivé. Le couple part à Paris pour mener une vie étudiante plus tournée vers le divertissement que l'étude. Au delà de la relation entre les deux amoureux quelque peu affectée par la liberté que lui s'accorde, conformément à la distinction sartrienne entre amour nécessaire et amours contingentes, mais riche de bonheur partagé au cours d'escapades au bord de l'océan ou en Catalogne, on découvre avant tout, avec eux, la capitale des années cinquante. Ils côtoient la vie populaire à travers quelques personnages hauts en couleurs et la misère des banlieues ouvrières ; ils choisissent l'adhésion et le militantisme au Parti communiste et les réseaux de soutien au FLN.

Vient ensuite le départ pour Rabat où règne encore une sorte de douceur de vivre, un mélange de cultures et d'identités alors que la guerre d'Algérie s'intensifie. Notre héroïne, dont le couple se délite, tombe alors amoureuse d'un ancien camarade de lycée de son premier compagnon, Hicham. Ce combattant algérien forgé à la clandestinité, à ses risques et à ses contraintes, n'est pas, lui, un habitué des conquêtes féminines.

L'indépendance, en juillet 1962 permet à Léa et Hicham de se retrouver à Alger dans un contexte politique porteur d'espérances. Le Président Ben Bella se veut favorable aux droits des femmes et décide la nationalisation des terres. On assiste à la bataille en faveur de l'autogestion à travers quelques figures de cette période exaltée comme le conseiller trotskiste Michel Raptis mais surtout aux difficultés quotidiennes des domaines autogérés confrontés à des problèmes d'approvisionnement en semences ou en matériel et à une commercialisation aléatoire de leurs produits. Pour le reste, la beauté d'Alger, les senteurs de la Méditerranée, les voyages en Kabylie ou dans le sud présentent beaucoup d'attraits. Mais l'Algérie frappe aussi, dès cette période, par l'absence de mixité, par les interdits touchant à la consommation d'alcool imposés d'ailleurs par le FLN pendant la lutte de libération, par les difficultés économiques et l'opportunisme d'une partie des nouvelles élites. La richesse culturelle, notamment artisanale, paraît moindre qu'au Maroc du fait d'une présence coloniale plus accentuée et sans doute d'une tradition moins ancrée.

Tandis que Chadly, le premier amour, est resté un ami très présent, l'évolution de la société algérienne contribue à fragiliser le couple que Léa forme avec Hicham. Avec le coup d'état de juin 1965 commencent arrestations, recherche de planques et expulsions. L'Algérie indépendante ne ressemble plus aux rêves de ceux qui ont lutté pour elle et auxquels N. Jean, restée fidèle à ses idéaux de jeunesse, dédie d'ailleurs son œuvre. Au-delà de son témoignage, l'auteure séduit aussi par son évocation forte et nostalgique du Maghreb.

Claude Journès

Ed. L'Harmattan, 2010, 268 et 305 pages, 24,50 et 28 €

Divorzio all'islamica a Viale Marconi

Amara Lakhous

À quinze ans Amara Lakhous découvre Flaubert. Il lit Mme Bovary en une seule nuit. Grande révélation pour ce garçon d'Alger, fils d'une famille nombreuse d'origine kabyle, ou les sœurs ne manquent pourtant pas.

« Ah, les femmes existent, elles ont aussi leur vie à elles. »

Il retient la leçon ! Dès son premier roman, *Le cimici e il pirata* (*Le pirate et les punaises*, éd. Arlem, Rome, 1998) il peint avec finesse une femme victime : une pauvre algérienne qui, pour échapper à un mari brutal, ne trouve d'autre refuge que le bordel où elle vit en prisonnière protégée.

Puis dans *Choc des civilisations pour un ascenseur Piazza Vittoria* (éd. Actes Sud 2007) roman choral où des émigrés d'Afrique, Asie et Amerique Latine décrivent leur vie difficile à Rome, Lakhous contrefait la voix d'une jeune péruvienne que des liaisons hâtives laissent souvent enceinte. Craignant de perdre son travail et son permis de séjour, cette femme qui pourtant adore les enfants, bat le record mondial des avortements. *Choc des Civilisations*, un best seller traduit en diverses langues, a fait la réputation de Lakhous en Italie, où il vit depuis 1995. Il a quarante ans et il est, depuis peu, citoyen italien.

Grand saut en avant avec son troisième roman, *Divorzio all'islamica a viale Marconi* (éd e/o, 2010) Lakhous invente un personnage divertissant, un sicilien arabophone achevé (il connait les 300 noms en Arabe pour le mot « épée ») envoyé comme espion par les services d'intelligence italiens au cœur du quartier égyptien de Rome (où Lakhous a vécu de 2002 a 2006) pour dépister une cellule terroriste. Premier narrateur du livre, ce faux arabe sympathique décrit la vie étriquée et aigre des émigrés égyptiens à Rome. Mais c'est l'autre narrateur, ou plutôt narratrice, qui domine le roman : Safia l'égyptienne, dite Sofia en Italie. Sofia s'est mariée avec un émigrant du Caire dans l'espoir de réaliser un rêve d'enfance : monter un salon de coiffure dans la capitale de la mode. Hélas, à Rome, son mari, tyran morose, lui impose le port du hijab – pas pour des raisons religieuses, mais pour signaler aux copains qu'il reste maître chez lui. Porter le hijab en Italie en 2005, c'est pourtant dangereux. Sofia n'ose pas s'asseoir seule au jardin public, par peur des insultes et des violences que lui attirent son habillement. Pire encore : son mari lui interdit de travailler en dehors de la maison.

Sofia, la mal mariée n'est pourtant pas une victime. Au contraire, c'est une héroïne, dotée par son créateur de toutes les qualités : la beauté éblouissante et le tempérament combatif de la jeune Sofia Loren, la réflexion féministe de Nawal Sadawi, le bagout bilingue d'Amara Lakhous. Elle vit l'émigration comme une libération. Elle apprend la langue italienne, lit attentivement les journaux du pays, discute de leurs problèmes avec ses sœurs italiennes (elle connait par cœur les statistiques ahurissantes sur l'abus contre les femmes en Italie). Ce brassage salutaire délie sa pensée et sa langue. Dans une série de tirades énergiques et lucides, elle dénonce les injustices faites aux femmes musulmanes depuis des siècles.

Si le fond est tragique, le ton est souvent drôle. Sofia s'exprime par des analogies tirées du football « Dans la société musulmane le mâle fait l'adversaire et l'arbitre en même temps », ou du monde des affaires. Une femme qui se marie, « c'est comme un commerce qui change de gestion. » Au paroxysme de l'indignation, là ou un homme aurait lâché un juron, elle s'exclame « *Allora ? Allora niente* ! » (Trad. approximative : Rien a faire !) Elle invente des jeux de mots, comme « *maschio subito* » (enfant mâle tout de suite !) pour décrire la menace qui pèse sur toute jeune mère de jeunes filles chez elle. Allusion suggestive au très catholique « *santo subito* » expression prônant l'élévation d'un grand personnage à la sainteté tout de suite après la mort.

Rien d'étonnant que Sofia, avec son éloquence, son énergie masculine pour ainsi dire, se sente une vocation d'imam, tout en sachant qu'on n'a pas encore vu de femmes imams en terre d'Islam. En attendant, elle poursuit un projet de sauvetage bien précis. Ses sœurs aînées ont subi à l'âge de sept ans, la mutilation génitale, fléau contemporain de l'Égypte, que Sofia compare, dans une plaidoirie passionnée, au viol et à la torture. Son mari lui défend de travailler, tant pis, elle travaille en cachette, comme coiffeuse à domicile (coiffeuse en hijab, pourquoi pas?) pour payer l'opération qui restaurera le corps mutilé de sa sœur aînée. (Voir le livre *Entière*, éd. Chèvre-feuille étoilée, 2008, où le Dr Pierre Foldes, chirurgien urologue, présente son travail de restauration auprès des femmes mutilées. C'est bien de lui qu'il s'agit dans ce roman !)

Son indépendance vaudra à Sofia une répudiation définitive de la part de son mari. S'ensuivent toutes les complications cocasses d'un divorce à l'islamique, présentées avec la verve comique de Pietro Germi dans le film *Divorzio all'italiana*, de 1963, mais aussi du comédien égyptien Adel Imam dans la pièce très appréciée dans le monde arabe, *Sayed el Saghir*.

« *Allora ? Allora niente !* » Cette phrase, mélange de désespoir et de détermination, donne son ton au livre « Rien à faire, il vaut mieux rire que pleurer ». Mais si, comme on dit, la femme est l'avenir de l'homme, Lakhous a monté autour de la belle Sofia, un roman foncièrement optimiste, et qui plus est, il l'a fait deux fois, en deux langues. Je cite ici la version italienne. La version arabe, du même auteur, a été publiée à Beyrouth l'été dernier, sous le titre *Al Qahira as - Saghira* (Petit Caire). La traduction française ne devrait pas tarder.

Suzanne Ruta New York nov 2010

Ed. e/o Rome 2010, 192 pages, 16 €

La Femme qui tremble
Siri Hustvedt

L'auteure a fait appel aux deux hémisphères de son cerveau – dont il est question dans cet essai ! – pour composer un livre vibrant d'intelligence et de sensibilité, de force et de sincérité, de lucidité et d'humaine humilité. Elle – la femme qui tremble – part à la recherche de « ce nous-mêmes qui toujours nous surprend, nous inquiète et nous émerveille » selon la poète Emily Dickinson. Siri Hustfedt « souvent (se) demande à qu'elle point (elle) a oublié », ce qu'elle sait réellement d'elle-même et si « lecture et écriture vont-*elles* de pair ? » Siri H. est une femme à la démarche empathique et généreuse, ouverte sur la vie. Elle ouvre grand les fenêtres – en jalonnant sa quête de questions – au lieu de les verrouiller dans les cadenas des meurtrières réductrices des réponses définitives… comme le font maints pédants théoriciens dans leurs ouvrages spécialisés !

Siri H. fait frissonner notre imagination et notre corps calleux !

La dernière page de la femme qui tremble m'a laissée les yeux humides et le corps frissonnant…

Nic Sirkis

Ed. Actes Sud 2010, 245 pages, 22 €

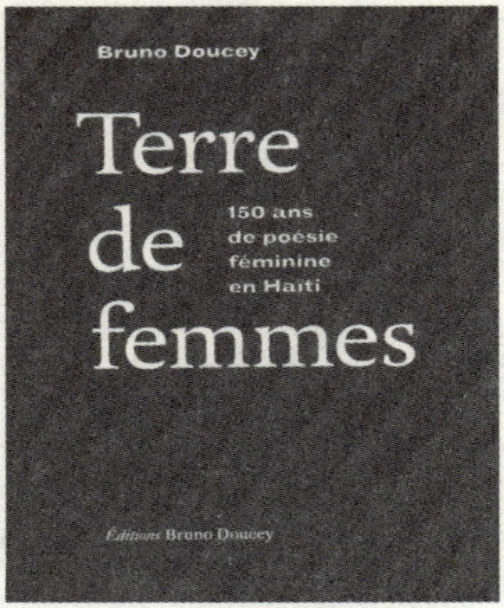

Terre de femmes

Bruno Doucey

Avant de créer sa maison d'édition, Bruno Doucey a dirigé les éditions Seghers. Cette anthologie est la première d'une liste à venir que nous espérons longue ! Elle présente 150 ans de poésie féminine en Haïti.
Nous vous présentons ici juste un extrait d'un poème de Marlène Riguad Apollon, *L'étrangère* qui aurait pu figurer dans notre revue.

Je suis retournée à mon pays natal

J'ai voulu revoir les montagnes de mon enfance / M'abandonner corps et âmes à la chaleur de leur étreinte / [...]

Les montagnes de mon enfance /Ne m'ont pas répondu [...]

Je suis allée revoir le peuple de mon pays natal, / Me glisser corps et âmes dans les recoins de leur misère. / Je me suis attendrie sur l'exotisme de leur vie / Et , émue, je me suis dit chez moi.

Le peuple de mon pays natal / M'a appelée touriste

[...

Ed. Bruno Doucey 2010, 294 pages, 19,50 €

Les cahiers de L'APA (association pour l'autobiographie et le patrimoine autobiographique) consacre leur numéro de juin 2010, N° 47, au Maghreb

Ce cahier thématique initié par Jacqueline Brisson reprend dans un ordre chronologique des témognages de français du XIXe siècle aux années 60 et termine par des témoignages de couples mixtes.

Je voudrais saluer le courage de cette association qui a tenu à ne pas censurer des lettres ou extraits de biographies très choquants. Dans le premier, « un médecin chef dresse un portrait accablant des Arabes, des Kabyles mais aussi des premiers colons : les socialistes, les détraqués, les dangereux et les malheureux du moment [1848]. » Il raconte même avec joie une chasse à courre à... l'arabe ! Les autres témoignages relatent la colonisation puis la guerre et le rapatriement.

Le dernier chapître de ce cahier est consacré aux témoignages des personnes entre deux rives. des histoires d'amour courageuses et souvent douloureuses...

Marie-Noël Arras

apa@sitapa.org http:/sitapa.org

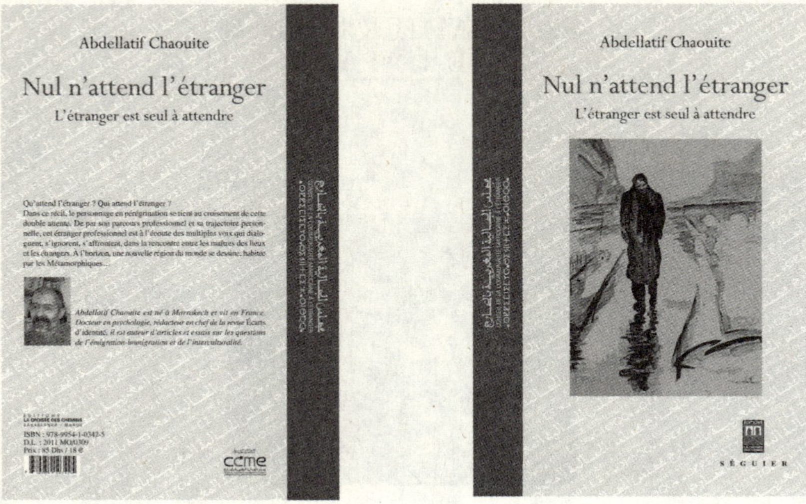

Nul n'attend l'étranger

L'étranger est seul à attendre

Abdellatif Chaouitte

Qu'attend l'étranger ? Qui attend l'étranger ?

Dans ce récit, le personnage en pérégrination se tient au croisement de cette double attente. De par son parcours professionnel et sa trajectoire personnelle, cet étranger professionnel est à l'écoute des multiples voix qui dialoguent, s'ignorent, s'affrontent, dans la rencontre entre les maîtres des lieux et les étrangers. À l'horizon, une nouvelle région du monde se dessine, habitée par les Métamorphiques…

Abdellatif Chaouite est né à Marrakech et vit en France. Docteur en psychologie, rédacteur en chef de la revue Écarts d'identité, il est auteur d'articles et essais sur les questions de l'émigration-immigration et de l'interculturalité. C'est aussi le président de l'Association des Revues Plurielles.

Éd. La croisée des chemins, Maroc, 85 Dhs / 18 €

Le voyageur nocturne
Jean-Michel Hirt

Quel livre, plus que celui-ci, pourrait s'inscrire dans cette problématique de l'étranger ? Si le mot « coran » est souvent – et peut-être trop souvent – évoqué par les médias ou par la multitude qui n'en a jamais ouvert une page, il ne l'est pas forcément par le désir de découverte de ce qu'il transmet de spiritualité, de message de paix, de trace de l'Histoire humaine. En cela, la démarche de Jean-Michel Hirt est salutaire. Elle permet de se réapproprier un texte et une voix qui n'ont rien à voir avec les instrumentalisations diverses qui les défigurent. Cet étranger qu'on nomme « coran » se désigne, s'expose ici comme une sonorité pacifique, poétique, apaisée.

La quatrième de couverture , ci-dessous, nous indique la lecture à faire de ce livre :

« Ce livre est une navigation à travers l'océan du Coran, cette œuvre universelle mais trop peu connue, voire suspecte, en Occident.

Beaucoup se demandent si le texte coranique apporte quelque chose de plus au message monothéiste de Moïse et Jésus ? Or le Coran énonce un discours sur les prophètes, depuis Adam jusqu'à Muhammad, qui prolonge et diffère de celui de la Bible. En partant, tel l'Ismaël de *Moby Dick*, à la recherche de la signification d'un ouvrage où se jouxtent et rivalisent prophétie et poésie, le lecteur est invité à un voyage spirituel. Ainsi s'invente un chemin pour mieux approcher le dessein de l'islam, en tant que rappel des révélations antérieures et leur recommencement infini. À l'heure où les religions sont instrumentalisées pour faire la guerre, où l'oiseau *Simorgh*, ce symbole divin, devient le nom d'une fusée iranienne et *Abraham* celui d'un char israélien, découvrir les enjeux prophétiques proclamés par le Coran est un acte de pensée contre la haine et l'ignorance. »

Éd. Bayard, 19 €

Liens de sang

Janine Teisson

Dans ce récit fantasmatique de sang et de douleur s'enlacent les destins de trois femmes : Djeyhmouna la rebelle, vendue à dix ans à un vieillard lubrique, Monique l'institutrice engagée qui perd son enfant sous la torture et Claudia le médecin humanitaire, qui retourne à Alger pour y retrouver son frère jumeau. L'arrière-grand-mère, la mère et la fille (semble-t-il) trois femmes de plus en plus déstabilisées, de moins en moins maîtresses de leur destin de génération en génération. Djeyhmouna est superbe, le simulacre de nuit de noce avec le vieillard à qui on l'a vendue est un récit magnifique d'indomptabilité sauvage, et les pages dont elle est la narratrice vibrent de la sensualité de son amour pour son second mari, Ismaïl, le roumi converti. Monique est déchirée par sa générosité, dans le tourbillon des horreurs de la guerre d'indépendance, mariée à un homme emporté, plus sectairement idéaliste que vraiment humain. Claudia est une enfant perdue, désorientée par la violence de son père, la maladie de sa mère et l'incertitude de ses origines.

Mais quels sont les liens qui lient ces trois narratrices ? En fait, ce sont ces ruisseaux de sang courant sur une terre qui en semble assoiffée (*Je vois l'Algérie comme une tache rouge sur la carte. Pays producteur de sang. Sa seule spécialité*) qui forment les vrais liens qui unissent ces trois femmes, car quels autres liens – *du* sang et non *de* sang – y a-t-il entre Monique et Claudia ou entre Béïa, la fille de Djeyhmouna et Monique ? Monique reçoit, de sa voisine de lit, Claudia en remplacement de son enfant mort, mais quelle est la filiation de Monique elle-même ? Entre Béïa, fille de Djeyhmouna et Ismaïl, malheureuse et rejetée comme bâtarde par la société étriquée du Second Empire, et Monique, l'institutrice affectée à un pauvre douar de bout du monde, il y a aussi solution de continuité, du moins dans le fil du récit. De même, Claudia n'aura pas de lien de filiation directe avec l'enfant de l'espoir qui lui sera confié, dans les dernières pages.

C'est que ce superbe roman ne parle qu'accessoirement de la violence des mâles ou de la maternité déçue. Dans une écriture incisive et forte, Janine Teisson traite avant tout de l'histoire sanglante de l'Algérie de la conquête à nos jours : politique de la terre brûlée de Bugeaud et de Lamoricière, torture des années cinquante et bégaiements terribles de l'histoire, avec à nouveau les massacres et les destructions de villages entiers dans les années quatre vingt dix – mais aussi premiers colons livrés sans soutien, sur une terre hostile, à la dysenterie et au paludisme, massacres des harkis, massacres d'Oran. *Egorgements, enfumages, razzias, viols, couper les oreilles, les couilles, les lèvres, couper, couper. Vider les femmes comme des poissons. La lame sur la chair bombée qui s'ouvre comme une grenade. Les morts là-bas ne se comptent pas. (...) Depuis 1830, qui a compté les morts ? Mécomptes, décomptes, oublis.*

Cette histoire de violence et de mort n'est adoucie que par la figure d'Ismaïl, inspirée du personnage historique de Thomas

Ismaÿl Urbain, descendant d'une mulâtresse libre, saint-simonien, interprète français converti à l'Islam, conseiller de Napoléon III et auteur, sous le nom de Georges Voisin, d'un ouvrage intitulé *L'Algérie pour les Algériens*, à l'origine du projet avorté de « royaume algérien ». De ce fait, son couple avec Djeyhmouna est emblématique des enfantements manqués de l'histoire : *J'aurais voulu que le meilleur de ma terre s'unisse au meilleur de la sienne… Pourquoi n'avons-nous pas enfanté l'Algérie* ? conclura Djeyhmouna à l'heure de sa mort, retrouvant ainsi un des thèmes du récit, cet échec de la colonisation qui n'engendre que le sang.

Michèle Perret

éd. Chèvre-feuille étoilée, 228 pages, 15 €

Plus loin que la nuit
Cécile Oumhani

Cette réédition du roman de cécile Oumhani ouvre avec bonheur l'édition *Chèvre-feuille étoilée poche.*

Chaque livre de Cécile Oumhani est pour moi un chant de voyage. Un chant d'amour aussi. Elle exprime son humanité, l'attention qu'elle porte aux autres et dépasse les frontières pour aller à la rencontre de la vérité de chacun de ses personnages. Elle dit à sa manière, sensible et forte, les désarrois, les failles, mais aussi les désirs et la lumière que nous portons en nous. C'est pourquoi nous nous sentons si proches d'Ahlam et de May que nous allons avec elles « Plus loin que la nuit ».

Maïssa Bey

Plus loin que la nuit fait partie de ces livres, rares, laissant après qu'on les ait refermés, une empreinte en soi.

Traversée de mots, dans une langue belle et exigeante, parlant à l'imaginaire, éclairant le réel. Roman de l'itinérance, de l'échappée des femmes résistantes, libres, douloureusement fragiles.

Un livre conduisant "plus loin", porté par le souffle des rêves survivants au vécu.

Hélène Pradas-Billaud

éd. Chèvre-feuille étoilée, 192 pages, 8 €

Libres paroles II
Claude Ber

C'est parce que Claude Ber articule la littérature, la poésie – qui sont présence au monde – et la réflexion sociale que ce livre est d'une importance particulière. Il s'ancre sur « l'interrogation obstinée du politique par le poïétique ». Entre l'épreuve brute du factuel et le théorique, Claude Ber choisit cet espace intermédiaire qui donne aux analyses les plus sérieuses cette liberté, où co-habitent les héritages des grands penseurs et écrivains, notamment de la Méditerranée, et le réel d'aujourd'hui façonné par l'héritage de la Révolution Française, de la décolonisation, des migrations, des métissages culturels..., bouleversant la myope quiétude que nous pourrions être tentés de continuer à revêtir.

Ce livre a la vertu essentielle d'ébranler nos certitudes et nous permet d'anticiper l'avenir.

Behja Traversac

éd. Chèvre-feuille étoilée, 360 pages, 10 €

La salle de bain d'Hortense

Janine Teisson

BAOUM ! En bas la porte de l'immeuble claque. La petite dame au bonnet rouge sursaute. Elle arrive sur le palier, frotte ses pieds sur le paillasson en sortant la clé de sa poche. BAOUM! Encore la porte. Cavalcade dans l'escalier. Elle pense : ce sont les petites qui jouent au satyre, et elle sourit. Sa porte est ouverte. Soudain elle est projetée en avant, poussée au dos par quelqu'un qui entre dans l'appartement, qui referme le verrou aussitôt derrière lui. La clé qu'elle tenait à la main a valdingué jusque dans la cuisine. La vieille dame est à genoux au milieu du couloir obscur.

— Bouge pas. Ne dis rien ou j'te bute.

[...]

Hortense ouvre la porte.

— Mais, mais, qu'est-ce que c'est ? C'est ça ta salle de bain ?

— Oui, c'est ça, et tout fonctionne. Mais ne prends pas de bain, seulement une douche pour aujourd'hui. Tu veux que je t'aide ?

Patricia ne répond pas. Elle est fascinée par la pierre verte veinée de noir qui luit sous les nombreuses petites ampoules hollywoodiennes qui entourent le grand miroir art déco. Le lavabo est immense, la pierre a été conservée brute à un coin. Pareil pour l'un des angles de la baignoire. Le tout lui paraît vaste et luxueux comme dans un film des années quarante.

— C'est de la malachite du Congo. Ne ferme pas à clé.

La rencontre improbable entre Patricia, une jeune fille en rupture poursuivie par « Trois types en cuir noir et crânes rasés », et Hortense, une très vieille dame qui a plus d'un tour dans son sac, va déclencher une série d'événements dangereux, drôles ou touchants.

Entourée de personnages truculents, ces deux héroïnes attachantes vont apprendre à s'apprivoiser, se connaître et s'aimer.

Une aventure incroyable qui nous fera voyager de Paris à Ouagadougou avec une multitude de personnages drôles et touchants.

Un superbe roman à rebondissements qu'il est difficile de quitter !

éd. Chèvre-feuille étoilée, 196 pages, 15€

Le dernier diabolo

Samira Negrouche

Deux femmes se rencontrent au hasard d'une escale à l'aéroport de Francfort.

Une jeune algéroise quitte Alger après avoir échoué à monter la pièce de théâtre de ses espérances.

Une militante et essayiste new yorkaise se retire d'une Amérique au seuil d'une nouvelle guerre irakienne.

Pendant trois jours, des bribes d'histoires se partagent, finalement pas si lointaines.

Si vous voulez savoir laquelle des deux joue du diabolo, il vous faudra lire ce livre, le premier roman d'une grande poète algérienne qui porte sa poésie à travers le monde !!

éd. Chèvre-feuille étoilée, 224 pages, 15€

partages

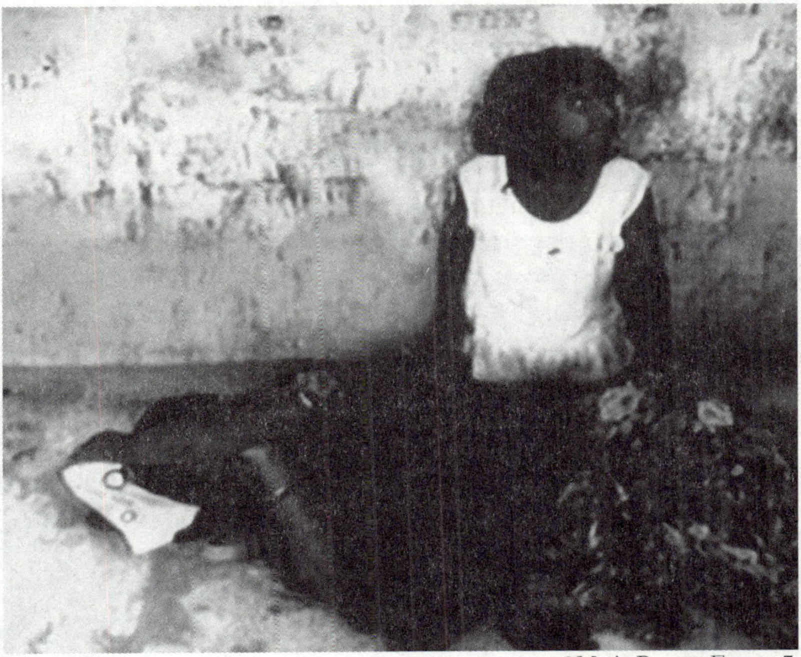

©Marie Bueno, *Errance 7*

©Anne-Marie Brenner avec *Maïssa et la lauréate, Tanéa Milesi*

©Anne-Marie Brenner, *séance de signatures !*

ch ch ch ch ch ch chut chut ! ! Ils ont commencé à écrire . . .

Annemarie Brenner

Depuis qu'elle est venue à Bourg Saint Andéol.. Ils se sont mis au travail ! ! Tout seuls, comme de vrais écrivains qu'ils sont en train de devenir... De temps en temps ils viennent demander une précision – c'est bien Masculin/ Féminin ? C'est pas Homme/ Femme ? –– ou bien un détail qui pour eux est d'une extrême importance. D'autres se croisent, le regard plein de sous-entendus ou un petit sourire au coin des lèvres, ils sont en écriture... Certains n'avaient jamais exhibé ces petits airs secrets et pourtant complices, cette mine un peu fébrile mais déjà téméraire, ces chuchotements coquins ou encore timides... Il paraît que le sujet les inspire : « Oh madame, ça y est, j'ai mon sujet ! Mais comment j'vais faire pour les fautes d'orthographe ? »…

Maïssa est venue, deux jours entiers. C'était la fête ! Ils voulaient tous la rencontrer, lui parler, lui poser des questions préparées à la lecture de « Sous le jasmin la nuit », « Bleu, blanc, vert » ou « Au commencement était la mer ! » Le professeur n'a pas toutes les réponses !

Maïssa est disponible, simple et si gentille, elle répond à toutes les questions ; aux plus récalcitrants, elle a même lu sa nouvelle « C'est quoi un Arabe ? », celle où sont évoquées l'arrestation puis la mort de son père. En classes de seconde et de première, sont abordés les thèmes très divers que comporte le programme : nouvelle, roman, littérature engagée, écrivains d'expression française, conditions d'écriture, édition, autobiographie, adaptation et réécriture du roman pour la scène, mais aussi les traditions de son pays, l'histoire de l'Indépendance de l'Algérie, la montée du F.I.S. et les années de plomb, les difficultés d'écrire, de dire l'insupportable, l'intolérable, l'horreur…

Riches, dynamiques, enthousiasmants, les échanges se sont enchaînés avec les classes des lycées général et professionnel lundi et mardi 22 et 23 novembre derniers.

Et puis, en coordination avec les libraires, une soirée de rencontres et de dédicaces a réuni élèves, parents, professeurs, libraires, permanents de la médiathèque voisine, lecteurs amoureux de l'Algérie, fervents de Maïssa et de ses romans humanistes et courageux. Un vrai succès ! La librairie, pourtant prévoyante, a épuisé son stock d'ouvrages. Quant à Tanéa Milesi, première lauréate, accompagnée de Maïssa, marraine de concours de nouvelles, elle signait aussi la revue, touchée et fière de cette première édition de son texte.

Merci Chèvre-feuille étoilée, merci Maïssa, Edith, Marie Noël et Behja.

À bientôt la prochaine édition !

Prof de Lettres
Lycée général Joseph Vernet
07700 Bourg Saint Andéol

***

©Anne-Marie Brenner, *Maïssa et la lauréate, Tanéa Milesi*

J'ai beaucoup aimé votre dernier numéro : les illustrations sont superbes. Je découvre le talent de Nicole Lantier. (merci à elle et Catherine Rossi pour les deux illustrations de mon texte sur le départ d'Algérie.) J'aime ces voix différentes qui forment un ensemble harmonieux. J'apprécie aussi la richesse des réflexions, des notes de lecture... Et quelle qualité de présentation ! Bravo, et un grand merci ! Courage pour poursuivre cette aventure unique. Amitiés,

Elisabeth Trouche - Besançon

J'aime la revue ! Elle est riche, je n'ai pas encore tout lu, je prends mon temps. Tout ne me parle pas mais les mots aussi s'apprivoisent. C'est la première fois que je découvre (je l'ai découverte au salon de Lyon l'année dernière, avec le numéro *Regards*) une revue pour laquelle j'ai envie d'écrire. Je me sens toute petite mais je sens mes mots à leur place, et ça me rend fière. J'aime ce mélange « sans étiquette » (prose, poésie, peinture) qui relie les regards de femme, dans une édition belle comme un livre. C'est bien qu'un tel espace existe. Bien amicalement,

Norlane Deliz - Lyon.

Merci à vous pour le beau numéro « Ce jour-là », si varié et en même temps témoin d'autant de cœurs battant à l'unisson,

Anne Guerber - Paris.

Marie-Noël & Behja, je tiens à vous remercier et vous féliciter pour ce nouveau n° d'Etoiles d'Encre (Je m'aperçois à l'instant que le sigle de cette revue : EE est le même que celui de mon 1er syndicat de jeune instit : EE pour... Ecole Emancipée !) EE qui va sortir et auquel vous me permettez de participer !

Ces jours et ces semaines dernières, j'étais tellement obnubilée par la « chasse aux coquilles » dans l'urgence des corrections... que je ne vous communiquais, dans le ping-pong de nos mails, que ce que j'avais pêché dans mon filet plongé dans le flot/flux des textes... comme petites rectifications nécessaires. Je ne communiquais avec vous que sur la *forme*, le côté technique de ce numéro et je ne vous ai pas du tout parlé du *fond,* du contenu de ce que je corrigeais ! Sachez que, par les lectures que j'ai faites de ce qui constituera ce numéro qu'on prépare, ces éléments d'un vaste patchwork que je découvrirai bientôt avec joie dans le numéro imprimé -comme un puzzle reconstitué dans son image globale, avec ses divers morceaux assemblés dans le mariage du camaïeu des couleurs, je suis dans la joie, l'émotion et l'émerveillement – en même temps que je corrige, même si j'essaye de rester concentrée sur la correction ! – quand je découvre les écrits divers de toutes ces femmes, dont certaines que j'ai déjà rencontrées et dont la signature me parle.

Je crois que ce N°45/46 sera un numéro magnifique et particulièrement réussi : c'est génial ! D'une part parce qu'avec votre travail d'abeilles industrieuses dans votre ruche méditerranéenne, vous avez courageusement, depuis 11 ans, construit un socle solide et qui tient la route. D'autre part parce que le thème de ce printemps : « ***L'ETRANGER*** » porte vers la générosité, le partage, les réflexions sur l'ouverture vers l'altérité et donne ainsi un gage de « positivité », d'espérance, en comparaison à des thèmes plus graves et difficiles, ceux qui menaient davantage, peut-être, vers la dénonciation incontournable des conflits, des affrontements et des douleurs sociétales (quand les thèmes traitaient, par exemple, de problèmes autour de la notion de couple, de l'exil, du secrets ou de sujets porteurs de douleurs intimes et de souvenirs cruels). Ces sujets sont beaux et nécessaires aussi, mais traitant davantage de l'intériorité introspective, ils n'ont pas la touche d'espoir, d'universalité, que je ressens dans ce N° 45/46 où il est question de rencontres, et d'horizons ouverts vers l'extérieur. « L'étranger » porte à sortir de l'égo de nos nombrils : c'est un numéro plus dans la convexité que dans la concavité – pour moi qui aime jongler avec ces 2 notions ! – et qui donc, je pense, gagnera un plus large public, mixte et intergénérationnel !

Et enfin, bien évidemment, ce numéro tombe génialement à pic (avec même le « Dégage ! » de Karima) C'est quelqu'un (e) qui bosse sur le hasard et la fameuse sérendipité qui vous le dit, comme vous l'avez constaté déjà bien-sûr vous aussi : tout ce qui se passe en ce moment autour de la Méditerranée, du Maghreb au Machreq et au-delà – et où les femmes ne sont pas en reste !!! – se marie miraculeusement avec ce numéro sur l'identité de l'autre, les questions de la difficile conquête de la démocratie, les miroirs des cultures et des civilisations qui se conjuguent. Ce nouveau cru 2011 de la revue porte vers ces rivages où les vagues remuent la grève, et surtout vers les peuples de ces rivages !

Voilà ! Je suis bien lyrique ce matin ! En pensant à Brassens, je vous dis que je suis fière, heureuse et ravie d'être montée avec « les copines d'abord » dans votre embarcation! J ! Je ne pouvais pas espérer plus belle jubilation (mot espagnol pour retraite !) Chèvrefeuillement vôtre, Nic-Noc, en ce mardi 22 février 2011

Nic Sirkis!, Paris, rue Charlot

Etoiles d'encre c'est aussi une équipe d'auteures qui s'agrandit au fil des ans, voici quelques souvenirs des trois derniers salons, celui des Revues en octobre, le marché de la poésie en novembre et le Maghreb des livres en février !

LES CONTRIBUTRICES À LA CARTE BLANCHE
FIGURENT DANS LA BIO-BIBLIOGRAPHIE DE LA CARTE BLANCHE

Marie-Noël Arras : Co-fondatrice des éditions Chèvre Feuille étoilée (cfe) et de la revue Etoiles d'Encre, elle en est directrice des publications. A publié *Entière ou la réparation de l'excision.*

Denise Bénaquin : Née à Alexandrie en Egypte. Elle vit à Paris, Meudon et Sèvres. Enseignante, psychothérapeute, conteuse, elle a fondé l'Association « Les Conteurs de Sèvres ». Elle anime des ateliers à partir des contes : « Le conte, un chemin vers soi et vers l'autre ». Elle publie des nouvelles dans Etoiles d'Encre dont *Sur la route du Désert*…

Karima Berger : Elle vit à Paris. Elle est écrivaine. Elle a publié plusieurs romans dont *Filiations dangereuses* à cfe en 2008, prix Alain Fournier ; *Eclat d'islam* chez Albin Michel en 2009 et *Rouge, sang, vierge* chez El Manar en 2010 ; elle est une contributrice de talent à Etoiles d'Encre où elle publie des nouvelles pour chaque numéro.

Maïssa Bey : Co-fondatrice des éditions Chèvre Feuille étoilée et de la revue Etoiles d'Encre, elle est écrivaine. Son dernier roman *Puisque mon coeur est mort* aux éd. de l'Aube.

Geneviève Briot : Elle vit dans la Drôme. Poésie, théâtre, récits, romans... Des séjours en Algérie dans les années 80 ont laissé une empreinte profonde dans sa vie et ses écrits. Derniers ouvrages : *Un livre à la mer* Marsa éditions, *Najib l'enfant de la nuit* L'Harmattan Jeunesse. Textes, poésies, publiés en revues Lieux d'être, Étoiles d'encre, Cairns…http://briot-aknin.hautetfort.com/

Marie Bueno: Enseignante et depuis toujours passionnée par les arts plastiques... le jour, elle enseigne et dés que décline le soleil, elle écrit des histoires pour enfants et de la poésie... C'est sa première contribution à Etoiles d'Encre.

Rosa Cortes: Née en Espagne, elle est sociologue. Arrivée à Alger enfant, elle y a fait ses études, y a vécu et y a travaillé jusqu'en 1976. Elle a également travaillé en Espagne et en France où elle a créé un centre de formation de langues à Lyon. Elle écrit pour Etoiles d'Encre depuis des années : L'*amphitryon ; Sac de temps ; La rencontre ; Eclats de silence ; Ecrire, dis-tu ?* etc.

Thérèse-Françoise Crasous : Elle fait partie de l'atelier d'écriture de Carole Menahem-Lilin, à Montpellier. Elle écrit des nouvelles pour Etoiles d'Encre notamment ; sa première contribution s'intitule *Rester là*.

Geneviève David: Elle vit à Montpellier. Elle a écrit à Paris dans la revue Dialogues (du Groupe Français d'Education Nouvelle) et à Montpellier avec Emmanuel Darley au Théâtre d'O et avec D. Gauthiez Rieucau. Elle vient de rejoindre les auteures d'Etoiles d'Encre avec les deux textes de ce numéro.

Norlane Deliz : Elle vit à Lyon. Elle a publié deux livres aux éditions du Manuscrit *Ma bouche tordue,* 2006, chronique intime mêlant prose et poésie. *Cajoleries aguicheuses,* 2009, recueil de poèmes sensuels, d'un érotisme léger. Elle travaille aussi sur des collages en lien avec sa poésie et espère poursuivre son chemin d'écriture de bien d'autres manières. http://l-iledelilie.over-blog.com

Edith Hadri : Elle gère l'administration et les relations publiques pour cfe. Elle est partie intégrante de l'équipe permanente dont elle constitue le point de convergence.

Anne Guerber : Elle vit en région parisienne. Elle a publié un premier recueil *Pulsations du temps, tambours de chair,* éd. Illador. Un second manuscrit est prêt d'où est extrait le texte de ce numéro. Elle continue son chemin dans l'écriture.

Catherine Jallet-Traverso : Chercheuse-écrivaine, elle travaille en Algérie comme traductrice freelance tout en poursuivant son étude de la correspondance de Lady Hester Stanhope, sujet de sa thèse soutenue en 2005. Elle a écrit un recueil de poèmes *Les visions fugitives.*

Magali Junique Ramirez : Elle travaille dans l'éducation nationale en France métropolitaine et en Guadeloupe ainsi qu'en Alliance française à Cuba et au Costa Rica. Elle anime un blog avec son époux, Yannier Ramirez Boza, et y alimente 3 rubriques : Chroniques d'ici, Chacun cherche son Che et Sex on the Story depuis octobre 2009. blog : http://paisdeorishas.blogspot.com

Nada Leil : Elle vit à Alger. En 2006, elle est lauréate du concours de poésie organisé par le Centre Culturel Français d'Alger. Elle lance avec une sœur de plume le groupe poético-musical *Aswat*. En 2010, son poème écrit en hommage à Marguerite Duras est sélectionné à l'issue du concours international *Poésie en liberté* pour figurer dans son anthologie annuelle. Elle est pharmacienne de formation.

Marie Malaspina : Elle est née en Algérie. Certifiée de lettres, elle a participé au développement de la pédagogie du jeu dramatique, animé de nombreux ateliers d'art dramatique, réalisé des mises en scènes de pièces contemporaines pour des troupes amateurs. Elle écrit pour Etoiles d'Encre depuis 2009 : *La cachette ; La petite dame aux fleurs ; Le silence des horloges ;* etc.

Françoise Martin-Marie : Architecte à Paris jusqu'à 40 ans, elle vit à Montpellier et se consacre à la géobiologie. Elle crée une association pour porter son projet (Ondelavie@free.fr). Elle a publié en 2008 une ballade poétique à l'intérieur du corps de la femme : *La magie de l'intime au féminin* aux éd. ALTESS et pour Etoiles d'Encre de très nombreux poèmes : *Corps tisane ; Bébé merveille* ; etc

Carole Menahem-Lilin : Elle anime à Montpellier, des ateliers d'écriture : http://atelierdecrits. canalblog.com. Elle a publié un livre d'artiste avec Marie-Lydie Joffre *ArTbre*, un recueil poétique et deux recueils de nouvelles *Enfermées*, éd. Guy Bouliane. Nombreux textes pour Etoiles d'Encre : *Maison entre deux jardins* ; *Rétrécie* ; *Héritage* ; etc.

Valéry Meynadier : Après avoir fait du cinéma, elle dirige des ateliers d'écriture. Elle est lauréate à Forum Femmes Méditerranée de Marseille. Elle a publié, *Ma mère toute bue* en 2007 et *Centaure* en 2010 aux éd. Chèvrefeuille étoilée. En 2009 elle a publié *Présent Défendu*, poèmes, photographies de Jason Girard & Valéry Meynadier, édité par La Villa des Cent Regards. Elle écrit pour Etoiles d'Encre.

Rose-Marie Naime : Elle vit dans le Lot et Garonne. Elle publie deux livres-douleur *Sylvaine* avec la collaboration graphique de Danièle Maffray. Elles signent deux recueils de poèmes *Couleurs d'ailes* et *L'éblouissement du jardin* (la colère des blessures faites aux humains en particulier aux femmes). Travaille actuellement au troisième recueil de SYLVAINE…

Samira Negrouche : Elle vit à Alger. Elle est poète et écrivain. Auteure de plusieurs recueils de poésie dont : *À l'ombre de Grenade et Cabinet Secret 2003*, 2005, *Iridienne* ; un livre d'artiste avec Enan Burgos, 2007. Elle est traductrice de poésie arabe. En collaboration elle publie *Mon père, ce passé présent*, cfe et *Il me sera difficile de venir te voir,* Vent d'ailleurs. Publications : 2009 *L'une et l'autre ;* 2010, *Le dernier diabolo,* cfe

Cécile Oumhani : Elle vit en région parisienne. Elle est romancière et poète. Auteure de plusieurs romans et recueils de poésie. Elle a publié à cfe *À fleur de mots ou la passion de l'écriture* en 2004. Dernières publications : *Le café d'Yllka* chez Elysad pour lequel elle a obtenu le Prix Littéraire Européen de l'ADELF en 2009 ; *Plus loin que la nuit*, cfe, coll. Poche 2010.

Sabine Peglion : Elle vit en région parisienne. Des études de lettres à Nice puis à la Sorbonne lui ont permis de concilier écriture, poésie et enseignement. Diverses revues ont accueilli ses poèmes : Voix d'encre, *Interventions à haute voix ;* Encres vagabondes, *Poésie Terrestre ; Les Lettres Françaises* in L'Humanité ; Etoiles d'Encre : *L'enfant s'avance au seuil ; Re-garder ; etc.*

Michèle Perret : Née en Algérie, elle vit à Paris. Agrégée de Lettres modernes, spécialiste de la langue du Moyen-Âge et d'histoire de la langue française, elle a publié plusieurs ouvrages de linguistique, des traductions de récits médiévaux, un roman pour enfants, *La légende de Mélusine* et chez L'Harmattan, une fiction, *Terre du vent*, inspirée de son enfance dans une ferme d'Oranie.

Hélène Pradas-Billaud : L'écriture accompagne sa vie dans ses engagements de femme, de mère et son métier de conseil en ressources humaines. Elle est l'auteure de différents textes publiés en revue dont à Etoiles d'Encre : *Les jours blancs* ou *Ecrire un jour* ; *C'est dans tes yeux que j'ai vécu*... et de deux manuscrits inédits.

Suzanne Ruta : Elle est américaine. Elle vit à New York. Elle est écrivaine et s'intéresse depuis longtemps à l'Algérie sur laquelle elle vient de publier un livre. Elle a réalisé la carte blanche du numéro d'Etoiles d'Encre sur le secret. Elle a découvert Etoiles d'Encre à la bibliothèque de New York.

Nic Sirkis : Elle vit à Paris. Elle a touché à tous les genres artistiques liés à la littérature et au théâtre. Auteure de nombreuses nouvelles publiées en revues dont à Etoiles d'Encre : *Clo ; une lueur d'espoir ; Pour Barbara*... ; aux éd. de l'A&A, Bacchanales... *Sorcières* (Les femmes vivent), *Voyelles*, *Types – paroles d'hommes*, *La nouvelle proue*, *Mémoire future sur le fil*... un manuscrit inédit en réserve...

Peggy Inès Sultan : Née à Héliopolis en Egypte, elle vit à Paris. Cofondatrice de la revue féministe *Elles voient rouge*, elle a publié deux recueils de poèmes : *Précaire le pays,* éd. Echo Optique et *La page suivante* à La Bartavelle ; contributions à diverses revues littéraires : textes et traductions en langue anglaise. Elle publie régulièrement des nouvelles dans *Étoiles d'Encre* depuis 2008 et en particulier le dossier sur Najia Mehadji pour *Célébrations*.

Angélique Thomine : Elle poursuit ses études d'anglais en tant que doctorante à la Sorbonne. Sa thèse porte sur la poésie des confessionnalistes américaines Sylvia Plath et Anne Sexton. En stage dans une maison d'éditions spécialisée dans la poésie, elle a lu quelques uns de ses poèmes au 4ème Festival International de Poésie de Paris.

Behja Traversac : Est cofondatrice des éditions Chèvre feuille étoilée et de la revue Etoiles d'Encre. Elle en est présidente. A publié *Amours rebelles*

Elisabeth Trouche : Née en Algérie, elle a vécu à Sidi-bel-Abbès et à Biskra et y retourne depuis peu. Elle écrit de nombreux textes en revue en relation avec l'Algérie et en particulier pour *Étoiles* d'Encre ou *Le journal de mes Algéries en France* de Leïla Sebbar : *Les Algériennes d'Elisabeth, Khaïra, Dzaïr, Aïcha*…

***Olivia Villon* :** Née en Algérie, elle a quitté le pays à 10 ans. Psychothérapeute à Reims. Elle se partage entre Reims et Montlaur dans les Corbières. Plusieurs des ses nouvelles ont été publiées dans Etoiles d'Encre dont *Fantasia ; Contre visite guidée ; Premier baiser...*

.

★★★

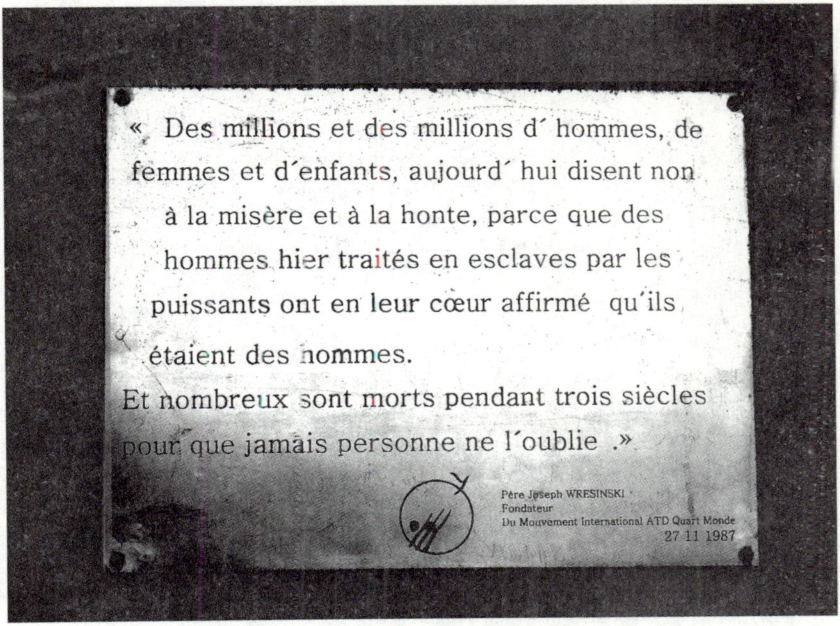

©Samira Negrouche, *Gorée*

Cet ouvrage
a été achevé d'imprimer
sur les presses de Pulsio
à Sofia en mars 2011
Dépôt légal : premier trimestre 2011

Mise en page et maquette de couverture :
Marie-Noël Arras

Rédactionnel
Behja Traversac

Corrections
Nic Sirkis

Imprimé en Bulgarie